The CERT® Guide
to System and Network
Security Practices

The CERT® Guide to System and Network Security Practices

Julia H. Allen

Addison-Wesley

Boston • San Francisco • New York • Toronto • Montreal
London • Munich • Paris • Madrid
Capetown • Sydney • Tokyo • Singapore • Mexico City

Carnegie Mellon
Software Engineering Institute

The SEI Series in Software Engineering

The publisher offers discounts on this book when ordered in quantity for special sales. For more information, please contact

Pearson Education Corporate Sales Division
201 W. 103rd Street
Indianapolis, IN 46290
(800) 428-5331
corpsales@pearsoned.com

Visit AW on the Web: www.awl.com/cseng/

Library of Congress Cataloging-in-Publication Data

Allen, Julia H.
    The CERT guide to system and network security practices / Julia H. Allen.
       p. cm — (SEI series in software engineering)
    Includes bibliographical references and index.
    ISBN 0-201-73723-X
    1. Computer security.   2. Computer networks—Security measures.   I. Title.   II. Series.
    QA76.9.A25 A454 2001
    005.8—dc21   2001022803

Text printed on recycled and acid-free paper.

ISBN 020173723X

2 3 4 5 6 7   MA   04 03 02 01

2nd Printing   December 2001

Contents

Preface

As the Internet and other international and national information infrastructures become larger, more complex, and more interdependent, both the frequency and severity of unauthorized intrusions into systems connected to these networks are increasing. Therefore, as much as possible and practical, it is critical to secure those networked systems of an organization that are connected to public networks.

The CERT®[1] Guide to System and Network Security Practices is a practical, stepwise approach to protecting systems and networks against malicious and inadvertent compromise.[2] The practices are primarily written for mid-level system and network administrators—the people whose day-to-day activities include installation, configuration, operation, and maintenance of systems and networks. The practices offer easy-to-implement guidance that enables administrators to protect and securely operate the systems, networks, hardware, software, and data that make up their information technology infrastructure. Managers of administrators are intended as a secondary audience; many practices cannot be implemented without active management involvement and sponsorship.

CERT security practices address critical and pervasive security problems. Practice topic selection is based on CERT's extensive data on security breaches (21,756 in 2000) and vulnerabilities (774 in 2000), which provide a field of vision not available to other security groups. These practices fill the gap left by the usual point solutions (typically

---

1. Registered in the U.S. Patent and Trademark Office.

2. Typically one or more violations of confidentiality, integrity, or availability.

operating-system-specific) or by general advice that lacks "how to" details. With CERT security practices, an administrator can act now to improve the security of networked systems.

By implementing these security practices, an administrator will incorporate solutions and protection mechanisms for 75–80 percent of the security incidents reported to CERT.[3] Each practice is written as a series of technology-neutral "how to" instructions that can be applied to many operating systems and platforms. However, since an administrator can only implement a solution using a specific host operating system, we have included examples of technology-specific implementation details in a separate appendix, as these tend to become outdated much sooner than the technology-neutral practices.

Wherever possible throughout the book, we emphasize planning[4] as a precursor to implementing. Ideally, an administrator and his or her managers (often including the chief executive officer and the chief information officer) need to undertake the following risk analysis activities before deciding what actions to take to improve security:[5]

1. Identify and assign value to information and computing assets.
2. Prioritize assets.
3. Determine asset vulnerability to threats and the potential for damage.
4. Prioritize the impact of threats.
5. Select cost-effective safeguards including security measures.

In our observation and as reflected in this book, the maintenance of system and network security is an ongoing, cyclical, iterative process of planning, hardening, preparing, detecting, responding, and improving—all of which require diligence on the part of responsible administrators. The ability to configure and operate systems securely at one point in time does not necessarily mean that these same systems will be secure in the future. Furthermore, no level of security can ensure 100 percent protection, other than disconnecting from public networks—and even then, the threat of attack from insiders still exists.

---

3. As determined by CERT vulnerability analysis and fourth quarter, 2000 incident analysis. The highest-priority practices that cover the majority of known vulnerabilities and incidents are Sections 2.4 Keep Operating Systems and Applications Software Up-to-Date, 2.5 Stick to Essentials on the Server Host Machine, and 3.3 Configure the Web Server with Appropriate Object, Device, and File Access Controls. In addition, the CERT security practices are periodically analyzed against top threat lists published by other organizations and consistently provide solutions for at least 80 percent of such threats.

4. Planning practices are not covered in detail; references are provided.

5. Taken from the presentation "CERT/CC Overview: Incident and Vulnerability Trends, Module 6 Site Security Policies," available at *http://www.cert.org/present/cert-overview-trends/cert-history-trends-2000-08-17.pdf,* page 214.

To get the most out of this book, you should already know how to install and administer popular operating systems and applications and be familiar with fundamental system security concepts such as establishing secure configurations, system and network monitoring, authentication, access control, and integrity checking.

The book is organized into two parts and two appendices.

- **Part I: Hardening and Securing the System.** Preventing security problems in the first place is preferable to dealing with them after the fact. This section covers the practices and policies that should be in place to secure a system's configuration. Chapter 2 contains guidelines for securing general-purpose network servers and workstations, while the following chapters provide additional guidance on securing public web servers and deploying firewalls.

- **Part II: Intrusion Detection and Response.** Even the most secure network perimeter and system configurations cannot protect against every conceivable security threat. Administrators must be able to anticipate, detect, respond to, and recover from intrusions, as well as understand how to improve security by implementing lessons learned from previous attacks. This section addresses practices required to carry out these measures.

- **Appendix A: Security Implementations.** The Appendix contains examples of several procedural and tool-based implementations that provide technology-specific guidance for one or more practices (the applicable implementations are referenced in the practices they support). The implementations chosen for this book are specifically geared to Sun Solaris (UNIX) operating environments, given CERT experience. They are intended to be illustrative in nature and do not necessarily reflect the most up-to-date operating system versions. The latest versions of over 70 UNIX and Windows NT implementations and tech tips are available on the CERT web site. Additional implementation development is planned for Windows 2000 and Linux.

- **Appendix B: Practice-Level Policy Considerations.** This Appendix contains all of the security policy considerations and guidance that are presented throughout the book. Having this material in one location may aid you in reviewing and selecting policy topics and generating policy language. You can also treat this appendix, along with the checklists appearing at the end of each chapter, as an overall summary of the entire book.

The most effective way to use this book is as a reference. We do not intend for you to read it from cover to cover, but rather to review the introductory sections of each part and chapter and then to refer to those chapters and practices that are of most interest to you.

The web site addresses (URLs) used in this book are accurate as of the publication date. In addition, we have created a CERT web site that contains all URLs referenced in the book. We plan to keep these URLs up-to-date, provide book errata, and add new references after book publication. At this book site (*http://www.cert.org/security-improvement/ practicesbk.html*) you will find links to all references, information sources, tools, publications, articles, and reports for which a URL exists and is mentioned in the book. We also regularly refer to CERT advisories, incident notes, vulnerability notes, technical tips, and reports, all of which can be found at the CERT web site *http://www.cert.org*. The phrase "the CERT web site" refers to this URL.

The content in *The CERT® Guide to System and Network Security Practices* derives from Carnegie-Mellon University's Software Engineering Institute (SEI) and CERT Coordination Center. CERT/CC, established in 1988, is the oldest computer security response group in existence. The Center provides technical assistance and advice to sites on the Internet that have experienced a security compromise, and it establishes tools and techniques enabling typical users and administrators to effectively protect systems from damage caused by intruders. The Software Engineering Institute is a federally funded research and development center with a broad charter to improve the practice of software engineering.

The material that serves as the primary content for this *Guide* has been posted and updated on the CERT web site over a period of five years. It has been reviewed and used by external security experts in commercial, federal government, and university-level academic organizations and by SEI staff members. All materials are periodically reviewed (and tested, where appropriate) for accuracy and currency.[6]

---

6. Security practices on the CERT web site undergo major updates every 18 to 24 months; technology-specific implementations more frequently. New practices and implementations are added annually.

Acknowledgments

The following Software Engineering Institute staff members (current and former) made significant contributions to the content of this book and supporting materials that reside on the CERT web site:

Greg Gravenstreter	Implementations
Robert Firth	Chapter 6
William Fithen	Chapter 4
Gary Ford	Chapter 2, Module and practice development process and format
John Kochmar	Chapter 5, Implementations
Suresh Konda	Chapter 2
Klaus-Peter Kossakowski	Chapters 2, 3, 5, 7, Implementations
Jerome Marella	Implementations
Larry Rogers	Implementations
Derek Simmel	Chapter 2, Implementations
Ed Stoner	Chapters 4, 5, 6
Bradford Willke	Implementations

The following people were also valuable contributors:

David Biber	Graphics
Matthew Desantis	Web content

Eric Hayes   Lead editor for all modules

Mindi McDowell   Editing support, conversions, web content

Barbara White   Editing support, conversions, web content

The following people were responsible for the leadership, management, and guidance for this work:

Barbara Fraser   Original practices manager; initiated CERT practices development work in 1996

Barbara Laswell   Current practices and training manager

Richard Pethia   Networked Systems Survivability and CERT program director

## Chapter 1

The CERT® Guide to System and Network Security Practices

The Problem—In the Large[1]

Networks have become indispensable for conducting business in government, commercial, and academic organizations. Networked systems allow you to access needed information rapidly, improve communications while reducing their cost, collaborate with partners, provide better customer services, and conduct electronic commerce.

Many organizations have moved to distributed, client-server architectures where servers and workstations communicate through networks. At the same time, they are connecting their networks to the Internet to sustain a visible business presence with customers, partners, and suppliers. While computer networks have revolutionized the way companies do business, the risks they introduce can be devastating. Attacks on networks can lead to lost money, time, products, reputation, sensitive information, and even lives.

The 2000 Computer Security Institute/FBI Computer Crime and Security Survey (CSI 00) indicates that the number of computer crime and other information security breaches is still on the rise and that their cost is increasing. For example, 70 percent of the 585 respondents reported computer security breaches within the last 12 months—

---

1. This Problem description is directly quoted from (Allen 00a).

up from 62 percent in 1999. Furthermore, the financial losses for the 273 organizations that were able to quantify them totaled $265,586,240—more than double the 1999 figure of $123,779,000.

Engineering for ease of use is not being matched by engineering for ease of secure administration. Today's software products, workstations, and personal computers bring the power of the computer to increasing numbers of people who use that power to perform their work more effectively. Products are so easy to use that people with little technical knowledge or skill can install and operate them on their desktop computers. Unfortunately, it is difficult to configure and operate many of these products securely. This gap between the knowledge needed to operate a system and that needed to keep it secure is resulting in increasing numbers of vulnerable systems. (Pethia 00)

Technology evolves so rapidly that vendors concentrate on time to market, often minimizing that time by placing a low priority on security features. Until their customers demand products that are more secure, the situation is unlikely to change.

Users count on their systems being there when they need them and assume, to the extent that they think about it, that their Information Technology (IT) departments are operating all systems securely. But this may not be the case. System and network administrators typically have insufficient time, knowledge, and skill to address the wide range of demands required to keep today's complex systems and networks up and running. Additionally, evolving attack methods and emerging software vulnerabilities continually introduce new threats into an organization's installed technology and systems. Thus, even vigilant, security-conscious organizations discover that security starts to degrade almost immediately after fixes, workarounds, and new technology are installed. Inadequate security in the IT infrastructures can negatively affect the integrity, confidentiality, and availability of systems and data.

Who has this problem? The answer is, just about everyone. In fact, anyone who uses information technology infrastructures that are networked, distributed, and heterogeneous needs to care about improving the security of networked systems.

Whether you acknowledge it or not, your organization's networks and systems are vulnerable to both internal and external attack. Organizations cannot conduct business and build products without a robust IT infrastructure. And an IT infrastructure vulnerable to intruder attack cannot be robust. In addition, users have an organizational, ethical, and often legal responsibility to protect competitive and sensitive information. They must also preserve the reputation and image of their organizations and business partners. All of these can be severely compromised by successful intrusions.

As depicted in Figure 1.1, in the 1980s the intruders were system experts with a high level of expertise who personally constructed the methods for breaking into systems. Use of automated tools and exploit scripts was the exception rather than the rule. By the year 2000, due to the widespread and easy availability of intrusion tools and exploit

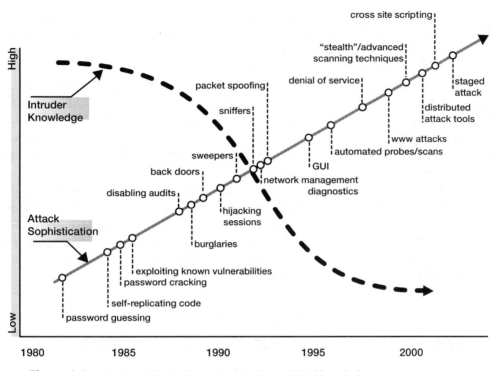

Figure 1.1   Attack sophistication versus intruder technical knowledge

scripts that can easily duplicate known methods of attack, absolutely anyone could attack a network. While experienced intruders are getting smarter, as demonstrated by increasingly sophisticated types of attacks, novice intruders require correspondingly decreasing knowledge to copy and launch known methods of attack. Meanwhile, as evidenced by distributed denial-of-service (DoS) attacks[2] and variants of the Love Letter Worm, both the severity and scope of attack methods are increasing.

In the early to mid-1980s, intruders manually entering commands on a personal computer could access tens to hundreds of systems; 20 years later they could use automated tools to access thousands to tens of thousands of systems. In the 1980s, it was also relatively simple to determine if an intruder had penetrated your systems and discover what he or she had done. By the year 2000, however, intruders could totally conceal their presence by, for example, disabling commonly used services and reinstalling their own versions, and erasing their tracks in audit and log files. In the 1980s and early 1990s, DoS

---

2. Refer to the CERT tech tip *Denial of Service Attacks* (available at *http://www.cert.org/tech_tips/denial_of_service.html*) and CERT advisories on this subject.

attacks were infrequent and not considered serious. Today, a successful DoS attack on an Internet service provider that conducts its business electronically can put that provider out of business. Unfortunately, these types of attacks occur more frequently each year.

Because of the explosion of Internet use, the demand for competent system administrators with the necessary technical experience far exceeds the supply of individuals either graduating from formal degree programs or with knowledge and skills acquired through hands-on experience. As a result, people who are not properly qualified are being hired or promoted from within to do the job. This trend is exacerbated by the fact that some skilled, experienced system administrators change jobs frequently to increase their salaries or leave the job market because of burnout.

Today's audit and evaluation products typically focus on the underlying system and network technologies without considering the organizational concerns (e.g., policies, procedures) and human aspects (e.g., management, culture, knowledge and skills, incentives) that can dramatically affect the security posture of IT infrastructures. As a result, companies often implement incomplete or narrow solutions with the expectation that these will completely solve the problem.

The Problem—As Viewed by Administrators

Systems, networks, and sensitive information can be compromised by malicious and inadvertent actions despite an administrator's best efforts. Even when administrators know what to do, they often don't have the time to do it; operational day-to-day concerns and the need to keep systems functioning take priority over securing those systems. Administrators choose how to protect assets, but when managers are unable to identify which assets are the most critical and the nature of the threats against them (as part of a business strategy for managing information security risk), the protections an administrator offers are likely to be arbitrary at best. Unfortunately, managers often fail to understand that securing assets is an ongoing process, not a one-shot deal, and, as a result, they do not consider this factor when allocating administrator time and resources. Even if an organization decides to outsource security services, it will probably continue to be responsible for the establishment and maintenance of secure configurations and the secure operations of critical assets.

Most system and network administrators have developed their knowledge of how to protect and secure systems from experience and word of mouth, not by consulting a published set of procedures that serve as de facto standards generally accepted by the administrator community; no such standards currently exist. For this reason and those stated above, administrators are sorely in need of security practices that are easy to access, understand, and implement. The practices in this book are intended to meet these needs.

We recognize that it may not be practical to implement all steps within a given practice or even all practices. Business objectives, priorities, and an organization's ability to manage and tolerate risk dictate where IT resources are expended and determine the trade-offs among security and function, operational capability, and capacity. However, we believe that by adopting these practices, an administrator can act now to protect against today's threats, mitigate future threats, and improve the overall security of the organization's networked systems.

How to Use This Book

The most effective way to use this book is as a reference. We have attempted to provide adequate cross-referencing from one practice to other, related practices; and we have deliberately included some repetition from practice to practice to allow each to stand alone.

All practices assume the existence of the following information:

- Business objectives and goals from which security requirements derive. These may require periodically conducting an information security risk analysis and assessment to help set priorities and formulate protection strategies (see Key Definitions below).

- Organization-level and site-level security policies that can be traced to the above business objectives, goals, and security requirements. If such policies do not currently exist, the development of such policies is recognized as essential and is under way. Charles Cresson Wood (Wood 00), among others, has prepared an extensive reference guide describing all elements of a security policy along with sample policy language. Each practice in this book contains a closing section describing the security policy language that must be considered to ensure successful implementation of the practice. This language will likely need to be tailored to reflect the specific business objectives and security requirements of your organization and its computing environment. Appendix B lists all policy-related language and guidance presented in this book.

> Security policies define the rules that regulate how your organization manages and protects its information and computing resources to achieve security objectives. Security policies and procedures that are documented, well known, and visibly enforced establish expected user behavior and serve to
>
> *continued*

inform users of their obligations for protecting computing assets. Users include all those who access, administer, and manage your systems and have authorized accounts on your systems. They play a vital role in implementing your security policies.

A policy must be enforceable to achieve its objectives. In most organizations, the system administrators responsible for the technological aspects of information security do not have the authority to enforce security policies. It is therefore necessary to educate your management about security issues and the need for policies in specific topic areas such as acceptable use (refer to Section 2.15), and then to obtain their commitment to support the development, rollout, and enforcement of those policies.

Designate an individual in your organization to have responsibility for the development, maintenance, and enforcement of all security policies. The person who fills this role must have enough authority to enforce these policies. In many large organizations, the chief information officer (CIO) is the appropriate choice. While the CIO will probably delegate the tasks of writing and maintaining the policy, he or she must retain the responsibility and authority to enforce it.

As a general rule, policies are more successful if they are developed in cooperation with the people to whom they apply. Users, for example, are in the best position to evaluate how various policy statements might affect how they perform their work. Although middle- or high-level managers may be responsible for setting overall information security policies, they need to collaborate with system administrators, operations staff, security staff, and users in order to define reasonable technological and procedural protection measures for information resources.

When a new policy is first adopted in an established organization, not everyone will want to make the behavioral changes to comply with it. The responsible executive must be sure to explain the motivation for the policy. Peers, including those who participated in the development of the policy, can help accomplish this.

Train new employees about the policy as part of their initial orientation and inform all employees whenever the policy changes, retraining them if necessary. Make sure they understand the consequences of noncompliance.

To ensure user acceptance of any policies that require their compliance, require each user to sign a statement acknowledging that he or she understands the policy and agrees to follow it.

The practices in Part I provide a strong foundation through establishing secure configurations of computing assets. If these are set up correctly *and maintained,* many of the common vulnerabilities typically exploited by intruders will be eliminated. Following these practices can thus greatly reduce the impact of a significant number of known, recurring attacks. Part II assumes that the practices in Part I have been implemented and provides guidance on what to do if something suspicious, unexpected, or unusual occurs. The practices presented in Parts I and II are technology-neutral, that is, independent of any specific operating system or version. Appendix A presents examples of practice implementations that are operating-system-specific.

How This Book Is Organized

Figure 1.2 serves as one top-level depiction of how to secure and protect information assets and serves as the organizing structure for this book. It includes steps to harden/ secure, prepare, detect, respond, and improve.

Harden/Secure

Systems shipped by vendors are very usable but unfortunately often contain many weaknesses when viewed from a security perspective.[3] Vendors seek to sell systems that are ready to be installed and used by their customers. The systems perform as advertised, and they come with most, if not all, services enabled by default. Vendors apparently want to minimize telephone calls to their support organizations and generally adopt a "one size fits all" philosophy in relation to the systems they distribute. First, therefore, an administrator needs to redefine the system configuration to match the organization's security requirements and policy for that system.

Taking this step will yield a hardened (secure) system configuration and an operational environment that protects against known attacks for which there are designated mitigation strategies. To complete this step, follow the instructions below in the order listed:

1. Install only the minimum essential operating system configuration, that is, only those packages containing files and directories that are needed to operate the computer.

---

3. Refer to the CERT vulnerabilities database (at *http://www.kb.cert.org/kb/*), CERT vulnerability notes (at *http://www.cert.org/vul_notes*), and the Common Vulnerabilities and Exposures (CVE) site at *http://cve.mitre.org* for detailed vulnerability information.

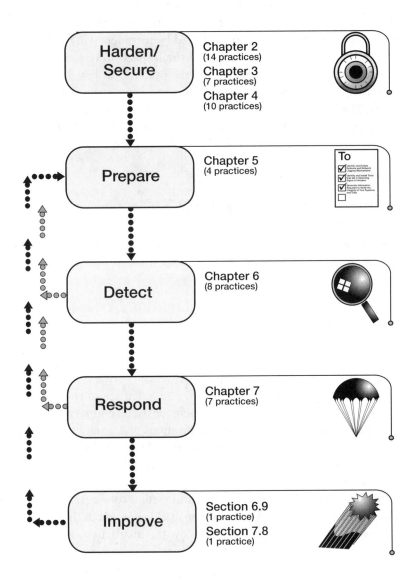

Figure 1.2   Securing information assets

2. Install patches to correct known deficiencies and vulnerabilities. Installing patches should be considered an essential part of installing the operating system but is usually conducted as a separate step.
3. Install the most secure and up-to-date versions of system applications. It is essential that all installations be performed before step 4, as any installation performed after privileges are removed can undo such removal and result in, for example, changed privileges or added accounts.
4. Remove all privilege and access and then grant (add back in) privilege and access only as needed, following the principle "deny first, then allow."
5. Enable as much system logging as possible to have access to detailed information (needed in the case of in-depth analysis of an intrusion)

Chapter 2 contains practices for hardening and securing general-purpose servers and workstations. These include configuring, minimizing deployed services, authenticating users, controlling access, performing backups, and performing remote administration in a secure manner. Additional hardening details can be found in the CERT implementation *Installing and Securing Solaris 2.6 Servers.*[4] Chapter 3 addresses more specific details for securing public web servers, such as web server placement, security implications of external programs, and using encryption. Chapter 4 provides guidance on deploying firewall systems, including firewall architecture and design, packet filtering, alert mechanisms, and phasing new firewalls into operation. The practices in Chapters 3 and 4 build upon and assume previous configuration of a secure general-purpose server as described in Chapter 2. This relationship is shown in Figure 1.3.

Prepare

The philosophy of the preparation step hinges on the recognition that a collection of vulnerabilities exists that are yet to be identified, requiring an administrator to be in a position to recognize when these vulnerabilities are being exploited. To support such recognition, it is vitally important to characterize a system so that an administrator can understand how it works in a production setting. Through a thorough examination and recording of a known baseline state and of expected changes at the network, system (including kernel), process, user, file, directory, and hardware levels, the administrator and his or her manager learns the expected behavior of an information asset. In addition, the administrator must develop policies and procedures to identify, install, and

---

4. Available at *http://www.cert.org/security-improvement* under UNIX implementations.

Chapter 2

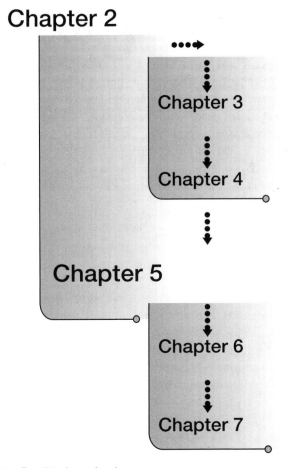

Figure 1.3   Practice dependencies

understand tools for detecting and responding to intrusions well before such policies, procedures, and tools need to be invoked.

One way to think about the distinction between the hardening and securing step and the characterization part of preparing is that hardening attempts to solve *known* problems by applying known solutions, whereas characterization helps identify new problems and formulate new solutions. In the case of characterization, the problems are identified through anomaly-based detection techniques, that is, departures from normal behavior, so that new solutions can be formulated and applied.

Chapter 5 contains practices for characterizing information assets, preparing to detect signs of intrusion, and preparing to respond to intrusions. As shown in Figure

1.3, the practices in this chapter are necessary precursors to those in Chapters 6 and 7. In addition, the practices in Part I (Chapters 2, 3, and 4) should be viewed as precursors to those described in Part II (Chapters 5, 6, and 7). This higher-level relationship is also depicted in Figure 1.3.

Detect

This step occurs during the monitoring of transactions performed by some asset (such as looking at the logs produced by a firewall system or a public web server). The administrator notices some unusual, unexpected, or suspicious behavior, learns something new about the asset's characteristics (see Section 5.3), or receives information from an external stimulus (a user report, a call from another organization, a security advisory or bulletin). These indicate either that something needs to be analyzed further or that something on the system has changed or needs to change (a new patch needs to be applied, a new tool version needs to be installed, etc.). Analysis includes investigating unexpected, suspicious behavior that may be the result of an intrusion and drawing some initial conclusions, which are further refined during the **Respond** step. Possible changes include a number of improvement actions (see **Improve** below):

- Installing a patch (rehardening)
- Updating the configuration of a logging, data collection, or alert mechanism
- Updating a characterization baseline to add unexpected but now acceptable behavior or remove no longer acceptable behavior
- Installing a new tool

Chapter 6 contains practices for detecting signs of intrusion in the following information assets:

- Detection tools
- Networks
- Systems (including processes and user behavior)
- Files and directories
- Hardware
- Access to physical resources

Chapter 6 practices assume that those described in Chapter 5 have been implemented.

Respond

For the purposes of this book, response includes recovery. In this step, an administrator further analyzes the effects of, scope of, and damage caused by an intrusion, contains these effects as far as possible, works to eliminate future intruder access, and returns information assets to a known, operational state—possibly while continuing analysis. Other parties that may be affected are notified, and evidence is collected and protected in the event of legal proceedings against the intruder.

Chapter 7 addresses response practices and assumes that the relevant practices in Chapter 5 have been implemented.

Improve

Improvement actions, described in Part II, Sections 6.9 and 7.8, typically occur following a detection or response activity. In addition to those noted under **Detect** above, improvement actions may involve the following steps:

- Holding a post-mortem review meeting to discuss lessons learned
- Updating policies and procedures
- Updating tool configurations and selecting new tools
- Collecting measures of resources required to deal with the intrusion and other security business case information

Improvement actions may cause you to revisit **Harden/Secure, Prepare,** and **Detect** practices.

Chapter Structure

Each chapter includes an overview of the problem being addressed and an introduction to possible solutions. The major sections within each chapter provide detailed descriptions of solutions that serve as security practices. Each security practice consists of an introduction, a series of practical steps presented in the order of recommended implementation, and a section covering policy considerations that complements these steps and helps ensure that they will be deployed effectively.

The recommended steps are addressed directly to a mid-level system or network administrator with several years of experience.[5] In some cases (policy considerations,

---

5. Refer to the SAGE (System Administrators Guild) job description for intermediate system administrators, available at *http://www.usenix.org/sage/jobs/jobs-descriptions.html#Intermediate.*

deployment plans, etc.), the person addressed is the manager responsible for system and network administration.

Each chapter closes with a checklist summarizing all of the practices and steps within each one. The checklist also serves as a table of contents that can be reviewed prior to reading each chapter.

Key Definitions

The following definitions are used throughout the book:

Assets generally include information, hardware, software, and people. Asset values are determined based on the impact to the organization if the asset is lost. Critical assets are those that are essential to meeting an organization's mission and business objectives. (Alberts 00) For the purposes of this book, assets include the information, hardware, and software that make up the information technology infrastructure of an organization.

Threat is defined as anything that may compromise an asset. This could be a person, such as an employee or a hacker, or it could be a competitor or anyone else with deliberate intent to compromise an asset. Threats also include anything that results in accidental disruption to an asset (such as a natural disaster), the means of access to do so, or any outcome or consequence that results in an unwanted effect such as disclosure, modification, destruction, loss, or interruption. (Alberts 00) Threats include vulnerabilities and risks of exposure.

Information security risk analysis and assessment methods help an organization identify important assets, threats against these assets, security requirements for these assets, and weaknesses or vulnerabilities in current practice that increase the likelihood of these assets being compromised. Refer to *Operationally Critical Threat, Asset, and Vulnerability Evaluation*^{SM}*(OCTAVE*^{SM}*) Framework, Version 1.0* (Alberts 99), *Survivable Network Analysis Method* (Mead 00), *Secure Computing* (Summers 97), *Network Intrusion Detection: An Analyst's Handbook* (Northcutt 99), and "Web of Worries" (Kessler 00) for more information on this subject. You can find additional guidance in a publication titled *Information Security Risk Assessment, Practices of Leading Organizations* (GAO/AIMD-00-33), published by the U.S. General Accounting Office (Washington, D.C., November 1999).

Attack connotes an action conducted by an adversary, the attacker, on a potential victim. From the perspective of the administrator responsible for maintaining a system, an attack is a set of one or more events that has one or more security consequences. From the perspective of a neutral observer, the attack can either be successful—an intrusion—or unsuccessful—an attempted or failed intrusion. From the perspective of an intruder, an attack is a mechanism to fulfill an objective. Intrusion implies forced entry, while attack implies only the application of force. Information-gathering probes and scans conducted by an intruder are considered attacks for the purposes of this book. (Allen 99)

An **incident** is a collection of data representing one or more related attacks. Attacks may be related by attacker, type of attack, objectives, sites, or timing. (Allen 99)

An **intrusion** refers to an actual illegal or undesired entry into an information system. Intrusion includes the act of violating the security policy or legal protections that pertain to an information system. (Allen 99) Additionally, an intrusion represents a deliberate event as a result of an intruder gaining access that compromises the confidentiality, integrity, or availability of computers, networks, or the data residing on them. *Breach* is used as a synonym. While a DoS attack does not constitute actual "entry" or "access," it does compromise the availability of the denied asset and is thus considered an intrusion for the purposes of this book.

Sources for This Book

The CERT series of security improvement modules listed below, all of which are available on the CERT web site, served as the primary source documents for this book.

Securing Network Servers (Allen 00b)

Securing Desktop Workstations (Simmel 99)

Securing Public Web Servers (Kossakowski 00)

Deploying Firewalls (Fithen 99)

Detecting Signs of Intrusion (Allen 00c)

Responding to Intrusions (Kossakowski 99)

The scope of and topics addressed by each module, and the set of modules as a whole, were explicitly chosen to address 75–80 percent of the practices designed to solve the problems that are reported to CERT. The practices describe the steps necessary to protect systems and networks from malicious and inadvertent compromise. The practice level (technology-neutral) was intentionally chosen to be as specific as possible while remaining broadly applicable and ensuring that the practices retain their utility and shelf life longer than the most up-to-date operating system version. To keep the size of each module manageable and easy to digest in a short period of time, each module addresses an important but *relatively narrowly defined* problem in network and system security.

Complete reference information is available in the Bibliography.

Other Sources of Information

There are many excellent sources of information about emerging intruder trends, attack scenarios, security vulnerabilities, vulnerability detection, and ways to mitigate their effects. The most common sources, which are referred to frequently throughout this book and are recommended for administrators wishing to stay current, are listed below.

- Vendor web sites
- CERT current activity, advisories, summaries, incident notes, vulnerability notes, and tech tips available at the CERT web site (see sidebar).
- Web sites of computer and network security organizations (see sidebar).
- Mailing lists, some of which are sponsored by vendors
- USENET news groups

Links to many of these sites can be found on the web sites for CERT and this book, as noted in the Preface.

Advisories address Internet security problems. They offer an explanation of the problem; information that helps a reader determine if his or her site has the problem; fixes or workarounds; and vendor information. All advisories published since 1988 are available from the CERT web site advisory archives. Advisories are available at *http://www.cert.org/advisories.*

Summaries are published each quarter. They contain information on the most frequent, high-impact types of security incidents and vulnerabilities that were reported to the CERT during the previous three months; they also provide pointers to more information. Summaries are available at *http://www.cert.org/summaries.*

Incident notes provide information about current intruder activity. Vulnerability notes provide high-quality, validated information about vulnerabilities. Because CERT's understanding of the scope of a vulnerability may change, information that originally appears in these notes may later become part of an advisory. Both contain information that might help to protect systems from intrusion, and both may be updated from time to time. Incident notes are available at *http://www.cert.org/incident_notes.* Vulnerability notes are available at *http://www.cert.org/vul_notes.*

continued

Tech tips contain information on a number of Internet security issues and guidance on specific topics to secure and protect UNIX and Windows NT systems. Tech tips are available at *http://www.cert.org/tech_tips.*

Implementations provide technology-specific guidance for carrying out steps in a practice. They are available for UNIX and Windows NT systems in specific topic areas. Implementations are available at *http://www.cert.org/security-improvement.*

Mailing lists and web sites appear, disappear, and change frequently. Be sure that the sources you consult are up-to-date and reliable. Links to many of these sources can be found on the book web site.

General security information. The following sources provide both broad and detailed information on a wide range of information, system, and network security topics:

AUSCERT (Australian Computer Emergency Response Team) at *http://www.auscert.org.au.*

Bugtraq and Security Focus at *http://www.securityfocus.com.* BugTraq is a full-disclosure, moderated mailing list providing detailed discussion and announcement of computer security vulnerabilities: what they are, how to exploit them, and how to fix them.

CERIAS (Center for Education, Research, and Information Assurance Security) at *http://www.cerias.purdue.edu* (formerly known as Computer Operations, Audit, and Security Team [COAST]).

CERT/CC (CERT Coordination Center) at *http://www.cert.org.*

CVE (Common Vulnerabilities and Exposures) at *http://cve.mitre.org.* CVE is a list or dictionary that provides common names for publicly known information security vulnerabilities and exposures.

CIAC (Computer Incident Advisory Capability) at *http://ciac.llnl.gov.*

CSI (Computer Security Institute) at *http://gocsi.com.*

DFNCERT (German Computer Emergency Response Team) at *http://www.cert.dfn.de/eng/.*

FIRST (Forum of Incident Response and Security Teams) at *http://www.first.org.* Contact information for FIRST teams can be obtained from *http://www.first.org/team-info.*

ICSA (Trusecure) at *http://www.trusecure.com.*

IETF (Internet Engineering Task Force) at *http://www.ietf.org.*

SANS Institute at *http://www.sans.org.*

Security Portal at *http://www.securityportal.com.*

USENIX Advanced Computing Systems Association at *http://www. usenix.org.*

Security fixes and patches. Monitor security fixes and patches that are produced by the vendors of your systems and obtain and install all that apply. A general index of vendor sites can be found at *http://www.cert. org/security-improvement/implementations/data/vendor_list.html.*

Advisories. Subscribe to advisories that are issued by various security incident response teams and update your systems against those threats that apply to your site's technology. Sites that publish such advisories include AUSCERT, CERT, and CIAC.

Mailing lists and USENET newsgroups. Read relevant mailing lists and subscribe to USENET newsgroups (*http://www.cert.org/othersources/usenet. html*) to keep up to date with the latest information being shared by fellow administrators.

Subscribers to mailing lists usually receive announcements about security problems and software updates soon after they are available. Web sites vary considerably in the timeliness of their announcements, so you need to determine how often to look for information there. Some news-oriented web sites are updated one or more times a day, so we recommend that you monitor these daily.

Security tools. It is important to review regularly sites that contain a wide range of useful and publicly available security tools. These include the following:

CERIAS at *ftp://ftp.cerias.purdue.edu/pub/tools/unix/*

CIAC at *http://ciac.llnl.gov/ciac/ToolsUnixSysMon.html*

Insecure.org at *http://www.insecure.org/tools.html*

TAMU (Computer and Information Services Network Group at Texas A&M University) at *http://www.net.tamu.edu/network/public.html*

Wietse Venema's site at *ftp://ftp.porcupine.org/pub/security/*

Summary

This chapter has set the stage for understanding and making effective use of the practices to follow by establishing the general context, describing the book's overall organization, and providing key definitions and information sources referenced throughout. The three chapters that constitute Part I address practices for establishing secure configurations of general-purpose servers, user workstations, public web servers, and firewall systems—necessary first steps before proceeding to the practices contained in Part II. The three chapters in Part II describe what preparation, detection, and response actions should be taken when an unexpected event or behavior occur.

Part I

Securing Computers

Many security problems can be avoided if administrators appropriately configure computers and keep those configurations up-to-date as problems and weaknesses are identified. Vendors typically set default hardware and software configurations to emphasize features and functions more than security so that most organizations' functional needs can be met with little or no additional effort beyond installing the operating system. Since vendors are not aware of your security needs, you must configure new computers to reflect your security requirements and reconfigure them as your requirements change.

Securing computers requires taking the following measures:

- Installing only the minimum essential operating system configuration, that is, only those packages containing files and directories that are needed to operate the computer

- Installing patches to correct known deficiencies and vulnerabilities

- Installing the most secure and up-to-date versions of system applications (while recognizing that new versions may introduce new vulnerabilities)

- Removing all privilege and access and then granting (adding back in) privilege and access only as needed, following the principle "deny first, then allow"

- Enabling as much logging as possible

Part I comprises the following chapters:

- Chapter 2: Securing Network Servers and User Workstations
- Chapter 3: Securing Public Web Servers
- Chapter 4: Deploying Firewalls

Chapter 2 contains practices for securing general-purpose servers and workstations, including the following:

- Addressing security requirements when selecting servers
- Keeping operating systems and applications software up-to-date
- Installing only the minimum essential operating system configuration
- Configuring for user authentication, access controls, backups, and secure remote administration
- Virus protection
- Guidance on acceptable use

Chapter 3 addresses more specific practices for securing public web servers, such as web server placement, the security implications of external programs, and encryption. Chapter 4 contains guidance for deploying firewall systems, such as firewall architecture and design, packet filtering, alert mechanisms, and phasing new firewalls into operation. The practices in Chapters 3 and 4 assume that you have first configured a secure general-purpose server as described in Chapter 2.

Many known vulnerabilities that serve as intruders' primary point of entry can be successfully eliminated or minimized by following the practices in Part I.

Chapter 2

Securing Network Servers and User Workstations[1]

Many security problems can be avoided if computers are appropriately configured. Default hardware and software configurations are typically set by vendors to emphasize features and functions more than security. Since vendors are not aware of your security needs, you must configure new and existing network servers and user workstations to reflect your security requirements and reconfigure them as these requirements change.

The development of computer networks has resulted in an important class of computers: network servers. The primary purpose of these machines is to provide services, including both computational and data services, to other computers on the network.

Because of its service role, it is common for a server to store many of an organization's most valuable and confidential information assets, as well as constituting a critical asset in and of itself. A server is also often deployed to provide a centralized capability for an entire organization, such as communication (electronic mail) or user authentication. Security breaches on a network server can result in the disclosure of critical

---

1. The terms *server* and *workstation* are used in this chapter to mean the combination of the hardware, operating system, network service, application software, and network connection. When it is necessary to be more specific, we explicitly mention one of these five components. We use the more generic word *computer* to mean "workstations, servers, or other computers." At times, we differentiate between guidance for user workstations and guidance for network servers.

information or the loss of a capability that can affect the entire organization. Therefore, securing network servers should be a significant part of your network and information security strategy.

Securing *user workstations* should be a significant part of your network and information security strategy because of the sensitive information often stored on workstations and their connection to the rest of the networked world.

The practices recommended in this chapter are designed to help you configure and deploy computers that satisfy your organization's security requirements. The practices may also be useful in examining and updating the configuration of previously deployed computers.

2.1 Overview

The practices covered in this chapter are applicable to your organization in the following situations:

- You operate or plan to operate a networked system of workstations that depend on servers for information or computation services.
- You operate or plan to operate a public network server (such as a public web site) connected to an external network (such as the Internet).
- Users of those workstations have network access to hosts inside your organization and to hosts outside through common Internet protocols.

We assume that you have the following security requirements for information assets stored on these servers or accessed by users or processes on these workstations:

- Some or all of the information is sensitive or proprietary. Access must be limited to authorized and properly authenticated users (inside or outside your organization).
- The integrity of this information is critical. It must not be compromised, that is, it must not be modified by unauthorized users or processes operating on their behalf.
- The information must be readily accessible by authorized users whenever they need it to perform their work.

We assume that you have the following security requirements for the services provided by these servers:

- Only authorized and properly authenticated users may use these services.
- Users must be able to access these services quickly.

These practices help you appropriately configure a computer and its operating system when it is first deployed. They do not attempt to address security issues for the following situations:

- The particular network service that will be provided by a server. For guidance that is specific to public web servers, see Chapter 3. For firewall systems, see Chapter 4.

- The network to which the server is attached. Network security practices are described in Chapters 5 and 6.

- Day-to-day operations of computers. We address operations in other chapters; for example, activities related to detecting signs of intrusion are covered in Chapters 5 and 6.

- Security of network services provided by third parties under contract to your organization.

- Wireless networking and its relationship to securing network servers.

- Portable workstations, laptop computers, workstations operating at geographically remote locations that connect to your site through the Internet or public telephone networks, and workstations that operate as network servers. Although many of the practices described here are applicable to these types of workstations, we do not include other practices that are unique to them.

- Computer physical security in detail (such as protection from theft and natural disasters).

The practices do not include the initial setup of the computer: unpacking it, confirming the hardware configuration, installing the default operating system as provided by the vendor (normally an automated procedure or script), and establishing the network connection. However, *some of the practices are most effective if performed during the process of installing the operating system.*

2.1.1 The Need for Secure Network Servers

Four major security issues need to be addressed when operating network servers:

1. Maintaining the confidentiality of information stored on the server. This involves ensuring that (a) only authorized users can access the services and information, (b) authorized users can access only the services for which they are authorized, and (c) information is disclosed only in accordance with policy.

2. Maintaining the integrity of information stored on the servers so that information is not destroyed or corrupted and systems operate as intended. This means ensuring that you can recognize and respond to breaches of integrity.
3. Maintaining the availability of the services and information. This involves ensuring that (a) access to services and information is uninterrupted even when there are hardware or software failures or during routine system maintenance, and (b) you can recognize and respond to security incidents in a timely manner.
4. Ensuring that the user is who he claims to be and that the network server host is who it claims to be, known as mutual authentication.

The common security requirements of confidentiality, integrity, and availability described above can be especially critical for network servers. Consider the following examples:

- File servers and database servers are often used to store your organization's most important information assets, which must be kept strictly confidential. Servers may also store information used for management decisions or customer billing, which demand a high level of integrity.

- Authentication servers store information about user accounts and passwords; any disclosure could compromise all the information on all of the hosts in your network.

- Public servers (such as web servers) can be a major component in the strategy your organization uses to represent itself to the public, so the integrity of the information on those servers is critically important.

- Servers used by customers for electronic commerce must be available and reliable to prevent loss of revenue.

- Servers that provide essential services for employees of your organization must be reliably available; otherwise people may be unable to work.

With respect to mutual authentication, user identities (ID, password) can be easily captured with network "sniffers" when passed in clear text. These identities can then be used by intruders to compromise your servers. Network server host identities can be redirected through IP (Internet Protocol) and DNS (Domain Name System) spoofing, enabling intruders to present their servers to legitimate users as though they were those belonging to your organization.

Several other aspects of network servers can make them tempting targets for intruders:

- Public servers often have publicly known host names and IP addresses.
- Public servers may be deployed outside an organization's firewall or other perimeter defenses.
- Servers usually actively listen for requests for services on known ports, and they try to process such requests.
- Servers often do not have an attending administrative user who notices signs of unusual activity.
- Servers are often remotely administered, so they willingly accept connections from administrator-level accounts.
- Servers are often configured to reboot automatically after some kinds of failures, which can offer opportunities for intruders.

2.1.2 The Need for Secure User Workstations

Three main security issues need to be addressed when operating user workstations:

1. Inappropriate disclosure of information stored on the workstation, violating *confidentiality*. This can happen when
   a. unauthorized users gain access to the workstation
   b. authorized users gain access to information that they are not supposed to see
   c. authorized users inappropriately transmit information via the network

2. A change, either accidental or malicious, in the *integrity* of information stored on the workstation.

3. Inability of authorized users to use the workstation, the network, or the information and services stored on each to perform their jobs, precluding *availability*. This can result when
   a. the information has been damaged, deleted, or otherwise rendered inaccessible (for example, by being encrypted or by having its access privileges changed)
   b. the computational resources of the workstation have been damaged or overloaded to the point of preventing authorized users' work
   c. access to services has been denied

2.1.3 An Approach to Securing Servers and Workstations

To secure a computer, we recommend a staged approach requiring the implementation of security practices in the following four areas:

1. Planning and executing the deployment of computers
2. Configuring computers to help make them less vulnerable to attack
3. Maintaining the integrity of deployed computers
4. Improving user awareness of security issues

The practices in this chapter are designed to improve security in three major ways:

1. Securing the configuration of each network server and workstation host, which provides a backup in case of the failure of perimeter defenses. Host security is also a first line of defense against internal threats, which generally have a higher probability of occurrence than external threats.
2. Assisting you in recognizing security incidents sooner, preparing you to respond to security breaches, and preventing similar breaches from recurring, thus reducing damages from security incidents. Refer to Chapters 6 and 7 for further details.
3. Promoting consistency. When the configuration and deployment of computers are consistent (the same from system to system), it is easier to manage security and to predict or identify use outside the norm. However, this can also result in the propagation of common vulnerabilities and other security weaknesses.

Within the context of this approach, Table 2.1 summarizes the recommended practices for securing computers. You will note that of the fourteen practices, eight are common to both servers and workstations, which are indicated by an X in both the network server (NS) and user workstation (UW) columns. Two practices apply only to NS and four apply only to UW. In addition, Sections 5.3, 5.4, and 5.5 provide logging and tool guidance for detecting and responding to intrusions, some of which affects configuring and installing computers.

Table 2.1　Securing Computers Practice Summary

Approach	Practice	Applicability		Reference
		NS	UW	
Planning	Address Security Issues in Your Computer Deployment Plan.	X	X	Section 2.2; page 28
	Address Security Requirements When Selecting Servers.	X		Section 2.3; page 36
Configuring	Keep Operating Systems and Applications Software Up-to-Date.	X	X	Section 2.4; page 39
	Stick to Essentials on the Server Host Machine.	X		Section 2.5; page 42
	Stick to Essentials on the Workstation Host System.		X	Section 2.6; page 46
	Configure Network Service Clients to Enhance Security.		X	Section 2.7; page 48
	Configure Computers for User Authentication.	X	X	Section 2.8; page 51
	Configure Operating Systems with Appropriate Object, Device, and File Access Controls.	X	X	Section 2.9; page 56
	Configure Computers for File Backups.	X	X	Section 2.10; page 59
	Use a Tested Model Configuration and a Secure Replication Procedure.		X	Section 2.11; page 62
Maintaining	Protect Computers from Viruses and Similar Programmed Threats.	X	X	Section 2.12; page 64
	Configure Computers for Secure Remote Administration.	X	X	Section 2.13; page 67
	Allow Only Appropriate Physical Access to Computers.	X	X	Section 2.14; page 70
Improving User Awareness	Develop and Roll Out an Acceptable Use Policy for Workstations.		X	Section 2.15; page 72

2.2 Address Security Issues in Your Computer Deployment Plan (NS, UW)[2]

Most deployment plans address the cost of the computers, schedules to minimize work disruption, installation of applications software, and user training. In addition, you need to include a discussion of security issues.

You can eliminate many networked systems vulnerabilities and prevent many security problems if you securely configure computers and networks before you deploy them. Vendors typically set computer defaults to maximize available functions, so you usually need to change defaults to meet your organization's security requirements.

You are more likely to make decisions about configuring computers appropriately and consistently when you use a detailed, well-designed deployment plan. Developing such a plan will support you in making some hard trade-offs between usability and security. Configuration consistency is a key factor in security, because it fosters predictable behavior. This predictability will make it easier for you to maintain secure configurations and help you to identify security problems (which often manifest themselves as deviations from predictable, expected behavior). Refer to Section 2.4.

2.2.1 Identify the Purpose of Each Computer

We assume that you are deploying workstations and servers in an existing infrastructure, which includes an existing network. The security issues related to the network architecture, including where you place servers and workstations on the network, are outside the scope of this chapter. As a general rule, subnets with differing security policies require some form of network separation such as firewalls (as described in Chapter 4).

Document how the computer will be used. Consider the following:

- What categories of information will be stored on the computer?
- What categories of information will be processed on the computer (but retrieved from and stored on another computer)?
- What are the security requirements for that information?
- What network service(s) will be provided by the computer?
- What are the security requirements for those services?
- What users and user groups will have access to the computer?
- What trust relationships need to exist between the computer and other computers?

---

2. Each practice title includes applicability to Network Servers (NS) and/or User Workstations (UW) as described in Table 2.1.

2.2.2 Identify Network Services That Will Be Provided

The network services you list in your deployment plan may include electronic mail, access to the web, domain name services, file transfers, and access to corporate databases. For each service, document whether the computer will be configured as a client, a server, or both (such as in the case of file and printer sharing).

Workstations are normally configured as *clients* for several network services. You should document the planned behavior of those clients: the levels and type (read, write, etc.) of access, and other aspects of the configurations required for client software.

As a general rule, a network *server* should be dedicated to a single service. This simplifies the configuration, which reduces the likelihood of configuration errors. It can also eliminate unexpected and unsafe interactions among the services that present opportunities for intruders.

In some cases, it may be appropriate to offer more than one service on a single computer. For example, the server software from many vendors combines FTP (File Transfer Protocol and HTTP (HyperText Transfer Protocol) services in a single package. For some organizations, it may be appropriate to provide access to public information via both protocols from the same server host, but we do not recommend this approach, as it makes for a less secure configuration. A compromise of the FTP service will result in a compromise of the HTTP service if they reside on the same server.

2.2.3 Identify Network Service Software to Be Installed

Many operating system vendors bundle network service software for both clients and servers. You may choose to use those packages. For major services, however, third-party vendors may provide products that offer much better security by not bundling service software. When making your choice, pay special attention to the ability of candidate packages to meet your security requirements, and document your selection.

Identify other application or utility software that will be installed on the computer. Include not only user-oriented application software but also system-related software and security-related software. Chapter 5 provides details on selecting some kinds of security-related software.

2.2.4 Identify Users

In the case of workstations, you will sometimes be able to identify an individual who will be the primary user, but more often you will have to define categories of users. The categories are based on user roles that reflect their authorized activity. The roles are often based on similar work assignments and similar needs for access to particular information assets—system administrators, software developers, data entry personnel, etc. If appropriate, you can include categories of remote users and temporary or guest users.

For network servers, document the categories of users that will be allowed access to the provided services. For public servers connected to the Internet, the category of users is probably everyone. For internal servers, you may need to categorize users by their organizational department, physical location, or job responsibilities. You also need a category of administrative users who will need access to administer the network server and possibly another category for backup operators.

Prevent the use of a network server as a workstation (except to deploy time-sharing services). A server's users should be restricted to those who are authorized to access the provided service and are responsible for server administration. Correspondingly, you should prevent having network services reside on and be provided by a user workstation (with X-windows being one exception). General users are typically not trained in network service administration.

2.2.5 Determine User Privileges

To document privileges, create a matrix that shows the users or user categories (defined in the previous step) cross-referenced to the privileges they will possess. The privileges are customarily placed in groups that define what system resources or services a user can read, write, change, execute, create, delete, install, remove, turn on, or turn off.

2.2.6 Plan Authentication

It is normal to authenticate workstation users via the authentication capability provided with the operating system.

For network servers, there are usually two kinds of authentication: (1) the kind provided with the operating system, commonly used for authenticating administrative users and (2) the kind provided by the network service software, commonly used for authenticating users of the service. A particular software implementation of a network service may use the authentication capability provided, and thus it may be necessary for users of that service to have a local identity (usually a local account) on the server.

Authentication mechanisms can be both procedural and technological. Passwords are the most frequently used mechanisms; but keys, tokens, and biometric devices (devices that recognize a person based on biological characteristics such as fingerprints or patterns of retinal blood vessels) can also be used.

Because authentication mechanisms like passwords require information to be accessible to the authentication software, you must carefully document how that information will be protected. Authentication data is critical security information that requires a high level of protection.

2.2.7 Determine Access Enforcement Measures

For many assets, such as program and data files, the access controls provided by the operating system are the most obvious way to enforce access privileges. You can also consider using encryption technologies to protect the confidentiality of sensitive information.[3] In some cases, protection mechanisms will need to be augmented by policies that guide users' behavior related to their workstations. See also Sections 2.7 and 2.15.

2.2.8 Develop Intrusion Detection Strategies

Many of the common intrusion detection methods depend on the existence of various logs that your systems produce and on the availability of auditing tools that analyze those logs. In your deployment plan, describe the kinds of information that will be collected and managed on each computer to reinforce security. This will help you install the appropriate software tools and configure these tools and the operating system to collect and manage the necessary information. Refer to Chapter 5 for detailed guidance.

2.2.9 Document Backup and Recovery Procedures

Maintaining recent, secure backup copies of information assets enables you to restore the integrity and availability of those assets quickly. Successful restoration depends on configuring the operating system, installing appropriate tools, and following defined operating procedures. You also need to document backup procedures, which include roles, responsibilities, and the ways in which the physical media that store the backup data are handled, stored, and managed. Consider using encryption technologies to protect backups.

Your backup procedures need to account for the possibility that backup files may have been compromised by an undetected intrusion. Verify the integrity of all backup files prior to using them to recover systems, as described in Section 7.7, before returning systems to normal operation.

---

3. However, also be aware of the vulnerabilities of cryptographic and encryption systems as discussed in "Why Cryptosystems Fail" (Anderson 93).

For some network servers, such as those providing public services like the World Wide Web, it is common to develop the information content used by those services on a different host. The authoritative version of this content is maintained (and backed up) on this second computer and then transferred to the public server. This method eliminates the need to perform file backups of the web page content itself. If the information is ever compromised, you can restore it by transferring a copy from the authoritative version. However, backups of web server logs are still required, as are backups of configuration and installation information, unless you have a configuration management system that can be used to recover or rebuild a system from a trusted baseline.

For more information, refer to Section 2.10.

2.2.10 Determine How Network Services Will Be Maintained or Restored After Various Kinds of Faults

Maintaining the availability of services essential to your business generally requires some level of redundancy. For example, you may want to specify when to use hot, warm, and cold backups or standbys. Hot backup systems create the ability to switch workload from the primary system to the standby system automatically and immediately, since the standby system is run in parallel with the primary system. A warm backup system requires some reconfiguration before the workload can be switched from the primary system, because it is not run in full parallel with the primary system. Cold backups are started from a shutdown state and need extensive configuration upgrades before being used.

Ensure, as part of your plan, that no single failure (natural disaster, sabotage, power supply outage, hardware or software failure, etc.) will make an essential service unavailable for a period of time you consider unacceptable.

2.2.11 Develop and Follow a Documented Procedure for Installing an Operating System

In your procedure, include steps to implement all the decisions you made in the steps above and describe all the parameters that are set during installation.

In many cases, the parameters are recorded in scripts or configuration files that are executed or read during various phases of the installation. Make all your parameter choices explicit, even if they match the vendor's current default settings. This step may seem unnecessary, but it can prevent security problems if you subsequently reuse your scripts or configuration files to configure workstations and servers. Your explicit choices will still be used even if the vendor's defaults have changed with new releases. Your installation procedure should also specify the vendor's security-related updates or patches that are to be applied to the operating system.

Make sure that your automated installation procedure contains the following steps in the order indicated:

1. Install only the minimum essential operating system configuration, meaning only those packages containing the files and directories needed to operate the server or workstation. Refer to Sections 2.5 and 2.6.
2. Install patches to correct known deficiencies and vulnerabilities. Installing patches should be considered an essential part of installing the operating system but is usually conducted as a separate step. Refer to Section 2.4.
3. Install the most secure and most up-to-date versions of system applications— for example, for UNIX systems, SSH (Secure SHell) replaces the Berkeley r-commands,[4] and the latest versions of sendmail and bind are installed. It is essential that all installations be performed before step 4, as any installation performed after privileges are removed can undo such removal and result in problems such as changed mode bits or added accounts.
4. Remove all privilege and access and then grant (add back in) privilege and access only as needed, following the principle "deny first, then allow." Refer to Sections 2.8 and 2.9.
5. Enable as much system logging as possible to have access to detailed information (needed when performing in-depth analysis of an intrusion). Refer to Chapter 5.

> Refer to the implementation *Installing and Securing Solaris 2.6 Servers*[5] and the *Solaris Security Step-by-Step Guide, Version 1.0* (SANS 99) for detailed guidance on securing Solaris servers.
>
> Refer to CERT tech tips *Windows NT Configuration Guidelines* and *Windows NT Security and Configuration Resources*[6] and the *Windows NT Security: Step-by-Step*, 2d ed. (SANS 00) for detailed guidance on securing Windows NT servers.

---

4. `rpc`, `rdate`, `rdist`, `remsch`, `rlogin`, `rsh`, `rksh`, `rup`, `ruptime`, `rusers`, `rwho`.

5. Available at *http://www.cert.org/security-improvement* under UNIX implementations.

6. Available at *http://www.cert.org/tech_tips/win_configuration_guidelines.html* and *http://www.cert.org/tech_tips/win_resources.html*, respectively.

2.2.12 Determine How the Computer Will Be Connected to Your Network

There are concerns relating to network connections that can affect the configuration and use of any one computer.

Many organizations use a broadcast technology such as Ethernet for their *local area networks (LANs)*. In these cases, information traversing a network segment can be seen by any computer on that segment. This suggests that you should place only "trusted" computers (i.e., known to be secure, implementing the same security policy) on the same network segment, or else encrypt information before transmitting it.[7]

Modems permit direct connectivity between one of your computers (and thus, potentially, your internal network) and the external networks reachable by the public telephone network. Many organizations forbid administrators to attach a modem to a server. We recommend that managers prohibit administrators from attaching a modem to any server connected to an internal network. However, if it is necessary to do this, deploy strong user authentication methods such as one-time passwords or token-based systems.

It is also important to document the use of modems on a network server. As a general rule, do not attach modems to any servers except those whose purpose is to provide dial-in access. Some vendors may require direct modem access to provide some level of service. In this case, we recommend establishing procedures that enable the vendor to access the server via modem, and disconnecting the modem when it is not in use. You should require strong user authentication methods for this type of access.

2.2.13 Identify the Security Concerns Related to Day-to-Day Administration

If your organization is small, it may be feasible to administer both workstations and network servers individually from their consoles. In most cases, however, workstations and servers are some distance from the offices of the system administrators. As a result, a significant amount of day-to-day administration takes place at the administrator's workstation via the network, using automated tools and procedures.

Providing the means for secure remote administration, as described in Section 2.13, typically requires configuring the operating system and installing various software tools.

---

7. However, note that most commonly used network protocols based on TCP/IP require at least part of the information in a packet (source, destination, port) to be unencrypted, which exposes the network to traffic analysis by a sniffer. By using specific protocols, such as IPSEC, in tunneling mode, you can further reduce the amount of cleartext information, thereby minimizing the potential for traffic analysis.

This step could involve configuring the tools to encrypt administration commands and data that traverse the network between the target computer and the administrator's workstation. You should define and document your administration procedures to configure the computer appropriately.

2.2.14 Protect Information Contained on Hardware That Is No Longer in Use

Determine the steps you must take to ensure the elimination, as far as possible, of information contained on hardware that is being updated, replaced, removed from service, or disposed of. For example, erase and reformat disks, rewrite tapes, and clear firmware passwords. The extensiveness of the actions you take depends on the sensitivity of the information. You may need to physically destroy hardware containing highly sensitive information to ensure that the hardware cannot be used and that the information cannot be accessed.

2.2.15 Keep Your Computer Deployment Plan Current

You need to update your computer deployment plan whenever relevant changes occur. Sources of change may include new technologies, new security threats, updates to your network architecture, the addition of new classes of users, or new organizational units, etc.

2.2.16 Policy Considerations

Your organization's networked systems security policy should require the following built-in protections:

- A detailed computer deployment plan will be developed, implemented, and maintained whenever computers are being deployed (or redeployed).
- Access to your deployment plan will be given only to those who require the information to perform their jobs.
- All new and updated computers will be installed, configured, and tested in a stand-alone mode or within test networks (i.e., not connected to operational networks).

- All computers will present a warning banner to all users indicating that they are legally accountable for their actions and that by using the computer they are consenting to having their actions logged.

- All computers (both workstations and servers) are to be configured securely prior to deployment.

2.3 Address Security Requirements When Selecting Servers (NS)

It is common to consider factors such as functionality, price, performance, and capacity when selecting computing technology. When you specify the requirements for selecting servers for your organization (including the host machine hardware, operating system, and server software), you should also include security considerations.[8]

There are many server vendors, and the security capabilities of their products vary. Many of the known and frequently exploited network server vulnerabilities apply only to certain products and platforms. If you consider security requirements when selecting servers, you may be able to choose products with fewer vulnerabilities or select better security-related features, which can result in a substantially more secure site. This makes the long-term operation of your site more economical, because you can reduce the expense associated with administration tasks (such as patching systems) as well as lower the costs that result from intrusions and their effects.

The selection of server products requires you to make trade-offs among competing requirements. To do this, you must first understand your organization's requirements.

For a general-purpose server, important performance requirements include response time (typically measured in terms of the number of connections per second that the server will allow) and throughput (typically measured in terms of the number of service responses that can be delivered to the network).

Typical functionality requirements include the ability to provide a range of services (such as web, e-mail, DNS, FTP, database access) and the ability to receive and process user information (such as authentication and access control). In addition, you will likely want the ability to administer the server software and the host system from another host on your network and, perhaps, remotely from outside your internal network.

---

8. Refer to the article "Toward Survivable COTS-Based Systems" (Mead 01) for detailed guidance on how to take security and survivability issues into account when acquiring COTS-based systems.

It is critical that you consider the availability of experienced staff to administer your server and server products when selecting a server. It is generally preferable to have capable, knowledgeable administrators working in a less secure, but familiar, server environment than to have to train staff to use an environment that is more secure, but unfamiliar—unless, of course, you plan to make a longer-term investment in the technology of the unknown environment.

Security requirements typically include the following conditions:

- The absence of known vulnerabilities used by common forms of attack against server hosts
- The ability to restrict administrative activities to authorized users only
- The ability to deny access to information on the server other than that intended to be available
- The ability to disable unnecessary network services that may be built into the operating system or server software
- The ability to control access to various forms of executable programs (such as CGI [Common Gateway Interface] scripts and server plug-ins in the case of web servers)
- The ability to log appropriate server activities for the purposes of detecting intrusions and attempted intrusions

2.3.1 Identify Functionality and Performance Requirements

Document the operating system features needed, even if you are confined to using one vendor's operating system. Include the requirements for both general and special security features. (General features might include capabilities for user authentication and file access controls, while special security features might include an encrypting file system or a built-in ability to erase memory and disk blocks before reallocating them.)

Keep in mind that technology diversity (i.e., selecting servers and operating systems offered by different vendors) can enhance overall security by not relying on a single solution with common weaknesses. Many of the more widespread attacks have been successful because of systems with the same implementation of services and operating systems. Of course, this creates a corresponding need for administrators with diverse skills and experience.

Document the applications software you intend to run on the server.

Given the operating system and applications software features, you should document the needed hardware, including the processor architecture, memory requirements, secondary storage requirements (such as hard disk drives and removable-medium drives), networking requirements (such as modems or network interface cards), and console requirements. Include requirements for server expansion and growth, and ensure that the hardware can accommodate this.

Document the hardware configuration to facilitate your selection and secure configuration of the software.

2.3.2 Review Server Product Features

Review the recommended practices that address the configuration and operation of the server product. Note the kinds of security problems that those practices are intended to help you avoid.

Where available, look at the sample implementations of those practices. Determine whether the implementations for a particular product are simple or complex, inexpensive or costly. These steps will help you carry out the necessary trade-offs.

Identify which specific security-related features you want in the server product, based on your organization's security needs. These may include types of authentication, levels of access control, support for remote administration, and logging features.

Check with available sources of incident data to help determine the likelihood of particular kinds of incidents and the vulnerabilities of specific servers. Vendor web sites often contain this information. CERT advisories, summaries, vulnerability notes, and incident notes will occasionally present information about new vulnerabilities in server software. See the end of Chapter 1 for additional sources of information for staying current.

Vendor sites may also present information about the operating systems under which servers operate.

2.3.3 Estimate the Differences in Operating Costs of Competing Products

Include the business costs of potential security incidents and the amount of staff effort required to operate, maintain, and use each product in a secure manner. A useful way to make an informed decision is to compare the cost of installing and maintaining security products with the cost of staff time needed to identify, analyze, and respond to a security incident, including lost productivity of other staff during the time they cannot use any compromised systems.

Select the technology that you believe offers the best balance of functionality, performance, security, and overall cost.

2.3.4 Policy Considerations

Your organization's networked systems security policy should require a security evaluation (including vulnerability assessment) as part of your computing and network technology selection procedures. Refer to Section 5.3 for more detailed guidance on identifying and selecting tools.

In addition, we recommend that your organization's purchasing guidelines mandate the specification of security requirements for all computing and network technologies.

2.4 Keep Operating Systems and Applications Software Up-to-Date (NS, UW)

You need to stay informed of vendors' security-related updates to their products, which may be called updates, upgrades, patches, service packs, hot fixes, or workarounds. Whenever an update is released, you need to evaluate it, determine if it is applicable to your organization's computers, and if so install it.

Because software systems are so complex, it is common for security-related problems to be discovered only after the software has been in widespread use. Although most vendors try to address known security flaws in a timely manner, there is normally a gap between the time the problem is publicly known and the time the vendor requires to prepare the correction; and additional time elapses before the update can be installed. This gap gives potential intruders an opportunity to take advantage of the flaw and mount an attack on your computers and networks. To keep this time interval as short as possible, you need to stay attuned to announcements of security-related problems that may apply to your systems; determine what immediate steps you can take to reduce your exposure to the vulnerability, such as disabling the affected software; and obtain permanent fixes from vendors.

Installing applicable vendors' updates can reduce your vulnerability to attack. Use vendor web sites and other commonly available sources of information to stay current (as described in Chapter 1). Consider purchasing comprehensive vendor services and support for critical assets.

2.4.1 Evaluate and Install Updates

Not all updates are applicable to the particular configuration of the computers and networks in your organization and your organization's specific security requirements.

Evaluate all the updates to determine their applicability, and weigh the cost of deploying an update against the benefits of so doing. Keep in mind that failure to install a vendor patch may result in a known vulnerability being present in your operational configuration.

Installing an update can itself cause security problems, such as the following:

- During the update process, the computer may temporarily be placed in a more vulnerable state.

- If the update is scheduled inappropriately, it might render a computer or information asset unavailable when needed.

- If an update must be performed on a large number of computers, there may be a period of time when some computers on the network are using different and potentially incompatible versions of software, which might cause information to be lost or corrupted.

- The update may introduce new vulnerabilities.

> As Matt Power of BindView's Razor security team notes, "A number of vendors do not offer patch authentication via any cryptographic method. This can make it very difficult for customers to verify that they have obtained a correct patch rather than a Trojan horse." (See Section 2.12 for information on Trojan horses.) Even if a vendor's server is not compromised, well-known vulnerabilities in Internet protocols can be exploited to deliver a Trojan horse patch to customers.[9]
>
> As a result, it is critical that you review the means by which you receive patches, authenticate them where possible, and review source code if it is provided.

Updates can also cause a number of problems in other installed software. We recommend installing updates in an isolated test environment and running a previously

---

9. Refer to *http://www.theregister.co.uk/content/4/15618.html* for more details.

developed regression test suite to compare current performance with past performance. Additionally, run a series of user trials before releasing the update on your operational systems. A less desirable but perhaps more practical approach would be to apply the update to a small number of less critical computers to see if any problems emerge before rolling out the change to all computers.

Software packages such as Tripwire (refer to Section A.2) are designed to reveal any differences in the system as a result of installing the update. We recommend that you use one of these packages so that you can fully understand and analyze the effects of the update on your systems.

In addition, you should always back up your system before applying any updates.

Any method of updating that depends on an administrator physically visiting each computer is labor intensive but will work for networks with a small number of computers. Automated tools are needed, however, to roll out updates to a large number of computers. Some of these tools are provided by vendors for their specific products. You may need to develop tools that are tailored to your environment if vendor tools are insufficient.

Given the number and diversity of operating systems and applications, the update process can become unmanageable if it is not supported by appropriate levels of automation. In such cases updates may not be performed, which in turn places your systems at risk by allowing intruders to take advantage of known vulnerabilities.

When using automated tools to roll out updates, the affected computers and the network are likely to be vulnerable to attack during the update process.

To lessen this vulnerability, you should use only an isolated network segment when propagating the updates; alternatively, consider using secure connectivity tools such as SSH. (Section A.3 provides a detailed description of SSH.)

Install updates using a documented procedure.

It is possible that you may not have enough information to decide whether or not to apply an update. You also may not have a comprehensive test environment in which to evaluate the effects of an update. In either of these situations, we recommend that you implement the steps in this practice as far as is both possible and practical. You should then try to recognize and manage any remaining risks of exposure.

2.4.2 Deploy New Computers with Up-to-Date Software

When new workstations and network servers are being deployed, it is common to install the operating system and other software from the original distribution media supplied by vendors. However, these software versions may not include recent security-related updates. Maintain an archive of updates that you have evaluated and chosen to install on existing computers, so that you can install them on new computers before deploying them.

Acquire and install the most current production-release driver software (often available from vendors' web sites) for all components and peripheral devices. Those drivers typically address performance and security issues that have been discovered since the components were packaged and shipped from the factory. Be sure to read all the release documentation associated with the updated drivers before using them. Whenever possible, verify the integrity and authenticity of the new driver software, using methods such as verifying your cryptographic checksums against those supplied by the vendor.

2.4.3 Create New Integrity-Checking Information

After making any necessary changes in a computer's configuration or its information content, create new cryptographic checksums or other integrity-checking baseline information for that computer.

Integrity checking tools (such as Tripwire, described in Section A.2) can identify changes made to files and directories when you install updates. By creating another baseline and subsequently monitoring these changes, you can learn more about how the system is working and, over time, identify unexpected changes that require further investigation.

Refer to Chapters 5 and 6 for additional information on the role of checking the integrity of baseline information to support intrusion detection.

2.4.4 Policy Considerations

Your organization's networked systems security policy should require system administrators to monitor the need for necessary security-related software updates and install them in a timely manner.

2.5 Stick to Essentials on the Server Host Machine (NS)

Ideally, each network service should be on a dedicated, single-purpose host. Many computers are configured by default to provide a wider set of services and applications than required to provide a particular network service, so you may need to configure the server to eliminate or disable these.

Offering only the essential network services on a particular host can enhance your network security in several ways:

- Other services cannot be used to attack the host and impair or remove desired network services. Each additional service added to a host increases the risk of compromise for all services on that host or for any computer trusting that host.

- Different services may be administered by different individuals. By isolating services so that each host and service has a single administrator, you will minimize the possibility of conflicts between the administrators (also known as separation of duties—a principle underlying a security policy [Summers 97]).

- The host can be configured to better suit the requirements of the particular service. Different services might require different hardware and software configurations, which could lead to needless vulnerabilities or service restrictions.

- Reducing services also reduces the number of logs and log entries, so detecting unexpected behavior becomes easier.

We strongly recommend that you use the configuration principle "deny first, then allow." That is, turn off as many services and applications as possible and then selectively turn on only those that are absolutely essential. We also suggest that you install the most minimal operating system configuration image that meets your business requirements. For additional information, refer to *Web Security & Commerce* "Minimizing Risk by Minimizing Services" (pp. 268–270; Garfinkel 97).

This practice is most effective if it is performed as part of the initial operating system installation and configuration.

2.5.1 Determine Functions

The services you enable on a selected host depend on the functions you want the host to provide. Functions could support the selected network service, other services hosted on this server, or development and maintenance of the operating system and applications. Providing multiple services or combining the role of workstation and server on the same machine results in a less secure configuration and makes maintaining security more difficult.

Determine the network server configuration for the following:

- File systems (e.g., whether any file services will be used by this host).

- System maintenance (e.g., whether, in the case of multi-user systems, all maintenance will be done only via the console or remotely).

- Server maintenance. In most cases, all server software maintenance should be done on another host and the updated files downloaded to this host. Limit the software on the server to what is required to administer the server. Carefully consider the need for compilers, editors, interpreters, shells, scripts, or other programming tools based on the server's use (providing specific services or applications, being used for internal development, etc.).[10]

- Network configuration. Consider including a list of trusted hosts and other computers, which will be in communication with the server. Be aware that this approach will take more time; information is replicated, and any updates must be performed on each host to keep this information consistent.

- Protocols offered (IP [Internet Protocol], IPX [Internetwork Packet Exchange], AppleTalk, etc.).

Depending upon the service, you can choose from several options:

- Limit the hosts that can access the service. Consider the use of tools such as TCP (Transmission Control Protocol) wrapper.[11]

- Limit the users who can access the service.

- Configure the service to allow only authenticated connections. The authentication should not rely solely on network data such as IP addresses and DNS names, which can easily be falsified (i.e., spoofed), regardless of whether or not the host is trusted.

- Limit the degree of access (especially in cases where that would permit a user to change the configuration of network services).

- If applicable, limit the range of facilities and functions offered by the service to those deemed necessary (e.g., if files will be shared via FTP, permit only file downloads and restrict file uploads).

- Isolate the service's files (configuration, data files, executable images, etc.) from those of other services and the rest of the system.

You may need to configure the server differently according to other features provided by the selected host operating system or environment. For example, certain operating systems provide extensive access control mechanisms that minimize or prevent the possibility of unauthorized access at relatively fine levels of granularity.

---

10. If programming tools are required, locate them in separate, protected directories. Locate public scripts in a single protected "execute only" directory.

11. Available at *http://www.cert.org/security-improvement/* under UNIX implementations.

2.5.2 Select the More Secure Alternative

On UNIX systems, for example, connectivity for remote system maintenance (i.e., not from the console) could be supported using remote shell (RSH) or SSH (see Section A.3). We recommend disabling all r-services[12] due to their inherent vulnerabilities (use of IP addresses for authentication). Therefore, select SSH, which is the more secure alternative.

Use wrapper tools such as TCP wrapper for controlling access to selected services by IP address and to log all connection attempts to those services (such as telnet). Be aware that TCP wrapper does not protect against IP spoofing (forging source addresses in IP packets; refer to CERT advisories); however, such connection attempts and successful connections would be logged.

2.5.3 Install Only the Minimal Set of Services and Applications

Either do not install unnecessary services or turn the services off and remove the corresponding files (source, binary, executable, configuration, and data files) from the server. Be careful with network service programs. Some provide multiple services, and you will have to reconfigure them or disable unnecessary services. For example, web server software often includes FTP along with HTTP. Disable FTP if you do not intend to support file transfers to and from your public web site. If you need to retain the FTP service, severely restrict access to it and carefully consider how anonymous FTP will be used.

When considering services to enable or disable, administrators typically think of those services that run as processes, for example, telnet, FTP, DNS, electronic mail, and web services. However, most of today's systems also provide services directly from the kernel. An example of this service is a netmask request. That request is typically broadcast onto the LAN, and all systems seeing that request answer it unless otherwise instructed. The kernel of those answering systems is providing the netmask service, more than likely unbeknownst to the administrator of that computer.

To reduce the risk of attack using TCP and UDP (User Datagram Protocol) network ports, eliminate all unnecessary services listening for incoming connections on these ports. Services listening on network ports can be identified using the netstat command on UNIX and Windows systems.

You need to determine what services the kernel and operating system respectively provide in order to configure those services. Since these services are frequently undocumented and uncontrollable, the best source of information is the system vendor.

---

12. Including `rpc`, `rdate`, `rdist`, `remsch`, `rlogin`, `rsh`, `rksh`, `rup`, `ruptime`, `rusers`, and `rwho`.

We recommend that you configure computers to offer only the services that your deployment plan specifies they should provide.

2.5.4 Create and Record Cryptographic Checksums

After you make all configuration choices, create and record cryptographic checksums or other integrity-checking baseline information for your critical system software and its configuration. Refer to Section 5.3 for descriptions of how to do this.

2.5.5 Policy Considerations

Your organization's networked systems security policy should require two important protection mechanisms:

1. Individual network servers, including public servers, should be configured to offer only essential services.
2. Each network service should be on a dedicated, single-purpose host wherever possible.

2.6 Stick to Essentials on the Workstation Host System (UW)

When you purchase a new workstation, usually a range of network service client, server, and application software is enabled by default to prepare the workstation for the following uses:

- As a personal workstation that uses network services only as a client
- As a personal workstation that provides and uses services from other workstations
- As a workstation that also functions as a public server (which introduces considerable risks)

Most workstations do not need all the settings enabled by default, so you need to configure the operating system to provide only the services specified in your deployment plan.

Workstations that perform services such as file sharing must recognize and "trust" those requesting service. Each service can be an entry point for unauthorized users and represents a potential security problem for that workstation and others on the local area network. It is important to enable only the software required for the workstation's intended use.

As already noted, we recommend that you be guided by the configuration principle "deny first, then allow," that is, turning off as many applications as possible and then selectively turning on only those that are absolutely essential. We recommend installing the most minimal operating system configuration image that meets your business requirements.

This practice is most effective if it is performed as part of the initial installation and configuration of the operating system. For the sake of completeness, some of the advice in this section refers to or duplicates recommendations contained in Section 2.5.

2.6.1 Determine Functions

The software you enable on a selected host depends on the functions you want the host to provide. Functions could support the use of a selected network service (by enabling the corresponding client), other services hosted on this workstation, specific applications, and software development. First, identify services provided by the system, such as Internet services (file transfer, web access, remote login, etc.), file services, computation services (such as remote procedure calls), electronic mail, and printing services. Next, review the documentation and the configuration files or settings to determine which services are on by default.

Combining the role of workstation and server on the same machine results in a less secure configuration and makes security maintenance more difficult. We do not recommend this.

You can now determine the workstation configuration for the following functions:

- Applications to be used on this workstation.
- File systems, e.g., whether any file services will be used by this host.
- Default settings for "small" servers, such as web access and FTP servers. These are becoming common parts of workstation operating systems. They are intended for file sharing within a workgroup, but it is possible to (mis)configure them to make local files visible to anyone (including intruders) via public networks.
- System maintenance, for example, whether all maintenance will be done only via the console or remotely.
- Network configuration. Consider including a list of trusted hosts and other computers that will be in communication with the server. Be aware that this approach will take more time; information is replicated, and any updates must be performed on each host to keep this information consistent.

- Protocols offered (IP, IPX, AppleTalk, etc.). It is useful to run a port-scanning tool from another connected computer to detect active TCP/IP network ports on the workstation and identify active services based on protocols other than TCP/IP, such as IPX or AppleTalk.

You may need to configure the workstation differently according to other features provided by the selected host operating system or environment. For example, certain operating systems provide extensive access control mechanisms that minimize or prevent the possibility of unauthorized access at relatively fine levels of granularity.

Select the more secure alternative as described in Section 2.5.

2.6.2 Install Only Essential Software

Either do not install unnecessary software or turn the software off and remove the corresponding files (source, binary, executable, configuration, and data files) from the workstation. Refer to Section 2.5 for guidance on enabling and disabling services residing on a computer (server or workstation).

We recommend that you configure workstations to offer only the services, clients, and applications software that your deployment plan specifies they should provide.

2.6.3 Create and Record Cryptographic Checksums

After you make all configuration choices, create and record cryptographic checksums or other integrity-checking baseline information for your critical system software and its configuration. Approaches for doing this are described in Section 5.3.

2.6.4 Policy Considerations

Your organization's networked systems security policy should require all workstations to be configured with only essential software and all other software to be disabled or removed.

2.7 Configure Network Service Clients to Enhance Security (UW)

Users typically need to access several network services from their workstations. Examples include centralized file services, electronic mail, web access, database access, collaboration or conferencing services, electronic bulletin boards, file transfers, and remote access to other workstations. You must configure the client software that accesses those services to operate securely, as far as is possible and practical. Many vulnerabilities can be eliminated by carefully configuring network service clients and installing vendors' patches and upgrades.

You must configure network service clients securely during the initial installation and setup of the operating system and carefully maintain the configuration thereafter.

Because there are many network services and different client software packages for using services, it is not possible to provide detailed configuration advice for each kind of client. The steps below offer general guidelines to help you configure network service clients to enhance security.

2.7.1   Identify Behaviors That May Lead to Security Problems

Address the following questions:

- Can the client be used to transmit confidential information (either personal or company data) over public networks? If so, you may need to use cryptographic software in conjunction with the client and institute policies limiting the number of users who are allowed to transmit information.

- Does the client software require increased user privileges? If so, misuse may result in other, more destructive actions at the higher privilege level.

- Can the client be used, either directly or indirectly, to download and execute software? Web browsers, for example, can be configured to execute ActiveX, Java, or JavaScript code from external web sites. ActiveX[13] and Java applets are known to have security vulnerabilities. You may want to disable them on browsers. If disabling ActiveX, Java, or JavaScript is not feasible or desirable, you should consider the use of a proxy server to intercept incoming web pages and not allow these applets to be passed to the requesting client.

- Can the client corrupt data because of improper configuration?

- Can the client disclose to servers confidential information about the client's host system configuration, network, or the user?

- When can users download and execute code from external sites, and when can they not do so?

---

13. Refer to the CERT report "Results of the Security in ActiveX Workshop," conducted August 22–23, 2000, and published December 21, 2000. The report is available at the CERT web site.

- Are there any private cryptographic keys or other authentication material on the client?
- Does the client have trust relationships with other users and computers?
- Is the client multi-homed (i.e., does it have more than one network interface)? Can it be used to bridge or route to other computers?

2.7.2 Maintain Awareness of Vendors' Updates

Vendors and organizations addressing network security issues often publish information related to recently discovered vulnerabilities in network service software (both clients and servers). You should actively seek this information and use it to help you configure or update network service clients. Refer to Chapter 1 and Section 2.4.

2.7.3 Configure the Client to Maintain Security

The details of this stage obviously vary widely among the software packages available for each network service. The following steps define a general configuration strategy:

1. Determine what is configurable.
2. Determine the likely threats to security presented by the software.
3. Turn off all software features except those absolutely necessary to provide the desired level of service.
4. Use access controls to inhibit the enabling of restricted settings.
5. Establish user policies to help maintain security where corresponding features of the software are lacking.

2.7.4 Policy Considerations

Your organization's workstation acceptable use policy (see also Section 2.15) should provide users with a clear explanation of the following:

- The precautions they should observe when using a web browser (for example, should Java and ActiveX be enabled or disabled?)
- The circumstances, if any, in which they may download and execute software from other hosts (inside or outside your organization)
- The limitations, if any, on the kinds of information that may be included in electronic mail

2.8 Configure Computers for User Authentication (NS, UW)

An organization's security policy for networked systems should specify that only authorized users may access the computers and the data and services they provide. To enforce this rule, you need to configure the computer to ensure that all users who attempt access can prove that they are authorized for such access.

Configuring computers for this authentication process usually involves configuring parts of the operating system, firmware, and applications such as the software that implements a network service. If your organization has authentication servers, configuring a new workstation or network server for user authentication may require you to make configuration changes on the authentication server. In special cases you may also use authentication hardware such as tokens, one-time password mechanisms, or biometric devices.

Your deployment plan (described in Section 2.2) documents the users or user categories and the approach to authenticating those users. The following steps describe how to implement that part of the plan.

This practice is most effective if you include it as part of the initial installation and configuration of the operating system.

2.8.1 Configure Hardware-Based Access Controls

If the computer's firmware offers the feature of requiring a password when the system is turned on, enable that feature and set the password. This feature is sometimes known as a BIOS (Basic Input/Output System) or EEPROM (Electrically Erasable Programmable Read-Only Memory) password.

Enabling this feature will require your intervention if the system crashes, because you can't configure the computer to restart automatically. This limitation is usually acceptable for workstations because if the user is not present, it is not necessary to restart the computer immediately. However, enabling this feature can present problems for network servers that operate 24 hours a day, because an administrator may not be available to restart the system when the system crashes.

2.8.2 Handle Accounts and Groups

The default configuration of the operating system often includes guest accounts (with and without passwords), administrator accounts, and accounts associated with local and network services. The names and passwords for those accounts are well known.

Remove or disable unnecessary accounts to eliminate their use by intruders, including guest accounts on computers containing sensitive information. If you do have the requirement to retain a guest account or group, eliminate it or severely restrict its access and change the password in accordance with your password policy.

For default accounts that you need to retain, consider changing the names (wherever possible and particularly for administrator accounts) and passwords. Default account names and passwords for such accounts are commonly known in the intruder community. However, even changed names and passwords can often be discovered by a moderately motivated intruder, and changing default administrator account names may affect other operating system functions.

Disable accounts (and the associated passwords) that need to exist but do not require an interactive login. For UNIX systems, disable the login shell or provide a login shell with NULL functionality (/bin/false).

Assign users to the appropriate groups. Then assign rights to the groups, as documented in your deployment plan. This approach is preferable to assigning rights to individual users.

Your deployment plan identifies who will be authorized to use each computer and its services. Create only the necessary accounts. Discourage or prohibit the use of shared accounts.

2.8.3 Check Your Password Policy and Ensure That Users Follow It

A password policy should cover five elements:

1. Length—it is common to specify a minimum length of eight characters.
2. Complexity—it is common to require passwords to contain a mix of characters, that is, both uppercase and lowercase letters and at least one nonalphabetic character.
3. Aging—how long a password may remain unchanged. It is common to require users to change their passwords periodically (every 30–120 days). The policy should permit users to do so only through approved authentication mechanisms.
4. Reuse—whether a password may be reused. Some users try to defeat a password-aging requirement by changing the password to one they have used before.
5. Authority—who is allowed to change passwords.

Document your password policy, communicate it to users, and train them always to follow the policy.

Configure the password-setting software to reject passwords that don't conform to your policy, if the operating system provides this feature.

If permitted by policy, for UNIX systems you may want to consider using npasswd.[14] This tool checks passwords as they are entered by users to ensure compliance with some aspects of your password policy.

Also if permitted by policy, an authorized system administrator can use tools such as crack[15] or l0phtCrack[16] to review all passwords to determine that they cannot be easily compromised and to ensure compliance with some aspects of your password policy.

2.8.4 Require Reauthentication After Idle Periods

This step is most useful for workstations, but consider it for network servers as well, especially if the server will be administered from the console.

Most operating systems include software to display a changing image (screensaver) on a monitor or software (locking screensaver) to power down monitors and disks (energy saver) after a short period of inactivity. This inactivity may indicate that the workstation is unattended, even though a user is still logged in. Requiring reauthentication when the user returns minimizes the risk of an unauthorized person using an active session while the authorized user is away.

If possible, configure the operating system to terminate a remote or terminal session (log out) and start a locking screen saver after a specified idle period (typically between two and ten minutes, depending on the sensitivity of access to the host). If this feature is not available, acquire and install third-party software to provide this capability.

Consider requiring users to shut down or lock computers when they leave them unattended. This precaution eliminates the period of vulnerability between the time the user leaves and the time the locking screensaver is activated. Hardware-based authentication systems such as chipcards can be used to lock computers when the user takes the chipcard out of its reader.

---

14. Available at *http://www.cert.org/security-improvement/* under UNIX implementations.

15. Available at *ftp://ftp.cerias.purdue.edu/pub/tools/unix/pwdutils/crack.*

16. Available at *http://www.l0pht.com/l0phtcrack/.*

2.8.5 Configure to Deny Login After a Small Number of Failed Attempts

It is relatively easy for an unauthorized user to try to gain access to a computer by using automated software tools that attempt to identify passwords.[17] If your operating system provides the capability, configure it to deny login after three failed attempts. Typically, the account is "locked out" for a period of time (such as 30 minutes) or until a user with appropriate authority reactivates it.

This is another situation that requires you to make a trade-off between security and convenience. Implementing this recommendation can help prevent some kinds of attacks, but it can also allow a malicious intruder to make failed login attempts to eliminate user access—amounting to a denial of service. You may consider this configuration unacceptable for network servers, because it renders the server unavailable to the authorized user whose account logins failed.

In some cases, you need to distinguish between failed login attempts at the console and those coming in through the network. Failed network login attempts should not prevent an authorized user or administrator from logging in at the console. Note that all failed login attempts should be logged (as described in Section 5.3).

2.8.6 Install and Configure Other Authentication Mechanisms

Consider using other authentication mechanisms such as tokens, one-time password systems, and biometric hardware and software. They can be expensive, but they may be justified in some circumstances and may be required to implement your security policies and procedures.

Passwords passed across a network in clear text can be easily captured by intruders using network sniffers. Consider implementing authentication and encryption technologies such as Kerberos,[18] SSH (see Section A.3), and SSL (Secure Socket Layer) (see Section 3.7). Configure the web server to use authentication and encryption technologies.

---

17. The time required to attempt to match a large number of passwords will depend on network speed and server performance capabilities, but an unauthorized user can certainly attempt to discover common passwords in a reasonable period of time.

18. Refer to *http://www.nrl.navy.mil/CCS/people/kenh/kerberos-faq.html* and *http://web.mit.edu/kerberos/www/* for further information.

The authentication capabilities of network service software packages vary. Note that some packages provide their own mechanisms for authenticating users, while others depend on the underlying operating system.[19] Be sure that both are configured appropriately and that they reinforce and do not conflict with one another.

2.8.7 Policy Considerations

Your organization's networked systems security policy should have the following characteristics:

- It should describe under what conditions an account is created and deleted. This description should cover what account actions are taken (disabled, deleted, transferred) and how files are handled when an employee, contractor, or vendor who has an account no longer works for your organization.

- It should require appropriate authentication of all users on all computers that can access information assets, including users of network services hosted by your servers.

- It should include an appropriate password policy.

- It should prohibit users from recording and storing passwords in places that could be discovered by intruders.

When writing a password policy, remember that requiring users to have complex passwords may result in the undesired situation whereby users write their passwords on paper that they keep near the computer (often stuck to the machine) or with personal papers (in a wallet, purse, or briefcase). If that paper is observed, lost, or stolen, it creates a potential vulnerability.

If a password policy is especially difficult to follow, it creates in users a desire to find ways around it. This attitude can negatively influence users' compliance with other aspects of security policies.

Your organization's acceptable use policy for workstations should require that users shut down or lock their unattended workstations. See also Section 2.15.

---

19. Be aware that proprietary, closed authentication mechanisms used by such packages are not necessarily secure.

2.9 Configure Operating Systems with Appropriate Object, Device, and File Access Controls (NS, UW)

Many operating systems enable you to specify access privileges individually for files, directories, devices, and other data or code objects. We recommend that you configure the settings on files and other objects to take advantage of this capability and protect information in accordance with your security policy.

By carefully setting access controls, you can reduce both intentional and unintentional security breaches. For example, denying read access helps protect the confidentiality of information, while denying unnecessary write (modify) access can help maintain its integrity. Limiting the execution privilege of most system-related tools to authorized system administrators can prevent general users from making configuration changes that could reduce security. This restriction can also make it harder for intruders to use those tools to attack the system or other systems on the network.

Some operating systems provide a number of file systems, each with different access control capabilities. It is important to choose the file system that best meets your needs for file access control. Your decision may affect the low-level formatting of storage devices and thus should be made early in the process of configuring the operating system.

Implement access controls during initial installation and configuration of the operating system. Carefully monitor and maintain them thereafter.

2.9.1 Identify the Protection Needed

One method that you can use to identify the protection you need is to construct a matrix with categories of files and objects on one axis and groups of users (defined by roles and access authority) on the other. Then record in the matrix the kinds of access privileges allowed for that class of objects and that class of users. The privileges are based on the security requirements (such as confidentiality, integrity, and availability) of the various classes of assets.

For example, you may have file categories that include administrative information (user names, passwords, privileges, etc.), applications, development tools, operating system files, and user data files. The latter may be further subdivided into categories such as customer accounts, inventory records, research data, and management reports. You may have user groups that include system administrators, network service daemons, and users from various departments.

As you begin to identify privileges, you may need to split some rows and columns. This need may occur, for example, when you discover that a single group of users is really two groups because their need to access a particular resource is not uniform.

Application programs may request, and be granted, increased access privileges for some of their operations—a change that is not obvious to the users of that application. You may not want all those users to have increased privileges. Therefore, it is important to take great care in assigning privileges to users and groups.

You may also want to distinguish local access privileges from network access privileges for a class of files.

You may identify categories of users not sufficiently detailed in the computer deployment plan (as described in Section 2.2). Configure the operating system to recognize the needed user groups, and then assign individual users (including network service daemons) to the appropriate groups.

2.9.2 Configure Access Controls

Configure access controls for all protected files, directories, devices, and other objects, using the matrix created in the step above as a guide. Every change or decision not to change each object's permission should be documented along with the rationale.

Consider the following:

- Disable write/modify access permissions for all executable and binary files.

- Restrict access of operating system source files, configuration files, and their directories to authorized administrators.

- For UNIX systems, there should be no world-writable files unless necessary application programs specifically require these. For Windows systems, there should be no permissions set such that "the Everyone group has Modify permissions to files."

- For UNIX systems, if possible, mount file systems as read-only and *nosuid* to preclude unauthorized changes to files and programs.

- Assign an access permission of immutable to all kernel files if assigning such permission is supported by the operating system (such as Linux and FreeBSD).

- Establish all log files as "append only" if that option is available.

- Aim to preclude users from installing, removing, or editing scripts (see Section 3.5) without administrative review. We realize that this restriction is difficult to enforce.

Pay attention to access control inheritance when defining categories of files and users. Ensure that you configure the operating system so that newly created files and directories inherit appropriate access controls, and so that access controls propagate down the directory hierarchies as intended when you assign them.

Many of an administrator's security directives can be overridden on a per-directory basis. The convenience of being able to make local exceptions to global policy is offset by the threat of a security hole being introduced in a distant subdirectory, which could be taken over by a hostile user. Administrators should disable a subdirectory's ability to override top-level security directives unless that override is required.

2.9.3 Install and Configure File Encryption Capabilities for Sensitive Data

Some operating systems provide optional file encryption; there are also third-party file encryption packages available, which may be useful if the operating system's access controls are insufficient to maintain the confidentiality of file contents. This situation can occur if the operating system provides few or no access control features, or when the relationships among categories of files and categories of users are so complex that it would be difficult to administer the security policy using only access controls.

Encryption adds complexity, so you need to weigh the need for it against the cost of using it.

The security provided by strong access controls is further enhanced by the use of encryption. However, when you use encryption, you must still dispose of unencrypted versions of the data that existed prior to encryption being performed, remain after decrypting, and are used in the encryption process.

Note that this recommendation pertains only to the encryption of files stored on the computer itself. Encryption of information for transmission over a network is a separate issue that is not within the scope of this practice.

2.9.4 Policy Considerations

Your organization's networked systems security policy should specify the following:

- Access privileges and controls for the information that will be stored on computers.
- How to access files that have been encrypted with a user key. This information is very important when that user no longer works for your organization.

- Access privileges and controls for administrative users, such as

    the authority and conditions for reading other users' e-mail

    access to protected programs or files

    disruption of service under specific conditions

    a ban on sharing accounts

    a ban on the unauthorized creation of user accounts

    the authority and conditions for using vulnerability testing tools

2.10 Configure Computers for File Backups (NS, UW)

Before deploying a computer, you need to develop a file backup and restoration plan and configure the computer to implement that plan.

File backups allow you to restore the availability and integrity of information assets following security breaches and accidents. Without a backup, you may be unable to restore a computer's data after system failures and security breaches.

2.10.1 Develop a File Backup and Restoration Plan

All system and user files should be backed up on a regular basis. You may need to perform a cost/benefit analysis to help you decide how to balance the speed of the backup process against the amount of storage needed for the backed-up files and the effort required to restore one or all files from backed-up versions.

Develop a plan that is broad enough to cover all the workstations and servers you plan to deploy.

If you have regularly created cryptographic checksums for all files[20] and have securely stored these checksums, you can plan to restore files from trusted backups against which such checksums have been calculated.

If you have no such checksums, you need to restore system, executable, and binary files from the original distribution media. Then you must reinstall site-specific modifications, relevant patches, and bug-fixes. You need to ensure that these modifications do not introduce additional defects or vulnerabilities. Exercise caution when restoring user

---

20. Refer to Sections 2.4 and 5.3.

files from untrusted backups, and instruct all users to check for any unexpected changes to their restored files.

For workstations, there are two common approaches:

1. Files are backed up locally at each workstation, often by the user(s) of that workstation. This approach has the advantage of not requiring that protected data traverse the network, which reduces the chances of its being monitored, intercepted, or corrupted. It has the disadvantage of requiring additional storage devices on each workstation, necessitating increased efforts to keep the many backup devices and media secure, and requiring that you train users to perform the backups.
2. Backups are centrally administered, with data copied from workstations via networks. Encryption tools can be used to protect data passing from a user workstation to a central backup host.

For network servers that provide information services dependent on automatic replication mechanisms,[21] a third approach is often used. The authoritative version of the information content of the server is created and maintained on a secure machine that is backed up. The information is periodically transferred to the server for access by clients. If the server is compromised and its content damaged, the information can be reloaded from the secure system that maintains the authoritative version. This approach is typically used for public servers, such as DNS, FTP, and web servers,[22] because the content changes at more predictable intervals than, for example, a server that provides e-mail and file-sharing services to user workstations (requiring a backup approach similar to those described above for workstations).

Determine the appropriate medium to contain your backup files based on your requirements for speed (both reading and writing), reliability, and storage duration. Options you should consider are magnetic tape, optical disk, and CD-ROM.

If you choose central administration and storage of backed-up files, ensure that the backup tools adequately protect data confidentiality and integrity as it travels across the network from the host to the backup device. We recommend that you use encryption technologies, although we recognize that this is not common practice.

The plan should specify that (1) source data are encrypted before being transmitted over a network or to the storage medium; (2) data remain encrypted on the backup storage media; and (3) storage media, including encryption keys, are kept in a physically secure facility that is protected from man-made and natural disasters.

---

21. The information is treated as though it resides on a WORM device (write once, read many).

22. This approach is more fully described in Chapter 3.

The plan should be designed to ensure that backups are performed in a secure manner and that their contents remain secure.

Be aware that file backups taken from compromised machines may contain damaged files, services, or other information left behind by an intruder (back doors, Trojan horses). Exercise caution when you use these backups to restore your computers.

Refer to Sections 7.6 and 7.7 for a discussion of approaches to consider when you are choosing backup methods.

2.10.2 Install and Configure File Backup Tools

Select file backup tools to allow you to implement your backup plan. You may need to use third-party software, given that the backup capabilities of most operating systems are not sufficient. You may also need to install storage devices, either centrally or on each computer, to store the backup copies.

The tools used to recover backed-up files should be kept both online and offline. If a computer has been compromised and you need to recover a file, you cannot trust the integrity of any of the tools on that computer, including the file recovery tools.

Tool configurations need to reflect your backup and restoration plan. Configure the tools to save access control settings along with file contents, if that feature is available.

Do the first full backup just before deploying the computer, and then confirm that you can perform a full restoration from that backup, as described in the following section on testing the ability to recover from backups.

In many organizations, file backups are completely automated, so system administrators tend to forget that they are happening. Therefore, confirm that the backup procedures for a newly deployed computer are being performed successfully.

2.10.3 Test the Ability to Recover from Backups

For many system administrators, recovering a file from a backup is an uncommon activity. This step ensures that if you need to recover a file, the tools and procedures will work.

Performing this test periodically will help you to discover problems with the backup procedures so that you can correct them before losing data.

Some backup restoration software does not accurately recover the correct file protection and file ownership controls. Check these attributes of restored files to ensure that they are being set correctly.

Periodically test to ensure that you can perform a full system recovery from your backups.

2.10.4 Policy Considerations

Your organization's networked systems security policy should both require the creation of a file backup and restoration plan and inform users of their responsibilities (if any) for file backup and recovery.

2.11 Use a Tested Model Configuration and a Secure Replication Procedure (UW)

When deploying several computers, especially workstations, across an organization, it is common to configure one appropriately and then propagate that configuration to all the others. You need to ensure that this is done in a secure manner, especially if the configuration is propagated via a network.

While a workstation is being configured, not all of its security features and controls are yet in place, thus making the workstation more vulnerable to attack. Performing the configuration on the model system in an isolated environment (not connected to your organization's networks or public networks) can prevent network-based attacks. Similarly, physical isolation during configuration limits who can access the computer.

Once the configuration is tested and found to satisfy your security requirements, it can be replicated on other workstations. This replication helps establish a consistent level of security on all workstations on your network, as well as facilitating the consistent updating of all workstations when necessary.

The replication process must be performed securely to prevent corruption of the configuration information and to prevent attacks on the other computers before they are fully configured.

2.11.1 Create and Test the Model Configuration

Do this on a single workstation in an isolated test environment. The isolated environment prevents intruders from gaining access to the workstation during the initial configuration process, while it is in a less secure state.

Many tests can be done in the isolated test environment. However, it may be necessary to do some final tests in a production environment. Be particularly vigilant for signs of intrusion during those tests. Also, the newly configured workstation may affect other computers or the network in ways that you did not expect.

2.11.2 Replicate the Configuration on Other Workstations

There are three approaches to replicating the configuration.

1. Record the steps performed to create the model configuration and then repeat those steps manually on each workstation. This may be the only secure way to install workstations in remote locations. It is, however, prone to human error and is not a manageable solution for a large number of workstations.
2. Save the configuration on a storage device that can be write-protected, moved to the other workstations, and used as a master copy. While this method is less error prone, it still requires considerable effort by the administrators and therefore does not scale up for a large number of workstations. It also requires the individual workstations' configurations to be modified before deployment, so that each workstation can be uniquely identified on the network.
3. Use the network to transfer the model configuration to the other workstations. This approach requires them to be already running in some default or minimal state that is likely to be less secure than the model configuration. Thus all the workstations and the network are likely to be vulnerable to attack during the process of replicating the model configuration. To lessen this vulnerability, you should use only an isolated network segment to propagate the model configuration during the configuration process.

2.11.3 Make Configuration Changes on a Case-by-Case Basis

Each workstation may have a different primary user, so you may need to create user accounts for each user on his or her particular system.

You can make these changes either at the workstation itself or from an administrator's workstation with secure network connectivity to the workstations being deployed.

2.11.4 Create and Record Cryptographic Checksums

After you make all configuration choices, create and record cryptographic checksums or other integrity-checking baseline information for your critical system software and its configuration. Approaches for doing this are described in Section 5.3.

2.12 Protect Computers from Viruses and Similar Programmed Threats (NS, UW)

Several kinds of software can surreptitiously breach computer security, either individually or in combination with one another.[23]

Viruses

A virus is a code fragment (not an independent program) that reproduces by attaching to another program. It may damage data directly, or it may degrade system performance by taking over system resources, which are then not available to authorized users.

Worms

A worm is an independent program that reproduces by copying itself from one system to another, usually over a network. Like a virus, a worm may damage data directly, or it may degrade system performance by consuming system resources and even shutting down a network.

Trojan Horses

A Trojan horse is an independent program that appears to perform a useful function but hides another unauthorized program inside it. When an authorized user performs the apparent function, the Trojan horse performs the unauthorized function as well (often usurping the privileges of the user). Several CERT advisories address specific Trojan horse behavior.

You should configure computers to take countermeasures against such threats; as e-mail filters, for example, look for and reject e-mail with suspicious attachments. In addition, you should establish policies and train users to help prevent these programmed threats from being installed on their workstations.

Programmed threats can cause significant damage. Your confidential information can be captured and transmitted, critical information can be modified, and the configuration of a computer can be changed to permit subsequent unauthorized access, leading to intrusions. Services provided by your organization can be interrupted for extended periods of time, your users and customers may lose confidence in your organization's ability to protect its information, and you can experience legal ramifications if

---

23. Definitions are adapted from *Computer Security Basics* (Russell 91).

your systems are used as launch points for broader distribution of programmed threat software.

Recovering from programmed threats can be expensive. Installing preventive measures and instituting user training can significantly reduce your exposure to these threats at a fraction of the cost that it would take to recover from them.

2.12.1 Develop a Programmed Threats Protection Plan

The plan should specify how much responsibility and authority users and system administrators should have to take specific actions to protect their computers against viruses and similar programmed threats.

The plan should also explain how users should use the available anti-virus tools for workstations and describe any limitations on the authority of users to download and/or install new software.

2.12.2 Install and Execute Anti-Virus Tools

Install selected anti-virus tools on your computers following a clean reboot and a full system check. This procedure is most effective if performed as part of the initial installation and configuration of the operating system.

Regularly check for viruses using the online version of tools.

Store copies of anti-virus tools offline in a secure manner. It is possible that a new virus could modify the detection and eradication software to prevent its own detection. Periodically use offline, trusted copies of the tools to scan your systems, particularly after new anti-virus signatures are added (see Section 2.12.4).

Regularly exercise anti-virus tools on all network servers and gateways. This can be done individually or from a central administration console.

2.12.3 Train Users[24]

Train users to understand how viruses and other programmed threats propagate and what they can do to help prevent further propagation. This training involves showing them how to use virus detection tools on software obtained from public sources (such

---

24. Note that this step is primarily applicable to workstations rather than network servers. For servers, the administrator is responsible for virus detection and eradication.

as shareware) before loading and executing it, and educating them to be alert to the possibility of such threats in e-mail attachments and downloaded web content.

Many viruses manifest themselves in predictable ways. Train users to recognize virus symptoms, report them, and run appropriate virus eradication tools (if your plan permits them to use these tools).

Keep users apprised of new programmed threats and related intrusion scenarios.

2.12.4 Update Detection Tools

Routinely check for and update programmed threat detection tools as needed, especially when new threats are discovered.

Many anti-virus tools use a database of known virus characteristics (signatures). Vendors frequently release updated versions of those databases on a weekly or monthly basis. Ensure that your computers have the most recent versions. Updating your anti-virus tools using vendor updates as they become available is one of the primary methods of preventing virus infections.

2.12.5 Policy Considerations

Your organization's workstation acceptable use policy (see also Section 2.15) or security policy for networked systems should do the following:

- Define users' authority (or lack thereof) to download and/or install software on the computer.

- Specify who has the responsibility to scan for and eradicate viruses—users or system administrators—and where to scan to include workstations, servers, and gateways.

- Prohibit users from running executable files that they have received as e-mail attachments or downloaded from untrusted sites. If such a file needs to be run, it should be run on a host that is isolated from your operational systems. The host should not contain sensitive information, and the file should be run through virus detection tools. In addition, determining the file originator, if possible, will aid in determining the level of trust.

2.13 Configure Computers for Secure Remote Administration (NS, UW)

Administering a workstation or network server includes updating user account information, examining the logs, installing new or updated software, and maintaining an appropriate configuration. These tasks can be performed locally from the workstation or server console, but they can also be performed remotely from a separate host via a network connection.

Although local administration is more secure (and we recommend it whenever feasible), remote administration is more typical, particularly when a large number of workstations or network servers (such as print servers and file servers) are being serviced. When performing remote administration, you need to consider the security of the administration host, the network, and the computer being administered.

Remote administration of computers is increasingly common because of the significant cost benefits—many tasks can be automated, and the administrator does not physically have to visit each computer. However, remote administration tools must be configured to operate securely.

Although the normal operational state of your computer may be secure, it may temporarily become vulnerable during the performance of administrative tasks. This is especially true when public servers that have been placed outside your firewall are remotely administered, requiring you to open a network connection through the firewall. Such a connection may be vulnerable to some forms of attack, and it may open the door to anyone on the Internet being able to "administer" your server. As a result, you could lose confidentiality or integrity of information assets on the server, or an intruder might gain access to resources on your internal network or be able to use your server or workstation as an intermediate host for attacks on other internal or external hosts.

2.13.1 Ensure That Administration Commands Originate from Only Authenticated Administrators and Hosts

Configure the computer to use a strong method to authenticate the identity of the user who is initiating any administrative process. In particular, avoid authentication methods that require the transmission of a password in clear text, unless it is a one-time password.

Authenticate the host in a manner that does not depend on network-resolved information such as IP addresses or DNS names, because intruders can falsify such information within packets sent to the computers being administered. We recommend the use of public key authentication using a tool such as SSH (see Section A.3).

Refer to Section 3.7 for a discussion of SSL, S/HTTP (Secure HTTP), and SET (Secure Electronic Transaction) for use with public web servers.

2.13.2 Ensure That All Administration Tasks Operate at the Minimum Necessary Privilege Level

Administration tasks sometimes require increased privilege levels. Take care to raise privilege levels only as needed.

Consider separation of duties among administrators to allow you to assign privilege levels as needed. This precaution eliminates the risk of one administrator becoming a single point of vulnerability.

2.13.3 Ensure That Confidential Information Cannot Be Intercepted, Read, or Changed by Intruders

Such information includes administration commands and system configuration information.

Methods such as encryption help to ensure that network packets travelling between the administrator's host machine and the computer being administered would not, if intercepted, provide sensitive information or permit system commands to be altered. Such actions could allow subsequent access to either the computer or your organization's internal network.

2.13.4 Use a Movable Storage Medium to Transfer Information

For some network servers, particularly those providing public services such as WWW, it is common to develop the information content of those services on a different host machine. The authoritative version of that content is maintained (and backed up) on that other machine and then transferred to the public server at appropriate intervals. The transfer can be performed by using a movable storage medium. This could include a CD-ROM, disk, hard disk cartridge, or tape. Since this procedure does not require a network connection through your firewall, it is more secure.

During the transfer, you may need to stop or disable your server. Some servers can be configured to continue operating and to send a "Service temporarily unavailable" message in response to all requests.

2.13.5 Use a Secure Method for Inspecting All Log Files

If you choose to inspect log files on a host other than the computer that generated the logs, use a secure method for transferring these logs. Movable storage media and file encryption are two suitable methods.

If you choose to inspect log files either by remotely accessing the computer from another host, or by remotely accessing a central log host that contains all log files, use appropriate authentication and encryption technologies as described above.

2.13.6 Create and Record Cryptographic Checksums

After making any changes in a computer's configuration or in its information content, create new cryptographic checksums or other integrity-checking baseline information for your server.

Refer to Chapter 6 for additional information on the role of checking the integrity of baseline information in support of intrusion detection.

2.13.7 Policy Considerations

Your organization's networked systems security policy should do the following:

- Require the use of secure procedures for administration of network servers and workstations
- Specify the circumstances in which third parties (vendors, service providers) are permitted to remotely administer your systems and how such administration is to be conducted

2.14 Allow Only Appropriate Physical Access to Computers (NS, UW)

In addition to the steps you take to prevent inappropriate electronic access to a computer, you should also strive to allow only appropriate physical access. What this involves can vary depending on the locations of computers, for example, whether they are in locked offices or in open-plan space. Physical access also includes activities such as installing or removing hardware.

If unauthorized persons can physically access a computer, the integrity of that system is at considerable risk. If the system is connected to internal networks, intruders can bypass all of your network perimeter defenses to access resources.

To preserve the confidentiality and availability of data, therefore, you must prevent the computer and its storage media from being removed from the facility by unauthorized persons.

Installing new hardware, such as a modem, may create new electronic access paths to the computer and thus make your network available to intruders.

2.14.1 Prevent Installation of Unauthorized Hardware

Installation of new hardware can lead to security problems in several ways:

- Installing a modem allows a direct connection from the computer to the public telephone network, which may then permit electronic access into your network from anywhere in the world, bypassing your perimeter defenses.
- Installing a removable-media storage device or printer makes it easy to copy information and carry it away from your site.
- Installing a boot device that precedes the authorized device in the boot sequence allows the computer to be restarted in a configuration that bypasses your security precautions.

You should lock the computer case, if possible. This may require third-party locking devices such as keys, cables, or racks. If a key is used, ensure that the key is protected, yet still accessible to authorized users. Make a backup key and protect it in a secure off-site location.

You may also want to remove or disable the external connectors on the computer.

2.14.2 Deploy the Computer in a Secure Facility

Deploying the computer in a secure facility helps to prevent theft, destruction, and unauthorized access. Methods of secure deployment may include using surveillance cameras or placing the computer in a locked room that uses controlled physical or electronic access, which is recorded.

Pay special attention to controlling access by vendors, contractors, and other visitors.

Do not deploy network servers in an individual's office.

Locate the computer in such a way that no unauthorized viewing of the monitor and keyboard can occur.

Secure the network wiring and other network connection components. Ensure that the network cabling is not placed in a physical location where it can be easily accessed. Note that this requires you to trade the convenience of access for the purposes of network maintenance for greater security.

If you need to protect against unauthorized monitoring, eavesdropping, or interference of electronic emanations coming from your computing equipment, you may need to consider physical protection technologies such as shielding and TEMPEST (Transient Electromagnetic Pulse Emanation Standard). Refer to *http://www.eskimo.com/ ~joelm/tempest.html* for further information on TEMPEST.

2.14.3 Policy Considerations

Your organization's networked systems security policy should indicate the following:

- Who is or is not allowed to install new hardware or modify existing hardware in a computer
- The circumstances in which users may or may not use storage devices with removable media
- The circumstances in which users may take storage media or printed information away from your site
- The need for network servers to be deployed in physically secure locations and for the access list to these locations to be kept short
- The circumstances in which third parties (vendors, service providers) are permitted to physically access your systems and how such access is to occur.

2.15 Develop and Roll Out an Acceptable Use Policy for Workstations (UW)

Organizations should develop a policy defining the acceptable uses of workstations. The policy should identify and encourage user behavior that can enhance security and discourage or prohibit user behavior that can reduce or breach security. You should help users understand the type of information you are protecting and their responsibilities in that protection.

The security of a workstation is ultimately the responsibility of the users. Their daily work usually requires them to access, manipulate, modify, and transmit protected information resources across networks. If your users don't understand their security responsibilities and your organization's expectations, the technological measures to enforce security may be ineffective.

Some of the security features built into operating systems or provided by third-party software products make it possible to enforce secure user behaviors. In the absence of such features, the only alternative may be to establish and enforce a policy prohibiting user actions that can reduce security.

2.15.1 Elements of an Acceptable Use Policy

The policy should cover all of the information technologies that your staff are likely to use. The policy needs to address corporate data, network access, and use of workstations, portable computers, home computers, modems, software packages, etc.

An acceptable use policy for workstations is best developed as part of an overall site security policy. Your policy should specify[25] the following:

- Workstations a user may or may not use
- Hardware changes the user may make
- Software the user may install or remove
- What kinds of work the user may perform on the workstation (such as manipulation of classified data or conducting personal business)
- Network services the user may or may not use
- Information the user may or may not transmit across the network (such as in electronic mail)

---

25. Refer also to Policy Considerations in Sections 2.7, 2.8, and 2.12.

- User responsibilities to operate the workstation securely, such as performing administrative tasks
- What kinds of configuration changes users may or may not make if they are given higher levels of privilege
- A ban on sharing of accounts
- The need to comply with your password policy
- Guidelines for accessing unprotected programs or files
- A ban on breaking into accounts and systems
- A ban on cracking passwords
- A ban on disruption of service
- Consequences for noncompliance

Review the policy on a periodic basis and update it to reflect changes in your business and networked systems technologies as events dictate.

2.15.2 Train Users

When a new policy is first adopted in an established organization, not everyone will want to make the behavioral changes to comply with it. You must be sure to explain the motivation for the policy. Peers, including those who participated in the development of the policy, can effectively accomplish this.

Train new employees about the policy as part of their initial orientation and inform all employees whenever the policy changes, retraining them if necessary.

User acceptance of the policy is typically accomplished by requiring each user to sign a statement acknowledging that he or she understands the policy and agrees to follow it.

2.15.3 Provide Explicit Reminders at Each Login

To avoid the risks of possible litigation and liability, it is essential that when users log in, they see a statement informing them that they must use the workstation in accordance with the acceptable use policy and that you may monitor their use to ensure compliance. This message may also help remind users of their responsibilities.

Chapter 2 Checklist

Practice	Step Number	Step Description	Yes	Partial	No
P2.2: Address Security Issues in Your Computer Deployment Plan (NS, UW)	S2.2.1	Identify the purpose of each computer			
	S2.2.2	Identify the network services that will be provided			
	S2.2.3	Identify network service software to be installed			
	S2.2.4	Identify users			
	S2.2.5	Determine user privileges			
	S2.2.6	Plan authentication			
	S2.2.7	Determine access enforcement measures			
	S2.2.8	Develop intrusion detection strategies			
	S2.2.9	Document backup and recovery procedures			
	S2.2.10	Determine how network services will be maintained or restored after various kinds of faults			
	S2.2.11	Develop and follow a documented procedure for installing an operating system			
	S2.2.12	Determine how the computer will be connected to your network			
	S2.2.13	Identify the security concerns related to day-to-day administration			
	S2.2.14	Protect information contained on hardware that is no longer in use			
	S2.2.15	Keep your computer deployment plan current			
	S2.2.16	Policy considerations			

Practice	Step Number	Step Description	Yes	Partial	No
P2.3 Address Security Requirements When Selecting Servers (NS)	S2.3.1	Identify functionality and performance requirements			
	S2.3.2	Review server product features			
	S2.3.3	Estimate the differences in operating costs of competing products			
	S2.3.4	Policy considerations			
P2.4 Keep Operating Systems and Applications Software Up-to-Date (NS, UW)	S2.4.1	Evaluate and install updates			
	S2.4.2	Deploy new computers with up-to-date software			
	S2.4.3	Create new integrity-checking information			
	S2.4.4	Policy considerations			
P2.5 Stick to Essentials on the Server Host Machine (NS)	S2.5.1	Determine functions			
	S2.5.2	Select the more secure alternative			
	S2.5.3	Install only the minimal set of services and applications			
	S2.5.4	Create and record cryptographic checksums			
	S2.5.5	Policy considerations			
P2.6 Stick to Essentials on the Workstation Host System (UW)	S2.6.1	Determine functions			
	S2.6.2	Install only essential software			

(continued)

Chapter 2   Checklist (*cont.*)

Practice	Step Number	Step Description	Yes	Partial	No
	S2.6.3	Create and record cryptographic checksums			
	S2.6.4	Policy considerations			
P2.7 Configure Network Service Clients to Enhance Security (UW)	S2.7.1	Identify behaviors that may lead to security problems			
	S2.7.2	Maintain awareness of vendors' updates			
	S2.7.3	Configure the client to maintain security			
	S2.7.4	Policy considerations			
P2.8 Configure Computers for User Authentication (NS, UW)	S2.8.1	Configure hardware-based access controls			
	S2.8.2	Handle accounts and groups			
	S2.8.3	Check your password policy and ensure that users follow it			
	S2.8.4	Require reauthentication after idle periods			
	S2.8.5	Configure to deny login after a small number of failed attempts			
	S2.8.6	Install and configure other authentication mechanisms			
	S2.8.7	Policy considerations			
P2.9 Configure Operating Systems with Appropriate Object, Device, and File Access Controls (NS, UW)	S2.9.1	Identify the protection needed			

Practice	Step Number	Step Description	Yes	Partial	No
	S2.9.2	Configure access controls			
	S2.9.3	Install and configure file encryption capabilities for sensitive data			
	S2.9.4	Policy considerations			
P2.10 Configure Computers for File Backups (NS, UW)	S2.10.1	Develop a file backup and restoration plan			
	S2.10.2	Install and configure file backup tools			
	S2.10.3	Test the ability to recover from backups			
	S2.10.4	Policy considerations			
P2.11 Use a Tested Model Configuration and a Secure Replication Procedure (UW)	S2.11.1	Create and test the model configuration			
	S2.11.2	Replicate the configuration on other workstations			
	S2.11.3	Make configuration changes on a case-by-case basis			
	S2.11.4	Create and record cryptographic checksums			
P2.12 Protect Computers from Viruses and Similar Programmed Threats (NS, UW)	S2.12.1	Develop a programmed threats protection plan			
	S2.12.2	Install and execute anti-virus tools			
	S2.12.3	Train users			
	S2.12.4	Update detection tools			
	S2.12.5	Policy considerations			

(continued)

Chapter 2   Checklist (*cont.*)

Practice	Step Number	Step Description	Yes	Partial	No
P2.13 Configure Computers for Secure Remote Administration (NS, UW)	S2.13.1	Ensure that administration commands originate from only authenticated administrators and hosts			
	S2.13.2	Ensure that all administration tasks operate at the minimum necessary privilege level			
	S2.13.3	Ensure that confidential information cannot be intercepted, read, or changed by intruders			
	S2.13.4	Use a movable storage medium to transfer information			
	S2.13.5	Use a secure method for inspecting all log files			
	S2.13.6	Create and record cryptographic checksums			
	S2.13.7	Policy considerations			
P2.14.1 Allow Only Appropriate Physical Access to Computers (NS, UW)	S2.14.1	Prevent installation of unauthorized hardware			
	S2.14.2	Deploy the computer in a secure facility			
	S2.14.3	Policy considerations			
P2.15 Develop and Roll Out an Acceptable Use Policy for Workstations (UW)	S2.15.1	Elements of an acceptable use policy			
	S2.15.2	Train users			
	S2.15.3	Provide explicit reminders at each login			

Chapter 3

Securing Public Web Servers

The World Wide Web is one of the most important ways for your organization to publish information, interact with Internet users, and establish an e-commerce business presence. However, if you are not rigorous in securely configuring and operating a public web site, you leave yourself and your organization vulnerable to a variety of security problems. Your organization may (at best) be embarrassed or (at worst) lose business because malicious intruders have changed the content of your web pages.

Compromised web sites have served as the entry point for intrusions into an organization's internal networks for the purpose of accessing confidential information. Your organization can face business losses or legal action if an intruder successfully accesses customer data. Denial-of-service (DoS) attacks[1] can make it difficult, if not impossible, for users to access your web site. This problem is especially critical if you are using your site to conduct business.

The practices recommended below are designed to help you mitigate the risks associated with these and several other known security problems. They build upon the assumption that you have first configured a secure general-purpose server (as described in Chapter 2).

---

1. Refer to CERT tech tip *Denial of Service Attacks* (available at *http://www.cert.org/tech_tips/denial_of_service.html*) and CERT advisories on this subject.

79

3.1 Overview

The practices covered in this chapter are applicable to your organization if you intend to operate your own public web site to conduct business with the Internet community and share information.[2] They are written for web server administrators and their managers.

We assume that you have the following security objectives for your web site:

- To maintain the integrity of all information resident on and accessible by your web site

- To prevent the use of your web host[3] as a staging area for intrusions into your organization's network that could result in breaches of confidentiality, integrity, or availability of information assets

- To prevent the use of the web host as a staging area for intrusions into external sites, which could result in your organization being held liable for damages

The practices outlined in this chapter do not cover all aspects of web technology use. In particular, they do not address the following topics:

- Securing a general purpose network server. Practices to accomplish this are described in Chapter 2.

- Firewalls and routers used to protect web servers. Some of the practices necessary to accomplish this are described in Chapter 4.

- Security considerations related to web client (browser) software. Section 2.7 provides some guidance in this area.

- Commercial transactions via the web, with the exception of a brief description of Secure Electronic Transaction (SET) in Section 3.7.

- Special considerations for very large web sites with multiple hosts.

- Contracting for or offering web-hosting services (such as those provided by a commercial Internet service provider).

- Other public information services, such as those based on the file transfer protocol (FTP).

---

2. Some of these practices may also be useful in securing an Intranet-based enterprise web server against insider attacks.

3. Throughout these practices, we use terms such as *host* and *host machine* to refer to the hardware and operating system that support a web site. The term *server software* refers to the application software that implements the HTTP protocol and any associated security layers. The term *server* generally means the combined hardware, operating system, and server software.

- Privacy protection and anonymity, specifically protecting personal identity and preferences that are available to web servers, such as name, location, computer used, browser used, last URL (Uniform Resource Locator) visited.

- Protection of intellectual property.

The practices addressed here assume the use of file-based web servers and data stores, in contrast to relational databases. We recognize, for example, that configuration management, URL semantics, and backup procedures may be significantly different if you are using relational databases to store data accessed by web servers.

3.1.1   The Need for Secure Public Web Servers

Your public web site not only gives high visibility to your organization, it also serves as an attractive target for attackers. The goal of the attacker may be to gain direct access to your web server, change web site contents, or deny user access to your web server. Attackers can target the web server host operating system, web server software, programs, scripts, or plug-ins used by web server software, as well as firewalls and routers that protect your public web site and your internal network. These targets include ISPs and other organizations providing network services.

There are three main security topics to consider when operating a public web site:

1. Improper configuration or operation of the web server can result in the inadvertent disclosure or alteration of confidential information, including information assets of your organization, information about the configuration of the server or network that could be exploited for subsequent attacks, and information about who requested which documents from the server sensitive customer or user information

2. If the host used for your web server becomes compromised, intruders could cause damage in a number of ways:
    - Change the information stored on the web server host machine, particularly the information you intend to publish
    - Execute unauthorized commands or programs on the server host machine, including ones that the intruder has installed
    - Gain unauthorized access to assets elsewhere in your organization's computer network
    - Launch attacks on external sites from your server host machine, thus concealing the intruders' identities and perhaps making your organization liable for damages

3. Users and customers are unable to access your web site if all of its resources are consumed by a DoS attack.

3.1.2 An Approach for Securing Public Web Servers

To improve the security of your public web site, we recommend a three-step approach:

1. Install a secure server (see Chapter 2).
2. Configure web server software and the underlying web server host operating system.
3. Maintain the web server's integrity.

Within the context of this approach, Table 3.1 summarizes the recommended practices for securing public web servers. The rest of this chapter covers these practices in more detail.

Table 3.1 Securing Public Web Servers Practice Summary

Approach	Practice	Reference
Configuring	Isolate the Web Server	Section 3.2; page 83
	Configure the Web Server with Appropriate Object, Device, and File Access Controls	Section 3.3; page 89
	Identify and Enable Web-Server-Specific Logging Mechanisms	Section 3.4; page 94
	Consider Security Implications for Programs, Scripts, and Plug-ins	Section 3.5; page 97
	Configure the Web Server to Minimize the Functionality of Programs, Scripts, and Plug-ins	Section 3.6; page 100
	Configure the Web Server to Use Authentication and Encryption Technologies	Section 3.7; page 105
Maintaining	Maintain the Authoritative Copy of Your Web Site Content on a Secure Host	Section 3.8; page 114

3.2 Isolate the Web Server

You have several choices for placing a public web server on your organization's network. We recommend that you place it on a separate, protected subnetwork. This will ensure that traffic between the Internet and the server does not traverse any part of your private internal network and that no internal network traffic is visible to the server.

A public web server host is a computer intended for public access. This means that many people will access the host (and its stored information) from locations all over the world. Regardless of how well the host computer and its application software are configured, there is always the chance that someone will discover a new vulnerability, exploit it, and gain unauthorized access to the web server host (e.g., via a user account or a privileged account on a host with a multi-user operating system). If such an incident occurs, you need to do everything you can to prevent intruders from (1) gaining access to internal hosts and possibly obtaining detailed information about them and (2) observing or capturing network traffic that is flowing between internal hosts. Such traffic might include authentication information, proprietary business information, personnel data, and many other kinds of sensitive data.

To guard against these two threats, the public web server host must be isolated from your internal network and its traffic, as well as from any other external public network.

3.2.1 Place the Server on an Isolated Subnet

Placing the web server on an isolated subnet allows you to better monitor and control network traffic destined for the web server subnet. It also helps in configuring any firewall or router used to protect access to the subnet, as well as detecting attacks and attempted intrusions. In addition, taking this precaution precludes the capture of internal traffic (accessible to all connected computers when using broadcast media such as Ethernet) by any intruder who gains access to your web server.

3.2.2 Use Firewall Technology to Restrict Traffic

You need to restrict traffic between an external public network such as the Internet and the web server, and between the web server and internal networks. The use of firewall technology (including packet filtering implemented by a router, discussed in Chapter 4) effectively restricts the traffic between all computers connected to the firewall in accordance with your security policy. Setting up firewall technology precludes many possible attacks but still allows anyone to access your public web server content.

A web server typically accepts TCP connections on port 80/tcp (http), the standard port. In general, no other connections from any external public network to the web server should be permitted. However, if the web server supports SSL-protected connections, port 443/tcp (https) should be permitted. Section 3.7 provides more details on the use of SSL.

You need to establish filtering rules that block TCP connections originating from the web server, as a web server typically does not depend on other services on an external public network. In general, all UDP and ICMP (Internet Control Message Protocol) traffic should be blocked. However, depending on the web server configuration, you may need to permit limited connections to UDP-based services such as DNS for host name lookup (permit port 53/udp).

> Given that UDP is a connectionless protocol, there is no concept of an "established" state. Therefore, there is no completely safe way to allow "return" UDP packets with traditional packet filtering—they simply cannot be positively associated with an outgoing packet. However, in spite of UDP's inherently less safe nature, a number of critical services depend on UDP packets. For example, the domain name service (UDP port 53) must be functional in order for your internal hosts to operate correctly. If possible, use stateful inspection features of the firewall software to filter connections based on state. If your firewall doesn't have stateful inspection features, it may be possible for you to determine the level of threat in permitting packets for each UDP service and thus make a risk-based decision whether to permit or deny the service.
>
> You should only permit connections from your web server to your internal DNS server (to conduct DNS lookups on an external public network). The internal DNS server can then relay requests to the appropriate external DNS server for resolution.

One recommended configuration is shown in Figure 3.1.

The router/firewall host can consist of a single computer or multiple computers, one of which may filter traffic to and from the web server, and one or more of which may filter traffic to and from the internal network.

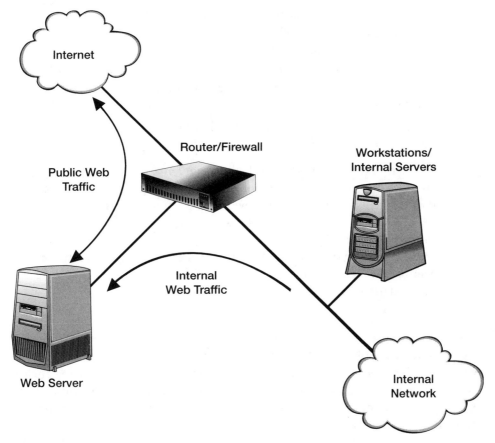

Figure 3.1   Network configuration for a public web server

3.2.3 Place Server Hosts Providing Supporting Services on Another Isolated Subnet

Public web sites rely on services that are likely to (or should) reside on other internal servers. As a result, you must consider the network placement of these server hosts when you determine the location of your web server.

Your web site may use e-mail, directory, or database services:

1. E-mail services, such as SMTP (Simple Mail Transport Protocol), to send data submitted by users using an HTML form to an internal address via a CGI

(Common Gateway Interface) script or program. The configuration (network, SMTP, firewall) should prohibit

the sending of e-mail to addresses outside your internal network, given that the e-mail was generated as a result of a user filling out a form. The user's information, as well as your organization's identity, needs to be protected.

receipt of e-mail on the web server itself, which may allow the SMTP server software to be compromised. This could then affect the web server.

2. Directory services, such as LDAP (Lightweight Directory Access Protocol), to retrieve previously stored user information, which provides customized information back to the user, or provide information such as X.509 certificates, which are used to authenticate users as they are accessing specific content services.
3. Database services, such as SQL (Structured Query Language), to retrieve up-to-date content information to support the generation of dynamic web pages and user-specified searches.

Place servers providing e-mail, directory, and database services in support of a public web site on protected subnetworks.

Use firewall technology to block any traffic between the Internet and these servers, prevent traffic between the web server and these other servers from traversing any part of your private internal network, and prohibit all users from connecting directly to any of these servers. Permitting such a connection may allow specific attacks against the software residing on these servers.

Restrict communication between these servers to that which is required to support your public web site.

One recommended network configuration for public web server database services is shown in Figure 3.2.

3.2.4 Disable Source Routing and IP Forwarding

Source routing is a function of IP routing that allows the packet originator to influence routing decisions as the packet traverses the networks. We recommend that you disable all source-routing functions in your firewalls and routers that protect your public web server and if possible deny any packets that have specified source-routing options.

Disable source routing on the public web server and any servers providing supporting e-mail, directory, and database services.

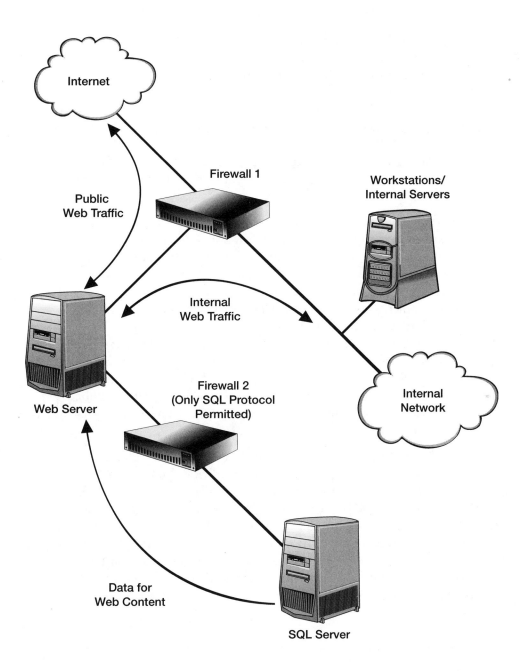

Figure 3.2 Network configuration for database services used in support of a public web server

In addition, disable IP forwarding on these servers. This step eliminates cases where packets can appear to have originated from a known (and trusted) host when they have in fact originated from an external public network (IP spoofing).

3.2.5 Alternative Architecture Approaches

Alternative public web server architecture approaches may mitigate the security risks mentioned above, but these approaches generate two other issues that you need to address.

1. You may choose to place the web server on an internal network and then use smart hubs or switches to separate it from internal network traffic. You could also choose to encrypt all internal traffic, so that even if the server is compromised, any traffic it sees will not be readable. However, neither of these approaches would prevent traffic from being sent from the web server host to other hosts on your internal network, unless you choose to use a virtual private network (VPN).

2. You may choose to have your public web server hosted by an external organization (such as an ISP), both to accomplish the separation of your public web site from your internal network and to take advantage of external expertise. If you take this approach, require your ISP to establish a protected subnet for your web server and any other services (e.g. e-mail, directory, or database) if these are also provided.

Servers that host these services should be located together with the web server. If, for example, you choose to keep the database server within your internal network, you may need to consider a VPN for more secure transfer of information between your externally hosted public web server and your internal database server. The details of this approach are beyond the scope of this practice.

In addition, require the use of strong authentication and encryption techniques to protect the connection from your internal hosts to your externally hosted public web server. This requirement is necessary when transferring web server content as well as when performing any server administration not done by the ISP.

3.2.6 Policy Considerations

Your organization's networked systems security policy should establish the following guidelines:

- Your public servers should be placed on subnets separate from external public networks and from your internal network.

- Servers providing supporting services for your public servers should be placed on subnets separate from external public networks, from your public servers, and from your internal networks.

- Routers and firewalls should be configured to restrict traffic between external public networks and your public servers, and between your public servers and internal networks

- Routers and firewalls should be configured to restrict traffic between servers providing supporting services for your public server and external public networks, your public server, and your internal networks

3.3 Configure the Web Server with Appropriate Object, Device, and File Access Controls

Most web server host operating systems provide the ability to specify access privileges individually for files, devices, and other data or code objects stored on that host.[4] Any information that your web server can access using these controls can potentially be distributed to all users accessing your public web site. Your web server software is likely to provide additional object, device, and file access controls specific to its operation. You need to consider from two perspectives how best to configure these access controls to protect information stored on your public web server:

1. How to limit the access of your web server software
2. How to apply access controls specific to the web server where more detailed levels of access control are required

A public web server typically stores information intended for widespread publication. It may also store information requiring restricted access, such as server log files, system software and configuration files, applications software and configuration files, and password files.

Using the access controls provided by both the server operating system and the web server software can reduce the likelihood of inadvertent disclosure or corruption of

---

4. Refer to Section 2.9.

information and violations of confidentiality and integrity. In addition, using access controls to limit resource use can reduce the impact of a DoS attack against your public web site, a violation of availability.

3.3.1 Establish New User and Group Identities

Establish new user and group identities to be used exclusively by the web server software.

Make this new user and new group independent and distinct from all other users and groups. This separation is a prerequisite for implementing the access controls described below.

Although the server may have to run as root (UNIX) or administrator (Windows) initially to bind to port 80, do not allow the server to continue to run in this mode.

3.3.2 Identify the Protection Needed

The general approach for identifying required access controls for files, devices, and objects specific to web servers is outlined in Section 2.9.

In addition, determine if your web server's operating system provides the ability to limit files accessed by the web services' processes. These processes should have read-only access to those files necessary to perform the service and should have no access to other files (such as server log files). If this feature is not available, you can skip some of the following steps. In this event, you need to implement other security controls (described below) to limit your exposure.

Use web server host operating system access controls to enforce the following rules:

- Public web content files can be read but not written by web service processes.
- The directories in which public web content is stored cannot be written by web service processes.
- Public web content files can be written only by processes authorized for web server administration.
- Web server log files can be written by service processes, but log files cannot be read or served as web content. Web server log files can be read only by administration processes.
- Any temporary files created by web service processes (such as those generated in the creation of dynamic web pages) are restricted to a specified and appropriately protected subdirectory.
- Access to any temporary files created by web service processes is limited to the service processes that created these files.

Some of these controls are reiterated below when they can be achieved using alternate methods.

3.3.3 Mitigate the Effects of DoS Attacks

Resource-intensive DoS attacks against a web server host operating system can involve several approaches, including the following:

- Taking advantage of the number of simultaneous network connections by quickly establishing connections up to the maximum permitted so that no new, legitimate users can gain access
- Filling primary memory with unnecessary processes to slow down the system and limit web service availability
- Filling file systems with extraneous and incorrect information (some systems will not function if specific assets, such as file systems, are unavailable)

Logging information generated by the web server host operating system may help in recognizing such attacks.

Institute the following controls to limit the use of resources by the web server host operating system and thus mitigate the effects of DoS attacks:

1. Network connection time-outs (time after which an inactive connection is dropped) should be set to a minimum acceptable time setting. Established connections will then time out as quickly as possible, opening up new connections to legitimate users. This procedure only mitigates the effects, however; it does not defeat the attack. If the maximum allowable open connections (or connections that are half-open, i.e., if the first part of the TCP handshake was successful) are set to a low number, an attacker can easily consume the available connections with bogus requests. By setting the maximum to a much higher number, the impact of such attacks may be reduced, but additional resources will be consumed.

2. Secure web servers often impose self-limiting constraints and are configured to make most processes unavailable. Assigning priorities to web service processes can help to ensure that high-priority processes obtain sufficient resources, even while under attack. Note, however, that doing so may create the potential for a denial of service on the lower-priority services.

3. It is unusual to be able to fill the available disk space of web servers. Requests are typically processed quickly, and other "writes" should be disabled. You can separate directories for log files and other information from system directories and user information. You can also establish effective

boundaries between these information objects by specifying separate partitions and/or disk locations.

These controls will not fully protect your web server against DoS attacks. However, by reducing the impact of these attacks, you may enable your web server to "survive" during the time period when the DoS attacks are occurring.

3.3.4 Protect Sensitive and Restricted Information

Configure the public web server so that it cannot serve files outside the specified file directory tree for public web content. This may be a configuration choice either in the server software or in how the server process is controlled by the operating system. Ensure as far as possible that such files (besides the specified directory tree) cannot be served, even if users know the names (URLs) of those files.

Avoid the use of links or aliases in your public web content file directory tree that point to files elsewhere on your server host or your network file system. If possible, disable the web server software's ability to follow links and aliases. As stated earlier, web server log files and configuration files should reside outside the specified file directory tree for public web content.

In the event that you do need to access sensitive or restricted files via your public web server, refer to Section 3.7.

3.3.5 Configure Web Server Software Access Controls

To configure the web server software access controls, perform the following steps:

1. Define a single directory and establish related subdirectories exclusively for web server content files, including graphics but excluding CGI scripts and other programs.
2. Define a single directory exclusively for all external programs executed as part of web server content.
3. Disable the execution of CGI scripts that are not exclusively under the control of administrative accounts. You can do this by creating and controlling access to a separate directory intended to contain authorized CGI scripts.
4. Disable the use of hard or symbolic links as ordinary files and directories.
5. Define a complete web content access matrix. Identify which pages are restricted and which pages are accessible (and by whom).

Most web server software vendors provide directives or commands that allow you to restrict user access to public web server content files. For example, the Apache web server software[5] provides a Limit directive, which allows you to restrict which optional access features (such as New, Delete, Connect, Head, and Get) are associated with each web content file. The Apache Require directive allows you to restrict available content to authenticated users or groups. Section 3.7 explains how to configure the web server to use authentication and encryption technologies.

Many of the directives or commands can be overridden on a per-directory basis. The convenience of being able to make local exceptions to global policy is offset by the threat of a security hole being introduced in a distant subdirectory, which could be controlled by a hostile user. You should disable a subdirectory's ability to override top-level security directives unless that override is required.

3.3.6 Disable the Serving of Web Server File Directory Listings

A common implementation of the web protocol (HTTP) specifies that a URL ending in a slash character is treated as a request for a listing of the files in the directory with that name. As a general rule, you should prohibit your server from responding to such requests, even if all of the files in the directory can be read by the general public.

Such requests may indicate an attempt to locate information by means other than that intended by your web site. Users may try this if they are having difficulty navigating through your site or if a link appears to be broken. Intruders may attempt this action to locate information hidden by your web site's interface. You may want to investigate requests of this type found in your server log files.

3.3.7 Policy Considerations

Your organization's networked systems security policy should require public servers to be configured to take maximum advantage of all available object, device, and file access controls to protect information as identified elsewhere in your security policy.

Your organization's information access control policy should address information residing on any public server, including web servers.

---

5. Refer to *http://www.apache.org*.

3.4 Identify and Enable Web-Server-Specific Logging Mechanisms

Collecting data generated by the web server provides you with critical information that is essential for analyzing the security of the web server and detecting signs of intrusion.

When you install web server software, you are normally presented with a number of choices for logging configuration options or preferences. Different systems provide various types of logging information, and some do not collect adequate information in their default configuration. You need to make choices based on your security policy and requirements.

The server host operating system may provide some basic logging mechanisms and data (see Sections 5.3 and 5.4). However, these mechanisms typically cannot provide sufficient data relevant to the performance of your public web server, such as web pages retrieved, or attacks intended to probe your web server for specific vulnerabilities. You should identify the types of logs available, along with the data recorded within each log, and then enable the collection of the desired data.

Log files are often the only record of suspicious behavior. Failure to enable the mechanisms to record this information and use them to initiate alert mechanisms will greatly weaken or eliminate your ability to detect intrusion attempts and to determine whether or not they succeeded. Similar problems can result from not having the necessary procedures and tools in place to process and analyze your log files.

As a general rule, system and network logs can alert you to the fact that a suspicious event has occurred requiring further investigation. Web server software can provide additional log data relevant to web-specific events. If you do not take advantage of these capabilities, web-relevant log data may not be visible or may require a great deal of effort to access.

The selection and implementation of specific web server software will determine which set of detailed instructions you should follow to establish logging configurations. Logging capabilities can be similar across several implementations. With this said, some of the guidance contained in the steps below may not be fully applicable to all vendors' web server software products.

3.4.1 Identify the Information to Be Logged

There are four possible different logs.

1. **Transfer Log.** Each transfer is represented as one entry showing the main information related to the transfer (see below). This is also known as the Access Log.

2. **Error Log.** Each error is represented as one entry, including some explanation of the reason for the error report.
3. **Agent Log.** If this log is available, it contains information about the user client software used in accessing your web content.
4. **Referrer Log.** If this log is available, it collects information relevant to HTTP access. This includes the URL of the page containing the link that the user client software followed to initiate the access to your web page.

Several log formats are available for Transfer Log entries. Typically, the information is presented in plain ASCII (American Standard Code for Information Interchange) without special delimiters to separate the different fields:

Common Log Format (CLF)

This format stores the following information related to one transfer (Transfer Log) in the indicated order:

1. Remote Host
2. Remote User Identity, in accordance with RFC (Request for Comment) 1413[6]
3. Authenticated User, in accordance with the Basic Authentication Scheme (see Section 3.7)
4. Date
5. URL requested
6. Status of the request
7. Number of bytes actually transferred

Combined Log Format

The Combined Log Format contains the same seven fields above. It also provides information normally stored in the Agent Log and the Referrer Log, along with the actual transfer. Keeping this information in a consolidated log format may support more effective administration.

Extended Log Format (ELF). This format provides a way to describe all items that should be collected within the log file. The first two lines of the log file contain the version and the fields to be collected.

---

6. Refer to *RFC 1413 Identification Protocol,* available at *http://www.ietf.org/rfc/rfc1413.txt.*

It appears in the log file as follows:

```
#Version: 1.0
#Fields: date time c-ip sc-bytes time-taken cs-version
1999-08-01 02:10:57 192.0.0.2 6340 3 HTTP/1.0
```

This example contains the date, time, originating IP address, number of bytes transmitted, time taken for transmission, and the HTTP version.

Other Log File Formats

Some server software provides log information in different file formats such as database formats or delimiter-separated formats. Other server software enables an administrator to define specific log file formats in the web server configuration file using a particular syntax (if the default CLF format is insufficient).

3.4.2 Determine If Additional Logging Mechanisms Are Needed

If your public web server supports the execution of programs, scripts, or plug-ins, you need to determine whether to capture specific logging data regarding the performance of these features. If you develop your own programs, scripts, or plug-ins, we strongly recommend that you define and implement a comprehensive and easy-to-understand logging approach based on the logging mechanisms provided by the web server hosting operating system. Log information associated with programs, scripts, and plug-ins can add significantly to the typical information logged by the web server.

3.4.3 Enable Logging

We recommend the following:

- Use the Combined Log Format for storing the Transfer Log or manually configure the information described by the Combined Log Format to be the standard format for the Transfer Log.
- Enable the Referrer Log or Agent Log if the Combined Log Format is not available.
- Establish different log file names for different virtual hosts that may be implemented as part of a single web server.
- Use the Remote User Identity as specified in RFC 1413 (although this may cause unacceptably slow performance).

- Some web server software allows the checking of specified access controls to be enforced or disabled during program startup. This level of control may, for example, be helpful in avoiding inadvertent alteration of log files as a result of errors in file access administration. You should determine the circumstances in which you may want to enable such checks if your web server software supports this feature.

3.4.4 Select and Configure Log Analysis Tools

Many commercial and public-domain tools (see Section 5.3.15, Table 5.3) are available to support regular analysis of Transfer Logs. Most operate on either the Common or the Combined Log Formats.

These tools can identify IP addresses that are the source of high numbers of connections, transfers, etc.

Error Log tools indicate not only errors that may exist within publicly available web content (such as missing files) but also attempts to access nonexistent URLs. Such attempts could indicate a number of suspect activities, such as probes for the existence of vulnerabilities to be used later in launching an attack, information gathering, or interest in specific content such as databases.

Any suspicious log file events should be forwarded to the responsible administrator or security incident response team as soon as possible for follow-up investigation, as described in Section 6.9.

3.5 Consider Security Implications for Programs, Scripts, and Plug-ins

In its most basic form, a web server listens for a request and responds by transmitting the specified file to the requestor. A web server may invoke additional mechanisms to execute programs or process user-supplied data, producing customized information in response to a request. Examples of these mechanisms include CGI scripts and server plug-ins. You need to consider security implications when selecting these mechanisms.

CGI is an accepted standard that supports the extension of web server software by adding external programs that are invoked by a request for a specific URL. CGI programs or scripts (see below) run as subtasks of the web server. Arguments are supplied in the environment or via standard inputs. Outputs of a CGI script are returned to the requesting web browser. CGI scripts can be used to interface to search engines and databases, create dynamic web pages, and respond to user input.

A **script** is a program written in a scripting language and executed by an interpreter. Examples of such languages include /bin/sh (bourne shell), PERL (Practical Extraction and Report Language), TCL (Tool Command Language), Python, JavaScript, and VBScript.

A **plug-in** serves as an extension of another program. Server side plug-ins provide additional functionality, such as SSL[7] or multimedia features (for example, video viewing), or improved server performance, such as PERL. In the case of a PERL CGI script, no external program needs to be started each time such a script is invoked.

Another commonly used term is **servlet.** Servlet programs are typically written in Java and are either invoked as CGI scripts or may accept a TCP connection and interact with the web browser directly.

Security vulnerabilities can be introduced in the acquisition, installation, configuration, deployment, and operation of programs, scripts, and plug-ins (collectively referred to as external programs in this practice). As a web server administrator, you may install a specific set of external programs that result in a unique configuration—one that has likely not been tested by the developers of your web server software or the external programs. Vulnerabilities may include poorly written programs never intended for widescale use or unexpected side effects that result when two or more programs are installed that were not intended to operate together. For example, many successful attacks on web sites have exploited known vulnerabilities in commonly available CGI scripts.

3.5.1 Perform Cost/Benefit Trade-offs

A number of factors need to be considered in weighing the costs and benefits of external programs:

- The functionality that each external program provides, and whether this functionality is important or just nice to have but not essential.

- The external program's ease of installation, configuration, testing, and maintenance

- The potential security vulnerabilities introduced by the external program and consequent risks to your public web site

- The potential security vulnerabilities introduced by two or more external programs when used in combination

---

7. Refer to Section 3.7.

3.5.2 Select from Trustworthy Sources

As far as possible, assess the trustworthiness of a variety of sources for external programs. If several programs provide the required functionality, choose one from the most trustworthy source. Avoid external programs produced by unknown authors or downloaded from unknown, untrusted Internet sites.

3.5.3 Understand All of the Functionality of an External Program

Some types of external programs (in particular CGI scripts) are distributed in source code form. If you have any doubts about the trustworthiness of the source or the authenticity of the code, conduct a thorough source code review.

When you examine a script, consider the following questions:[8]

- How complex is the script? The longer it is, the more likely it is to have problems.

- Does the script read or write files on the host system? Programs that read files may inadvertently violate access restrictions or pass on sensitive system information. Programs that write files may modify or damage documents, or even introduce Trojan horses.

- Does the script interact with other programs? For example, many CGI scripts send e-mail in response to form input by opening up a connection with the sendmail program. Is it doing this in a secure way?

- Does the script run with suid (set-user-id) privileges? In general, this is not recommended and should not be permitted if at all possible.

- Does the script author validate user inputs from forms? Strip meta-characters? Deny, then allow? Use secure forms of popen (C) or open (Perl)? If so, the author is thinking about security.

- Does the author use explicit path names when invoking external programs? Relying on the PATH environment variable to resolve partial path names is not recommended.

---

8. This list is taken from *The World Wide Web Security FAQ* (Stein 99), specifically Q34.

3.5.4 Review Publicly Available Information to Identify Vulnerabilities

As described in Chapter 1, various organizations research network and system security topics and periodically publish information concerning recently discovered vulnerabilities in service software. This software includes web server software and supporting technologies such as scripting languages and external programs. External programs that are in wide use are regularly analyzed by researchers, users, and security incident response teams, as well as by members of the intruder community.

Intruders will often publish exploit scripts that take advantage of known vulnerabilities in web service software and external programs commonly used by public web servers. You need to review public information sources frequently and be aware of all relevant security information about any external programs that you are considering.

For further information, refer to Section 2.4 as well as to *The World Wide Web Security FAQ* (Stein 99), specifically Q35. Consult CERT advisories for information about CGI scripts that are known to contain security holes.

3.5.5 Policy Considerations

Your organization's networked systems security policy should require a security evaluation (including vulnerability assessment) as part of your web server software selection procedures. See Section 5.3.15 and Table 5.3.

3.6 Configure the Web Server to Minimize the Functionality of Programs, Scripts, and Plug-ins

Programs, scripts, and plug-ins (collectively referred to as external programs in this practice) can add valuable and useful functionality to your public web service. They are widely available from many different sources, and you can add them to the web server at any time without having to modify the server code. If you cannot meet your web service requirements without using external programs, you must thoroughly review and determine how these external programs will be configured, used, and administered. Your goal should be to restrict their functionality to the greatest extent possible to keep potential security risks to a minimum. See also Section 3.5.

As a web server administrator, you need to reduce the likelihood of a security compromise by ensuring that you limit the access rights, functionality, and potential for damage by such external programs.

3.6.1 Verify That the Acquired Copy of an External Program Is Authentic

Typically, the authenticity of a copy can be verified using cryptographic checksums, digital signatures, or similar technologies provided by the external program's distributor.

Scan all external programs for computer viruses and Trojan horses.

3.6.2 Use an Isolated Test Machine

Exercise all acquired external programs on a test machine isolated from your internal network prior to operational use.

3.6.3 Limit Your Exposure to Vulnerabilities

Execute tools and include mechanisms that limit your exposure to vulnerabilities in external programs. Refer to Section 5.3.15 and Table 5.3 for examples of such tools.

Many of the known vulnerabilities in external programs result from poor programming practices and use in environments that are not designed for secure operation. These include buffer overflows,[9] misuse of character input,[10] and others.[11]

---

9. Input data exceed the size of their allocated program memory buffer because checks are lacking to ensure that the input data are not written beyond the buffer boundary. For examples, refer to CERT advisory CA-1999.07 *IIS Buffer Overflow* or CERT advisory CA-1997.24 *Buffer Overrun Vulnerability in Count.cgi cgi bin Program* at the CERT web site.

10. Input characters change the way input data are interpreted or cause the execution of an unexpected function within the external program. Examples include "meta" characters that invoke a specific function instead of being used as input and "escape" characters that change the interpretation of the character, which follows them. Quotation of character strings can also be a problem. For an example, refer to CERT advisory CA-1997.25 *Sanitizing User-Supplied Data in CGI Scripts* at the CERT web site. Also refer to the CERT tech tip *How to Remove Meta-characters from User-Supplied Data in CGI Scripts* at *http://www.cert.org/tech_tips/cgi_metacharacters.html*.

11. Refer to the chapter "Secure CGI/API Programming," pp. 293–310, in *Web Security & Commerce* (Garfinkel 97).

Tools are available that (1) scan for and identify the presence of problematic input characters and (2) serve as a "wrapper" around a potentially vulnerable external program, limiting possible inputs to avoid buffer overflows.[12]

You should execute these tools in your test environment and review their results before you deploy any external programs on your public web site (and also on a regular basis once external programs are deployed).

Mechanisms such as the PERL interpreter's "tainting" feature allow you to restrict operations (open files, system calls) when using user-supplied input.[13]

3.6.4 Mitigate the Risk of Distributing Malicious Code

Even if the web server does not contain any vulnerabilities, it may inadvertently distribute malicious code to an unaware user. This is not necessarily a "server" problem, as the results will almost always impact the user receiving the malicious or manipulated web pages. However, attacks[14] can be constructed in such a way as to reveal information to unauthorized users, for example by embedding references to other web sites.

The problem, as described in CERT advisory CA-2000-02, *Malicious HTML Tags Embedded in Client Web Requests* (available at the CERT web site) arises when the user sends a request from an untrustworthy source to a trusted web server. The source may be a web page, an e-mail message, a netnews message, or a web page previously stored on disk or distributed via other media such as CD-ROM.

The user's request may contain malicious data that is modified and sent back to the user's browser, where it can cause damage, execute programs, or present the requested page with missing or manipulated information.

There are controls that can help prevent the insertion of malicious code when they are built into the web server. These controls can (1) facilitate the appropriate encoding of all output elements, (2) filter content sent to the server, and (3) check cookies.

Refer to the CERT tech tip *Understanding Malicious Content Mitigation for Web Developers* (CERT/CC).

---

12. One example of such a program is CGIWrap, available at *http://www.unixtools.org/cgiwrap*.

13. Refer to *Web Security & Commerce* (Garfinkel 97), specifically the chapter "Secure CGI/API Programming," pp. 293–310.

14. These are often called cross-site scripting attacks, although this name does not correctly describe this problem.

3.6.5 Disable or Restrict the Use of Server Side Include Functionality

Server side include functionality is used to reference dynamic information that is determined at the time a web page is generated. Examples of functions that can be invoked through the use of server side includes are (1) adding the timestamp of the last modification to the web page and (2) executing arbitrary external programs (which may have been supplied by an intruder) to produce content that is incorporated into the web page. We recommend disabling all server side include functionality wherever possible to reduce the risk that intruders will be able to access external programs or place programs they created into your web content for later execution.

If you need to selectively deploy some functions associated with server side includes, we recommend that you do not deploy those that enable the execution of external programs.

3.6.6 Disable the Execution of External Programs Present in Your Web Server Configuration

The execution of specific external programs is often called out in your default web server configuration. You need to locate and disable any of these that are not essential. This includes disabling "example" scripts, which may be useful for demonstration purposes but are not required for your operational configuration.

3.6.7 Restrict Access to External Programs

Configure web server host operating system and web server software access controls to severely restrict access to all external program files that reside on your public web server. None of these should be accessible by internal or external users requesting web site content.

Typically, all external programs are located in the configured CGI-BIN directory. They can be directly invoked from that directory even if they are not referenced in one of your HTML pages. All the attacker needs to know is the name of the program or how to obtain responses that indicate whether or not the name guessing is successful.

Often, interpreters such as PERL are also placed in the CGI-BIN directory. While this may make installation easier, it is neither necessary nor recommended. Interpreters, shells, scripting engines, and other extensible programs should never reside in a CGI-BIN directory. In addition, you need to establish access controls that prohibit interpreters from being executed indirectly via CGI programs or scripts, as described in CERT advisory CA-1996.11, *Interpreters in CGI Bin Directories* (available at the CERT web site).

Refer to Sections 3.3 and 2.9 for further guidance and details.

3.6.8 Ensure That Only Authorized Users Can Access External Programs

All external programs should reside in directories that are tightly controlled and protected. Such directories should be accessible only to the administrators who are responsible for installing, configuring, and maintaining these programs. The one exception to this rule is if your public web site is designed for the purpose of supporting users who are authorized to provide their own functionality through such programs as the generation and maintenance of private home pages for access by internal users.

3.6.9 Execute External Programs Under Unique Individual User and Group IDs

Assign separate and unique individual user and group IDs and access permissions for the execution of external programs in your web server configuration. In addition, make sure that these IDs and permissions are not the same as those assigned for normal web server software execution. This precaution will help prevent external programs from performing unauthorized actions against the web server or its content.

If your web server host operating system or web server software does not provide this capability, other tools are available, such as the use of `chrootuid` on UNIX systems.

3.6.10 Restrict the Access of External Programs to Only Essential Files

In addition to the execution access controls described above, you may need to further restrict the access of external programs to those files that are required for such programs to perform their functions. These may include files within web content directories and other external programs but should not include system files such as log files. You need to review carefully the files that each external program can access to ensure that an intruder cannot abuse this access.

3.6.11 Create Integrity-Checking Information for All External Programs

Integrity-checking tools (such as Tripwire, described in Section A.2) can identify changes made to files and directories when you install updates. By monitoring changes made to external programs, you can determine whether they were modified as you intended and identify unexpected changes that require further investigation.

Section 5.3 contains additional information on the role of establishing a trusted baseline, and Section 6.5 discusses checking the integrity of that baseline to support intrusion detection.

3.6.12 Policy Considerations

Your organization's networked systems security policy should require a security evaluation (including vulnerability assessment) as part of your web server software selection and/or implementation procedures. Refer to Section 5.3.15 and Table 5.3.

3.7 Configure the Web Server to Use Authentication and Encryption Technologies

Your public web server may need to support a range of technologies for identifying and authenticating users with differing privileges for accessing information. Some of these technologies are based on cryptographic functions that can also provide an encrypted channel between a web browser client and a web server that supports encryption. Candidate technologies include SSL (Secure Socket Layer), S/HTTP (Secure Hypertext Transport Protocol), and SET (Secure Electronic Transaction).[15]

Before placing any sensitive or restricted (i.e., not for public consumption) information on your public web server, you need to determine the specific security and protection requirements and confirm that the available technologies can meet these requirements.

---

15. Refer to *Secure Electronic Commerce* (Ford 97) for a more detailed discussion of the various protocols and related topics, such as Public Key Infrastructure (PKI) and certificates.

User training is required to ensure that sensitive or restricted information is not inadvertently placed on your public web site in a directory that provides broad public access. You will likely want to establish procedures that require at least two people to review all material on a "preview" server prior to public posting.

You may need to install additional cryptographic enhancements or choose alternate web server software depending on your requirements.

Without strong user authentication, you will not be able to restrict access to specific information by authorized users. All information that resides on your public web server will be accessible to anyone who accesses that server.

Without strong server authentication, users of your public web server cannot determine if they have connected to an authentic web server or to a bogus version operated by an intruder. In the latter case, the user may receive and act upon false information assuming that it originated from your web server, perhaps even providing sensitive information such as a credit card number.

Encryption can protect information traversing the connection between a web browser client and a public web server. Without encryption, anyone with access to network traffic (accomplished via the use of a sniffer) can determine, and possibly alter, the content of sensitive and restricted information, even if the user accessing the information has been carefully authenticated. As a result, the confidentiality and integrity of critical information may be violated.

3.7.1 Determine Access Requirements for Sensitive or Restricted Information

Review all information objects accessible via your public web server and determine their specific security requirements. In the process of doing so, identify information objects that share the same security and protection requirements. For sensitive or restricted information objects, determine the users or user groups that legitimately need to access each set of objects.

Implement one or more of the steps described below to meet your security requirements.

If you are planning a new web site or an enhancement to an existing site, you may want to anticipate the need to limit access to specific information (by specific users, user groups, or by subscription) by requiring implementation of one or more of the technologies described below. Sections 3.3 and 2.9 provide further guidance and details.

3.7.2 Establish Trust Between Clients (Users) and Web Servers

External users (clients) need to be sure of the following conditions:[16]

- They are communicating with the correct server.
- What they send is delivered unmodified.
- They can prove that they sent the message.
- Only the intended receiver can read the message.
- Delivery is guaranteed.

In turn, the web server needs to be sure of the following conditions:

- It is communicating with the right client.
- The content of the message received is correct.
- The identity of the author is unmistakable.
- Only the real author could have written the message.
- It acknowledges receipt of the message.

3.7.3 Understand the Limitations of Address-Based Authentication

Most server software supports access controls based on IP addresses or hostnames. However, both IP and DNS spoofing limit the effectiveness of these controls (refer to advisories at the CERT web site). Whenever possible, use authentication and encryption in addition to or in place of IP address or hostname access checking.

3.7.4 Understand Authentication and Encryption Technologies

Based on well-established standards, four technologies are available to restrict access to information residing on a public web site:

1. Basic Authentication
2. Secure Socket Layer

---

16. This material is taken from the article "Web of Worries" (Kessler 00).

3. Secure HTTP
4. Secure Electronic Transaction

Basic Authentication

This technology uses the web server content's directory structure by typically configuring all files in the same directory with the same access privileges. A requesting user provides a recognized user ID and password for access to files in a given directory. More restrictive access control can be enforced at the level of a single file within a directory, given that the web server software provides this capability. Each vendor's web server software has its own method and syntax for defining and using this basic authentication mechanism.

From a security perspective, the main drawback of this technology is that all password information is transferred in an encoded rather than an encrypted form. Anyone who knows the standardized encoding scheme[17] can decode the password after capturing it with a network sniffer. Furthermore, any web content is transmitted as unencrypted clear text, which can be captured as well, thus violating confidentiality.

Basic Authentication is supported by any standards-compliant web browser.

Secure Socket Layer (SSL)[18]

SSL is composed of two subprotocols called SSL record protocol and SSL handshake protocol. The handshake protocol is used to exchange any information about cryptographic capabilities and keys used. The record protocol is used to exchange the actual data.

SSL provides a range of security services: server authentication, client authentication, integrity, and confidentiality.

SSL uses public key cryptography. Certificate authorities (CAs) can be used to verify the relationship between users and organizations. Some CAs may also be able to verify a specific user's relationship to specific server keys. Both of these verification actions allow CA users to have a higher level of trust in the relationships and the keys, based on their trust in the CA and the CA's compliance with regulations directing their actions.[19] However, keep in mind that some CAs severely limit what they offer and may explicitly disclaim any responsibility to bind a specific person to a specific encryption key.

---

17. Known as base64, described in *RFC 2617 HTTP Authentication: Basic and Digest Access Authentication,* available at *http://www.ieft.org/rfc/rfc2617.txt.*

18. Indicated by the use of URLs beginning "https://www.xyz.net."

19. Browsers often come with a pre-installed list of CAs. Based on the pre-installed configuration, the browser accepts SSL certificates as "trusted" without alerting the user. Users therefore need to remove manually any CA key that they do not want to accept as "trusted."

The SSL protocol resides at the transport layer and is effectively "plugged" between the web server/browser and TCP/IP. As a result, it also has the potential to protect other TCP services such as FTP, SMTP, and telnet.

SSL is in the process of becoming an IETF (Internet Engineering Task Force) standard under the name TLS (Transport Level Security). SSL is supported by most of the well-known web browsers.

Secure HTTP (S/HTTP)[20]

Secure HTTP, an alternative approach to SSL, was developed in 1993–94 (earlier than SSL). Designed as a security enhancement of the HTTP protocol, it contains four features:

1. Authentication
2. Encryption
3. Cryptographic checksums
4. Digital signatures

Secure HTTP has greater functionality than SSL because it is integrated into the HTTP protocol, but users need to install a specific web browser to use S/HTTP.

As reference implementations became available, SSL became the preferred choice of major vendors, with S/HTTP receding into the background as a result.

Secure Electronic Transaction (SET)

Developed by two major credit card companies, SET provides a protocol and infrastructure specification supporting bank payments that can be integrated into any web site. SET provides three capabilities:[21]

1. It encrypts payment instructions that preclude exposure of a user's credit card number (both on the network and on the merchant's system).
2. It authenticates merchants to users to protect against impostors.
3. Optionally, it authenticates users to protect against unauthorized attempts to initiate a bank payment.

SET depends on the infrastructure elements, which certify the use of keys and the relationship between users, merchants, banks, etc., and the appropriate keys.

---

20. Indicated by the use of URLs beginning "shttp://www.xyz.net."

21. The infrastructure necessary to support SET is complex; the details are not included here.

To use SET, users need to obtain a software tool (often called a wallet) and other supporting information from their credit card organization.

The technologies described above can be used to meet a range of security requirements and can be deployed individually or in conjunction with one another.

Table 3.2 indicates the requirements that can be satisfied by technology currently in use.

Follow these guidelines when selecting authentication and encryption technologies:

- Basic Authentication can be used to authenticate users. SSL encryption needs to be added to protect against sniffers and intruders posing as authorized users.

- SSL User Authentication provides a "stronger" solution than Basic Authentication. This technology provides a more secure and complete description of a user's attributes, and it relies on a user-specified passphrase as opposed to a single, typically shorter, password. It does, however, require some form of PKI (Public Key Infrastructure) for verifying certificates and managing keys.

- SET is recommended if credit card information needs to be protected. The use of SET requires cooperation with the banking industry. SSL provides a much simpler solution if you only need to protect the transfer of credit card information against sniffers.

- To protect users against bogus web sites, use SSL server authentication in conjunction with an SSL server certificate from a trusted CA.

- Use SSL to protect against network sniffers and the unauthorized alteration of web content during transmission.

Table 3.2   Security Requirements Supported by Authentication and Encryption Technologies

Technology/ Requirement	Basic Authentication	SSL	SET
User Authentication	Yes (cleartext passwords)	Optional (certificates)	Optional (certificates)
Server Authentication	No	Yes (certificates)	Yes (certificates)
Confidentiality	No	Yes	Yes (for credit card information
Integrity	No	Yes (with Server Authentication)	Yes

3.7.5 Support the Use of SSL

1. Install and configure the web server software to support the use of SSL if confidentiality is needed.

SSL is typically not included with most web server software. Therefore, you will need to add an available plug-in or extension or replace your web server software with another product that includes SSL. You may want to consider implementing the SSL-enabled version of your web server software on another host. This procedure is consistent with a previous guideline to have separate services reside on different hosts (Section 3.2); however, it might not be practical to maintain your public web site's content on two different machines.

If you do choose to install and deploy SSL-enabled web server software, all practices contained in this chapter apply and need to be followed.

2. Create an SSL server key and the related certificate request. Arrange for a CA to provide a certificate for your public SSL server key.

An SSL-enabled web server encrypts the data exchanged between browser and server, but this encryption does not by itself ensure the authenticity of the connection.

Verifying the authenticity of a SSL web server depends on either distributing the public SSL server key in a secure manner to all users or requesting a certificate from a trusted third party (CA) able to verify that the public key does indeed belong to the specified web server.[22]

Typically, SSL-enabled web browsers come with a list of recognized CAs, which you may want to treat initially as untrustworthy. By arranging with a CA to sign your public SSL web server key, you can allow users to verify that the connection they have established is truly with your web server.

3. Assuming that you have deployed SSL to encrypt the connection between a browser and your public web server and that you have deployed the use of certificates to authenticate the server side of any connection, you can now use Basic Authentication to further authenticate the user to the web server. The user ID and password[23] are passed in an SSL-encrypted, and thus protected, form, and any request can therefore be granted or denied based on their legitimacy.

---

22. The details of this certification process are covered under the broader topic of operating a public key infrastructure (PKI). This topic is complex, controversial, and considered out of scope for this practice.

23. Password policies such as login limits, minimum password length, diverse character set, and password expiration time apply here (although such policies must be explicitly set because they are not supported by default).

4.   If a stronger authentication mechanism is needed (given that user passwords can be easily broken), consider using SSL client certificates.

The use of client certificates requires all users to have a personal SSL client key, which is then signed by a CA. The CA can be internal to your organization (requires resources, staff expertise) or a trusted third party.

SSL client certificates are best used in conjunction with smart cards, which effectively protect the user's keys. At the same time they support the use of these keys on all workstations (as opposed to only the user's personal workstation if the key is stored on the workstation's hard disk).

5.   Configure the web server to support the use of SSL or SET if credit card information needs to be transmitted. The credit card information must be transmitted in a very secure manner.

SSL may be the most straightforward technology to apply, especially if you already have an SSL-enabled web server. Credit card information can be safely transmitted between the web browser and the web server based on the SSL server certificate and the use of encryption.

Unencrypted credit card information may reside on the web server during a transaction. We strongly recommend that you transfer this information to a more secure system for any further processing and remove this information from your public web server as soon as possible. If you intend to keep and process credit card information on your public web server, it must be encrypted to ensure its confidentiality. Use public key technology to avoid compromising user private/secret keys, which are required when using private key technology.

SET provides additional benefits as compared with SSL. Public web sites do not receive the credit card information; it is passed directly and electronically to the SET infrastructure (banks, etc.). The payment is handled automatically via credit card. This minimizes the effort required to transfer credit card information from one system (SSL) to another. We recommend the use of SET for e-commerce sites that have large numbers of credit card transactions. Using SET may require establishing an interinstitutional relationship with a financial or SET-infrastructure provider.

6.   This practice does not discuss the strength of cryptographic algorithms used in SSL and SET. Until fairly recently, encryption software exported from the United States was restricted to keys of no more than 40 bits (later increased to 56 bits). New legislation has lifted this restriction for public domain products and products for the mass market.

Both SSL and SET protocols provide strong security against attacks on confidentiality and authenticity. This conclusion is based on the standards for SSL and SET as well as expert consensus regarding the underlying cryptographic algorithms. In the past, several SSL-related vulnerabilities were discovered. The majority of these were based on implementation errors.

3.7.6 Policy Considerations

Your organization's networked systems security policy should mandate the review of all information prior to its posting on your public web site and ensure that access to sensitive or restricted information via the web site is protected at the level required (using, for example, the encryption and authentication technologies described above).

3.7.7 Other Cryptographic Approaches

Three other cryptographic approaches are available, but they lack wide public acceptance and use:

1. Digest Authentication was introduced with Apache 1.1 for HTTP/1.1 to complement Basic Authentication. It is based on the MD5[24] message digest algorithm (hence the name) and a shared secret. Technically, it is a challenge response approach, which solves the problem of cleartext transmission. However, MD5 is falling into disfavor due to the reduced effort necessary to find collisions (two text strings having the same MD5 message digest). Depending on the implementation, Digest Authentication may provide protection against replay attacks—or it may not. For example, if the server does not keep track of distributed challenges, no protection is provided.

2. Pretty Good Privacy (PGP), along with other software producing ASCII digital signatures, can be used to authenticate web pages. To do so, the PGP-specific lines containing the delimited digital signature can be "hidden" from the web browser by surrounding them with HTML comment statements. To check the authenticity of the web page, users must run PGP after saving the web page on their computer. However, it may not be practical to use this approach. More information on PGP can be found at *http://www.pgp.com.*

3. Digital watermarking is a software method used to mark graphic and sound files for later verification of origin and ownership. It is performed in such a way that the marking is not noticeable to the user. Accompanying software at the browser end can be executed to verify the author or owner of a graphic or sound file. These file types can then be distributed while protecting the interests of the owner.

---

24. Available at *http://www.cert.org/security-improvement* under UNIX implementations.

3.8 Maintain the Authoritative Copy of Your Web Site Content on a Secure Host

The authoritative (i.e., verified, correct, trusted) copy of your public web site content needs to be stored on a host that is separate from, and more secure than, your public web server. The more secure host will likely be one that is on your internal network and protected behind one or more firewalls. If the integrity of the information on your public web server is ever compromised, you can restore it from the authoritative copy using a secure transfer procedure.

News reports regularly describe intruder attacks on well-known, commercial web sites, causing them at the very least to be defaced, or, worse, to present erroneous information that appears to be accurate. Organizations that rely on their web sites to transact business must be able to restore their authentic version quickly; otherwise, they run the risk of losing business and customer confidence.

The authoritative copy of your public web site content is less likely to be compromised by an intruder if it is stored in a relatively secure location and therefore likely be correct and available when you need to restore the publicly accessible version.

3.8.1 Restrict User Access

Restrict the number of users with access to the authoritative version of your public web site's content. Access should be granted only to users authorized to create and update web content and perform whatever administrative tasks are necessary to ensure the secure operation of the server where the content resides.

All authorized users should receive adequate training in the secure creation and maintenance of web site content and should have the opportunity to work safely with web content to gain experience (perhaps with a partner or mentor).

The list of authorized users should be reviewed and updated on a regular basis, particularly when an authorized user leaves your organization.

3.8.2 Implement and Enforce Access Controls

Your public web server content will likely be divided into different subdirectories, such as those containing home page information, project-related materials, and CGI scripts and programs. Implementing individual user and group access controls at the level of these subdirectories (and below, if necessary) will further protect your web content (see Section 3.3).

3.8.3 Enforce the Use of Strong User Authentication

Once users gain access to your authoritative version, there will likely be no further attempts to authenticate those users. Therefore, you need to ensure that user authentication has been accomplished prior to granting access. Strong authentication technologies include smart cards, tokens, and one-time passwords.

We strongly recommend against allowing remote authoring tools for content to reside directly on your public web site. However, you may be able to deploy these tools securely for use within the more protected environment where the authoritative copy resides if appropriate authentication and access control mechanisms are enforced.

3.8.4 Accept Authenticated and Encrypted Connections

Configure your public web server to accept an authenticated and encrypted connection initiated by the secure host where the authoritative copy is stored. If you choose to transfer the authoritative copy of your public web server content via a network, you need to implement the following four security measures:

1. Initiate all connections to the public web server by the secure host (not by the public web server). This prevents the public web server from being used to launch an attack directed at the secure host.
2. Implement firewall technology limiting the connectivity between the secure host and the public web server to allow the transfer of only authoritative web server content. You can use protocol-aware filtering proxies (such as those available for FTP) to accomplish this.
3. Use cryptographic measures to encrypt and authenticate the transferred content.
4. Additional measures such as restricting transfer time can further improve security for this type of transaction.

3.8.5 Establish Manual Procedures for Transferring Web Content

You need to develop alternative procedures for transferring web content from the secure host where the authoritative copy resides to your public web server in cases where you cannot use a network, either because higher-priority tasks override security requirements or due to other technical problems.

Such procedures may necessitate the following steps:

- Storing an encrypted archive on disk or CD-ROM and uploading the files directly at the public web server's console (with appropriate authentication and access controls)
- Transferring an encrypted ZIP archive on disk or CD-ROM to another workstation within the internal network, using the workstation's connectivity to upload the files to the public web server

It is preferable to use write-once read-many (WORM) media (such as CD-ROM) rather than media that can be rewritten.

3.8.6 Policy Considerations

Your organization's networked systems security policy should establish the following guidelines:

- Identical, authoritative copies of all information residing on public servers should be securely maintained. This information includes the current version of public server content as well as previous versions and their update/transfer history. Include the transfer date, time, user ID, reason for the transfer, and any related observations.
- The transfer of authoritative content to public servers should use strong authentication and encryption.

3.8.7 Additional Information

Consult the CERT advisories and tech tips listed in the Bibliography at the end of the book for information on common web server vulnerabilities that can be exploited by intruders.

Chapter 3 Checklist

Practice	Step Number	Step Description	Yes	Partial	No
P3.2: Isolate the Web Server	S3.2.1	Place the web server on an isolated subnet			
	S3.2.2	Use firewall technology to restrict traffic			
	S3.2.3	Place server hosts providing supporting services on another isolated subnet			
	S3.2.4	Disable source routing and IP forwarding			
	S3.2.5	Alternative architecture approaches			
	S3.2.6	Policy considerations			
P3.3: Configure the Web Server with Appropriate Object, Device, and File Access Controls	S3.3.1	Establish new user and group identities			
	S3.3.2	Identify the protection needed			
	S3.3.3	Mitigate the effects of DoS attacks			
	S3.3.4	Protect sensitive and restricted information			
	S3.3.5	Configure the web server software access controls			
	S3.3.6	Disable the serving of web server file directory listings			
	S3.3.7	Policy considerations			

(continued)

Chapter 3 Checklist (*cont.*)

Practice	Step Number	Step Description	Yes	Partial	No
P3.4: Identify and Enable Web-Server-Specific Logging Mechanisms	S3.4.1	Identify the information to be logged			
	S3.4.2	Determine if additional logging mechanisms are needed			
	S3.4.3	Enable logging			
	S3.4.4	Select and configure log analysis tools			
P3.5: Consider Security Implications for Programs, Scripts, and Plug-ins	S3.5.1	Perform cost-benefit trade-offs			
	S3.5.2	Select from trustworthy sources			
	S3.5.3	Understand all of the functionality of an external program			
	S3.5.4	Review publicly available information to identify vulnerabilities			
	S3.5.5	Policy considerations			
P3.6: Configure the Web Server to Minimize the Functionality of Programs, Scripts, and Plug-ins	S3.6.1	Verify that the acquired copy of an external program is authentic			
	S3.6.2	Use an isolated text machine			

Practice	Step Number	Step Description	Yes	Partial	No
	S3.6.3	Limit your exposure to vulnerabilities			
	S3.6.4	Mitigate the risk of distributing malicious code			
	S3.6.5	Disable or restrict the use of server side include functionality			
	S3.6.6	Disable the execution of external programs present in your web server configuration			
	S3.6.7	Restrict access to external programs			
	S3.6.8	Ensure that only authorized users can access external programs			
	S3.6.9	Execute external programs under unique individual user and group IDs			
	S3.6.10	Restrict the access of external programs to only essential files			
	S3.6.11	Create integrity-checking information for all external programs			
	S3.6.12	Policy considerations			
P3.7: Configure the Web Server to Use Authentication and Encryption Technologies	S3.7.1	Determine access requirements for sensitive or restricted information			
	S3.7.2	Establish trust between clients (users) and web servers			
	S3.7.3	Understand the limitations of address-based authentication			
	S3.7.4	Understand authentication and encryption technologies			

Chapter 3   Checklist (*cont.*)

Practice	Step Number	Step Description	Yes	Partial	No
	S3.7.5	Support the use of SSL			
	S3.7.6	Policy considerations			
P3.8: Maintain the Authoritative Copy of Your Web Site Content on a Secure Host	S3.8.1	Restrict user access			
	S3.8.2	Implement and enforce access controls			
	S3.8.3	Enforce the use of strong user authentication			
	S3.8.4	Accept authenticated and encrypted connections			
	S3.8.5	Establish manual procedures for transferring web content			
	S3.8.6	Policy considerations			

Chapter 4

Deploying Firewalls

A firewall is a combination of hardware and software used to implement security policies governing the network traffic between two or more networks, some of which may be under your administrative control (e.g., your organization's networks) and some of which may be beyond your control (e.g., the Internet). A network firewall commonly serves as a primary line of defense against external threats to your organization's computer systems, networks, and critical information. Firewalls can also be used to partition your organization's internal networks, thus reducing your risk from insider attacks.

The term *firewall* is taken from the structural analog whose purpose is to slow the spread of fire in a building. In the computer literature, popular press, and vendor marketing materials, the term is used in many ways. Some people use it to identify a specific hardware component or software package, while others consider the entire collection of systems and software deployed between two networks to be parts of a firewall.

Throughout this chapter, we will generally use the term *firewall* as an adjective modifying a noun (such as system, hardware, software, product) to make the reference clear. When we use the term *firewall* as a noun, we mean the general concept of a technological mechanism for the enforcement of a network traffic security policy. While these distinctions may seem cumbersome at times, we believe they will increase your understanding of our intent.

The practices described in this chapter build upon the assumption that you have first configured a secure general-purpose server (as described in Chapter 2).

4.1 Overview

The practices described in this chapter are applicable to your organization if its information infrastructure either includes or will soon include interconnections between internal networks and networks not under its administrative control, such as the Internet or business partner networks and interconnections among internal networks with different security requirements.

The purpose of this chapter is to cover the fundamentals of firewall functionality (packet filtering) and the deployment process. The practices assume that your desired firewall architecture includes packet filtering as a first step. Advanced firewall capabilities, such as proxies, stateful inspection or dynamic packet filtering, virtual private networks, and vendor-specific information are beyond the scope of this chapter.

This chapter assumes the existence of a site security policy, including the policy to be enforced by the firewall. It does not address the evaluation and selection of specific firewall products, post-deployment operation and maintenance of firewall products, networking and system management fundamentals, or cryptography and encryption technologies.

4.1.1 The Need for Firewalls

Increasingly, organizations are connecting to the Internet to establish an electronic commerce presence and to access information rapidly. When your organization's networks are connected to the Internet without adequate security measures in place, you become vulnerable to attacks from external adversaries. Without firewalls, you will be unable to prevent many forms of undesirable access to your networks, systems, and information assets, and you will expose your organization to a number of risks, including the following:

- Loss of confidentiality of business information (e.g., financial records, strategic planning data, engineering models and prototypes, marketing plans, medical records, as well as inability to guarantee the integrity of such information)

- Loss of availability of mission-critical services such as EDI (electronic data interchange), ERP (enterprise resource planning), just-in-time inventory controls, and electronic mail

- Exposure of critical data about your information infrastructure that your adversaries can use in planning their attacks

- Legal liability, regulatory liability, or public loss of confidence when your adversaries use one of your computers to carry out attacks against other organizations

- Vandalism of public information services (such as your public web site)

The use of firewall technology provides you with one of the most effective tools available to manage your networks' risk by providing you with access control mechanisms that can implement complex security policies.

4.1.2 An Approach to Deploying Firewalls

To effectively deploy firewall technology, we recommend a four-part approach, which requires implementing security practices in the following areas:

1. Preparing for firewall system deployment
2. Configuring your firewall system to reflect your security policy
3. Testing your firewall system to ensure it performs according to your specifications
4. Deploying the correctly configured firewall system

Within the context of this approach, Table 4.1 summarizes the recommended practices for deploying firewalls. The rest of this chapter covers the practices in more detail.

Table 4.1 Deploying Firewalls Practice Summary

Approach	Practice	Reference
Prepare	Design the Firewall System	Section 4.2; page 124
Configure	Acquire Firewall Hardware and Software	Section 4.3; page 139
	Acquire Firewall Training, Documentation, and Support	Section 4.4; page 142
	Install Firewall Hardware and Software	Section 4.5; page 144
	Configure IP Routing	Section 4.6; page 148
	Configure Firewall Packet Filtering	Section 4.7; page 150
	Configure Firewall Logging and Alert Mechanisms	Section 4.8; page 157
Test	Test the Firewall System	Section 4.9; page 160
Deploy	Install the Firewall System	Section 4.10; page 171
	Phase the Firewall System into Operation	Section 4.11; page 173

4.2 Design the Firewall System

Designing a firewall requires that you understand and identify the boundaries between security domains in your network. A network security domain is a contiguous region of a network that operates under a single, uniform security policy. Wherever these domains intersect, there is a potential need for a policy conflict resolution mechanism at that boundary. This is where firewall technology can help.

The most common boundary where firewalls are applied today is between an organization's internal networks and the Internet. When establishing an Internet firewall, the first thing you must decide is its basic architecture, assuming that you have previously established your firewall requirements and the security policy the firewall is intended to implement.[1] Four main topics need to be considered:

- Identification of the users of services you intend to offer to and request from the Internet
- Firewall availability and performance
- Choice of who will manage the firewall system and how they will manage it
- Choice of system and network growth that the firewall system will need to accommodate in the future

Refer to the section on policy considerations at the end of this chapter for policy-related guidance.

In this context, architecture refers to the inventory of components (hardware and software) and the connectivity and distribution of functions among them. There are two classes of firewall architectures, *single-layer* and *multiple-layer* architectures.

In a single-layer architecture (see Figure 4.1), one network host is allocated all firewall functions and is connected to each network for which it is to control access. This approach is usually chosen when containing cost is a primary factor or when there are only two networks to interconnect. The advantage of this approach is that everything there is to know about the firewall resides on that one host. In cases where the policy to be implemented is simple and there are few networks being interconnected, this approach can also be very cost-effective over time. The greatest disadvantage of the single-layer approach is its susceptibility to implementation flaws or configuration errors—depending on the type, a single flaw or error might allow firewall penetration.

In a multiple-layer architecture (see Figure 4.2), the firewall functions are distributed among a small number of hosts, typically connected in a series, with (Demilitarized

---

1. Other considerations can be found in *Firewalls Complete* (Goncalves 98) and the *Third Annual Firewall Industry Guide* (ICSA 98).

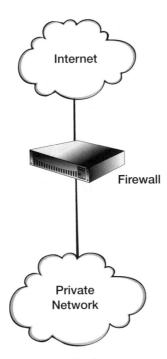

Figure 4.1 Example of a single-layer architecture

Zone) networks between them. This approach is more difficult to design and operate, but it can provide substantially greater security by diversifying the defenses you are implementing. Although more costly, we advise using different technology in each of these firewall hosts to reduce the risk that the same implementation flaws or configuration errors will exist in every layer. The most common design approach for this type of architecture is an Internet firewall composed of two hosts interconnected with one DMZ network.

Having chosen the basic architecture (i.e., the number of hosts, the method in which they are connected, the tasks that each will perform), the next step is to select the firewall functions to be implemented in these hosts. The two most basic categories of firewall function are packet filtering and application proxies. These functions can be used separately or jointly and can be implemented on the same or on different firewall hosts. Recently, packet filtering firewall products have gained some of the features of application proxies and are generally referred to as stateful inspection packet filters. See *Building Internet Firewalls, Version 2* (Zwicky 00), *Firewalls Complete* (Goncalves 98), and "Firewalls Fend Off Invasions from the Net" (Lodin 98) for a more detailed explanation of the different types of firewall architectures and functions.

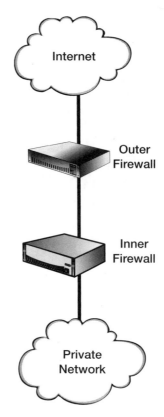

Figure 4.2   Example of a multi-layer architecture

There are good reasons to use both packet filtering and application proxies. Certain services (e.g., SMTP, HTTP, or NTP [Network Time Protocol]) are usually safe to control via packet filters, whereas others (e.g., DNS, FTP) may require the more complex features available only in proxies. Packet filtering is fast, whereas application proxies are generally slower. In cases where greater access control is required and the poorer performance of proxies cannot be tolerated, stateful inspection packet filters may be an acceptable compromise. In any case, one should plan to have as many of these different functions (i.e., packet filters, proxies, and stateful inspection) available as possible, applying each where appropriate.

Ideally, the design of your firewall architecture should precede firewall hardware and software selection. However, we recognize that in some organizations, some form of firewall may already be in place.

Your ability to enforce your organization's security policies accurately can be severely impaired if you have not chosen an appropriate and effective firewall architecture. This design will determine which policies can and cannot be enforced, as well as how well the firewall will accomplish its objectives over time. Firewall architectures are difficult and expensive to change after deployment, so there is considerable value (cost savings) in creating an effective, scalable, and manageable design at the outset.

Firewall systems provide a policy enforcement mechanism at a security domain boundary. If an adversary can exploit another, less protected boundary to gain access into your network (for example, a modem on a user workstation or via a partner's network), any firewall systems you have deployed on other boundaries to control access to that network will be ineffective.

4.2.1 Document the Environment

The generation and use of diagrams are extremely important while designing your architecture. They are good communications mechanisms and excellent tools to help you avoid mistakes later. The basic rule of thumb is, "if you cannot draw it, you cannot build it." Do not skip or scrimp on this step. One effective method is to use an electronic whiteboard with a group of knowledgeable people to generate possible diagrams.

4.2.2 Select Firewall Functions

Firewall functions available in today's products include packet filtering, application proxies, and stateful inspection filtering. Each of these functions implies a certain range of possible choices for deployment platforms. A firewall deployment platform is the combination of the particular hardware and operating system on which the desired firewall functions execute. In some cases the choice of function and platform can be made independently, while in others the choice of one forces a choice in the other. The following sections describe each of these functions and the platform choices available.

Packet Filtering

Since routers are commonly deployed where networks with differing security requirements and policy meet, it makes sense to employ packet filtering on routers to allow only authorized network traffic as far as possible. The use of packet filtering in those routers can be a cost-effective mechanism to add firewall capability to an existing routing infrastructure. As the name implies, packet filters specify packets to filter (discard) during the routing process. These filtering decisions are usually based on contents of the individual packet headers (e.g., source address, destination address, protocol, port). Some packet filter implementations offer filtering capabilities based on other information, which are considered under the heading of stateful inspection below.

Generally speaking, packet filtering routers offer the highest-performance firewall mechanism. However, they are harder to configure because they are configured at a lower level and therefore require a detailed understanding of protocols.[2]

Packet filtering is typically implemented on two kinds of platforms (refer to Table 4.2): (1) general-purpose computers acting as routers and (2) special-purpose routers.

We have found that cost is not a major consideration in choosing a platform for packet filtering.

Special-purpose router vendors have added packet filters to their router products to provide limited access controls as a result of customer demand and minimal implementation effort. However, they are router vendors, not security product vendors, so when they make a design trade-off between routing functionality and security functionality, they choose routing. In this context, performance is a routing functionality issue, not a security issue, so it always ranks near the top of the list of design priorities for these routers. In addition, adding filtering to a router can negatively impact routing, and therefore networking, performance and may require additional memory.

General-purpose computers and the operating system software that runs on them are not typically designed to act as high-performance routers, with or without packet filtering. A general-purpose computer is most commonly chosen for the following reasons:

Table 4.2   Principal Advantages and Disadvantages of Each Platform

	General-Purpose Computer Acting as a Router	**Special-Purpose Router**
Advantages	Unlimited functional extensibility	Highest performance
		Large number of interfaces
Disadvantages	Moderate performance	Minimal functional extensibility
	Small number of interfaces	May be more expensive
	OS vulnerabilities	

2. The difficulty primarily arises because of how quickly the rule sets grow in complexity. Low-level debugging is hard and requires detailed knowledge of how the router parses the rules you have defined.

- Firewall mechanisms and packet filtering can be used on the same host.
- In-depth knowledge of the chosen platform already exists.
- The filtering load can be eliminated on a special-purpose router.
- Source code is available.

Application Proxies

An application proxy is an application program that runs on a firewall system between two networks (see Figure 4.3). The host on which the proxy runs need not be acting as a router. When a client program establishes a connection "through" a proxy to a destination service, it first establishes a connection directly to the proxy server program. The

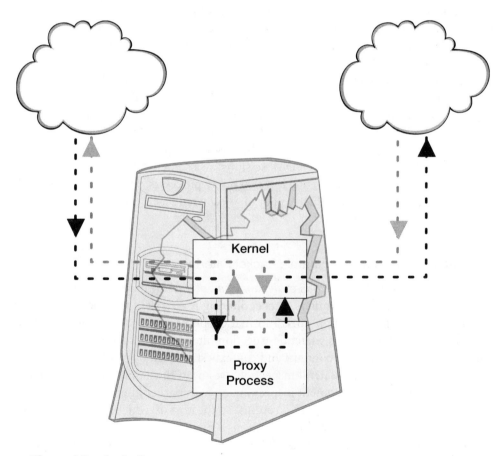

Figure 4.3   Application proxy

client then negotiates with the proxy server to have the proxy establish a connection on behalf of the client between the proxy and the destination service. If successful, there are then two connections in place: one between the client and the proxy server and another between the proxy server and the destination service. Once established, the proxy then receives and forwards traffic to and from the client and the service. The proxy makes all connection-establishment and packet-forwarding decisions, rendering any routing functions that are active on the host system irrelevant. In order to take advantage of a proxy server, client programs must be able to be configured so that they can send their packets to the proxy server instead of to their final destination.

As with packet filtering, application proxies are available on both special-purpose proxy machines and general-purpose computers. Generally speaking, application proxies are slower than packet filtering routers. However, application proxies are in some ways inherently more secure than packet filtering routers. Packet filtering routers have historically suffered from implementation flaws or oversights in the operating system's routing implementation on which they depend. Since packet filtering capabilities are "add-ons" to routing, they cannot correct or compensate for certain kinds of routing flaws.

As a result of making more complex filtering and access control decisions, application proxies can require significant computing resources and an expensive host upon which to execute. For example, if a certain firewall technology running on a UNIX platform needs to support 200 concurrent HTTP sessions, the host must be capable of supporting 200 HTTP proxy processes with reasonable performance. Add 100 FTP sessions, 25 SMTP sessions, some LDAP sessions, and some DNS transactions, and you have a host that needs to sustain 500 to 1,000 proxy processes. Some proxies are implemented using kernel threads, which can dramatically reduce resource requirements, but resource demands remain high.

Stateful Inspection or Dynamic Packet Filtering

We use the terms *stateful inspection* or *dynamic packet filtering* to refer to a more capable set of filtering functions on routers. Packet filtering is restricted to making its filtering decisions based solely on the header information on each individual packet, without considering any prior packets. Stateful inspection filtering allows both complex combinations of payload (message content) and context established by prior packets to influence filtering decisions. By stateful inspection, we mean the ability to use information extrinsic to the packet, not content inspection. As with packet filtering, stateful inspection is implemented as an "add-on" to routing, so the host on which the stateful inspection function is executing must also be acting as a router.

The principal motivation for stateful inspection is a compromise between performance and security. As a routing "add-on," stateful inspection provides much better performance than do proxies. It also provides a greater level of firewall function than simple packet filtering. Like proxies, much more complex access control criteria can be specified; and like packet filtering, stateful inspection depends on a high-quality (i.e., correct) underlying routing implementation.

Refer to "Stateful Inspection Firewall Technology Tech Note" (Check Point 98) and "Application Gateways and Stateful Inspection: A Brief Note Comparing and Contrasting" (Avolio 98) for more information about stateful inspection and dynamic packet filtering. Additional information on all firewall functions and the pros and cons of each can be found in *Firewalls and Internet Security* (Cheswick 94), *Building Internet Firewalls* (Chapman 95), *Firewalls Complete* (Goncalves 98), *Third Annual Firewall Industry Guide* (ICSA 98), and *Internet Security Policy: A Technical Guide* (NIST 98). A summary of thirteen vendor firewall products and the functions they support can be found in "Firewalls Market Survey" (SC 99).

Transparent Proxies

A transparent proxy combines packet filtering, packet rewriting, and traditional applications proxies. Packet headers matching specific criteria are rewritten so that they are directed to the proxy. Packets can then be sent to a proxy server without requiring clients to reconfigure their applications.

Approach

We recommend using a combination of packet filtering, stateful inspection, and transparent proxies to achieve the proper level of security. A good strategy is to start by implementing packet filter rules. In places where these rules don't sufficiently protect the infrastructure, add stateful inspection. In places where stateful inspection doesn't sufficiently protect the infrastructure, add transparent proxies.

For example, you may have public DNS, web, and mail servers that can be accessed by external users. Web and mail servers can be adequately protected using packet filtering. Access to DNS servers occurs using the UDP protocol, which is stateless—that is, you cannot infer the state of a connection with a single UDP packet as you can with a TCP packet. Therefore, you need to use stateful inspection to verify the contents of the packet. If you have a requirement to monitor web sites visited by internal users and restrict their browsing to certain locations, you need to use a proxy to intercept and properly direct their request, preferably using transparent proxies so that changes to web browser client configurations are not required.

A layered firewall design (using packet filtering, stateful inspection, and transparent proxies where required) allows an administrator to understand and correlate more easily the logs generated by these defensive mechanisms.

4.2.3 Select the Firewall Topology

While the firewall functions described above can be deployed in a wide variety of ways, there are only a small number of commonly deployed architectures. They are presented here in order of increasing effectiveness.

Basic Border Firewall

As shown in Figure 4.4, this is the starting point for all firewalls. A basic border firewall is a single host connecting an organization's internal network to some untrusted

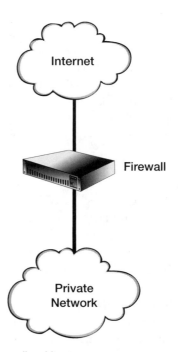

Figure 4.4   Basic border firewall architecture

network, typically the Internet. In this configuration, the single host provides all firewall functions.

Untrustworthy Host

To the basic border firewall (see Figure 4.5.), add a host that resides on an untrusted network where the firewall cannot protect it. That host is minimally configured and carefully managed to be as secure as possible. The firewall is configured so that both incoming and outgoing traffic must go through the untrustworthy host. The host is referred to as untrustworthy because it cannot be protected by the firewall; therefore, hosts on the trusted networks can place only limited trust in it.

DMZ Network

In a DMZ network (see Figure 4.6.) the untrusted host is brought "inside" the firewall but placed on a network by itself (the firewall host then connects three networks). This

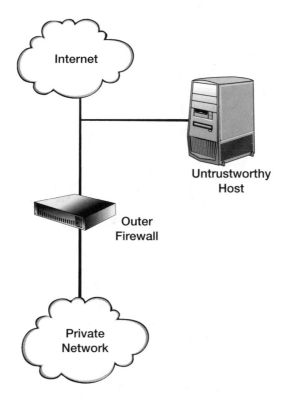

Figure 4.5 Basic firewall with untrustworthy host architecture

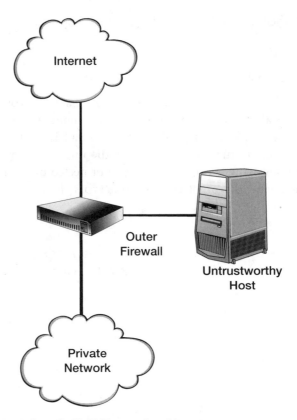

Figure 4.6   Basic firewall with DMZ network architecture

increases the security, reliability, and availability of the untrusted host, but it does not increase the level of trust that other "inside" hosts can afford it. Other untrustworthy hosts for other purposes (for example, a public web site or FTP server) can easily be placed on the DMZ network, creating a public services network.

Dual Firewall

The organization's internal network (see Figure 4.7.) is further isolated from the untrustworthy network by adding a second firewall host. By connecting the untrustworthy network to one firewall host, the organization's internal network to the other, and the DMZ between, traffic between the internal network and the Internet must traverse two firewalls and the DMZ.

In each of these architectures, firewalls are used to control access at the border of your network mainly for the purpose of protecting your network from an untrusted network. Firewalls deployed entirely within your network can also be used to provide

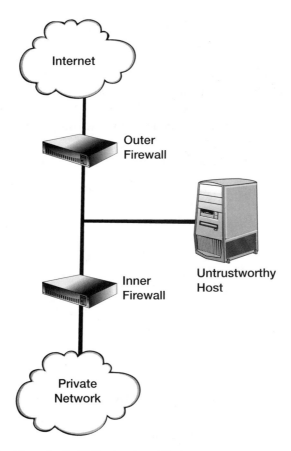

Figure 4.7 Dual firewall with DMZ network architecture

mutual protection among subnets of your network. Controlling access between internal subnets is no different from controlling access between your network and the Internet, so all of the above architectures can be used as internal firewall architectures as well.

Additional information on these firewall architectures and their respective pros and cons can be found in *Firewalls and Internet Security* (Cheswick 94), *Building Internet Firewalls* (Zwicky 00), *Firewalls Complete* (Goncalves 98), "Firewalls Fend Off Invasions from the Net" (Lodin 98), and *Internet Security Policy: A Technical Guide* (NIST 98).

4.2.4 Perform Architectural Trade-off Analysis

Firewalls are typically thought of in their restrictive or protective sense. That is, they protect your network from the Internet or restrict access to your network from the Internet. In today's Internet-enabled organizations, firewalls are more frequently thought of as safely empowering the organization to interact with the Internet. As such, firewalls are very much part of an organization's mission-critical infrastructure and need to be designed accordingly.

As a result, you must make the same architectural trade-offs in designing your firewall that are commonly made in other mission-critical systems. Architectural characteristics that must be considered include the following:

- Availability
- Performance
- Reliability
- Security
- Cost
- Manageability
- Configurability
- Function

Refer to "The Architecture Tradeoff Analysis Method" (Kazman 98) and "Experience with Performing Architecture Tradeoff Analysis" (Kazman 99) for more information on performing architectural trade-offs.

Availability

You can achieve availability through a combination of reliability and redundancy. Start by choosing hardware and software components that are reliable. If the level of reliability achieved is insufficient, consider using redundant components to meet availability requirements.

A hot backup/standby system is one redundancy approach that provides the ability to switch workload, automatically and immediately, from the primary system to the standby system, which is run in parallel with the primary system. A warm backup system requires some reconfiguration before the workload can be switched from the primary system, because it is not run in full parallel with the primary system. Cold backups are started from a shutdown state and need extensive configuration upgrades before being used. Having a hot standby firewall system will minimize downtime and maximize the ability to test broken systems offline.

Performance

Based on the expected traffic through the firewall system, you may need multiple firewall hosts to distribute the load and handle traffic at an acceptable rate.

Security

Weigh the use of single versus dual firewall systems at your network perimeter. Consider the following factors:

- Ability to have outside traffic passing through two firewall systems instead of one (benefits versus cost)
- Ability to monitor traffic and the monitoring locations
- Ability to respond to compromises, including disconnecting one firewall system while keeping the other operational
- The need for and number of network ports
- Performance
- Failure characteristics
- Expense
- Complexity of firewall system operations and maintenance
- Advisability of using multiple firewall systems from different vendors to reduce exposure to vulnerabilities inherent in a single product (survivability through diversity)

4.2.5 Protect Your Firewall System from Unauthorized Access

If you need to administer your firewall systems remotely, you must use strong authentication and data encryption technologies to prevent adversaries from compromising your firewall systems. The firewall administrator should be authenticated using technologies such as one-time passwords or recognized cryptographic protocols rather than cleartext passwords or replayable authenticators. All administrator communications to and from the firewall systems must be strongly encrypted. Consider strongly encrypting any sensitive information (passwords, configuration data) stored on the firewall system or on all administrative systems (such as the network management system).

Ensure that you have appropriate physical access controls for the work areas that house the consoles for your infrastructure management and administration systems. Unauthorized users who have physical access to these systems could use them to access your firewall systems. Ensure you have equivalent physical access controls for the work areas that house your firewall system consoles.

4.2.6 Policy Considerations

Your organization's networked systems security policy should address the following topics:

- The risks you are trying to mitigate with the firewall (i.e., the information assets and resources you are trying to protect and the threats that you are trying to protect against based on the security requirements that specify how these assets are to be protected)
- The services you intend to offer to untrusted networks from your protected network (these could be offerings to the Internet or to other internal networks)
- The services you intend to request from untrusted networks via your protected network (these could be requests to the Internet or to other internal networks)
- All incoming and outgoing network traffic must go through the firewall (that is, no traffic that bypasses the firewall is permitted, for example by using modems)—or, conversely, specific loopholes are permitted and under certain conditions (such as through the use of modems, tunnels, or connections to ISPs)

When offering and requesting services, your policy should ensure that you allow network traffic only if it is (1) determined to be safe and in your interests and (2) minimizes the exposure of information about your protected network's information infrastructure.

For additional information on policy-related topics, refer to *Firewalls Complete* (Goncalves 98).

4.3 Acquire Firewall Hardware and Software

You need to ensure that you have all of the hardware and software necessary to install, test, operate, monitor, and audit your firewall system prior to its deployment. In addition, make sure that you have adequate physical space to accommodate the equipment and that it can be connected properly in both its test and operational states. Seek expert advice if you are unfamiliar with the hardware and any aspects of its configuration, the software, or the physical environment in which it will operate.

Be aware that installing and configuring firewall hardware and software are difficult and complex processes. Each firewall product is different. It is critically important that you carefully read and understand all documentation provided by product manufacturers. For example, some products require specific hardware (e.g., graphic adapters) or specific software patches to be present for a successful installation.

You cannot operate your firewall mechanisms effectively, or perhaps at all, if key hardware or software components are missing. If you do not ensure that you have all components on hand prior to deployment, you are likely to experience delays in ordering and acquiring missing components, thus increasing the time needed to deploy your firewall system.

4.3.1 Determine Required Hardware Components

The hardware components you need may include the following:

- Appropriate processors on which to run the firewall software with sufficient processing speed to meet performance requirements
- Adequate RAM to meet performance requirements
- Devices necessary for software installation (e.g., CD-ROM, floppy drives, keyboard, display, mouse)
- Sufficient hard disk space to accommodate the operating system, the firewall software, and additional requirements such as log files
- Firewall client administration workstation(s)
- Network interface cards
- Backup devices and media
- Physical space such as rack mount space
- Appropriate power (e.g., plug strips, redundant power supplies, continuous power)

- Appropriate cabling (e.g., network and console cables)
- Testing devices (e.g., network traffic generators and monitors)
- Surrounding network infrastructure (e.g., routers, switches, and hubs)
- Telecommunications facilities
- Spare parts as required

Processor, memory, and disk capacities should be determined on a cost/benefit basis. Order the maximum that you can afford. Firewall software processing is typically very resource-intensive, and you will continue to require increased capacity as your network grows and your traffic or security needs increase.

Obtain sufficient adapter slots for all of the networks that will connect to your firewall system in both test and operational modes. Ensure that they operate at the data rates you require. If you have very high traffic at your site, you may need to consider multiple parallel gateways with automatic load balancing so that your firewall systems do not become a bottleneck.

Ensure that you have sufficient spare equipment on hand to meet your firewall redundancy, availability, and failure recovery requirements. For example, if you plan to maintain a hot standby or backup of your firewall system, you need sufficient equipment to operate a fully redundant system.

4.3.2 Determine Required Software Components

The software components you need may include the following:

- Host operating systems
- Patches and fixes to secure the operating system and bring it up to the most current version
- Device drivers for all adapters and interfaces required
- Any tools that are required to perform software reconfiguration
- Firewall software components
- Support utilities
- Network-monitoring tools such as tcpdump to view network traffic during testing and operations
- Patches and fixes to secure all software components

4.3.3 Determine Required Testing Components

Just as the operational environment for the firewall system must be designed, so must the test environment. Refer to Section 4.9 for information about determining testing requirements. The test environment should be designed to be as realistic as possible without running the risk of compromising your operational network or the firewall systems under test.

Hardware components may include equipment that fulfills the function of some or all of the networks that the firewall systems will eventually connect, as well as equipment used for the purposes of generating simulated traffic.

Software components may include tools to simulate network traffic that will exercise firewall rules.

While it is theoretically possible to test a firewall policy exhaustively by generating and monitoring network traffic, it is not practical to do so. Therefore, the policy must be tested via traffic sampling. Two possible techniques are to capture or replay existing traffic and to generate simulated traffic.

We recommend generating simulated traffic for the following reasons:

- You can choose and predictably generate traffic of most interest at any point in time.

- You are not distracted by traffic that is irrelevant to the test you are currently conducting.

- You do not need to characterize the captured traffic to ensure that it adequately covers your areas of interest.

- You do not need to sanitize traffic, as it does not represent actual communication.

- Most approaches to firewall testing are likely to include a review of log files and the use of network traffic generators and sniffers. Section 4.8 provides more information about logging practice.

4.3.4 Acquire All Components

Ensure that you have all hardware and software components available before attempting firewall system deployment.

Conduct a preliminary installation of the firewall software and operating system on the target hardware to ensure that nothing is missing. It is particularly important that you do this upon receipt of hardware and software if your deployment is delayed, so that if something is missing, you have time to correct the omission before deployment deadlines. If you skip this step, you may not realize the omission until much later. Plan to do this type of preliminary installation many times. The more comfortable you are with the installation process, the quicker you can perform major reconfigurations or recoveries.

If your firewall operating system (OS) resides in nonvolatile memory (e.g., flash memory), make sure that you can erase its contents completely and rewrite the OS image onto the hardware. Do this for both your primary and all spare OS hardware. This step will ensure that your OS hardware works correctly and that you can load a new version of the operating system once the firewall system is deployed.

If you have limited experience with the target hardware or operating system, bring in a knowledgeable consultant or vendor. Document your understanding, the actions that the advisers take, and the recommendations that they make. Have the consultant/vendor sign this document in the event you encounter problems in the future. It may give you some leverage to have them return without incurring additional expense.

4.4 Acquire Firewall Training, Documentation, and Support

Depending on the firewall architecture you design, you may need some level of training or vendor support when you are deploying a new firewall system. You need to evaluate a range of choices in order to determine your requirements for these information sources.

If you are unfamiliar with the technologies that make up your new firewall, you are likely to make potentially costly mistakes. Such errors can cause delays in all aspects of installing, configuring, deploying, operating, and maintaining your firewall system. While the most serious mistakes result from incorrect security configurations (exposing your network to a range of possible consequences), even maintaining the underlying hardware and software can be complex enough to warrant training or support.

4.4.1 Determine Your Training Requirements

You can almost always acquire training services and materials on the various technologies that make up your firewall system from the firewall product vendor. You may also be able to acquire what you need from other organizations that specialize in such training. Start by assessing the skills available within your organization. If staff with the requisite skills are not available, the best way to understand what is needed is to ask the personnel who are candidates for the training; they are most likely to know what they don't know. Assess existing skills and plan to supplement them as necessary in the following areas:

- TCP/IP protocols, services, and routing
- Network architecture
- Hardware on which the firewall runs or depends
- Software on which the firewall runs or depends, including the operating system
- The firewall software
- Network security and survivability
- Network monitoring

> system management techniques
>
> installation
>
> maintenance
>
> backup and recovery
>
> system security
>
> auditing, logging, and monitoring

Training is a relatively expensive commodity; make sure you get what you need—no more, no less.

Be sure to consider a range of training delivery methods, such as classroom instruction, including on-site learning and the use of web-based or video-conferencing technologies; self-paced learning (conventional or computer based); books and manuals; journals and magazines; conferences and user groups; and use of the World Wide Web.

Make sure to consider your future training requirements, including those for new personnel, in your plan.

Depending on the extent of your requirements as described above, we recommend that you schedule training well in advance of any firewall deployment activities but close enough to the start of deployment to be applied.

4.4.2 Determine Your Support Requirements

Vendor support may be essential when you are troubleshooting complex problems. Vendor support can also be used in lieu of training to address specific questions whose answers are not clear or present in available documentation.

Vendor support is generally negotiated in the form of a service-level agreement.[3] It can come in several forms: access-controlled web site support, phone support, and on-site support. Telephone support will likely offer the following options:

- A choice of 24 hours a day, seven days a week or during your normal business hours (Monday–Friday, 8:00 A.M. to 5:00 P.M.)
- A number of specified individuals who can call for support or an unlimited number of callers
- A specified period of support (one month, six months, one year)
- The use of a more in-depth service or on-site support if telephone support personnel cannot solve your problem
- A flat monthly or annual rate for telephone support or an hourly rate for in-depth or on-site support that is billed on a per-use basis

As with training, be sure to consider product support, such as support for the operating system, in addition to the firewall system. We recommend that you obtain vendor support as soon as you have selected your firewall systems and before you actually start testing and deployment.

4.5 Install Firewall Hardware and Software

Install and configure the operating system that will execute the firewall software; then install and configure the firewall software. These two steps should be performed on the firewall hardware you intend to use in your production environment but while it is deployed in the test environment and configuration (refer to Section 4.9. for information on using a test configuration). You need to ensure that all hardware and software are properly configured and operate as expected to the extent possible in the test configuration.

Configure the operating system on your firewall host in the minimum essential configuration so that only those services necessary for firewall operation and maintenance are included. You need to include all applicable patches or fixes for both the operating system and the firewall software.

The most common cause of firewall security breaches is misconfiguration of the firewall system. Various references on penetration testing show that well over half the

---

3. For more information on developing a service level agreement, refer to *http://www.gtlaw.com.au/pubs/negotiating.html* and *http://www.gtlaw.com.au/pubs/negotiatingservice.html.*

firewall systems regularly tested are not properly configured. According to ICSA,[4] 70 percent of sites with certified commercial firewalls are still vulnerable to attacks due to misconfiguration or improper deployment.

Exercising your installation and configuration procedures in a test environment will allow you to learn what you need to do to install and configure both the operating system and your firewall software efficiently while minimizing the impact on your operational systems. Such a test will highlight any hardware that may be missing in your initial configuration.

If you do not install the operating system and your firewall software with a minimal service configuration and with all applicable patches, you risk exposing your organization's network to intrusions that exploit well-known vulnerabilities for which patches exist. You also run the risk of not being able to get support from your vendor. Vendors almost always require the underlying system to be current before they will answer questions. Finally, you risk not having a stable platform on which to run the firewall software. Many patches are related to reliability and recovery.

4.5.1 Install a Minimum Acceptable Operating System Environment

Ensure that your firewall system configuration includes only those packages and services that are required for firewall system operation. This can be accomplished by either (1) removing all software that is not needed (if this can be determined) after installation, or (2) including only that software which is needed, selectively adding specific packages and services back in as you determine that they are required.

Examples of services that are typically included in a default operating system configuration that should be removed are X Windows services, telnet (assuming SSH is installed and configured), NFS for Unix-based operating systems, and NetBios for Microsoft NT operating systems.

For some firewall products, the process of installing the firewall software will force a minimal configuration of the operating system, such as removing unnecessary services, if this was not done before the installation process.

Keep in mind that packet filtering functions typically run in the operating system kernel (for performance reasons); therefore, packet filtering software is fairly sensitive to a specific kernel version and release number.

Once you are satisfied that the operating system and the firewall software are successfully installed, repeat the sequence to ensure that the process can be done again. The

---

4. January, 1999, quote.

second time, document it. Finally, have an outside person who was not involved in the first two installations follow the documentation to see if it is correct and complete.

Take appropriate steps to ensure that any redundant systems are in a state consistent with the systems to be used in production. Ensure that you can easily switch between your primary firewall system and any redundant systems.

Your installed environment may not have all of the necessary troubleshooting and support tools necessary to determine what has happened if anything goes wrong during the installation process. If you run into problems, you may need to install the firewall system on another host that has better diagnostic tools. After you understand the problems and know how to compensate for them, you can complete the installation on the production hardware.

4.5.2 Install All Applicable Patches

Information on patches is available from your operating system and firewall software vendors. Determine how to deliver patches securely to the firewall system. Some products require that you do this using removable media (disk, CD-ROM), not via a network.

As an operational consideration, if your redundancy requirements result in your having an identical hot backup or standby firewall system (which we strongly recommend), you can consider installing and testing any new patches on the redundant system and then switch from the current operational system to the redundant system.

Your vendor service-level agreement should state that the firewall software will always be fully functional if all of the operating system patches are installed.

In addition, you need to ensure that those responsible for your firewall operating system and software set aside time periodically to review applicable public and vendor information sources for security patch updates. Refer to Chapter 1 and Section 2.4.

4.5.3 Restrict User and Host Access

The only users who should have access to your firewall system are the firewall system administrator, those authorized by policy, and individuals involved in operating and maintaining your information technology infrastructure.

For some firewall products, the process of installing the firewall software will automatically disable access to the firewall system by all users (except those mentioned above) if you have not already disabled their access before installation.

We recommend that you allow remote access to your firewall system only via mechanisms that are strongly authenticated and encrypted, even on your organization's internal networks. Some firewall products enable you to restrict the administrative client to a specific IP address and a specific port. We do not believe that this is adequate security; encryption is required as well. IP addresses and ports are too easily spoofed.

4.5.4 Disable Packet Forwarding

Make sure packet forwarding is disabled until after the firewall software is operational.

While you are booting firewall hosts, there may be an interval between the time when the operating system and networking are functional and the time when the firewall software is functional. During this interval, packets may flow freely through the firewall system. You can make sure that no packets are forwarded before the firewall software is functioning by doing one or both of the following:

- Disabling IP routing before any interfaces are enabled (refer to Section 4.6)
- Not enabling network interfaces before the firewall software is functional

4.5.5 Back Up Your System

When installation is complete, perform a backup of the entire firewall system. Use this backup to restore the production system (or one identical to the test firewall system) for operation. Verify that both the operating system and the firewall software operate properly from the restored backup version. Refer to Section 2.10 for more information.

4.5.6 Policy Considerations

Your organization's networked systems security policy should establish the following guidelines:

- Timely evaluation, selection, and installation of patches and other corrections that you need to operate securely
- Limitation of access to the firewall system by authorized personnel only via authorized, strongly authenticated mechanisms
- Installation of the firewall system in an environment isolated from your operational networks
- Regular backups of your firewall system

4.6 Configure IP Routing

Routing is the process of deciding the disposition of each packet that a router handles. It applies to incoming packets, outbound packets leaving your network for external destinations, and those packets being routed among your internal networks.

There can be only two dispositions: forward or discard. The routing mechanism decides between these two, using the destination IP address in the packet header. This decision process is governed by a data structure called the routing table. The routing mechanism should not be used to implement security policy; it is too dynamic and unreliable. Routing functions and supporting structures are designed to route packets efficiently and reliably, not securely.

A firewall system's routing configuration reflects its view of the topological configuration of the networks to which it is attached. Most firewall systems' routing configurations are static, changing only rarely.[5]

You should have a routing configuration that reflects your network topology so that your firewall system will be able to deliver legitimate packets to their desired destinations.

4.6.1 Obtain IP Addresses

Obtain a unique IP address for each interface on each firewall system.

Each network to which a firewall system is attached has a procedure to obtain new IP addresses. For the Internet, the address is obtained from the ISP that will connect to your firewall. For internal networks, including any DMZ networks you intend to establish, you must obtain IP addresses from within your organization.

4.6.2 Establish Routing Configuration

A firewall system's routing table contains a list of IP network addresses for which the firewall system is intended to provide routing services. Each row of the table describes one network. The index used to access a row in the table is the destination network address of the packet currently being routed. If table lookup is successful, the table

---

5. Dynamic updates to routing configurations do occur. However, we state them as static here because the large majority of firewalls today have two interfaces—one to the Internet and one to the organization's internal network. In this case, routing is static. Most ISPs handle all dynamic routing, presenting a static interface to their customers' systems at all times.

provides either the address of the next router to which to send the packet or the interface you should use to send the packet out. That next router is used as the intermediate destination and the packet is forwarded there. If the table lookup fails, the packet is discarded. An ICMP "unreachable" message may be returned to the source indicating that the packet was undeliverable.

If you are replacing an existing firewall system or router, thoroughly examine the routing configuration of your system to determine the network topology that it describes. Ensure, as a first step, that the routing configuration of the new firewall system is consistent with your current system before departing from that configuration.

Full information on routing protocols and the process of establishing a routing configuration is given in *Internetworking with TCP/IP, Volume 1: Principles, Protocol and Architecture,* 3d ed. (Comer 95).

4.6.3 Policy Considerations

Your organization's networked systems security policy should (1) require that configuring IP routing for your firewall system be performed in an environment isolated from your operational networks and (2) specify what connectivity is to be permitted, explicitly stating that all other connectivity is denied.

Your routing configuration is derived from your network topology. You should not attempt to implement aspects of your security policy with routing. It is too imprecise, exercises insufficient control of your incoming and outgoing network traffic, and has no support for auditing and logging.

4.6.4 Considerations in Formulating IP Routing Configuration and Packet Filtering Rules

If your firewall design is based on a multiple-layer firewall architecture with a DMZ so that all inbound and outbound packets travel through both firewall systems, you need to take the following factors into account:

- For the outside firewall system (the one that sits between the external world and the inside firewall system), the routing configuration is more complex and the packet-filtering rules are more simple. Formulating the routing configuration and the filtering rules needs to be done separately and somewhat sequentially.

- For the inside firewall (the one that sits between the outside firewall and your internal networks) the routing configuration is more simple and the packet filtering rules are generally more complex (depending on the policy you are implementing). You need to formulate the routing configuration and the filtering rules concurrently.

Take these recommendations into account when performing the steps described here as well as in the next section (4.7).

4.7 Configure Firewall Packet Filtering

Packet filtering is the process of deciding the disposition of each packet that can possibly pass through a router with packet filtering (firewall host).[6] For this discussion, assume there are only two dispositions: accept and reject. IP filtering provides the basic protection mechanism for a routing firewall host, allowing you to determine what traffic passes through it based on the packet's contents and thereby potentially limiting access to each of the networks controlled by the firewall.

The criteria used in each filtering rule for determining the disposition can be arbitrarily complex. For a router with packet filtering, the rules may be applied at multiple points in the routing process; typically, they are applied at the time a packet is received in the case of arriving packets, and immediately before a packet is transmitted in the case of departing packets. There may be different rule sets at each point where filtering is applied.

Your firewall's packet filtering rules should implement some portion of your organization's network security policy. If the entire policy can be implemented in packet filters, other firewall mechanisms may not be required. If some elements of your policy cannot be implemented with packet filters, consider additional firewall mechanisms. We suggest first adding stateful inspection features. Then, if additional protections are still required, add transparent proxies. Refer to Section 4.2 for additional information about these mechanisms.

Packet filtering can be a high-performance, low-cost way to implement a substantive portion of your network security policy.

4.7.1 Design the Packet Filtering Rules

In general, controlling what packets are forwarded can be achieved in two ways. You can deny packets you know are unacceptable and permit everything else; or you can permit packets you know are acceptable and deny everything else. Logically, these approaches are

---

6. Filtering uses a range of information in the packet header (for example, source and destination IP addresses, port, and protocol), while routing uses only the destination IP address.

equivalent. Operationally, however, they are quite different. Given that there are a potential of 131,070 TCP and UDP services on any given host, it is not operationally feasible to determine which of these might be acceptable or unacceptable. Fortunately, your users will tell you what is acceptable (usually in the form of complaints). We believe that taking advantage of your users' suggestions leads to the best practice for packet filtering today, that is, explicitly to permit packets you know to be acceptable (and reflective of your policy) and to deny everything else.

Intrinsic and Extrinsic Information

The criteria that are available to influence the content of the rules you design come from two sources: information intrinsic to a packet and information extrinsic to a packet. Intrinsic information is contained within a packet itself. Two examples of intrinsic information are (1) packet header information—source address, destination address, protocol, source port, destination port, packet length, and connection state information—and (2) packet payload (message content).

Some or all of this information may be referenced in filter rules, depending on the actual implementation of the packet filter mechanism in the firewall software you have selected. Most packet filters only support references to information in headers.

Extrinsic information is information that exists outside a packet, for example:

- Arrival interface on the router or firewall
- Departure interface on the router or firewall
- Context maintained by the firewall software that pertains to a packet (for use in stateful inspection)
- Date and time of packet arrival or departure

Packet filters cannot generally reference extrinsic information. Most packet filters are implemented as separate sets of rules for each interface, sometimes with separate sets for arriving and departing packets. By placing a given rule in the appropriate interface's rule set, you are using extrinsic information in the design of your rules.

A Design Approach

When designing rules for a new network interconnect (one that does not currently exist in firewalled or unfirewalled form), we recommend the following approach:

1. You can generally assume that the last rule in every rule set of every firewall system is to deny all packets. However, we recommend explicitly adding this

rule to remind you that this is the policy you are implementing and to express the rule set more completely.

2. Design anti-spoofing rules and put them at the top of each rule set. Refer to *http://www.ietf.org/rfc/rfc2267.txt* (Ferguson 98) for more information about spoofing and designing antispoofing rules.

3. Canvass the potential users of this interconnect to find out what they expect to be doing. Collect this list into a table of protocols, ports, and source and destination addresses. Select those that implement your security policy.

4. Sort the table by protocol and then by port.

5. Collapse the rows of matching protocols and consecutive ports together into one new row that specifies a range for the port.

6. Convert this table into a set of rules and insert them between the anti-spoofing rules and the "deny all" rule at the end of the rule set.

Design Guidelines

In implementing the design approach, keep in mind the guidelines discussed earlier in this section.

For some firewall software, installing an empty set of packet filtering rules does not mean that all traffic is allowed to pass through; rather, it instructs the firewall to block all traffic (including firewall configuration session packets). If this happens, you will need physical access to the firewall management console to recover the system.

Watch for default packet filtering rules that may come with the firewall software. These are sometimes not obvious and will likely not comply with your security policy. Carefully review your firewall software documentation.

If your firewall has separate rule sets for arrival and departure on each interface, repeat the rules in the arrival rule set of each interface and in the departure interface of the others. This reduces the possibility of an oversight.

You can automatically generate rules for one interface from the other as long as your firewall has only two interfaces. This process becomes more difficult, however, as the number of interfaces increases, eventually becoming computationally infeasible.

For anti-spoofing rules to work as intended, your firewall must be able to distinguish between arrival and departure on each interface independently. You need to specify sets of rules that reference interfaces and direction; otherwise, you cannot implement anti-spoofing rules without interfering with other rules.

Check to see if your firewall system is capable of generating anti-spoofing rules automatically from routing tables. The advantage of this approach over manually designed rules is that the rules may be able to adapt automatically to routing changes. This is important if your firewall has multiple routes to the same destinations (e.g., multiple connections to the Internet). If you do not automatically generate antispoofing rules, then routing changes may adversely affect your ability to reach certain destinations, since routing and filtering could then be in conflict.[7]

Remember that packet filters must be based on IP addresses, not host names or use of DNS services. If your firewall software allows you to specify addresses in the form of host names, the names must be converted to addresses, which are then used in filters before filters can take effect. If a host's address changes, the firewall will not recognize the change until the filter configuration is reloaded and the names are converted to addresses again.

IP implementation flaws can compromise the effectiveness of a packet filtering firewall. Such flaws include fragmentation reassembly errors and incorrect interpretation of invalid packet headers. Several of the references in the Bibliography at the end of the book contain more information on the dangers of broken IP implementations.

If your filtering software allows you to refer to established TCP connections, you may wish to use this feature to allow return traffic to be forwarded for established connections. This feature is useful for allowing packets returning from TCP connections originating within your internal network to the Internet back into your network. Note that this feature is not foolproof. It is possible for an adversary to forge such packets, thereby getting them through your firewall and into your network. If all of your internal systems have properly operating TCP implementations, they will discard these forged packets. But this is a risk you must decide to accept or reject.

Given that UDP is a connectionless protocol, it has no concept of an "established" state. Therefore, there is no completely safe way to allow "return" UDP packets with traditional packet filtering—they simply cannot be positively associated with an outgoing packet. However, in spite of UDP's inherently less safe nature, a number of critical services depend on UDP packets. For example, the domain name service (UDP port 53) must be functional in order for your internal hosts to operate correctly. If possible, use stateful inspection features of the firewall software to filter connections based on state. If your firewall doesn't have stateful inspection features, it may be possible for you to determine the level of threat in permitting packets for each UDP service and thus apply risk management to decide whether to permit or deny the service.

ICMP is also a connectionless protocol. Therefore, it suffers from the same types of filtering limitations and threats as UDP. However, there are only thirteen types of ICMP packets. For each type, you should explicitly decide what you are willing to permit and

---

7. Be aware that routing topology changes may create conflicts between routing and filtering policies for non-spoofing-related filter rules. This is the primary reason that most firewalls operate with a static routing configuration.

then apply stateful inspection technology to filter any remaining types based on connection state, if possible.

Source routing is a function of IP routing that allows the packet originator to influence routing decisions as the packet traverses networks. We recommend that you disable all source-routing functions in your firewall's router and, if possible, deny any packets that have specified source-routing options.

Refer to *TCP/IP Illustrated, Volume 1: The Protocols* (Stevens 94) for details on TCP, UDP, and ICMP.

4.7.2 Document the Packet Filtering Rules

Document packet filtering rules so that anyone reading the documentation and configuration data is able to see how each filtering rule enforces its part of the firewall policy. Explain why each rule is included.

Specifying the detailed rules that implement your firewall policy can be a very complex and time-consuming process. It is common for several rules to be required to achieve one integral function. Group the rules that go together and include comments or other documentation that explains what the group does (to the extent that the filter syntax permits).

Most commercial firewall products provide complex configuration managers and user interfaces for specifying rules. Some products enable the user to aggregate related sets of rules into groups. However, the language used to express the rules is typically network-based, not policy-based. This means that you can specify a rule and understand what it does from a network perspective, but you may still have little idea of the policy implications.

In many current products, firewall system performance deteriorates as the number of filtering rules increases. So you may be forced to combine rules to optimize performance (make sure to include good documentation to explain what the optimized rule set does and how it performs). This process contributes to further obfuscation of the rules from a policy perspective. Establishing and maintaining your understanding of the rules from both a policy and a network viewpoint at the same time is very difficult.

One strategy for addressing this complexity is to maintain your firewall policy and the rules that implement it in a policy language of your own design. We know of no products that can do this. Developing a language that works for the firewall and system administrators in your organization might be worth the effort, as it simplifies the operation and maintenance of your firewall system and reduces the probability of introducing errors over time.

It is easy to make mistakes in altering rules as your requirements change. We recommend keeping the rule sets under revision control (using a tool such as RCS (Revision

Control System) or SCCS (Software Configuration Control System) so that you can look back to prior configurations when necessary.

4.7.3 Install Packet Filtering Rules

Now that you have one or more sets of rules, install them in your firewall test environment. Most firewall software has a mode of operation that allows the installed filters to be dumped to a file for examination. Become familiar with this feature. Install your filters, dump them, and compare the two. Sometimes you will find ambiguities in the input language that result in your implementing something different from what you intended. Continue this install-dump-compare cycle until you are satisfied that you have installed what you intended to install.

In actual use, all three steps of this practice (design, document, install) are performed in parallel using a process of successive refinement. It is also common to perform initial rule-specific testing during this activity to ensure that each rule does what you expect it to do. Refer to Section 4.9 for more information on testing.

4.7.4 Policy Considerations

It is rare for packet filtering to be able to implement an organization's security policy exactly. Your managers must decide what level of accuracy and precision is required in implementing your security policy. We suggest adding stateful inspection to packet filters as a first attempt at implementing the policy more accurately. If this is not sufficient, you may need to implement proxies.

Your organization's networked systems security policy should state that (1) all network traffic that is not explicitly permitted should, by default, be denied and (2) configuration of packet filtering for your firewall system must be performed in an environment isolated from your operational networks.

> The following example represents a text-based firewall policy to protect a local user workstation on the ABC network. It assumes that all traffic not explicitly permitted is denied.
>
> Permit all traffic to and from local host.
> Permit all inbound SSH traffic.
> Permit all AFS client traffic (AFS is the site file system).

Permit all Kerberos 4 client traffic.

Permit all Kerberos 5 client traffic.

Permit all DNS client traffic.

Permit all NTP client traffic to ntp1.abc.org.

Permit all NTP client traffic to ntp2.abc.org.

Permit all NTP client traffic to ntp3.abc.org.

Permit all syslog traffic to log-server.abc.org.

Permit all ICMP traffic.

Permit fragments from ABC networks inbound.

Permit all outbound TCP connections.

The following example represents a text-based firewall policy to protect a public web server. Like the example above, it assumes that all traffic not explicitly permitted is denied:

Permit all traffic to and from localhost

Permit all inbound web (http and https) traffic

Permit all inbound SSH traffic

Permit all AFS client traffic

Permit all Kerberos 4 client traffic

Permit all Kerberos 5 client traffic

Permit all DNS client traffic

Permit all NTP client traffic to ntp server

Permit all syslog traffic to logging server

Permit all ICMP traffic

You should take care to minimize the amount and usefulness of information about your information infrastructure disclosed to those outside the firewall by addressing the following points in your policy:

- Limit the use of your organization's internal networks and services by users who are not members of your organization. If you are providing services, such as access to your public web site, specifically for use by nonmembers, your policy should require that they be isolated from your internal systems. This decreases your risk even if one of the services is vulnerable to attack, because access is strictly controlled.

- Address access requirements by members of your organization who are located on untrusted networks, such as mobile users on the Internet and employees located at a business partner's site. You may need to allow mechanisms to be implemented granting these people appropriate access through the firewall system to your internal networks or systems. If so, require the use of strong authentication and encryption.

4.8 Configure Firewall Logging and Alert Mechanisms

You want your firewall systems to log activities pertinent to firewall operation and the rules the firewall will enforce. For significant firewall events, you want the system to alert you in real time that these events have occurred.

You need to specify the following types of logging for your firewall systems:

1. Logging associated with the packets arriving and departing the firewall (e.g., packet denied, packet forwarded)
2. Logging associated with the operation of the firewall software and the system on which it runs (e.g., no more disk space, no more memory, firewall logs are full)

For most firewall software, there are logging options associated with each individual packet-filtering rule. Every packet processed by such a rule has these options applied to it for the purposes of logging. An example is to log packets denied by the firewall software. Logging options can also be used to specify the level of logging, which commonly includes real-time alert mechanisms such as paging, electronic mail, or executing an arbitrary program.

The most important reason for logging is to ensure the continued operation of the firewall system. Logged events related to the operational status of the firewall are critically important in preventing and recovering from failures. They are also an important auditing tool to ensure that the proper security configurations (e.g., packet filters, proxies) are installed on the firewall system. Logs of this sort are generally small and can have long-term value for a variety of purposes.

Quite independently from firewall operational concerns, logs can be useful in intrusion detection. See Sections 5.3 and 5.4 for more information about logging.

Since log files are typically voluminous and difficult for humans to process, you should use alert mechanisms to notify you of any significant event. It is generally impractical to depend on manual analysis of logs to detect significant events.

4.8.1 Design the Logging Environment

You need to determine the following factors:

- The location of firewall log files—both on the firewall system itself and on a remote logging host accessed via a network
- The expected size of log files
- The rate at which data are logged to the log files
- Who needs access to the log files, and the level of access required
- Whether or not logging is to be encrypted
- How log files are to be backed up and recovered

We recommend the following as general heuristics to guide your design:

- If you log to a host other than the firewall host, make sure your packet filter logging does not create log entries for log packets. This will create an infinite logging loop. See the next step.
- Log to both local log files on the firewall host and a central log host. Log as much information as you can locally and keep it for as long as disk space permits. Log only information that you need or will use to the central log host.
- Use a separate logging-only network to log to the central logging host. This action prevents logging from affecting normal traffic. You can use this logging-only network to log intrusion detection traffic as well.
- Do not allow disk space requirements to be a constraining factor for logging. Disks are inexpensive, so make sure you have enough disk space on both the firewall host and the central log host for local logging.

4.8.2 Select Logging Options for Packet Filter Rules

Design the logging options on each packet filter rule. You need to decide what purpose is served by logging packets affected by the rule. Generally, logging for its own sake is not a wise use of resources.

Logging options for each rule may include packets that are denied upon arrival at the firewall system, denied upon departure from the firewall system, or arrive or depart within a specified time or date interval.

In addition to logging options for each rule, you might be able to configure other aspects of logging that relate to packets being filtered. For example, your firewall software may support summarization of individual filter logs. These can be useful for seeing trends, and it is generally more worthwhile to keep these for an extended period than it is to keep the individual log entries.

Although it is not typical practice to log packets that are permitted by filter rules, it is occasionally interesting to track a particular kind of traffic. For this purpose, you might consider adding a redundant filter rule (one that either permits or denies packets that are already permitted or denied by another rule) just so that you can specify different logging options for that rule. If you do this, make sure to document the fact that the rule is redundant and not essential to the implementation of your security policy.

If you are replacing an existing firewall system, thoroughly examine the logging options specified by your existing system. Consider retaining those logging options for rules in the new configuration that are consistent with your security policy.

4.8.3 Design the Alert Mechanism Configuration

You should design the real-time alert function of your firewall system to ensure that important event notifications are delivered to the appropriate people as quickly as possible with a minimum number of false notifications.

These notifications may cover the following events:

- Unsuccessful user and host login attempts
- Modification or disabling of packet filters in the firewall system
- Successful logins to the firewall system
- Changes to certain files on the firewall system
- Operational events (e.g., logs full, memory or disk shortages, system reboots)

If you followed our recommendation above to establish a central log host, we further recommend that you establish a central alert mechanism that also operates on the central log host. It may be that if you choose this approach, the firewall alert mechanism can be disabled and all alerts can be handled by one system.

If you are replacing an existing firewall system, thoroughly examine the alert options specified by your existing system. Consider retaining those parts of the alert mechanism configuration that remain consistent with your current security policy and your firewall system operation policy.

4.8.4 Acquire or Develop Supporting Tools

Acquire or develop tools that monitor your log files, and summarize the content of your log files beyond those provided by the vendor. These actions will allow you to review only those events of interest.

You will need to develop log file archive mechanisms unless your design includes enough disk capacity to retain log records until they are discarded. We recommend that you use WORM devices for all archiving.

4.8.5 Policy Considerations

Your organization's networked systems security policy should establish the following guidelines:

- Your firewall system should record all significant activity (such as administrative changes and attempts to breach filter rules) by doing thorough auditing and logging.

- Configuration of the logging and alert mechanisms for your firewall system should be performed in an environment isolated from your operational networks.

- Designated administrators should be notified of suspicious behavior that can be detected by the firewall system. Such behavior would include events related to the firewall system, such as failed login attempts and requests to disable filter rules.

- Guidelines should be specified for handling archived log information, deciding how long information should be retained, and discarding log information.

4.9 Test the Firewall System

The purpose of the test activity is to verify that the firewall system works as intended. You should take the following three steps:

1. Plan testing activities to demonstrate that routing, packet filtering, and logging and alert capabilities perform as designed.
2. Test recovery plans for firewall system failures.
3. Design your initial regression-testing suite.

The features that must be tested include the following:

- Hardware (processor, disk, memory, network interfaces, etc.)
- Operating system software (booting, console access, etc.)
- Firewall software
- Network interconnection equipment (cables, switches, hubs, etc.)
- Firewall configuration software—including routing rules, packet filtering rules, and associated logging and alert options

Testing your firewall system and verifying that it operates properly should help to increase your confidence that it will perform as designed. You should understand both the types of failures that can occur in each system component and the recovery techniques available for each type of failure. This knowledge will allow you to exercise your response and recovery processes when and if these failures occur once the firewall system becomes part of your operational infrastructure.

The most common cause of firewall security breaches is a misconfiguration of your firewall system. Knowing this, you need to make thorough configuration testing—both of the firewall system itself and of the routing, packet filtering, and logging capabilities—one of your primary objectives.

4.9.1 Create a Test Plan

You need to test both the implementation of the firewall system and the policy being implemented by the system. Testing the implementation of the system involves three steps:

1. Create a list of all field-replaceable system components whose failure would significantly interfere with the ability of the firewall to meet its mission goals.
2. For each such component, create a short list of the modes of failure most likely to affect firewall operations. De-emphasize components whose failure modes are unlikely to occur or may occur but are unlikely to have an impact on firewall operations.
3. For each relevant failure mode, design a test scenario that would either directly cause or simulate the failure and a mitigation strategy that minimizes the impact of the failure.

An example of a test scenario is to assume that the host system on which the firewall software runs has an unrecoverable hardware failure preventing it from performing any packet forwarding, a situation that might occur if the network adapter failed. A way to test this scenario might be simply to unplug the network from the interface to simulate the failure.

An example of a recovery strategy would be to maintain a totally redundant firewall system, switching to the redundant host when failures occur to minimize the time period during which packet transmittal is affected.

Testing the policy installed in the system is more difficult. It is not feasible to undertake exhaustive tests of an IP packet filter configuration; there are too many possibilities. We recommend that you use boundary tests instead. In these tests, you identify boundaries in your packet filter rules and then sample-test the regions immediately adjacent to each boundary.

To do this for each rule, you identify every boundary in the rule. In general, each constrained parameter in a rule contributes either one or two boundaries. The space being partitioned is a multidimensional packet attribute space. Common attributes include protocols, source addresses, destination addresses, source ports, and destination ports. Basically, every attribute of a packet that can be independently checked in a packet filter rule defines one dimension of this space. For example, a rule that permits TCP packets from any host to your Web server host on port 80 has checked three attributes (protocol, destination address, and destination port), partitioning the attribute space into three regions: TCP packets to Web server at ports less than 80, port 80, and ports greater than 80.

To do this for each region, you generate some test traffic that you have engineered to stay within that region. You verify that the firewall either rejects or forwards all traffic for a given region. Within a single region, all traffic should be rejected or forwarded; that is the purpose of partitioning the packet attribute space.

For a complex set of rules, this can be a tedious process and may not be practical. If it is not practical to test the rules, request that several people review them and ask one person to explain to the others what each rule does.

The test plan needs to include the test cases, configurations, and expected results for the following situations:

- Testing the routing configuration, packet filtering rules (including service-specific testing), and logging and alert options
- Testing the firewall system as a whole (hardware/software failure recovery, sufficient log file sizing, proper archival of logs, performance monitoring)
- Exercising both normal conditions and excursion (anomaly) conditions

You also need to describe the tools you intend to use (such as scanners, monitoring tools, and vulnerability detection tools) and the tests you intend to run using those tools.

4.9.2 Acquire Testing Tools

Develop firewall test tools if your firewall product does not come with these capabilities. There are several types of firewall test tools (see sidebar):

- Network traffic generators (such as SPAK (Send PAcKets), ipsend, or Ballista)
- Network monitors (such as tcpdump and Network Monitor)
- Portscanners (such as strobe and nmap)
- Vulnerability detection tools (a range of public domain and commercial tools available from various sources)
- Intrusion detection systems such as snort (refer to Section A.9), NFR (Network Flight Recorder), and Shadow

Tool	Available at
SPAK	*ftp://ftp.cerias.purdue.edu/pub/tools/unix/netutils/spak*
ipsend	*http://www.openbsd.com*
Ballista is now part of Cybercop Scanner from Network Associates.	*http://www.nai.com under Products*
tcpdump	*http://www.cert.org/security-improvement* under UNIX implementations
Network Monitor is a packet sniffer.	included with Microsoft's Systems Management Server
strobe	*ftp://ftp.cerias.purdue.edu/pub/tools/unix/scanners/strobe/*
nmap	*http://www.insecure.org*
NFR	*http://www.nfr.com*
Shadow is an intrusion detection system developed by the U.S. Navy.	Information at *http://www.nswc.navy.mil/ISSEC/CID/step.htm* A step-by-step guide for Shadow can be ordered from SANS at *http://www.sansstore.org.*

See also Section 5.3.15, and Table 5.3. Links to many of these tools can be found on the book's web site.

4.9.3 Test the Firewall Functions in Your Test Environment

Establish a test configuration so that your firewall system is interconnected between two isolated hosts, one playing the role of the external world and the other playing the role of your internal hosts (see Figure 4.8). Ensure that the default gateway for the internal host is set to the firewall system under test. If you have chosen an architecture that supports centralized logging (which we recommend), place both the internal host and a log host on your internal network so that you can test logging options. If logging is performed on the firewall host, you can connect the internal host directly to the firewall host.

Have scanning or network-sniffing tools in place on your outside and inside hosts to capture all traffic in both directions (inside to outside, outside to inside).

Do the following:

1. Disable packet filtering.
2. Inject packets that will exercise all routing rules and send these through the firewall system.
3. Ensure that packets are routed correctly by examining the firewall logs and your scanner results.
4. Turn on packet filtering.
5. Inject network traffic that is an appropriate sampling of all possible source and destination IP addresses, across all ports, and for all protocols.
6. Ensure that packets intended to be blocked (denied) are blocked. For example, if all UDP packets are to be blocked, ensure that none gets through. Ensure that packets intended to enter or exit (permitted) do enter and exit. Do this by examining your firewall logs and scanner results.
7. Scan for open and blocked ports to ensure that your firewall system is performing as intended.
8. Examine all of the network traffic that is logged and verify that the logging options associated with each packet filtering rule are operating as intended.
9. Examine all of the network traffic that is logged, and verify that the alert options associated with each logging option are sending alerts to the designated destination (such as the firewall administrator) using the specified mechanism (such as paging or e-mail).

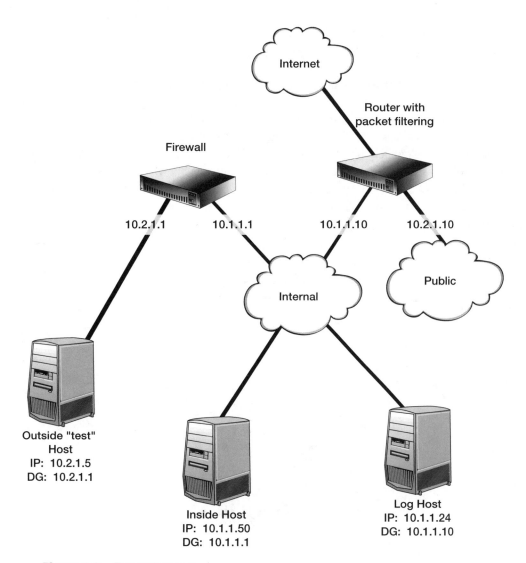

Figure 4.8 Test environment

Plan to conduct this step and the next with at least two people: the original implementer of the routing configuration, packet filtering rules, logging options, and alert options, and an independent person who reviews what has been implemented, understands the intent, and agrees that the network topology and security policy have been reflected correctly.

4.9.4 Test the Firewall Functions in Your Production Environment

This step assumes that you are migrating from a single-layer firewall architecture (see Figure 4.9) to a multiple-layer architecture (see Figure 4.10). This step also assumes that you have a network topology of one or more private networks and one or more public networks. The public networks typically connect hosts that respond to internal and external requests for service such as WWW (HTTP), FTP, e-mail (SMTP), and DNS. These hosts may also respond to internal requests for service such as SNMP, file access, and logging. The public network as described here can serve as your DMZ. The private network typically connects hosts that service your internal users, including individual user workstations (see Figure 4.11).

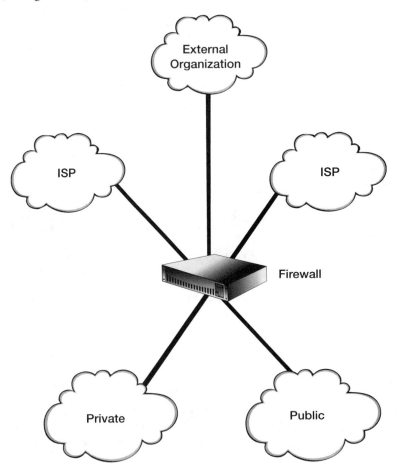

Figure 4.9   Single-layer firewall architecture

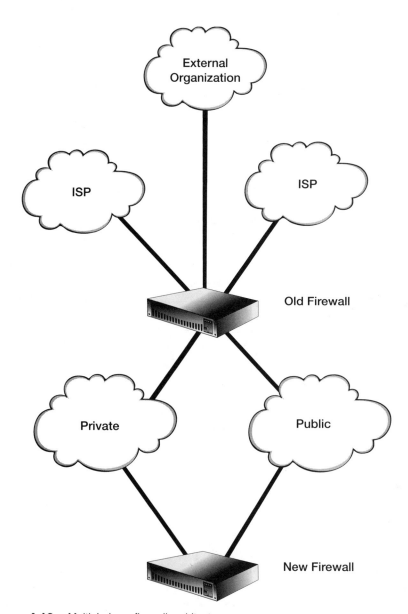

Figure 4.10   Multiple-layer firewall architecture

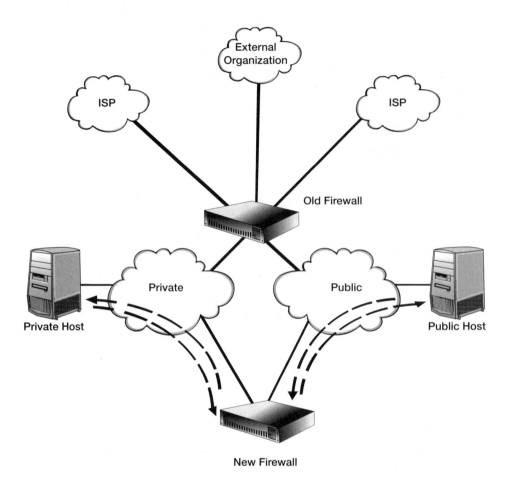

Figure 4.11 Production environment

Do the following:

1. Connect your firewall system to your public and private networks.
2. Set the routing configuration on selected public and private network hosts to direct traffic through the firewall system. The selection is on a service-by-service basis, for example, the web server on your public network and the host storing the files that the web server needs to access on your private network. Cycle through the selection and exercise of all services such as web, file access, DNS, mail, and logging (see Figure 4.11).
3. Log the firewall system's incoming and outgoing network traffic. Use a scanner or network sniffer to observe what is happening.

4. Ensure that packets intended to be blocked (denied) are indeed blocked. For example, if all UDP packets are to be blocked, ensure that none gets through. Ensure that packets intended to enter or exit (permitted) do enter and exit. Do this by examining your firewall logs and scanner results.

5. Scan all hosts in a selected portion of your network that includes the firewall system. Verify that you cannot gain any undesired information due to the scanning packets being blocked (denied). Attempt source port scanning using a well-known port such as the FTP data port (port 20) to ensure that you cannot use the port for a service other than the one intended.

6. You can use intrusion detection system tools in a simulated network traffic or live network traffic test to aid you in determining if your packet filtering rules are protecting your systems and networks from known attacks. You will need to run these tools for some time and review the results on a regular basis. You may want to defer this level of testing to normal operations once you have fully deployed the new firewall system.

7. Examine all of the network traffic that is logged, and verify that the logging options associated with each packet filtering rule are operating as intended.

8. Examine all of the network traffic that is logged, and verify that the alert options associated with each logging option are sending alerts to the designated destination (such as the firewall administrator) using the specified mechanism (such as paging or e-mail).

You cannot do a final test of your routing configuration before connecting the firewall system to your operational external interfaces (refer to Sections 4.10 and 4.11). As a result, you should run live packets through your internal networks using the new firewall system as far as possible before connecting to the outside world. To mitigate the risk of unexpected problems in this final test phase, you should initiate the operational connections for a small subset of hosts (such as those used by your system and firewall administrators) before connecting large numbers of user workstation or server hosts.

4.9.5 Select and Test Features Related to Log Files

When log files are full, you need to select how the firewall system will respond. Possible options are one or more of the following:

- Shutting down all external interfaces connected to the firewall
- Continuing to operate, overwriting the oldest entries
- Continuing to operate without logging

The first option is preferred but may not be available with all firewall products. Simulate a firewall log full condition and ensure that the firewall system behaves as expected based on the option you selected.

Select and exercise the appropriate settings for archiving log files. The settings may include the log file destination (e.g., a local file on the firewall host or a central log file on a remote host), the number of days before a specified log file is archiving, and the number of days before an archived version of a specified log file is purged.

4.9.6 Test the Firewall System

For each relevant failure mode described in the test plan (see the first step), execute the test scenario causing or simulating the failure, and exercise the mitigation strategy to check that it has the desired effect.

4.9.7 Scan for Vulnerabilities

Use vulnerability detection tools to scan your firewall system to determine the presence of known vulnerabilities. If patches exist for vulnerabilities that a tool detects, install these on your firewall system and re-execute the tool. This ensures that the vulnerability has been eliminated.

4.9.8 Design Initial Regression-Testing Suite

Select a subset of test cases to be used for regression-testing purposes during normal operations. These should include cases verifying that all incoming and outgoing packets are being routed, filtered, and logged as expected, as well as service-specific cases verifying that packets requesting specific services (WWW, e-mail, FTP, etc.) are being routed, filtered, and logged as expected.

Once the new firewall system is part of normal operations, you can use selected regression test cases to verify that a change does not affect operational capabilities that worked successfully prior to the change.

4.9.9 Prepare System for Production Use

Create and record cryptographic checksums or other integrity-checking baseline information of your firewall system once you have completed testing as described in Section 5.3.

Once you have completed testing, back up your operational configuration as described in Section 2.10.

4.9.10 Prepare to Perform Ongoing Monitoring

Given the complex nature of networks, their traffic, and firewall systems, ongoing monitoring is the only way to ensure that you have specified the correct security policy and that the policy is being implemented properly.

Ensure that you have the necessary policies, procedures, tools, and staff resources in place to monitor your networks and systems, including your firewall system.

4.9.11 Policy Considerations

Your organization's networked systems security policy should establish the following guidelines:

- The firewall system should be tested in an environment isolated from your operational networks.
- The firewall system should be retested after every configuration change and periodically using the regression test suite.
- The regression test suite should be kept up-to-date to exercise the current firewall system configuration.
- The inventory of all applications software, operating systems, supporting tools, and hardware should be kept up-to-date.
- Monitoring of all network and systems, including your firewall system, should be performed on a regular basis.

4.10 Install the Firewall System

A tested firewall system has to be installed in the production environment, given that there are generally differences between the test and production environments.

There are two cases to consider:

1. The firewall system is being installed to provide new connectivity between the networks that it was designed to interconnect.
2. The firewall system is being installed as a replacement for an existing system that already provides connectivity between these networks.

The approaches for these two cases differ and are described below.

It is important to plan the installation carefully and execute a defined plan to minimize interruptions in existing services.

4.10.1 Install New Connectivity

Do not allow unfiltered traffic through the firewall system during installation. Turn off the firewall system, reinstall it, bring it back up carefully, and perform sample tests to prove that it is forwarding and filtering as expected.

Make sure that the networks are prepared to be interconnected. Take into account, for example, IP addressing, routing, and DNS. Refer to *Firewalls and Internet Security* (Cheswick 94), *Building Internet Firewalls* (Zwicky 00), and *Firewalls Complete* (Goncalves 98) for additional information.

Consider making any new services available incrementally. The easiest way to accomplish this gradual increase is to insert a "deny all" filter into each rule set immediately after the services you wish to make available. To make more services available, move the "deny all" rule further down the rule sets until it gets to the bottom, at which point it should be redundant, and then remove it.

4.10.2 Install Replacement Connectivity

Install the new firewall system in parallel with the existing system. Try not to cause any changes to the environment when inserting the new firewall system into your production environment.

Do not allow unfiltered traffic through the new firewall system during installation. Turn off the firewall system, reinstall it, bring it back up carefully, and perform sample tests to prove that it is forwarding and filtering as expected.

During initial installation, maintain the existing system once it is disconnected. You can then switch back to it if the new system does not operate properly.

4.10.3 Policy Considerations

Your organization's networked systems security policy should ensure that the firewall system installation/deployment plan and schedule are consistent with your site infrastructure business plan and schedule of infrastructure upgrades.

4.11 Phase the Firewall System into Operation

Once you have physically installed your tested firewall system into your production environment, you can then integrate it into your operational networks. This practice addresses the case where your firewall system is replacing an existing firewall or router. In this configuration, no hosts are aware of the newly installed firewall. Each host that is intended to send traffic through the firewall must be made aware of the new firewall's existence. You then make sure that the packet filters perform as expected in the production environment.

There are two subcategories to consider:

1. The replacement firewall system may be installed using the same IP addresses as the original system.
2. The replacement firewall system may be installed using IP addresses different from the original system.

This practice includes steps for installing the new replacement firewall system, using different IP addresses, as this is the more complex case.

The hosts on all of the networks that your firewall system controls must be configured to send traffic to and from the new firewall system, or the firewall will not serve its purpose.

4.11.1 Prepare for Transition to the Replacement Firewall System

There are generally three ways to update all hosts connected to the new, replacement firewall with the routing information they each need to route traffic through this firewall.

1. Manually configure the routing information on each host.
2. Use one or more routing management protocols, for example, RIP (Routing Information Protocol) or OSPF (Open Shortest Path First), to transmit routing information from the firewall to hosts.
3. Use a client management protocol, for example, DHCP (Dynamic Host Configuration Protocol) to reconfigure hosts from a central server.

DHCP is supported by most TCP/IP stacks provided by operating systems; in addition, a DHCP server responds to requests for IP addresses. You can configure your

DHCP server to provide default route addresses to clients. Change the default route for specified hosts that are to send their traffic to and from the new firewall.

Alternatively, you may choose to distribute routing information to your client hosts via a routing protocol. The two most common protocols for this purpose are RIP and OSPF. The choice between these two protocols is beyond the scope of this document, but most TCP/IP routing texts cover both in depth. For our purposes here, they are equivalent: Both can distribute a default route to hosts that are listening for it.

In the absence of these capabilities (DHCP, RIP or OSPF), you will need to reconfigure each host to change the host's default route address manually.

You should maintain a fallback configuration to continue operations if the firewall system does not work as intended. Otherwise, you run the risk of incurring network outages that may affect the ability of your organization to conduct business that relies on internal and external communication via networks and through the firewall system. You should plan to perform the transition during nonbusiness hours, perhaps over a weekend.

4.11.2 Notify Users

Alert your users that the firewall system is being brought into your operational environment.

Inform them that the default gateways on their hosts will be changed to route network traffic through the firewall system and that this modification should be invisible to them. Indicate that they should inform their system or firewall administrator if they encounter any problems.

4.11.3 Enable Private Traffic Through the New Firewall System

This step assumes that you are migrating from a single-layer firewall architecture (see Figure 4.9) to a multiple-layer architecture (see Figure 4.10). The old firewall system becomes the interface to the external world, while the new one serves as the interface to your internal networks. This step also assumes that you have a network topology of one or more private networks and one or more public networks. The public networks typically connect hosts that respond to internal and external requests for service, such as WWW (HTTP), FTP, e-mail (SMTP), and DNS. These hosts may also respond to internal requests for services such as SNMP and logging. The public network described here can serve as your DMZ. The private network typically connects hosts that service your internal users, including individual user workstations.

Configure and enable packets generated by the hosts on your private network to pass through the new firewall system:

1. Connect your public and private networks to the new firewall system (see Figure 4.10).
2. Change the default gateway of the hosts on the private network from the old firewall system to the new one (see Figure 4.12).

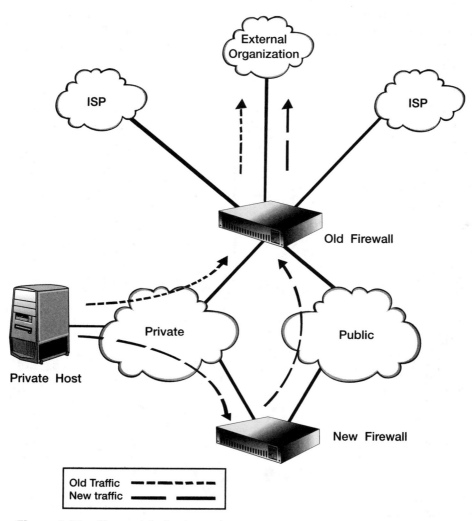

Figure 4.12   Change default gateway

3. Update the routing table on all public network hosts to route private network traffic through the new firewall system as opposed to the old one (see Figure 4.13).

4. Disable the interface to the private network on the old firewall. Add a route to the old firewall system's routing table to route private network traffic through the new firewall system (see Figure 4.14).

5. Ensure that traffic is being routed and filtered as expected (see Section 4.9).

6. Unplug the private network interface to the old firewall system.

If you are replacing an existing firewall system, maintain the physical connectivity through your existing system when you bring the new one online. This will allow you to

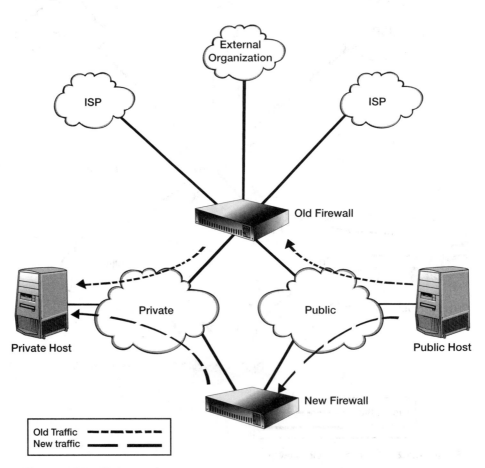

Figure 4.13   Update routing

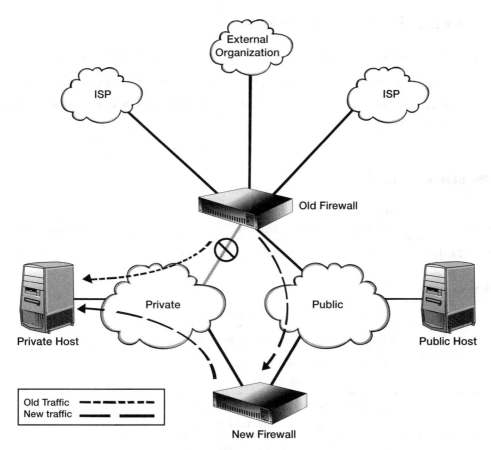

Figure 4.14 Disable old interface; add new route

determine if there are any hosts on your private network that have not had their routing configuration updated to interface with the new firewall system (as their traffic will continue to flow through the old firewall system). It will also allow you to make sure that everything is working as expected (i.e., all private network traffic is now being routed through the new firewall system).

If this does not work as intended, do the following:

1. Unplug the new firewall system hardware.
2. Plug the old firewall system hardware back into the private network.
3. Change the old firewall system's private network interface address to the one used by the new firewall system, given that all of your private network hosts are now using it.
4. Add the route for the private network in the old firewall system's routing table.

4.11.4 Policy Considerations

Your organization's networked systems security policy should do the following:

- Require your users to be notified of firewall system service outages in advance
- Specify the person to be notified in the event of firewall system anomalies once deployment is complete

Chapter 4 Checklist

Practice	Step Number	Step Description	Yes	Partial	No
P4.2: Design the Firewall System	S4.2.1	Document the environment			
	S4.2.2	Select firewall functions			
	S4.2.3	Select the firewall topology			
	S4.2.4	Perform architectural trade-off analysis			
	S4.2.5	Protect your firewall system from unauthorized access			
	S4.2.6	Policy considerations			
P4.3: Acquire Firewall Hardware and Software	S4.3.1	Determine required hardware components			
	S4.3.2	Determine required software components			
	S4.3.3	Determine required testing components			
	S4.3.4	Acquire all components			

Practice	Step Number	Step Description	Yes	Partial	No
P4.4: Acquire Firewall Training, Documentation, and Support	S4.4.1	Determine your training requirements			
	S4.4.2	Determine your support requirements			
P4.5: Install Firewall Hardware and Software	S4.5.1	Install a minimum acceptable operating system environment			
	S4.5.2	Install all applicable patches			
	S4.5.3	Restrict user and host access			
	S4.5.4	Disable packet forwarding			
	S4.5.5	Back up your system			
	S4.5.6	Policy considerations			
P4.6: Configure IP Routing	S4.6.1	Obtain IP addresses			
	S4.6.2	Establish routing configuration			
	S4.6.3	Policy considerations			
P4.7: Configure Firewall Packet Filtering	S4.7.1	Design the packet filtering rules			
	S4.7.2	Document the packet filtering rules			
	S4.7.3	Install packet filtering rules			
	S4.7.4	Policy considerations			

(continued)

Chapter 4   Checklist (*cont.*)

Practice	Step Number	Step Description	Yes	Partial	No
P4.8: Configure Firewall Logging and Alert Mechanisms	S4.8.1	Design the logging environment			
	S4.8.2	Select logging options for packet filter rules			
	S4.8.3	Design the alert mechanisms configuration			
	S4.8.4	Acquire or develop supporting tools			
	S4.8.5	Policy considerations			
P4.9: Test the Firewall System	S4.9.1	Create a test plan			
	S4.9.2	Acquire testing tools			
	S4.9.3	Test the firewall functions in your test environment			
	S4.9.4	Test the firewall functions in your production environment			
	S4.9.5	Select and test features related to log files			
	S4.9.6	Test the firewall system			
	S4.9.7	Scan for vulnerabilities			
	S4.9.8	Design initial regression-testing suite			
	S4.9.9	Prepare system for production use			
	S4.9.10	Prepare to perform ongoing monitoring			
	S4.9.11	Policy considerations			

Practice	Step Number	Step Description	Yes	Partial	No
P4.10: Install the Firewall System	S4.10.1	Install new connectivity			
	S4.10.2	Install replacement connectivity			
	S4.10.3	Policy considerations			
P4.11: Phase the Firewall System into Operation	S4.11.1	Prepare for transition to the replacement firewall system			
	S4.11.2	Notify users			
	S4.11.3	Enable private traffic through the new firewall system			
	S4.11.4	Policy considerations			

Online Resources

Information on firewall issues can be found at the mailing list archive maintained by Gnac at *http://lists.gnac.net/firewalls/*. This site includes a link to the Internet Firewalls FAQ (frequently asked questions).

Check the CERIAS web site at Purdue University (Center for Education, Research, and Information Assurance Security—formerly known as Computer Operations, Audit, and Security [COAST]). Firewall-related materials can be found at *http://www.cerias. purdue.edu/coast/firewalls/*. The site lists relevant books, papers, articles, reports, guides, research, products, firewall testing results, firewall tools, network tools, system monitoring tools, mailing lists, newsgroups, conferences, and frequently asked questions.

Part II

Intrusion Detection and Response

A general security goal is to prevent intrusions, which can be achieved to some extent by implementing the practices described in Part I. However, intruder attack methods are constantly evolving, posing new threats to your systems and networks, and because no prevention measures are perfect, you also need an effective strategy for handling intrusions. The main elements of such a strategy are preparation, detection, and response. Part II identifies advance preparations that will enable you to obtain indicators of a successful or attempted intrusion, steps to analyze these indicators to determine if an intentional or inadvertent compromise has occurred, and actions to recover your systems as quickly as possible.

Part II comprises the following chapters:

- Chapter 5: Setting Up Intrusion Detection and Response Practices
- Chapter 6: Detecting Signs of Intrusion
- Chapter 7: Responding to Intrusions

Chapter 5 addresses decisions, policies, procedures, tasks, and tools that you should consider carefully and put in place before (ideally) and after (more likely) connecting your systems and networks to a public network such as the Internet. We recognize that in the face of today's pressure to have an Internet presence, prior implementation may not be possible; it is important, however, to recognize your risk of exposure if you choose not to take these steps. The chapter recommends five preparatory actions:

1. Establish policies and procedures, including the roles and responsibilities for their execution and enforcement.
2. Identify all of the data that need to be collected to detect and respond and the mechanisms that need to be put in place to ensure comprehensive collection.
3. Manage these data collection and logging mechanisms.
4. Identify what constitutes an asset characterization baseline and establish that baseline, which is critical for use in future configuration comparisons.
5. Identify tools for detection and response, install and configure these tools properly, and exercise them before an intrusion takes place

Chapter 6 provides guidance on effective monitoring of all types of information assets: networks, systems, processes, users, network and system performance, files and directories, hardware, and access to physical resources. The practices show how to determine if something suspicious or unexpected has occurred and identify steps to take in such cases, including ways to improve the detection process. The practices presented in Chapter 6 assume that those described in Chapter 5 have been implemented.

Chapter 7 describes recommended steps for responding to an intrusion:

1. Analyze the effects of, scope of, and damage caused by an intrusion.
2. Contain these effects to the extent possible.
3. Work to eliminate future intruder access.
4. Return information assets to a known, operational state possibly while continuing analysis.

Other parties that may be affected are notified, and evidence is collected and protected in the event of legal proceedings against the intruder.

Chapter 7 describes ways to improve the response process, assuming that the practices described in Chapter 5 have been implemented and that signs of an intrusion have been detected as described in Chapter 6.

Often, as discussed in Chapter 1, the outcome of preparation, detection, and response practices is to iterate back to configuration hardening and securing as described in Part I. You need to institute a continuous cycle of successive refinement to achieve as secure an operation of systems and networks as is possible and practical. This cycle never ends. Administrators, their managers, and senior executives need to understand this and plan for it in the operation and regular review of all elements of their organization's information technology infrastructure.

Chapter 5

Setting Up Intrusion Detection and Response Practices

It is essential that those responsible for your organization's information systems and networks be adequately prepared to detect evidence of breaches in security and respond. Without advance preparation, it will be difficult, if not impossible, to determine (1) if there has been—or still is—an intruder, (2) the extent of the damage caused by the intrusion, and (3) how to return affected systems to a known, trusted state.

Thorough preparation will permit you to detect an intrusion or an intrusion attempt during or soon after it occurs and return affected systems to a trustworthy, reliable state of operation as soon as possible. Such preparation involves your security policies and supporting procedures, your critical business information, your systems, your networks, your user community (internal and external), and the tools to be employed in detecting and responding to intrusions.

This chapter identifies advance preparations you must make to enable you to obtain evidence of an intrusion or an intrusion attempt and respond as quickly as possible. These include configuring your data, systems, networks, workstations, tools, and user environments to capture the necessary information for detecting and responding to intrusions.

5.1 Overview

These practices are intended primarily for system and network administrators, managers of information systems, and security personnel responsible for networked information resources. They are applicable to your organization if its networked systems infrastructure includes any of the following:

- Host systems providing services to multiple users (file servers, time-sharing systems, database servers, web servers, etc.)
- Local area or wide area networks
- Direct connections, gateways, or modem access to and from external networks, such as the Internet

These practices do not cover the establishment of initial configurations of applications, operating systems, networks, or workstations. Refer to Chapter 2 for securing network servers, to Chapter 3 for securing public web servers, and to Chapter 2 for securing user workstations.

5.1.1 The Need for Intrusion Detection and Response Preparation

If you are not adequately prepared to detect and respond to intrusions, it is difficult, if not impossible, to determine later if your systems have been compromised. If the information necessary to detect an intrusion is not being collected and reviewed, you probably will not be able to determine which of your sensitive data, systems, and networks are being attacked and what breaches in confidentiality, integrity, or availability have occurred. Specifically, insufficient preparation can result in the following situations:

- You are unable to detect signs of an intrusion in a timely manner (if at all) due to the absence of necessary warning mechanisms.
- You are unable to identify intrusions due to the absence of characterization information (refer to Section 5.3) with which to compare your current operational state. Differences between this expected configuration and your current state can provide an indication that an intrusion has occurred.
- Your staff members may not understand their roles and responsibilities and, therefore, may be unable to execute detection and response procedures without confusion, omissions, and errors.

Adequate preparation can lead to your staff and systems being able to detect signs of an intrusion or an intrusion attempt in a timely manner. As a result, you are then able to mitigate your exposure to the intrusion and the possible damage caused to your data or systems.

We recognize that it may not be practical to implement all steps within a given practice or even all preparation practices. Business objectives, priorities, and an organization's ability to manage and tolerate risk dictate where information technology resources are expended and what trade-offs will be made among security and function, operational capability, and capacity.

5.1.2 An Approach for Detect and Response Preparation

The practices in this chapter make the following assumptions:

- You have performed security planning—such as policy formulation, disaster recovery and business continuity planning, risk assessment, identification of critical information assets—that addresses your organization's business objectives.

- You have performed trade-off analyses to determine the cost of protecting versus the cost of reconstituting critical assets (data, systems, networks, workstations, tools) in the event of an intrusion. Protecting an asset includes considering the loss of confidentiality and customer confidence if the asset is disclosed (e.g., confidential, competitive information). It is probably not feasible to protect all assets.

- You have documented disaster recovery policy and procedures that include determining what assets are critical to protect and with what priority. The policy identifies who has responsibility for and authority to access each asset that needs to be recovered, under what conditions, and by what means.

To prepare to detect and respond to intrusions, we recommend a two-step approach:

1. Define the required level of preparedness necessary to meet your business objectives.
2. Implement selected steps that prepare your staff and systems to detect and respond to intrusions.

Table 5.1   Setting Up Intrusion Detection
and Response Practices Summary

Approach	Practice	Reference
Define level of preparedness	Establish policies and procedures	Section 5.2; page 188
Implement preparation steps	Identify characterization and other data for detecting signs of suspicious behavior	Section 5.3; page 198
	Manage logging and other data collection mechanisms	Section 5.4; page 216
	Select, install, and understand tools for response	Section 5.5; page 221

5.2 Establish Policies and Procedures

Security policies define the rules that regulate how your organization manages and protects its information and computing resources to achieve security objectives. One of the policy's primary purposes in detecting and responding to intrusions is to document important information assets and the threats to those assets that your organization chooses to address.

Preparation procedures include taking the actions necessary to observe systems and networks for signs of unexpected behavior, including intrusion, and to implement response policies throughout your organization. Observation can take the form of monitoring, inspecting, and auditing, while response policies include determining whom to notify, when to notify them, and what types of information to send.

From these procedures, all concerned parties should be able to determine the operational steps they need to take to comply with your policies. These steps form the foundation for the security state of your organization's information and networked systems.

> Monitoring is the observation of data streams for specific events. Inspection is the examination of a system, application, data object, or process. Auditing is the systematic examination of data against documented expectations of form or behavior. Refer to *An Approach for Selecting and Specifying Tools for Information Survivability* (Firth 97).

Security policies and procedures that are documented, well known, and visibly enforced establish expected user behavior and serve to inform users of their obligations for protecting computing assets. Users include all those who access, administer, and manage your systems and have authorized accounts on your systems. They play a vital role in detecting and responding to intrusions.

The practice steps contained in this section cover a subset of the topics that your intrusion detection and response policies and procedures should address. Additional policy and procedure information is contained in the other practices of this chapter and in Chapters 6 and 7 where they are most applicable. All policy and procedure language presented here needs to be tailored to reflect the specific business objectives and security requirements of your organization and its computing environment. The details of procedures used to address specific types of intrusions may vary.

Having intrusion detection/response policy language and procedures in place in advance allows you to use these procedures in a timely, managed, and controlled way and eliminates potential errors or omissions in advance of an attack. You do not want to be caught trying to determine what actions to take, what data to gather and preserve, and how to protect your systems from further damage while under attack or after the fact. With advance planning, documentation, and education, trained staff members can more effectively coordinate their activities and responses when detecting suspicious activity, an intrusion, or an intrusion attempt. Without the proper knowledge and skills, users may inadvertently expose parts of the organization to security threats.

Note that we use the verb "document" in the steps below to mean both creating specific information and recording it in a form that can be used as a reference.

5.2.1 Address Intrusion Detection and Response in Your Security Policies

Document the important and critical information assets and the level of protection (confidentiality, availability, integrity) required for each. Designations for the level may range from "cannot be compromised under any circumstances" (maximum protection) to "contains no sensitive information and can be easily restored" (minimal protection).

Document the types of threats or events that indicate possible signs of intrusion, as well as how you intend to respond to them if they are detected. Types of threats may include the following:[1]

- Attempts (either failed or successful) to gain unauthorized access to a system or its data
- Unintended and unauthorized disclosure of information
- Unwanted disruption or denial of service
- The unauthorized use of a system to process, store, or transmit data
- Changes to system hardware, firmware, or software characteristics without your or the asset owner's knowledge or consent

Recognize that some threats are difficult to protect against if your systems are connected to the Internet. You need to determine what actions you will take if these occur. Threats of this type include the following:

- Resource starvation such as e-mail bombing (sending a large volume of electronic messages to a targeted recipient until the system fails) and flood attacks (filling a channel with garbage, thereby denying others the ability to communicate across that channel or to the receiving host). These may result in the loss of availability, i.e., a denial of service.
- Programmed threats, such as new viruses not yet detected and therefore not eliminated by virus-checking tools, and malicious software in the form of CGI scripts, plug-ins, servlets, or applets[2] (see Sections 3.5 and 3.6).
- Intruders probing or scanning your systems, possibly with the intent to exploit any vulnerabilities they discover for use in attempting an intrusion

Document the requirement to establish and maintain secure, reliable configuration information for all assets that represent your known, expected operational state. This requirement includes taking inventory and tagging all physical computing resources. Refer to Section 5.3. Periodically compare this information with your current state to determine if anything has been altered in an unexpected way. Refer to Sections 6.3, 6.4, and 6.5.

---

1. Refer to CERT summaries, advisories, incident notes, and vulnerability notes and to *How to Eliminate the Ten Most Critical Internet Security Threats: The Experts' Consensus* (SANS 00).

2. Also refer to the CERT report *Results of the Security in ActiveX Workshop,* conducted August 22–23, 2000, and published December 21, 2000. The report is available at the CERT web site.

If a critical machine is compromised as a result of an intrusion, having redundant equipment in place enables you to restore service quickly while preserving all of the evidence on the compromised machine and performing ongoing analysis. You need to describe, for example, where and when to use hot, warm, and cold backups. Refer to Section 4.2.4. Ensure that this configuration redundancy policy is consistent with your business continuity policy and document it.

The value of establishing management guidelines and rules for responding to intrusions cannot be overstated. These guidelines and rules can be categorized as follows:

Priority and Sequence of Actions

Document the priority and sequence of actions to be taken when dealing with an intrusion. Actions necessary to protect human life and safety are likely to have priority over those that ensure operational and service continuity, protect classified and sensitive data, or prevent damage to systems. Document the factors that can alter the priority and sequence of actions, for example, time, additional information (such as the extent of an intrusion), and awareness that an intrusion you are analyzing interacts with one or more other intrusions and/or organizations.

A number of actions can be taken:

- Deny access to an intruder, possibly by disconnecting the affected system from the network and shutting down the system
- Contain an intrusion and limit the actions of an intruder
- Continue operation to gather additional information
- Restore the affected service

For the last action, you need to specify the order in which services will be restored, if this is a consideration (for example, you may choose to restore your e-mail service before restoring FTP). This ensures that the order meets your business objectives and priorities while minimizing negative effects on users whenever possible.

Authority to Act

This guideline should indicate what types of responses to an intrusion require management approval and which are preapproved.

Document the circumstances in which you need authorization to do the following:

- Stay connected to pursue an intruder by gathering additional information
- Protect your systems by disconnecting and shutting down
- Conduct covert monitoring of network traffic and file access

Ensure that the individuals or team responsible for intrusion response are pre-authorized by management to disconnect from the network and shut down the affected service(s) and system(s), if appropriate. This will cause a denial of service to the affected assets until they are returned to operation.

Document the necessary authority and actions to be taken in dealing with intrusions involving remotely connected computers used by your employees and vendors if these actions differ from those taken for other types of intrusions.

Intrusion Response Resources

Determine how you will structure, staff, and support your intrusion response. One option is to create a computer security incident response team (CSIRT). For this option, determine if the team will be distributed across organizational units or centralized within one unit and/or at one site. Identify the roles to be filled by team members based on your organization's security policies and procedures. Identify qualified people to assume these roles and determine how much of their time will be devoted to team activities. Ensure that you have a knowledgeable team trained and in place to handle the full intrusion response process.

Refer to the *CSIRT Handbook* (West-Brown 98) for more information on this subject, including a full range of procedures to consider when operating such a team.

If you choose not to create a CSIRT, ensure that all response roles and responsibilities are clearly assigned to system and network administrators, security personnel, and other staff.

5.2.2 Document Procedures That Implement Your Intrusion Detection Policies

In general terms, document what data you plan to collect, why you want to collect it, and where and when you will collect it, as described in Section 5.3.

- Document what you want to discover by collecting the data. Typically, you should verify that levels of performance (function, throughput, load) are as you expected them to be and that there are no errors and suspicious or unexpected behavior that cannot be explained (see Chapter 6).

- Document where best to collect each type of data. We recommend collecting data as close to the source of its generation as possible, ideally on all hosts. If this is not possible because it would impact performance, collect the data as close to the host as possible. For example, if you cannot place an intrusion detection system on the firewall host, place it on another host that monitors network traffic on both the external (Internet) side of the firewall host and the internal (organizational network) side of the firewall host.

- Document when to collect the data. As an ideal (but potentially impractical) starting point, we recommend collecting everything you possibly can, at every available source location, 24 hours a day, seven days a week. While this approach is likely to produce excessive amounts of data, you can manage the process by automating the deletion of data that you normally do not need to process or analyze further under normal conditions of operation. However, by inserting a delay between the time of collection and the time of deletion, in the event that a suspicious event occurs, you can then analyze further data you would normally delete. A reasonable delay might be one to two weeks, but this depends on your operation, review schedule, and data storage capacity. Refer to Section 5.4 for more information on handling log files.

Document any special handling procedures for each type of collected data. This is particularly important for data that may be used as evidence in subsequent legal proceedings. Refer to Section 7.4.

Document how you plan to conduct your review of all collected data. Because a large volume of system and network data can be collected, and because there are increasing demands on an administrator's time, you need to determine carefully the following factors:

- The order in which specific data will be reviewed
- The frequency of data review
- Tools and other mechanisms, such as alerts, that can aid in better identifying suspicious and unexpected behaviors
- The types of events that warrant further investigation and in-depth analysis
- Administrator authority, actions to be taken, and what circumstances warrant what actions
- How you will track the status of open events to resolution and closure

In particular, document the following:

- The procedure(s) by which monitoring is performed, i.e., the observation of data streams for specific events. This procedure specifies

    the data streams to be monitored

    the monitoring locations on systems and networks

    the times and frequencies with which monitoring is to be performed the activation of monitoring after the occurrence of what types of events

the operational activities necessary to alert appropriate personnel to act upon the suspected intrusion

- The procedure(s) by which regular inspection and auditing of recorded data (e.g., logs) are performed to identify evidence of intrusions or intrusion attempts
- The procedure by which physical audits of installed hardware and software are performed
- The procedure by which integrity checking is performed (comparing the current operational state with a previously generated, secure, reliable, and known state). Specify what files are to be checked; how integrity information is securely generated, maintained, and tested; and the frequency with which integrity checking is performed.
- The procedure by which correlation of intrusions is performed, i.e., determining when suspicious activity occurring in one part of your infrastructure may be related to activity in another part. Performing some level of correlation analysis during the intrusion detection process will assist you in determining the full extent of any compromise and its characteristics. Refer to Section 7.2.
- The procedure for the acquisition and secure installation, configuration, and maintenance of all tools necessary to implement your monitoring, inspection, auditing, and integrity-checking procedures. Refer to Section 5.3 for more detailed guidance on identifying and selecting tools.

5.2.3 Document Procedures That Implement Your Intrusion Response Policies

Such procedures include the following steps:

- Analyze all available information to characterize an intrusion, including assessing the damage and extent of an intrusion and an intruder's activities
- Communicate with all parties that need to be aware of an intrusion and participate in handling it, taking into account that an intruder may be able to access and monitor your means of communication
- Collect and protect information associated with an intrusion
- Contain an intrusion and determine what actions to take
- Eliminate an intruder's means of access and any related vulnerabilities

- Return your systems to normal operation
- Follow up with a postmortem review of events as they occurred and a review of your policies and procedures

Ensure that your intrusion response procedure is consistent and integrated into your business continuity and disaster recovery processes.

5.2.4 Document Roles and Responsibilities

Document the roles, responsibilities, and authority of system administrators, security personnel, and users regarding the use and administration of all assets when they participate in detecting and responding to intrusions.

Document the roles, responsibilities, authority, and conditions for the testing of intrusion detection tools, the execution of intrusion detection procedures, and the examination of assets suspected of having been compromised. We strongly recommend that your policies require all such activity to be conducted in a test environment isolated from production systems and networks.

For each policy, procedure, and step, document the roles, responsibilities, and authority of system administrators, security personnel, and users. Identify who performs each procedure activity, when, and under what conditions.

5.2.5 Conduct a Legal Review

A legal review of your policies and procedures should be performed by your organization's legal counsel. Such a review is intended to ensure that your policies and procedures meet the following standards:

- Are legally defensible and enforceable.
- Comply with overall company policies and procedures.
- Reflect known industry best practices demonstrating the exercise of due care.
- Conform to federal, state, and local laws and regulations.
- Protect your organization from being held legally responsible in the event of compromise. This part of the review should consider the legal implications of continuing to allow intruders access as you gather additional information about their activities. The risk is that they might continue to use your system to attack others.

- Require the preservation of critical evidence, including a defensible, documented chain of custody for all artifacts that may be used in legal proceedings (see Section 7.4).

Ensure that your legal counsel is able to address the following topics:

- When and how to sue an intruder
- What procedures should be followed to protect privacy
- What procedures should be followed to ensure the admissibility of evidence
- When to report an intrusion to local, state, or national law enforcement agencies

5.2.6 Train Users

Users are those who access, administer, and manage your systems and have authorized accounts on your systems. During the training process, users should learn the following:

- What is expected of them
- How to identify suspicious behavior and whom to notify
- What behaviors can reduce the exposure of systems to possible compromise, such as[3]

> not opening unsolicited e-mail attachments without verifying their source or checking their content in an isolated environment
>
> working with system administrators to install security patches for commonly used applications (such as web browsers)
>
> not downloading and installing software from untrusted sources
>
> making and testing backups
>
> not using modems while connected through a local area network
>
> protecting passwords and sensitive data
>
> knowing how to respond to social engineering attacks such as a caller's attempt to gain your password by pretending to be an authorized administrator

- What types of information are being gathered as part of routine security procedures, and the degree to which this information gathering may affect them

---

3. Refer to *http://www.sans.org* for more information on the five worst security mistakes committed by the average user.

- How to communicate appropriately with the news media, including forwarding inquiries to your organization's public relations staff

- How to report a suspected intrusion, including whom to notify, by what means (web, e-mail, phone), and what information to report

- The use of intrusion response tools and environments based on their roles and responsibilities

Create and conduct periodic training on your policies and procedures regarding how to handle intrusions. This training should be mandatory for all new employees and should be tailored to the employee's knowledge and responsibilities.

Test the effectiveness of the training and each employee's readiness. Conduct practice drills (e.g., detecting viruses, responding to break-ins) that test procedures and execute operational activities, making sure all staff members are aware of their roles and responsibilities. Conduct postmortem meetings with trainees. Provide remedial training as required.

Regularly conduct mandatory security awareness refresher training. Highlight recent changes in policies or procedures and summarize recent attack methods and countermeasures. Make this subject a recurring topic at executive and management meetings to maintain awareness.

Obtain information from the FBI and local law enforcement about preserving the chain of custody of the evidence.[4] Ensure that your system and network administrators, intrusion response staff, and their managers are aware of this information.

To keep pace with the rapid rate of technological change, ensure that system and network administration staff have time set aside to maintain the knowledge, skills, and currency in technical topics required to implement your policies and procedures.

5.2.7 Keep Your Policies, Procedures, and Training Current

Periodically review your policies, procedures, and training. Take into account the following:

- System changes and upgrades, including the introduction of new software

- Changes in critical assets

- Changes in security requirements

---

4. Refer to the CERT tech tip *How the FBI Investigates Computer Crime,* available at *http://www.cert.org/ tech_tips/FBI_investigates_crime.html.*

- Changes in key roles and responsibilities
- Public and vendor information sources

Use vendor web sites and other commonly available sources of information to stay current (see Chapter 1).

If your organization suffers an intrusion, review your policies, procedures, and training to determine if revisions are necessary to ensure that future intrusions of the same type can be more readily detected and controlled, if not prevented. Refer to Section 7.8.

5.3 Identify Characterization and Other Data for Detecting Signs of Suspicious Behavior[5]

Collecting data generated by system, network, application, and user activities is essential for analyzing the security of your information assets and detecting signs of suspicious and unexpected behavior. Log files contain information about past activities. You should identify the logging mechanisms and types of logs (system, file access, process, network, application-specific, etc.) available for each asset and identify the data recorded within each log.

Different systems provide various types of logging information; some systems do not collect adequate information in their default condition. It is important to supplement your logs with additional collection mechanisms that watch for signs of intrusions or intrusion attempts. The logs should also alert responsible parties when events occur. Include mechanisms that do the following:

- Monitor and inspect system resource use
- Monitor and inspect network traffic and connections
- Monitor and inspect user account and file access
- Scan for viruses
- Verify file and data integrity
- Probe for system and network vulnerabilities
- Reduce, scan, monitor, and inspect your log files

---

5. Includes any unauthorized action taken to learn about or access your systems, intrusion attempts, and intrusions.

Capturing an accurate, reliable, and complete characterization of your systems when they are first created, and as they evolve, establishes the expected state against which to compare your current systems. The information to be captured includes a known, expected state for all assets, among them your network traffic, system and network performance, processes, users, files and directories, and hardware. This includes information that characterizes past behavior derived from system logs and monitoring tools, which is available once you have been operational for some period of time. This trusted record is periodically compared with your current systems to determine if assets are behaving as expected, in other words, to verify the integrity of your systems and to identify any deviations from expected behavior.

Characterizing your software, hardware, and information assets is a time-consuming, complex, and ongoing task. You need to determine in advance, therefore, the level of resources you can commit to this activity.

Approaches to detecting signs of suspicious or unexpected behavior are often based on identifying differences between your current operational state and a previously captured and trusted expected state.

You need to know where each asset is located and what information you expect to find in each location. You also need to be able to verify the correct or expected state of every asset. Without this information, you cannot adequately determine if anything has been added, deleted, modified, lost, or stolen.

You may not be able to rebuild a critical component that has been compromised without up-to-date, available, trusted characterizations.

Log files may be the only record of suspicious behavior. Failure to enable the mechanisms to record this information and use them to initiate alert mechanisms will greatly weaken or eliminate your ability to detect intrusion attempts and to determine whether or not they succeeded. Similar problems can result from not having the necessary procedures and mechanisms in place to process and analyze your log files.

You may need your logs to do a number of tasks:

- Alert you to suspicious activity that requires further investigation
- Determine the extent of an intruder's activity
- Help you recover your systems
- Provide information required for legal proceedings

It is possible that the logging and monitoring mechanisms provided with your systems may not produce all of the information necessary to detect signs of an intrusion in a timely manner. Even if adequate information is provided, the volume of data may be so overwhelming that it requires automated analysis to reduce it to a manageable subset before you can examine it for signs of intrusive activity. In either case, you will need to add tools to your systems to adequately detect signs of suspicious or unexpected behavior that require further analysis. Sections 6.3, 6.4, and 6.5 offer examples of suspicious and unexpected behaviors that can be determined based on the data you collect.

5.3.1   Determine What Data Is Most Useful to Collect

You need to balance the importance of recording system, network, and user activities against the resources available to store, process, review, and secure them. The following questions may help you determine the usefulness of collected data:

- What is the priority of this asset (hardware, software, information)? How important is it to collect data related to this asset? How important is it to characterize this asset?

- What is the system's sole or primary purpose? (For example, if a host is acting as a web server, you want to capture web logs.)

- How many users are assigned to the system, and how important is it for you to know who is logged on? This information helps you decide how much login/logout information to capture.

- How important is it to be able to use your logs and other data to recover a compromised system? (Knowing this helps you set the priority for capturing information such as data and file transaction logs.)

- What is the range of services that can be performed on this system? Process accounting information is useful to detect unauthorized services and intruder actions.

- What is your organization's ability and capacity to process and analyze all collected data to obtain useful information when it is needed?

5.3.2   Identify the Data to Be Collected

Table 5.2 contains data categories and possible types of data to collect.

Table 5.2   Data Categories and Types of Data to Collect

Data Category	Types of Data to Collect
Network performance	Total traffic load in and out over time (packet, byte, and connection counts) and by event (such as new product or service release)
	Traffic load (percentage of packets, bytes, connections) in and out over time sorted by protocol, source address, destination address, other packet header data
	Error counts on all network interfaces
Other network data	Service initiation requests
	Name of the user/host requesting the service
	Network traffic (packet headers)
	Successful connections and connection attempts (protocol, port, source, destination, time)
	Connection duration
	Connection flow (sequence of packets from initiation to termination)
	States associated with network interfaces (up, down)
	Network sockets currently open
	Whether or not network interface card is in promiscuous mode
	Network probes and scans
	Results of administrator probes
System performance	Total resource use over time (CPU, memory [used, free], disk [used, free])
	Status and errors reported by systems and hardware devices
	Changes in system status, including shutdowns and restarts
	File system status (where mounted, free space by partition, open files, biggest file) over time and at specific times

(continued)

Table 5.2   Data Categories and Types of Data to Collect (*cont.*)

Data Category	Types of Data to Collect
	File system warnings (low free space, too many open files, file exceeding allocated size)
	Disk counters (input/output, queue lengths) over time and at specific times
	Hardware availability (modems, network interface cards, memory)
Other system data	Actions requiring special privileges
	Successful and failed logins
	Modem activities
	Presence of new services and devices
	Configuration of resources and devices
	System call data
Process performance	Amount of resources used (CPU, memory, disk, time) by specific processes over time; top "x" resource-consuming processes
	System and user processes and services executing at any given time
Other process data	User executing the process
	Process start-up time, arguments, file names
	Process exit status, time, duration, resources consumed
	The means by which each process is normally initiated (administrator, other users, other programs or processes), with what authorization and privileges
	Devices used by specific processes
	Files currently open by specific processes
Files and directories	List of files, directories, attributes
	Cryptographic checksums for all files and directories

Data Category	Types of Data to Collect
	Accesses (open, create, modify, execute, delete), time, date
	Changes to sizes, contents, protections, types, locations
	Changes to access control lists on system tools
	Additions and deletions of files and directories
	Results of virus scanners
Users	Login/logout information (location, time): successful attempts, failed attempts, attempted logins to privileged accounts
	Login/logout information on remote access servers that appears in modem logs
	Changes in user identity
	Changes in authentication status, such as enabling privileges
	Failed attempts to access restricted information (such as password files)
	Keystroke monitoring logs
	Violations of user quotas
Applications	Applications- and services-specific information such as network traffic (packet content), mail logs, FTP logs, web server logs, modem logs, firewall logs, SNMP logs, DNS logs, intrusion detection system logs, database management system logs
	Services-specific information could be used for the following:
	FTP requests: files transferred and connection statistics
	Web requests: pages accessed, credentials of the requestor, connection statistics, user requests over time, which pages are most requested, and who is requesting them. Refer to Section 3.4
	Mail requests: sender, receiver, size, and tracing information; for a mail server, number of messages over time, number of queued messages

(continued)

Table 5.2   Data Categories and Types of Data to Collect (*cont.*)

Data Category	Types of Data to Collect
	DNS requests: questions, answers, and zone transfers
	A file system server: file transfers over time
	A database server: transactions over time
Log files	Results of scanning, filtering, and reducing log file contents
	Checks for log file consistency (increasing file size over time, use of consecutive, increasing time stamps with no gaps)
Vulnerabilities	Results of vulnerability scanners (presence of known vulnerabilities)
	Vulnerability patch logging for the purpose described in Section 6.4

5.3.3 Identify the Data to Be Captured Using Logging Mechanisms

Identify the types of information you can log, the mechanisms used for logging, where the logging is performed, and where the log files are stored.

Use Table 5.2 as a guide to the types of information to log (although not all systems are able to log every type in the table). Tailor logging selections to meet your site's specific policies and security requirements.

For all data categories, capture alerts and any reported errors.

If possible, do not log passwords, even incorrect ones. Logging correct passwords creates an enormous potential vulnerability if an unauthorized user or intruder accesses log files. Recording incorrect passwords is also risky, as they often differ from valid passwords by only a single character or transposition. Turning off password logging may require resetting a system default. If you cannot turn off password logging, you need to exercise special care in protecting access to log files that contain this information (refer to Section 5.4). However, you may want to log data about password use, such as the number of failed attempts, accesses to specific accounts, etc.

Determine the logging mechanisms available for the systems at your site. Identify what types of information each logging mechanism can capture and whether collectively these are sufficient to capture the required information. There may be differences in the log file contents provided by different vendors, even for similar types of systems.

Determine where each logging mechanism stores data. Identify how the log files are named and where they are located. The names of these log files can differ even among versions of the same operating system delivered by a single vendor, so it is important that you verify this each time you upgrade your systems.

5.3.4 Identify the Data to Be Captured Using Additional Data Collection Mechanisms

Use Table 5.2 as a guide to the types of information you need to collect beyond that which is available using logging mechanisms. Tailor additional data selections to meet your site's intrusion detection policies and procedures.

Monitoring is the observation of data streams for specific events, whereas logging systematically records specified events in the order in which they occur. Monitoring generally connotes more of a "real-time" analysis activity, while inspecting[6] log files generally occurs as more of an "offline" or after-the-fact activity. Monitoring is often preferable where there are large quantities of data, such as network traffic. In most circumstances, it isn't feasible to store every network packet, but monitoring the network traffic for specific types of events and connections is very desirable.

Real-time intrusion detection systems,[7] including log file monitoring tools, can detect possible intrusions or access violations as they are occurring and generate alerts in any of the Table 5.2 data categories. Real-time intrusion detection occurs while an intruder is attempting to break in or is still present on your system. Offline intrusion detection, on the other hand, is performed after the intrusion has occurred, usually through inspecting various system and network log files and performing data and system integrity tests.

A host- or system-based intrusion detection system (IDS) examines data such as log files, process accounting information, and user behavior and generates alerts based on specified configuration information. A network IDS examines network traffic, including packet headers and content.

Both types of ID systems can employ one or more analysis approaches to determine whether or not an intrusion has occurred. There are two common analysis approaches:

1. Attack signature detection (sometimes called "misuse detection"), which identifies patterns (signatures) corresponding to known attacks.

---

6. Inspection is the examination of a data resource or process.

7. Refer to *State of the Practice of Intrusion Detection Technologies* (Allen 99).

2. Anomaly detection, which identifies any unacceptable deviation from expected behavior. Expected behavior is defined in advance by a manually or automatically developed profile of system, network, and user behavior.

It is difficult to provide guidance about additional data selection and collection mechanisms, because the selection criteria vary based on organizational policy and security requirements. This problem is complicated by a lack of uniformity in the intrusion characterizations used by common collection mechanisms.

In most cases you will need to perform manual analysis along with the automated data collection and reporting performed by any mechanism.

5.3.5 Determine Which Events Should Produce an Alert

Events that require immediate administrator attention and need to be given the highest priority should be designated as alerts. Alerts can take the form of a message displayed on your workstation, someone stopping by your office, a phone call or voice mail, e-mail, or pager messages. Most data collection mechanisms provide some form of alerting capability for specified events.

5.3.6 Recognize That Data Collection and Characterization Are Iterative Processes

Initially, you want to collect as much data as possible because you do not know which data will be most meaningful. Over time, you begin to identify filtering approaches that allow you to successively refine what data you choose to examine. In addition, you begin to identify trends in behavior and specific activities and events that constitute normal behavior. This behavior can then be captured as part of your current characterization baseline (see the following steps). However, it is important to note that systems and the operations that users perform on them are always changing (for example, through the addition of new software or changes in user privileges due to new assignments), so you need to examine your characterization information periodically to determine if it needs to be updated.

Having a trusted characterization baseline is critical for identifying departures from normal and expected behavior that warrant further investigation. In addition, data that reveal normal and expected behavior can be eliminated from further consideration, allowing an administrator to focus attention on a smaller set of data demonstrating any unexpected behavior, including potential intrusions.

5.3.7 Document and Verify Your Characterization Trust Assumptions

As you generate all characterization information (for both baselining and comparison purposes), explicitly document your trust assumptions and continually verify that you can trust the results they produce.

Trust assumptions will likely address the following elements:

- The operating system kernel (loaded from virus-free, secure distribution media)
- The media where your data collection and characterization tools are stored and from which they are installed
- Cryptographic checksums and authoritative reference data that constitute characterization data

5.3.8 Characterize Typical Network Traffic and Performance

Document the procedure by which you intend to verify that the network traffic traversing your networks is as expected and reflects, for example, trusted source and destination addresses, and legitimate ports and protocols.

The types of network traffic information you should capture include network performance and other network data described in Table 5.2, and should answer the following questions:

- What traffic is typically produced by my system?
- What traffic is typically consumed by my system?
- What are the ranges of acceptable performance levels provided by my networks?

Comparing previous network performance information with current information allows you to determine if any network performance characteristic is beyond tolerable or acceptable limits, as described in Section 6.3.

5.3.9 Characterize Expected System Behavior and Performance

Document the procedure by which you intend to verify that your systems are performing as expected.

The types of performance information you want to capture answer the question, "What is the range of acceptable performance levels provided by my systems?" and include the system performance data and other system data described in Table 5.2.

Comparing previous system performance information with current information allows you to determine if any system performance characteristic is beyond tolerable or acceptable limits. Refer to Section 6.4.

5.3.10 Characterize Expected Process and User Behavior

Document the procedure by which you intend to verify that the processes executing on your systems are operating only as expected and can be attributed only to authorized activities of users, administrators, and system functions.

The types of process information you want to capture answer the question, "What processes are normally running on my system?" and include process and user data as described in Table 5.2.

Comparing previous process and user information with current information allows you to determine if any process is behaving in an unexpected or suspicious manner. Refer to Section 6.4.

5.3.11 Characterize Expected File and Directory Information

Document the procedure you will use to verify that the files and directories on your systems are as you expect them to be and that they were created, modified, accessed and deleted as you expected.

For each file and directory, the type of information you want to capture should include the file and directory data described in Table 5.2 and should answer the following questions:

- What files are on my system (name, type, attributes, etc.), and where do they reside?

- How are files and directories affected during normal system operation (created, deleted, contents changed, accessed, permissions changed, location changed)?

Capture a cryptographic checksum for all files and directories. For example, Tripwire[8] (refer to Section A.2) will generate this. Tripwire will also inform you of the state

---

8. Tripwire is a registered trademark of the Purdue Research Foundation.

of the collection of files on your system (added or deleted), changes in state (protection changes), and the fact that changes to file contents have or have not occurred (but not what the actual changes are). Commercial versions of Tripwire are available for UNIX and Windows NT systems.[9] MD5[10] and other one-way hashing functions (such as SHA-1, RIPEMD-160, and HAVAL[11]) can also be used to generate cryptographic checksums.

Keep in mind that Tripwire updates access time stamps for all files that it examines. This is normally not a problem for routine system administration. However, time stamps are an important element in any legal investigation. We recommend that you mount file systems as read-only when executing Tripwire on files and directories that may be used as evidence, as described in Section 7.4.

It is important to characterize the following files and directories:

- Operating systems and configuration files
- Access control lists
- Applications
- Security tools and data, such as those used for integrity checking and detecting signs of intrusion
- Organizational data such as financial reports and employee information
- User data
- Public information such as web pages

Some operating systems provide the ability to make files immutable, that is, unchangeable by any process on the system, including system and administrative processes. All operating system and other files that don't need to be modified when a system is running should be made immutable wherever possible.

Comparing previous file and directory information with current information allows you to determine if any file or directory has changed in an unexpected or suspicious manner. Refer to Section 6.5.

---

9. Refer to *http://www.tripwiresecurity.com.*

10. Refer to the CERT implementation *Using MD5 to Verify the Integrity of File Contents,* available at *http://www.cert.org/security-improvement* under UNIX implementations.

11. References for SHA-1 (Secure Hashing Algorithm), RIPEMD-160, and HAVAL (Hashing Algorithm with VAriable Length) can be found at *http://www.users.zetnet.co.uk/hopwood/crypto/scan/md.html.*

5.3.12 Generate an Inventory of Your System Hardware

If you have not already done so, create an inventory of all of your computing hardware assets. This is most easily accomplished by performing a physical audit. Use a tool (e.g., a database management system or spreadsheet) to record the initial inventory and keep it up-to-date. Select a tool that will easily allow you to perform comparisons with subsequent inventories.

Ensure that procedures are in place to update your hardware inventory when the physical location of equipment changes, when its hardware configuration is upgraded (e.g., through adding more memory), and when equipment is added to or removed from your systems.

Produce and maintain complete, up-to-date network infrastructure information that captures the architecture, connectivity, and identity of all network devices, including information on the following:

- The layout or topology of all network devices
- Network architecture
- Network and device connectivity
- Network and device configuration
- Administrative domains
- Physical location of all network devices
- Intermediate public networks, if any
- Additional details such as MAC addresses, IP addresses, host names, ports on routers, hubs and switches, contact telephone numbers, and external devices and servers your network depends on (e.g., ISP routes, DNS servers, and WWW cache)

Identify network monitoring and management mechanisms to keep this information up-to-date and to alert you to anomalies.

Use automated tools to detect installed hardware and compare the results with your physical inventory. For PC-based systems, the Windows 95, 98, or NT operating systems provide a complete hardware inventory capability as part of system properties. There are also a variety of vendor and public domain tools available (refer to Table 5.3). Tools such as daemon dialers[12] can help determine what modems are connected to your telephone lines, systems, and networks.

---

12. An article that addresses several sources for daemon dialers can be found at *http://www.infosecuritymag.com/articles/june00/features1.shtml.*

Refer to the implementation *Establishing and Maintaining a Physical Inventory of Your Computing Equipment.*[13]

5.3.13 Protect Your Asset Information and Keep It Up-to-Date

Keep authoritative reference copies of files and checksums on write-protected or read-only media stored in a physically secure location. You may want to consider using a tool such as PGP (Pretty Good Privacy) to "sign" the output generated by your checksum tool.

Consider making paper copies of configuration files and cryptographic checksums in case you are unable to recover uncorrupted electronic versions.

If you transmit authoritative reference data over unsecured network connections, make sure to verify the data upon arrival at the destination host (e.g., by using MD5). Consider encrypting the reference data at the source host to reduce the likelihood of the information being compromised and to protect confidentiality and privacy.

Encrypt your asset characterization information, authoritative reference data, and hardware inventory if your organization's security requirements demand this level of protection.

Keep your asset characterization information, authoritative reference data, and system inventory up-to-date.

5.3.14 Policy Considerations

Your organization's networked systems security policy should require your system administrators to create an accurate, reliable, and complete characterization of those assets you have selected. This should be done when they are first created and at well-defined events when you modify, add to, and replace elements of your systems or determine that the characterization of normal, expected behavior needs to change.

5.3.15 Additional Information

1. *Characterization development and maintenance.* It is difficult to estimate both the time required to develop an initial characterization baseline and the additional time required to keep it updated. One good guideline is to periodically observe a host's behavior for three to six months and then derive the initial

---

13. Available at *http://www.cert.org/security-improvement* under "General Implementations."

characterization baseline from that observation, using some of the data collection mechanisms described in this practice. Another good guideline is to allow 15 days of observation for characterizing the first host, 12 days for the second host, 9 days for the third host, and 7 days for the fourth and all subsequent hosts. It may take a year or more for an administrator to observe the network traffic traversing a large network and to develop a characterization baseline representing normal traffic behavior. Once an administrator understands how to develop a characterization baseline, developing subsequent baselines should proceed more quickly.

2. For information on log filtering, analysis, and alerting approaches, refer to Chapters 6 and 7. See also State of the Practice of Intrusion Detection Technologies (Allen 99).

3. *Tool selection.* You may find it useful to categorize and select tools using a set of activities associated with common approaches for detecting signs of suspicious or unexpected behavior. These activities would include the following:
   - Filtering—examining a data stream and removing from it items that are deemed undesirable or inappropriate
   - Probing—attempting connections or queries
   - Scanning—iteratively probing a collection of systems or data for known vulnerabilities
   - Monitoring—observing a data stream for specified events
   - Inspecting—examining a data resource or process
   - Auditing—systematically examining system data against documented expectations of form or behavior
   - Integrity checking— verifying that the contents of a data resource are exactly as created, stored, or transmitted
   - Notifying—alerting a designated recipient to the occurrence of a specific event

Refer to *An Approach for Selecting and Specifying Tools for Information Survivability* (Firth 97).

4. *Evaluation criteria.* It is difficult to provide specific guidance on tool selection, as the selection criteria vary broadly based on each organization's needs. This difficulty is compounded by the lack of uniformity in characterizations of common security tools. Some guidance on evaluation criteria for selecting monitoring systems and tools is available in "System and Network Monitoring" (Sellens 00). Possible criteria include the following:
   - size and complexity
   - scalability
   - reliability

- cost
- number and type of probes
- configuration complexity and flexibility
- exception reporting style
- exception reporting tools
- logging and data storage
- reporting mechanisms

5. *Examples of tools that can aid in detecting signs of intrusion.* In each of the tool types described below, a series of events, mechanisms, and desired data are provided that will help you decide whether or not you require a tool of this type to implement your intrusion detection policies and procedures. Refer also to Table 5.2.

In most cases, the identified tools require manual analysis in conjunction with the automated data collection and reporting performed by the tool.

Links to all of these tools can be found at the book web site. Appendix A provides sample implementations for Tripwire (Section A.2), logsurfer (Section A.6), spar (Section A.7), tcpdump (section A.8), and snort (Section A.9).

Table 5.3   Examples of Tools That Can Aid in Detecting Signs of Intrusion

Event Type	Tool Type Description	Example Tools
System	Monitor and inspect for use of system resources (e.g., changes to file systems) and suspicious activity (e.g., unusual or unexpected open files, successful and failed administrative logins, unexpected shutdowns and restarts, unusual modem activities, unusual or excessive email activities)	watcher klaxon lsof (LiSt Open Files) nfswatch showid loginlog
	Active intrusion detection systems, including active log file monitoring, that detect possible intrusions or access violations while they are occurring	snort asax (Advanced Security audit trail Analysis on uniX) swatch logsurfer tklogger

(continued)

Table 5.3   Examples of Tools That Can Aid in Detecting
Signs of Intrusion (*cont.*)

Event Type	Tool Type Description	Example Tools
Network	Monitor and inspect network traffic and connections (e.g., what kinds of connections, from where, and when) both for attempted connections that failed as well as for established connections, connections to/from unusual locations, unauthorized network probes, systematic port scans, traffic contrary to your firewall setup, and unusual file transfer activity	tcp wrapper tcpdump argus arpmon arpwatch snort courtney gabriel logdaemon rfingerd clog pidentd enhanced portmap/rpcbind
	Detect whether or not your network interface card is in promiscuous mode	ifstatus cpm (Check Promiscuous Mode)
	Detect new, unexpected services and verify the expected, available services on your network	nmap fremont strobe iss (Internet Security Scanner) satan (System Administrator Tool for Analyzing Networks) saint (Security Administrator's Integrated Network Tool)[14] sara (Security Auditor's Research Assistant)[15]

---

14. SAINT (Security Administrator's Integrated Network Tool) is a registered trademark of WWDSI (World Wide Digital Security, Inc.) and is available at *http://www.wwdsi.com/saint*.

15. SARA (Security Auditor's Research Assistant) is a registered trademark of Advanced Research Corporation and is available at *http://www.www-arc.com/sara*.

Event Type	Tool Type Description	Example Tools
User-related	Check account configurations, such as authentication and authorization information	cops (Computer Oracle and Password System) tiger checkXusers chkacct
	Monitor and inspect user activity, such as the login activity and repeated, failed login attempts, logins from unusual locations, logins at unusual times, changes in user identity, unauthorized attempts to access restricted information	noshell ttywatcher logdaemon
Verify data, file, and software integrity	Inspect operating systems and tool configurations for possible signs of exploits, such as improperly set access control lists on system tools, etc.	cops tiger secure-sun-check
	Detect unexpected changes to the contents or protections of files and directories	Tripwire L5 hobgoblin RIACS Auditing Package (Research Institute for Advanced Computer Science)
	Scan for Trojan horses	trojan.pl
Examine systems in detail, periodically or as events warrant	Reduce and scan log files to enhance the immediate detection of unusual activity[16]	top sps (Special Process Status) spar (Show Process Accounting Records) logsurfer logcheck

(continued)

16. Refer also to Sections A.4 and A.5 in Appendix A.

Table 5.3   Examples of Tools That Can Aid in Detecting
Signs of Intrusion (*cont.*)

Event Type	Tool Type Description	Example Tools
	Check log consistency for possible tampering	chklastlog
		chkwtmp
		loginlog
		trimlog
	Check for known vulnerabilities	nessus
		satan
		saint
		sara
		cops
		iss
		tiger
	Aid in conducting forensic analysis	TCT (The Coroner's Toolkit)

5.4 Manage Logging and Other Data Collection Mechanisms

Once you have identified the data to be collected (as described in Section 5.3), you need to enable the corresponding logging and data collection mechanisms, as well as log filters and alert tools. All of these mechanisms can produce a large volume of recorded information. You need to determine how best to capture, manage, and protect all recorded information, as well as how to alert security staff and administrators when appropriate.

Select and enable data collection mechanisms based on your site's security policy and security requirements.

Failure to enable the necessary data collection mechanisms will greatly weaken or eliminate your ability to detect suspicious behavior and intrusion attempts and to determine whether or not such attempts succeeded.

Failure to configure and secure the volume of data produced by these mechanisms will place the data at risk of compromise and make subsequent review and analysis difficult, if not impossible.

5.4.1 Enable Logging

Using the logging mechanisms provided by the vendor and any supplemental tools, enable all logging that you have selected. For help, refer to the administration documentation for your systems to learn how to enable each of the logging mechanisms, and refer to any documentation that accompanies relevant tools. This documentation will specify whether these mechanisms need to be enabled only once, each time the system is rebooted, or at regular intervals during the system's normal operation. Some logging mechanisms let you select different levels of detail.

Pay attention to the location of the log data: Some tools allow you to choose a file or directory where the data is logged, while others write their data to a predefined default location. Make sure that you have sufficient space for the data that are generated. Ensure that the logged data are protected, based on previously determined ACLs (access control lists) and your security policy.

Be aware that multiple logging mechanisms may contribute log records to a single log file, such as syslog in UNIX systems. This feature is specified within your system configuration file. Refer to Section A.4.

5.4.2 Protect Logs

To protect sensitive information, ensure that log files are protected from being accessed or modified by unauthorized users. Confirm that only authorized users can access utilities that reconfigure logging mechanisms; turn the utilities on and off; and write to, modify, and read log data.

It is important to collect and archive log files so that they cannot be accessed by an intruder to remove or alter signs of an intrusion or add erroneous information. Use the following methods to ensure that log files are not modified:

- Log data to a file on a separate host that is dedicated solely to log collecting. The log host should reside in a physically secure location that is not easily accessible from the network. For example, capturing log data using a computer via a dedicated serial line provides a way of storing the log files more securely than if they were written on the logging host's disks.

- Log selected data to a write-once/read-many device such as a CD-ROM or a specially configured tape drive, or to a write-only device such as a printer to eliminate the possibility of the data being modified once it is written.

- If supported by your systems, set selected log file attributes that enable only new information to be appended to the log files (i.e., new records can be added, but those already recorded cannot be modified).

- Encrypt log files, particularly those that contain sensitive data or those being transmitted across a network.

Direct logging to disk on the local host is the easiest method to configure, allowing instant access to file records for analysis, but it is also the least secure. Collecting log files on a write-once device requires slightly more effort to configure but is more secure. However, data are not as easily accessed using this method, and you need to maintain a supply of storage media.

Printing the logging results is useful when you require hard copies of log files, but printed logs can be difficult to search, require manual analysis, and potentially need large storage space.

When the host generating the logging data is different from the host recording it, you must secure the path between them. For environments where short distances separate the generating host from the recording host, you can connect them with single point-to-point cable(s). For environments where this approach is not practical, minimize the number of networks and routers used to make the connection, or encrypt sensitive log data as it is generated.

To protect the log files on your log host, place the host on a separate, secure subnet that is protected by a firewall and make log files "read only" from the log host console.

You need to prepare systems that perform logging to ensure that they do not stop functioning in the event of a logging DoS attack. For UNIX systems, an intruder could launch an attack that fills up the syslog files so that when the logging partition is full, logging ceases. For NT systems, an intruder could overwrite the oldest log file entries after filling all available storage.

To prepare a system so that it continues functioning, create separate file partitions for different log information and filter network messages to decrease the likelihood of such attacks. Refer to Section 4.7.

In addition, some systems have the ability to shut down (or prohibit anyone but the system administrator from logging in), and produce a warning when the log files are full. However, this is not normally the default configuration, so it must be explicitly specified.

5.4.3 Document Your Management Plan for Log Files

Handle the Total Volume of Logged Information

We recommend that you log as much as possible for your systems and networks. While log files can very quickly consume a great deal of storage (which is relatively inexpensive), it is difficult to predict which logs will be critical in the event of an intrusion. Based on your log collection and storage approach, you may want to compress log files to allow them to remain accessible online for easier review and to conserve space.

Rotate Log Files

This step consists of the following tasks:

- Make a copy of the active (online) log files at regular intervals (ranging from daily to weekly)
- Rename the files to prevent further augmentation of information contained in them
- Reset file contents
- Verify that logging still works

Rotating log files allows you to limit the volume of log data you have to examine at any given time. It also allows you to keep log files open for a limited duration so that damage is contained if an active log file is compromised. In this way you create a collection of log files that contain well-defined time intervals of recorded data.

You can then consolidate logs from different systems by matching time intervals. This process will help you gain a networkwide perspective on the activities. To perform this consolidation, you will likely need to merge log files from different systems into a central log file.[17] To avoid having to adjust the time stamps used in each, use a master clock system such NTP (Network Time Protocol) or another time synchronization protocol system.[18] Make sure to take into account different time zones and formats for recorded time.

---

17. Refer to Section 7.2 , especially the step describing how to examine logs generated by firewalls, network monitors, and routers (7.2.5).

18. Refer to *http://www.eecis.udel.edu/~ntp/*.

Back Up and Archive Log Files

Move your log files to permanent storage or capture them as part of your regular backup procedure. This step will allow you to retrieve them later if the need arises. Document the method you use to access archived log files. To minimize loss of logging data, create backups before you execute any automated tools that truncate and reset the log files.

Encrypt Log Files

We recommend encrypting log files that contain sensitive data as the log data are being recorded. Protect the encryption software and place a copy of your encryption keys on a floppy disk or WORM (write once, read many) CD-ROM in a secure location such as a safe or safety deposit box. If the keys are lost, the log files cannot be used. If possible, use public key encryption.

The logs can be encrypted using the public key (which can be safely stored online); the corresponding private key (stored offline) can then be used to decrypt the logs.

Ensure that you have the system and personnel resources necessary to analyze logs on a regular basis (at least daily in most cases) and on demand (such as when alert events occur).

Dispose of Log Files

Ensure that all media containing log file data are securely disposed of (e.g., shred hard-copy output, sanitize disks, destroy CD-ROMs).

5.4.4 Protect Data Collection Mechanisms and Their Outputs

Make sure you obtain tools from a reliable source and verify their software integrity through digital signatures, cryptographic checksums, or by using trusted copies from secure media. Intruders have been known to modify tools installed by authorized administrators so that the tools, when used, do not identify the presence of the intruder.

Once you have verified the software, you need to configure it for use at your site. The installation should be performed on a secure system to eliminate the possibility of the tool being tampered with before you have had a chance to deploy it. You should make a cryptographic checksum of these tools. Using this information, you can then verify that your original configuration has not been compromised. You need to protect these tools by ensuring that they have the appropriate access control lists set to allow use and modification only by authorized users. The reports produced by these tools also need to be protected so that only authorized users can use them.

5.4.5 Consider Special Procedures to Preserve Evidence

Such procedures are required in the event that an intrusion has actually occurred and your organization decides to take legal action against the intruder.

Refer to Section 7.4.

5.4.6 Policy Considerations

Your organization's networked systems security policy should establish the following guidelines:

- You should document a management plan for handling log files. This plan should include what to log, when and why to log, where to log, and who is responsible for all aspects of the plan.

- Approved sources should be identified for acquiring tool software (Internet, shareware, purchased from vendor, etc.) and acceptable use practices related to tools.

5.5 Select, Install, and Understand Tools for Response

Response preparation includes selecting, installing, and becoming familiar with tools that will assist you in the response process and help you collect and maintain data related to an intrusion. You need to perform these preparation steps well in advance of an intrusion. You also need to understand and know how to use a range of tools to support your response procedures, including the following:

- Tools that capture data, configurations, backups, and cryptographic checksums about the systems involved in an intrusion. The outputs produced by these tools help you to analyze the system and provide information for system recovery.

- Tools and data that directly support your response procedures, such as an isolated computer system to test artifacts that were found on compromised systems and a contact database for those you need to keep informed about an intrusion.

You need to ensure that all tools and related data are available, taking into account that the systems involved in an intrusion may not be working reliably or may not be available until an intrusion is contained and the recovery is successfully accomplished.

To do so, you may have to make additional systems available for tool execution or take additional steps to ensure that your tools are reliable and can be executed securely on the compromised system (as described in Section 6.2).

You will not be able to respond to an intrusion efficiently if you do not have the appropriate tools and data available before the intrusion is detected. You will likely enact your response procedures later than desired, potentially increasing the extent and damage of an intrusion and making recovery more difficult. If you wait until an intrusion occurs before identifying and installing needed tools, you may not be able to obtain a working version of the tools within the time required. It may then be difficult to create the correct set of data needed for tool execution. Analysis results that would help you clarify your current situation may not be available. You may not be able to restore a compromised system to its previous operational state if trusted backups are not accessible.

Tools may not operate predictably and effectively if they are not kept up-to-date, and they may not operate reliably if they are not protected in a way that ensures their authenticity and integrity. Their results could have been manipulated to hide signs of an intrusion. If they are not protected to ensure their availability, you will not be able to access them to assist you in your response procedures.

5.5.1 Build Archives of Boot Disks and Distribution Media

An archive of original or trusted boot disks (or CD-ROMs) provides the ability to restart a specific computer from a known, preexisting configuration. This ensures, to a large extent, that compromised files, programs, and data are not reloaded onto the system.

There are often incompatibilities in different operating system versions that may preclude, for example, full access to systems disks. Therefore, it is important to have all operating system versions in the archive in order to rebuild your system successfully and include the original distribution media for each. This information allows you to (1) reinstall a specific version of the operating system when necessary and (2) install the trusted version on a test machine and compare files (trusted versus installed, possibly compromised) for unexpected changes.

All media should be hardware-write-protectable to avoid intentional or inadvertent tampering.

5.5.2 Build an Archive of Security-Related Patches

Every new version of every operating system or application contains some unknown vulnerabilities and errors. Vendors provide security-related patches (also called bug-fixes, hot-fixes, etc.) to correct these. Usually, they provide such patches free of charge to their customers.

Having an archive of patches allows you to initiate a specific operating system or application in a known, secure configuration by applying patches whenever the software is initially installed or subsequently reinstalled. Refer to Section 2.4 for further guidance on keeping operating systems and applications software up-to-date.

5.5.3 Identify and Install Tools That Support Reinstallation

These tools include the following:

- Installation servers containing trusted, generic versions of the original distribution for all operating systems, applications, and versions. The reinstallation process can be executed from these servers for a network with a large number of hosts, with prompting for any host-specific information such as an IP address.

- All tools that are needed to retrieve, unpack, verify, and install software patches intended to correct errors and eliminate vulnerabilities.

5.5.4 Ensure Adequate Backup Procedures

During daily operations, the generation of backups provides you with copies of the system and its data. You depend on these copies to be able to restore the most recent version of the system or specific data files in the event of damage to your systems or data. You need to have high confidence that the restored assets are as you intended by regularly testing your ability to restore these assets from previously stored backups. Also refer to Section 2.10.

Ensure that high-capacity, removable and hardware-write-protectable media and supporting equipment are available to make and restore system backups. The media that you use to store backups must have sufficient capacity to contain all backup information.

Backups made as part of your response procedures are used for a number of reasons:

- To save the latest version of data and configuration information. This is necessary to restore systems to their last known state, which will include the most recent modifications made by users and system administrators not available from the routine backups.

- To ensure that evidence on compromised systems is preserved.

- To provide an easy way to establish the compromised environment on other systems required to conduct analysis (for example, on an isolated test network).

To make backups and load them on other systems, all of the necessary devices, cables, plugs, and terminators need to be available, as does the software that was used to create the backups.

If possible, use media that cannot be written again once used (i.e., protected for read-only access such as WORM media). This method safeguards the information and avoids accidental overwriting.

5.5.5 Build an Archive of Test Results

We recommend that for comparison purposes you prepare a set of test results that describe the expected state of your systems. This step will give you some level of confidence that your systems have been properly restored after an intrusion occurs. The results may include a scan for services on the network level (building up an authoritative list of such services) and a file of cryptographic checksums for critical configuration files (building up an authoritative list of such checksums).

5.5.6 Build and Maintain Sources and Methods for Contact Information

The database should contain contact information for all individuals and organizations called out in your information dissemination policy and procedure, as described in Section 7.3. These contacts include response teams within your organization and those that operate nationally and internationally, as well as your public relations and legal staff.

> The Forum of Incident Response and Security Teams (FIRST) brings together a variety of computer security incident response teams from government, commercial, and academic organizations. FIRST has the following goals:
>
> - To foster cooperation among information technology constituents in the effective prevention of, detection of, and response to computer security incidents
>
> - To act as a channel for communicating alert and advisory information on potential threats and emerging incident situations
>
> - To facilitate the actions and activities of the FIRST members, including research and operational activities

> • To facilitate the sharing of security-related information, tools, and techniques
>
> Currently, FIRST has 70 members. Contact information for FIRST teams can be obtained from *http://www.first.org/team-info.*

Design the contact database so that it can be easily accessed and updated. Keep all contact information up-to-date, including public encryption keys or shared private keys.

To ensure database availability during an intrusion, store a backup copy offsite, have a copy available on an accessible system that is not connected to any network such as a laptop, and have hard copies available. Having access to a trusted version of your contact's database is critically important when you need to communicate with those involved. Protect the database as you would any other type of critical information. It can reveal a great deal about how you conduct your response process.

Not all contact information can be derived prior to the occurrence of an intrusion. If an intrusion originates from an Internet host, you will need to search for the appropriate contacts for that host. Directories such as "whois"[19] or DNS (Domain Name System) provide information about organizations that are present on the Internet.[20]

Various telephone directories are also present on the Internet. These can be accessed using web browsers or with tools targeted for specific databases.

Tools that access these sources of information need to be included in the resource kit described below.

5.5.7 Set Up Secure Communication Mechanisms

You need to determine with whom you will need to communicate using secure mechanisms during the handling of an intrusion. Communication may take place using electronic means such as e-mail. All points of contact need to agree on what technology to use, and must exchange authenticated encryption and signature keys in advance. You may want to consider protecting other communication mechanisms such as fax or phone lines using encryption technology.

---

19. Refer to *http://rs.internic.net/whois.html.*

20. Refer to the CERT tech tips *Finding Site Contacts, Registry Databases by Domain Name,* and *Registry Databases by IP Number,* all available at *http://www.cert.org/tech_tips.*

Be aware that the mere act of two people communicating could alert intruders to the fact that they have been detected. A sudden flurry of encrypted e-mail from your internal security group to users, system administrators, CSIRTs, and others is a sure sign that something is happening. Your response procedures need to take this into account, perhaps by forgoing e-mail and conducting all communications via phone and fax.

If you depend on secure communication mechanisms that use encryption, you need to manage all keys and authenticate those keys. This means verifying that the keys belong to the identified point of contact and are not compromised prior to or during key exchange. If you are dealing with a large number of contacts, exchanging and authenticating keys can be quite burdensome. You may be able to locate commercial certificate authorities (CAs) that will certify keys for all points of contact, or at least those outside your organization; however, most CAs do not currently provide this service.

In the event that you cannot communicate via the Internet or your organization's intranet, ensure that you establish alternate paths for communication with critical sites, such as phone lines with direct modem connections.

5.5.8 Build a Resource Kit

The resource kit should contain all tools that you may need to use in the response process. Examples of such tools include those that make and restore backups, compare files, build and compare cryptographic checksums, take system snapshots, review system configurations, list services and processes, trace the path to the attacking site and their ISP, etc. Ensure that the resource kit is available on clean, hardware-write-protectable media.

Ensure that hardware devices such as printers or laptops are reserved for use in the event of an intrusion. Hard copies of materials are often required as part of an intrusion log and archives. For example, laptops can be used to monitor your network for suspicious activity, to retrieve contact information from Internet directory servers, and to access previously collected information such as default configurations and user ID lists.

5.5.9 Ensure That Test Systems and Networks Are Properly Configured and Available

Using compromised systems for any kind of analysis or test may expose these systems to further damage; given that the systems have already been compromised, any results produced by them are unreliable. In addition, using such systems may inadvertently inform an intruder of the tests you are executing through the generation of network messages by malicious or compromised programs.

We recommend that you use test systems and test networks that are both physically and logically separated from any operational system and network. If you have sufficient resources available, you may choose to move the compromised systems to a test network and deploy newly installed and fully patched and secured systems so as to continue operations. Newly installed systems may have the same vulnerability that an intruder used to gain access. However, making the original systems available for analysis may give you an advantage over other approaches for reconstituting the compromised systems on your test network. In addition, the newly installed system will not contain any software that the intruder may have left behind.

If your equipment is limited or you do not want equipment to be idle when no analysis is being performed, you may choose to have a plan and process in place to configure a test environment quickly, on an as needed basis.

After analysis is complete, clear all disks to ensure that any remnant files or malicious programs do not impact future analysis, affect any ongoing work on the test system, or inadvertently become transferred to other operational systems. This is particularly critical in the event that your test system is used for other purposes.

Make a backup of all analyzed systems to protect the results of your analysis in case you need to do further analysis in the future.

5.5.10 Policy Considerations

Your organization's networked systems security policy should establish the following guidelines:

- Designated system administrators, network administrators, and response team members should be trained in the use of intrusion response tools and environments. This training should include participation in response practice drills or simulations using the tools and environments.

- The inventory of all applications software, operating systems, supporting tools, and hardware should be kept up-to-date.

- Quick access to backups should be available in an emergency, even if they are stored at a remote site. This requirement may include defining procedures that give specific managers the responsibility to authorize such access.

- Staff members dealing with an intrusion should be able to gain access to restricted systems and data. This policy may include

  specifying how staff access is granted and how they will obtain administrator passwords and encryption keys

  establishing the authority for staff access

establishing the authenticity of the staff member obtaining access

requiring that all access is documented and tracked

Chapter 5   Checklist

Practice	Step Number	Step Description	Yes	Partial	No
P5.2: Establish Policies and Procedures	S5.2.1	Address intrusion detection and response in your security policies			
	S5.2.2	Document procedures that implement your intrusion detection policies			
	S5.2.3	Document procedures that implement your intrusion response policies			
	S5.2.4	Document roles and responsibilities			
	S5.2.5	Conduct a legal review			
	S5.2.6	Train users			
	S5.2.7	Keep your policies, procedures, and training current			
P5.3: Identify Characterization and Other Data for Detecting Signs of Suspicious Behavior	S5.3.1	Determine what data is most useful to collect			
	S5.3.2	Identify the data to be collected			
	S5.3.3	Identify the data to be captured using logging mechanisms			

Practice	Step Number	Step Description	Yes	Partial	No
	S5.3.4	Identify the data to be captured using additional data collection mechanisms			
	S5.3.5	Determine which events should produce an alert			
	S5.3.6	Recognize that data collection and characterization are iterative processes			
	S5.3.7	Document and verify your characterization trust assumptions			
	S5.3.8	Characterize typical network traffic and performance			
	S5.3.9	Characterize expected system behavior and performance			
	S5.3.10	Characterize expected process and user behavior			
	S5.3.11	Characterize expected file and directory information			
	S5.3.12	Generate an inventory of your system hardware			
	S5.3.13	Protect your asset information and keep it up-to-date			
	S5.3.14	Policy considerations			
P5.4 Manage Logging and Other Data Collection Mechanisms	S5.4.1	Enable logging			
	S5.4.2	Protect logs			

(continued)

Chapter 5 Checklist (*cont.*)

Practice	Step Number	Step Description	Yes	Partial	No
	S5.4.3	Document your management plan for log files			
	S5.4.4	Protect data collection mechanisms and their outputs			
	S5.4.5	Consider special procedures to preserve evidence			
	S5.4.6	Policy considerations			
P5.5 Select, Install, and Understand Tools for Response	S5.5.1	Build archives of boot disks and distribution media			
	S5.5.2	Build an archive of security-related patches			
	S5.5.3	Identify and install tools that support reinstallation			
	S5.5.4	Ensure adequate backup procedures			
	S5.5.5	Build an archive of test results			
	S5.5.6	Build and maintain sources and methods for contact information			
	S5.5.7	Set up secure communication mechanisms			
	S5.5.8	Build a resource kit			
	S5.5.9	Ensure that test systems and networks are properly configured and available			
	S5.5.10	Policy considerations			

Chapter 6

Detecting Signs
of Intrusion

Intruders are always looking for new ways to break into networked computer systems. They may attempt to breach your network's perimeter defenses from remote locations or try to infiltrate your organization physically to gain access to information resources. Intruders seek old, unpatched vulnerabilities as well as newly discovered vulnerabilities in operating systems, network services, and protocols; and they take advantage of both. They develop and use sophisticated programs to penetrate systems rapidly. As a result, intrusions and the damage they cause can be achieved in seconds.

Even if your organization has implemented a number of the more popular information security protection measures, such as firewalls and intrusion detection systems, it is essential that you closely monitor your information assets and transactions involving these assets for signs of intrusion. Monitoring may be complicated, because intruder attack methods are constantly changing, and intruders often hide their activities by changing the systems they break into. An intrusion may have already happened without your noticing because everything seemed to be operating normally.

The practices contained in this chapter are designed to help you detect intrusions by looking for unexpected or suspicious behavior and "fingerprints" of known intrusion methods.

6.1 Overview

These practices are intended primarily for system and network administrators, managers of information systems, and security personnel responsible for networked information resources.

The practices are applicable to your organization if its networked systems infrastructure includes any of the following:

- Host systems providing services to multiple users (file servers, time-sharing systems, database servers, web servers, etc.)
- Local area or wide area networks
- Direct connections, gateways, or modem access to and from external networks, such as the Internet

The practices do not address the following issues:

- Protecting user privacy while in the process of detecting signs of intrusion
- Using security monitoring and reporting services provided by outside (third-party) organizations

6.1.1 The Need for Detecting Signs of Intrusion

If you do not know that an intrusion or an intrusion attempt has occurred, it is difficult, if not impossible, to determine later if your systems have been compromised. If the information necessary to detect an intrusion is not being collected and reviewed, you cannot determine what sensitive data, systems, and networks are being attacked and what breaches in confidentiality, integrity, or availability have occurred. As a result of an inadequate ability to detect signs of intrusion, your organization may face the following problems:

- Inability to determine either the full extent of the intrusion and the damage it has caused, or whether or not you have completely removed the intruder from your systems and networks. This will significantly increase your time to recover.
- Legal action. Intruders make use of systems they have compromised to launch attacks against others. If one of your systems is used in this way, you may be held liable for not exercising adequate due care with respect to security.
- Lost business opportunities, coupled with loss of reputation.

If you are adequately prepared and have the necessary policies and procedures in place to detect signs of intrusion, you can mitigate your risk of exposure to such problems.

6.1.2 An Approach for Detecting Signs of Intrusion

The practices in this chapter assume that you have implemented the detection preparation practices described in Chapter 5. The general approach to detecting intrusions is threefold:

1. Observe your systems for anything unexpected or suspicious.
2. Investigate anything you find to be unusual.
3. If your investigation finds something that isn't explained by authorized activity, immediately initiate your intrusion response procedures as described in Chapter 7.

While this process sounds simple enough, implementing it is a resource-intensive activity that requires continuous, automated support and daily administrative effort. Furthermore, the scale of intrusion detection practices may need to change as threats, system configurations, or security requirements change. In all cases, however, four areas must be addressed:

1. The integrity of the software you use to detect intrusions
2. Monitoring of the behavior of your systems and the traffic on your networks
3. Physical forms of intrusion to your computer systems, offline data storage media, and output devices
4. Follow through, including the investigation of reports by users and other reliable sources (such as incident response teams) and action following unexpected activities

As you look for signs of intrusion, keep in mind that information from one source may not appear suspicious by itself. Inconsistencies among several sources can sometimes be the best indication of suspicious behavior or intrusions.

Table 6.1 Detecting Signs of Intrusion Practice Summary

Approach	Practice	Reference
Integrity of intrusion detection software	Ensure that the Software Used to Examine Systems Has Not Been Compromised	Section 6.2; page 234
Behavior of networks and systems	Monitor and Inspect Network Activities	Section 6.3; page 237
	Monitor and Inspect System Activities	Section 6.4; page 243
	Inspect Files and Directories for Unexpected Changes	Section 6.5; page 251

(continued)

Table 6.1   Detecting Signs of Intrusion Practice Summary (*cont.*)

Approach	Practice	Reference
Physical forms of intrusion	Investigate Unauthorized Hardware Attached to the Network	Section 6.6; page 254
	Look for Signs of Unauthorized Access to Physical Resources	Section 6.7; page 257
Follow through	Review Reports of Suspicious System and Network Behavior and Events	Section 6.8; page 258
	Take Appropriate Actions	Section 6.9; page 261

6.2 Ensure That the Software Used to Examine Systems Has Not Been Compromised

When you look for signs of intrusions on your systems, and when you examine your systems in general, you should use a verified, reference set of software—one that contains only trusted copies of software that have not been modified—and perform a clean boot (start the system from a known, virus-free image of the operating system). In addition to executable programs, the verified set of software must include all the operating system kernel, system libraries, configuration and data files, and system utilities on which the programs depend. You should avoid relying on software that resides on systems being examined (unless you can verify that the software and its supporting libraries, configuration files, and data files have not been modified).

Intrusion detection depends heavily on the reliability of the information you gather about the state and behavior of your systems. Therefore, it is essential that you use only software that you know to be reliable and accurate in its reporting of such information.

Intruders often replace software that would reveal their presence with substitutes that obscure or remove such information. Intruders are known to have replaced programs, libraries, and other utilities called by the programs. If a program used in detecting intrusions has been tampered with or replaced with a substitute, obviously you cannot rely on its output.

Ensuring that you are using only verified software may be very difficult. Intruders can make extremely devious system modifications that make things appear normal when in fact they are not. They can create, substitute, modify, and damage files on systems to which they have gained access. For example an intruder can use the rootkit tool set[1] to replace the *ps* command on a UNIX system with one that does not display the intruder's process; similarly, an editor can be replaced with one that reads a file other than the one specified, which the intruder may have hidden and replaced with another version. Intruders modify system log files to remove traces of their activities and may modify software that is executed at system boot and shutdown, complicating your ability to take a system safely offline for more detailed analysis. Viruses often do this. By masking their presence on a compromised system, intruders prolong the time they have to use that system for their purposes. In several notable cases, the presence of intruders on compromised systems was not discovered until many months after the initial intrusion occurred.

> Any examination or alteration of a suspect system could destroy data that may be useful during any legal investigation or proceedings. However, to determine the cause of the problem and return a system to operations as soon as possible, the system administrator may have no choice but to destroy such data. If you require legal evidence to be preserved, we recommend that you initiate your intrusion response procedures immediately, as described in Chapter 7.

The guiding principle for this practice is that you maintain a certain level of suspicion. Question everything you observe, and be able to answer these questions:

- What software is producing this output?
- What other software does it rely on?
- What software can I trust?

You can use five different approaches to achieve the goal of using a verified set of software. In all cases, the verified software should be located on physically write-protected media (e.g., CD-ROM or write-protected disk), so that it cannot be modified by a user or by software running on the system being examined. Each approach listed below has advantages and disadvantages, so you should choose a method appropriate to your current circumstances.

---

1. For Windows NT, refer to *http://www.rootkit.com*. For Linux, refer to *http://www.securityfocus.com/tools/1489*. To check for signs of the presence of rootkit, refer to *http://www.securityfocus.com/tools/1646*.

1.   Move the disk from the system suspected of having been compromised to a write-protected, verified system, and examine the disk's contents using the software on the verified system.

The advantage of this method is that you do not need to rely on the integrity of any part of the operating system or the hardware on the suspect system. The method is effective and reasonable when you suspect that a particular system has been compromised and you want to analyze it. However, it may not be practical for automated procedures or for checking a large number of systems.

Be careful when shutting down the suspect system, since this act may in and of itself cause the evidence you are seeking to be hidden or lost. Before shutting down the suspect system, look at any programs that will run at shutdown for signs that they were modified (for example in some UNIX operating systems, the */etc/shutdown* program should be examined). However, be aware that just looking at the file may be misleading, since you are relying on the suspect system's software. You may want to execute verified copies of shutdown programs and their data files (taking care to save the original files for later analysis). Other alternatives are to execute the shutdown from external media, force the system to halt immediately, or just pull the plug.

2.   Attach to the suspect system a write-protected, verified system disk that contains the operating system and all necessary software, and then reboot the system using the verified operating system. This method has advantages and disadvantages similar to those of method 1 but relies on the trustworthiness of the suspect system's hardware.

3.   Generate an image of the suspect system disk, mount it on a verified system, and examine it there. This method is acceptable if you have a verified system that you can use to examine the suspect system disk. This approach has the advantage of not affecting the operational environment of the suspect system (because what you're examining is an image of it on another system) and preserving the original evidence for subsequent legal proceedings.

4.   Use external media containing a verified set of software to examine the suspect system.

To use this method, you need to use a CD-ROM or a write-protected disk containing verified software when examining the suspect system. A significant concern with this approach is that you will still be using the suspect system's operating system (e.g., the UNIX kernel), and it is highly unlikely that you have provided every needed operating system program, utility, and library on the CD-ROM or write-protected disk. As a result, the outcome of such analysis is suspect.

5.   Verify the software on the suspect system first, then use the verified software to examine the suspect system.

This method requires you to compare the software on the suspect system with a reference copy (either complete files or cryptographic checksums as described in Section 5.3). However, take care to use a verified comparison program or cryptographic checksumming program. The program used to verify the software should be located on physically write-protected media. This approach has the same problem as that noted in method 4 with respect to using the suspect system's operating system.

6.2.1   Policy Considerations

Your organization's networked systems security policy should specify the level of verification that is required when examining each class of data and service provided by the organization's systems.

6.2.2   Additional Information

Some operating systems have the ability to make files immutable, that is, unchangeable by any process on the system, including system and administrative processes. All operating system files that don't need to be modified when a system is running should be made immutable wherever possible.

When you are examining your system through a remote access connection, make sure that you have established a secure channel to the system (as described in Section 2.13). Configure servers for secure remote administration and use of SSH (as described in Section A.3), so that only authorized personnel use the channel and nothing is changed or revealed in transit.

6.3   Monitor and Inspect Network Activities

Data about network activities (traffic, performance, etc.) can be collected from a variety of sources, including the following:

- Administrator probes (Internet control message protocol [ICMP] pings, port probes, simple network management protocol [SNMP] queries)
- Log files (routers, firewalls, other network hosts and devices)
- Alert reports
- Error reports

- Network performance statistics reports
- The outputs of tools used to support in-depth analysis

You should watch for unexpected network behavior, such as the following:

- Unexpected changes in network performance such as variations in traffic load at specified times
- Traffic coming from or going to unexpected locations
- Connections made at unusual times
- Repeated, failed connection attempts
- Unauthorized scans and probes
- Nonstandard or malformed packets (protocol violations)

Monitoring messages as they traverse your network gives you the ability to identify intrusive activity as it is occurring or soon afterwards. By catching suspicious activity as early as possible, you can immediately begin to investigate the activity and hopefully minimize and contain any damage.

Logs of network traffic may contain evidence of unusual, suspicious, or unexpected activities, indicating that someone has compromised or tried to compromise a system on your network. By inspecting log files on a regular basis, you may be able to identify intruder reconnaissance in advance of an intrusion. You may also identify attempted or successful intrusions soon after they occur. However, if an intruder has altered log files, the data may no longer be present.

If you permit access to your systems and networks by third parties (vendors, contractors, suppliers, partners, customers, etc.), you must monitor their access to ensure that all their actions are authentic and authorized. This step includes monitoring and inspecting their network activities.

6.3.1 Notify Users

Inform authorized users of your systems about the scope and kinds of monitoring you will be doing and the consequences of unauthorized behavior.

A common method for communicating this message is the presentation of a banner message immediately before user login.

Without the presentation of a banner message or other warning, you probably cannot use log files and other collected data in any action you may choose to take against a user.

For further information on setting up monitoring banners for Windows NT, refer to the implementation *Setting Up a Logon Banner on Windows NT 4.0.*[2] Here's one example of banner language taken from this implementation:

> This system is for the use of authorized users only. Individuals using this computer system without authority, or in excess of their authority, are subject to having all of their activities on this system monitored and recorded by system personnel. In the course of monitoring individuals improperly using this system, or in the course of system maintenance, the activities of authorized users may also be monitored. Anyone using this system expressly consents to such monitoring and is advised that if such monitoring reveals possible evidence of criminal activity, system personnel may provide the evidence of such monitoring to law enforcement officials.

6.3.2 Review Network Alerts

Review and investigate notification from network-specific alert mechanisms (such as e-mail, voice mail, or pager messages), for example:

- Users and other administrators, via e-mail or in person
- Operating system alert mechanisms
- Network and system management software traps, such as those that can be set via SNMP (simple network management protocol)
- Intrusion detection systems
- Custom alert mechanisms from service or application programs (including tools)

6.3.3 Review Network Error Reports

These types of notifications are typically produced by one of the following devices:

- Operating system error reporting mechanisms
- Log file filtering tools

---

2. Available at *http://www.cert.org/security-improvement* under Windows NT implementations.

- Vendor or custom-developed management software
- Custom error-reporting mechanisms from service or application programs (including tools)

Often an administrator will be able to configure error reporting at a number of criticality, severity, or priority levels when installing the network system, service and application programs, and supporting tools.

6.3.4 Review Network Performance

Statistics are generally produced by vendor or custom performance-monitoring tools. Typical statistics include the following (refer to Section 5.3, Table 5.2):

- Total traffic load in and out over time (packet, byte, and connection counts) and by event (such as new product or service release)
- Traffic load (percentage of packets, bytes, connections) in and out over time sorted by protocol, source address, destination address, other packet header data
- Error counts on all network interfaces
- Comparison of previous network performance statistics with current statistics for the same time frame

Look for the following extraordinary occurrences:

- Unexpected changes in performance between current and previously captured statistics, for example, unusually high or low network traffic compared with expected levels for the day of the week and time of day
- Unexpected deviations from authoritative network traffic characterization information, for example (refer to Section 5.3):

    traffic coming from unexpected source addresses or using unexpected ports or protocols

    traffic going to unexpected destination addresses or using unexpected ports or protocols

    excessively high or low traffic volume for the day of the week and time of day

- Unexpected loss of connectivity
- Unusual modem activity or availability, which can indicate intruder access through overlooked entry points (ports) or intruder use of daemon dialers

6.3.5 Review Network Traffic

Identify any unexpected, unusual, or suspicious network traffic and the possible implications. From network log files and other network traffic collection mechanisms, look for the following extraordinary occurrences:

- Reconnaissance (probes, scans, use of mapping tools) in advance of an attack. These activities can indicate attempts to identify your configuration (hosts, operating systems, network topology, externally accessible paths into your systems, etc.) and your Internet service provider(s) (ISP), along with their configuration.

- Connections to or from unusual locations. For example, if a server host is dedicated to a single service (such as serving a public web site), any requests it makes for outbound connections are suspicious. Such requests may indicate that an intruder has compromised the server and that it is being used to launch an attack on another host.

- Protocol violations. These include, but are not limited to, invalid option bits in a transmission control protocol (TCP) packet, invalid sequence numbers in a TCP packet, invalid flags in a TCP packet (ACK before SYN), and invalid fragments. There is no good reason to violate the Internet protocol (IP), TCP, ICMP, and user datagram protocol (UDP) specifications. These types of protocol violations often result when an intruder uses a network scanner in an attempt to bypass your firewall (that may just check for an established bit set on a packet) and to identify the type of systems on your networks (since different host IP stacks will respond to the error in different ways). A DoS condition can occur, for example, when an intruder's host creates TCP half-open connections by sending a flood of SYN packets with no corresponding ACK packets.[3]

- Packets with source and destination addresses external to your network. Your firewall should always be configured to prevent this. If it occurs, it may indicate that an intruder has bypassed the firewall, possibly by compromising the firewall host, and is routing his or her traffic through your network, perhaps to take advantage of a network-level trust relationship. It may also indicate the presence of an inside intruder.

- Packets with an internal source address that actually originate from an external source. This can indicate an IP spoofing attack that may have bypassed your firewall.

---

3. Refer to CERT advisories CA-2000-21, *Denial-of-Service Vulnerabilities in TCP/IP Stacks* and CA-1996-21, *TCP SYN Flooding and IP Spoofing Attacks*, available at *http://www.cert.org/advisories*.

- Unusual port combinations in TCP and UDP packets. This type of traffic could indicate an unexpected service running on the network (such as a backdoor program). It could also indicate that the intruder has bypassed your firewall. Packets with the same source address and a sequence of destination ports often indicate that an intruder is trying to discover both the firewall policy and what services are available on your systems.

- Unusual address resolution protocol (ARP) traffic. In a switched network, an intruder can alter the ARP cache on one or more hosts so that any host on the same segment can see traffic on that segment (similar to a network interface card in promiscuous mode on a shared Ethernet segment). The intruder can then gain access to passwords and other unencrypted information sent over the network.

- Unusual dynamic host configuration protocol/boot protocol (DHCP/BOOTP) traffic. An intruder can cause a host to send bogus DHCP replies and convince other hosts that it is their default gateway. The compromised host will then receive all of the traffic for outbound networks and gain access to unencrypted information sent over the network.

- Packets with unusual protocol or port numbers sent to broadcast addresses. This type of traffic can indicate a DoS attack.

- An unusually high number of ICMP port unreachable packets from a single host. This indicates that an intruder is scanning the host looking for available services.

- Connections made at unusual times

- Unusual use of Internet Relay Chat (IRC), a common means of communication used by intruders

If you are reviewing network traffic on a system other than the one being monitored, ensure that the connection between them is secure, as described in Section 2.13.

6.3.6 Policy Considerations

Your organization's networked systems security policy should specify the following:

- The need for users to be notified that you will monitor network activities
- Your objectives for monitoring
- Which data streams will be monitored and for what purposes
- The responsibilities and authority of system administrators for handling notifications generated by monitoring and logging software

- What forms of unexpected network behavior users should watch for and the need to report any such behavior to their designated security officials and system administrators

6.3.7 Additional Information

1. For further UNIX- and NT-specific network monitoring and network data collection guidance, refer to CERT tech tips at the CERT web site, including the *Intruder Detection Checklist* and *Steps for Recovering from a UNIX or NT System Compromise.* A list of network-monitoring tools is presented in Section 5.3.15, and Table 5.3.
2. When possible, analyze and correlate data collected from multiple sources (as described in the other practices of this chapter). Performing some level of correlation analysis during the intrusion detection process, such as determining when suspicious activity occurring in one part of your infrastructure may be related to suspicious activity in another part, will assist you in determining the full extent of any compromise and its characteristics. Refer to Section 7.2 for further guidance.

6.4 Monitor and Inspect System Activities

System activities include those associated with system performance, processes, and users. Programs executing on your networked systems typically include a variety of operating system and network services, user-initiated programs, and special-purpose applications such as database services. Every program executing on a system is represented by one or more processes. Each process executes with specific privileges that govern what system resources, programs, and data files it can access, and what it is permitted to do with them. The execution behavior of a process is demonstrated by the operations it performs while running, the manner in which those operations execute, and the system resources it uses while executing. Operations include computations; transactions with files, devices, and other processes; and communications with processes on other systems via your network. User activities include login/logout, authentication and other identification transactions, the processes they execute, and the files they access.

If you are reviewing system activities on a host other than the one being monitored, ensure that the connection between them is secure, as described in Section 2.13

You need to verify that your systems are behaving as expected and that the processes executing on your systems are attributed only to authorized activities by users, administrators, and system functions. Unexpected or anomalous system performance may indicate that an intruder is using the system covertly for unauthorized purposes. The intruder may be attempting to attack other systems within (or external to) your network, or running network sniffer programs. A process that exhibits unexpected behavior may indicate that an intrusion has occurred. Intruders may have disrupted the execution of a program or service, causing it either to fail or to operate in a way other than the user or administrator intended. For example, if intruders successfully disrupt the execution of access-control processes running on a firewall system, they may access your organization's internal network in ways that would normally be blocked by the firewall.

If you permit access to your systems and networks by third parties (vendors, contractors, suppliers, partners, customers, etc.), you must monitor their access to ensure that all their actions are authentic and authorized. This step includes monitoring and inspecting their system activities.

6.4.1 Notify Users

Inform authorized users of your systems about the scope and kinds of monitoring you will be doing and the consequences of unauthorized behavior.

A common method for communicating this message is to present a banner message immediately before user login, as described in Section 6.3.1.

Without the presentation of a banner message or other warning, you probably cannot use log files and other collected data in any action you may choose to take against a user.

6.4.2 Review System Alerts

Review and investigate notifications from system-specific alert mechanisms (such as e-mail, voice mail, or pager messages), including the following:

- Users and other administrators, via e-mail or in person
- Operating system alert mechanisms
- System management software traps
- Intrusion detection systems
- Custom alert mechanisms from service or application programs (including tools)

6.4.3 Review System Error Reports

These types of notifications are typically produced by the following devices:

- Operating system error-reporting mechanisms
- Log file filtering tools
- Vendor or custom-developed management software
- Custom error-reporting mechanisms from service or application programs (including tools)

Often an administrator will be able to configure error reporting at a number of criticality, severity, or priority levels when installing the system, service and application programs, and supporting tools.

6.4.4 Review System Performance Statistics

Statistics are generally produced by vendor or custom performance-monitoring tools. Typical statistics include the following (refer to Section 5.3, Table 5.2):

- Total resource use over time—CPU, memory (used, free), disk (used, free)
- Status reported by systems and hardware devices such as print queues
- Changes in system status, including shutdowns and restarts
- File system status (where mounted, free space by partition, open files, biggest file) over time and at specific times
- File system warnings (low free space, too many open files, file exceeding allocated size)
- Disk counters (input/output, queue lengths) over time and at specific times
- Hardware availability (modems, network interface cards, memory)
- Performance statistics meaningful for a specific server or host[4]
- Comparison of previous system performance statistics with current statistics

Unexpected shutdowns, reboots, and restarts can indicate the presence of a Trojan horse program that requires a shutdown or restart of a system or service.

Investigate anything that appears anomalous.

---

4. For example, for a web server, these statistics include pages accessed, connection statistics, user requests over time, which pages are most requested, and who is requesting the pages.

6.4.5 Monitor Process Activity and Behavior

The examination of processes is complex, time-consuming, and resource-intensive. The degree to which you are able to identify suspicious processes depends on your knowledge of what processes you normally expect to be executing on a given system and how they should behave.

Due to the large number of processes and their rapidly changing natures, it is impractical for you to monitor them continually yourself. In addition, the amount and value of information that you can gather from a snapshot of currently executing processes may be very limited. This means that you must employ a variety of information-gathering and monitoring mechanisms to help you collect and analyze data associated with processes, and to alert you to suspicious activity.

One common approach with multi-user systems is to set up consoles (or separate terminal windows on workstations) that display the current status of processes and are updated at short intervals. Ideally, these consoles should be hard-wired to the systems for which they are displaying information. With strategic placement of these displays, you can take advantage of the experience of system administrators to notice unexpected activity that may not be picked up by your more immediate alert mechanisms.

Identify any unexpected, unusual, or suspicious process behavior and the possible implications. As a general guideline, you should look for the following:

- Missing processes
- Extra processes
- Unusual process behavior or resource utilization
- Processes that have unusual user identification associated with them

Data from log files and other data collection mechanisms will help you to analyze the process behavior, for example (refer to Section 5.3, Table 5.2):

- User executing the process
- Process start-up time, arguments, file names
- Process exit status, time duration, resources consumed
- The amount of resources used (CPU, memory, disk, time) by specific processes over time; top "x" resource-consuming processes
- System and user processes and services executing at any given time
- The means by which each process is normally initiated (administrator, other users, other programs or processes), with what authorization and privileges
- Devices used by specific processes
- Files currently open by specific processes

Look for processes that are operating in one of the following ways:

- Running at unexpected times
- Terminating prematurely
- Consuming excessive resources (wall clock time, CPU time, memory, disk), which may warn you of an impending DoS condition or the use of a network sniffer
- Password cracking, network packet sniffing or any other process not due to normal, authorized activities
- Unusually formatted in their output or arguments (for example, on UNIX systems, a process running as `./telnetd` instead of `/usr/sbin/telnetd`)
- New, unexpected, or previously disabled, possibly indicating that intruders have installed their own version of a process or service or are running IRC services, web services, FTP services, and so forth to allow them to distribute tools and files they have stolen (such as password files) to other compromised hosts.
- Being spawned by inactive user accounts using CPU resources
- A terminal process exhibiting abnormal input/output behavior
- Without a controlling terminal and executing unusual programs
- Unusually large in number

Pay close attention to the processes associated with intrusion detection and other security tools. Intruders regularly compromise these tools to gain greater leverage and information and to generate decoy alerts to distract and waste the time of system administrators.

6.4.6 Monitor User Behavior

Identify any unexpected, unusual, or suspicious user behavior and the possible implications.

Data from log files and other data collection mechanisms will help you to analyze user behavior, for example (refer to Section 5.3, Table 5.2):

- Login/logout information (location, time): successful, failed attempts, attempted logins to privileged accounts
- Login/logout information on remote access servers that appears in modem logs
- Changes in user identity
- Changes in authentication status, such as enabling privileges

- Failed attempts to access restricted information (such as password files)
- Keystroke-monitoring logs
- Violations of user quotas

Look for the following types of intrusions and intrusion attempts:

- Repeated failed login attempts, including those to privileged accounts
- Logins from unusual locations or at unusual times, including unusual or unauthorized attempts to log in via a remote access server
- Unusual attempts to change user identity
- Unusual processes run by users
- Unusual file accesses, including unauthorized attempts to access restricted files
- Users logged in for an abnormal length of time (both short and long)
- A user executing an unexpected command
- A user working from an unusual terminal

If you notice unusual activity associated with particular users, initiate supplemental data collection mechanisms to gather detailed information about their activities. Many multiuser systems provide mechanisms to audit all processes associated with a particular user. Since process accounting logs tend to generate a great deal of information rapidly, you will need to allocate sufficient resources to store the data collected. Similarly, detailed network logging of all activity associated with all the systems accessed by a specific user can be voluminous, and you will need to allocate resources accordingly. Review the newly collected data often (at least daily) and rotate files regularly to minimize the amount of information that you have to analyze at any given time (as described in Section 5.4).

6.4.7 Monitor for the Presence of Network Sniffers

One thing intruders commonly do is to gather information from the traffic on your networks to find user account names, passwords, and other information that may facilitate their ability to gain access to your systems. They do this by breaking into one system on your network and installing and executing a sniffer program. This program collects information about connections established between systems from network data packets as they arrive at or pass by the compromised system. To hide this illicit activity on compromised systems, intruders typically modify log files and replace programs that would reveal the presence of the sniffer program with Trojan horse versions. The substitute programs appear to perform the same functions but exclude information associated with the intruders and their activities. In many documented cases of this type of intrusion, the intruders' activities went unnoticed for a considerable amount of time, during which they collected enough information to gain privileged access to several other systems.

Detecting the presence of distributed network sniffers may not be possible. Some operating systems (but not all, or even most) respond differently to an ICMP echo request when the interface is in promiscuous mode than when it is not, thus providing some indication that something is amiss. Even when this indication is present, however, the computer is under intruder control and will behave as the intruder directs. Without sophisticated analog electronic signaling techniques, it's probably impossible to detect a distributed sniffer externally.

This reality underscores the importance of using verified software to examine your systems (as described in Section 6.2) and the need to verify the integrity of your files (as described in Section 6.5). Unfortunately, intruders can use several sophisticated collections of programs to gain rapid access to systems and "set up shop" to install and execute a sniffer. In such cases the only way you may be able to catch such activity is to use verified software to examine processes on your systems for unexpected behavior (as described in Section 6.4), although this method is not effective against kernel modifications.

Processes associated with a sniffer will typically have transactions with a network interface that has been placed in promiscuous mode, as well as a file or network connection to which the information gathered from network packets is being sent. However, keep in mind that legitimate network monitors and protocol analyzers will set a network interface in promiscuous mode as well.

> Network interfaces on most systems normally operate in nonpromiscuous mode, which means that they ignore network packets not explicitly addressed to them. In promiscuous mode, no packets are ignored, that is, all packets that traverse the network segment to which the system is attached are read by its network interface and are accessible to processes executing on that system.

Refer to CERT advisory CA-1994.01, *Ongoing Network Monitoring Attacks,* at the CERT web site.

6.4.8 Run Network Mapping and Scanning Tools

The purpose of running network mapping and scanning tools is to understand what intruders who use such tools can learn about your networks and systems. We recommend carrying out this task periodically during nonbusiness hours and when you are physically present, because mapping tools can sometimes affect systems in unexpected ways. Eliminate or make invisible (if possible) any aspect of your network topology and system characteristics that you do not want to be known by intruders who use mapping tools.

6.4.9 Run Vulnerability Scanning Tools on All Systems

The purpose of running vulnerability scanning tools on all systems is to check for the presence of known vulnerabilities. We recommend running such tools periodically during nonbusiness hours and when you are physically present, because scanning tools can sometimes affect systems in unexpected ways. Eliminate all vulnerabilities identified by these tools wherever possible. Many of these can be dealt with by updating configuration file settings and installing vendor-provided patches as described in Section 2.4.

Consider using scanning tools that include password analysis as part of their vulnerability assessment. Such analysis may include the identification of weak, nonexistent, or otherwise flawed passwords, such as those that can be determined using brute force or dictionary-based attacks.

Refer to CERT vulnerability notes at the CERT web site and *How to Eliminate the Ten Most Critical Internet Security Threats: The Experts' Consensus, Version 1.25* (SANS 00) for a description of some of the more prevalent vulnerabilities.

6.4.10 Policy Considerations

Your organization's networked systems security policy should specify the following:

- The need for users to be notified that process and user activities will be monitored and state the objective of such monitoring
- The responsibilities and authority of designated systems administrators and security personnel to examine systems, processes, and user activity for unexpected behavior

- What forms of unexpected behavior users should watch for and require users to report any such behavior to their designated security officials and system administrators.

- What software and data users and administrators are permitted to install, collect, and use, with explicit procedures and conditions for doing so

- What programs users and administrators are permitted to execute and under what conditions

6.4.11 Additional Information

1. If you are reviewing system activities on a host other than the one being monitored, ensure that the connection between them is secure, as described in Section 2.13.

2. Whenever possible, analyze and correlate data collected from multiple sources, as recommended in the other practices of this chapter. Performing some level of correlation analysis during the intrusion detection process, such as determining when intrusion activity occurring in one part of your systems may be related to activity in another part, will assist you in determining the full extent of any compromise and its characteristics as described in Section 7.2.

3. Logging information produced by vulnerability patches (updated software that corrects or closes a vulnerability), if provided by the vendor and if turned on, can help identify a pattern in which an intruder exploits more than one vulnerability before gaining access. For example, a failed logged attempt to probe for an old vulnerability (produced by the vulnerability patch) could be followed by a successful probe for a new vulnerability that is not logged. The presence of the vulnerability patch logging information, along with other mechanisms such as integrity checking, could alert you to this type of intruder action.

6.5 Inspect Files and Directories for Unexpected Changes

The file systems in your network environment contain a variety of software and data files. Unexpected changes in directories and files, especially those to which access is normally restricted, may indicate an intrusion. Changes could include modifying, creating, or deleting directories and files. What makes such changes unexpected may depend on who changed them and where, when, and how the changes were made.

Private data files and files containing mission-critical information are common targets of modification or corruption by intruders. Information about your organization that is accessible to the public or to subscribers via public networks and the Internet is also a common target. Numerous documented cases exist of prominent organizations that have had their web sites modified to include offensive content and other erroneous information.

Intruders often create, substitute, modify, and damage files on systems to which they have gained access, as described in Section 6.2 Introduction. Intruders may create new files on your systems. For example, they may install backdoor programs or tools used to gain privileged access on the system. Intruders may make use of the disk space on compromised systems to store their tools and other artifacts.

If you permit access to your systems and networks by third parties (vendors, contractors, suppliers, partners, customers, etc.), it is critical that you actively monitor their access to your systems and networks as well as any processing they do. This precaution helps ensure that all actions are authentic and authorized. Monitoring access includes examining all relevant directories and files.

6.5.1 Verify Integrity

Examine the directories and files on your system and prioritize how frequently you should check them. The more mission- or security-critical the file, the more frequently you should check it.

We recommend checking at least daily, perhaps at the start of the business day, to cover all processing done during the preceding 24 hours.

Compare the attributes and contents of files and directories to the authoritative reference (either complete copies or cryptographic checksums). Identify any files and directories whose contents or other attributes have changed, as described in Section 5.3.

Always access authoritative reference data directly from its secured, read-only media. Never transmit authoritative reference data over unsecured network connections unless you use mechanisms such as digital signatures and cryptographic checksums to verify data integrity.

6.5.2 Identify Unexpected Changes and Their Implications

Data from log files and other data collection mechanisms will help you to analyze changes to files and directories. These include the following (refer to Section 5.3, Table 5.2):

- Cryptographic checksums for all files and directories
- Lists of files, directories, attributes
- Accesses (open, create, modify, execute, delete), time, date
- Changes to sizes, contents, protections, types, locations
- Additions and deletions of files and directories
- Results of virus scanners

Also look for the following extraordinary occurrences:

- Unexpected file or directory access, creation, or deletion.
- Unexpected changes to file or directory protections or access control lists. Identifying these can aid, for example, in detecting the creation of files in user home directories that can be later used for backdoor access. Improperly set access control lists on system tools may indicate that an intruder has located and executed security tools that were installed by the authorized system administrator.
- Unexpected changes to file or directory sizes, contents, and other attributes. These may signify that a file or service has been replaced with the intruder's version, including the installation of a Trojan horse or backdoor. An intruder inadvertently enabling debugging can easily quadruple the size of a file.
- Unexpected changes to password files, such as unauthorized creation of new accounts and accounts with no passwords.
- Unexpected changes to system configuration files and other restricted and sensitive information, including firewall-filtering rules.
- Unusual or unexpected open files. These can reveal the presence of sniffer logs or programs.
- Violations of log file consistency (unexpected changes in file size, gaps in time between log records).
- The presence of viruses, backdoors, and Trojan horses detected by scanning tools, as described in Section 2.12.

Intruders can use compromised systems that support a promiscuous network interface to collect host and user authentication information that is visible on the network.

Sniffers are able to capture user keystrokes containing host, account, and password information. The presence of some sniffers can be detected by looking for Trojan horse programs, suspect processes, and unexpected modifications to files. See the discussion on network sniffers in Section 6.4.7.

6.5.3 Policy Considerations

Your organization's networked systems security policy should establish the following guidelines:

- Users should be notified that files and directories will be examined, and informed of the objective of such examinations.
- The responsibilities and authority of designated systems administrators and security personnel to examine files and directories on a regular basis for unexpected changes should be specified.
- Users should report any unexpected changes to their software and data files to system administrators or your organization's designated security point of contact.

6.5.4 Additional information

1. Some types of important files, such as log files and database tables, are expected to change frequently (perhaps several times per second). In general, the techniques described above will not be useful in distinguishing normal changes to these file types from those that might have been caused by intruders. Techniques based on transaction auditing are more useful in these cases.
2. As noted in Sections 6.3 and 6.4, whenever possible you should analyze and correlate data collected from multiple sources, as described in the other practices of this chapter. Refer to Section 7.2.

6.6 Investigate Unauthorized Hardware Attached to the Network

Unauthorized hardware may include computers connected to network segments or hubs and peripheral communication or input/output equipment such as modems, terminals, printers, and disk or tape drives.

Intruders actively attempt to circumvent network perimeter defenses. If they can gain physical access to your organization's internal network, they can install their own equipment and software. Alternatively, intruders may learn of insecure (unauthorized) equipment added by users that they can use to gain access to your organization's network. For example, users might install modems for the purpose of remote access to their office computers from home. Intruders often use automated tools to identify modems attached to public telephone lines. If the configuration of the dial-up access and the traffic through it is not secured, intruders may use such back doors to gain access to the internal network, bypassing preventive measures that may have been put in place to restrict external connections to your organization's network. They may then capture network traffic, infiltrate other systems, disrupt operations, and steal sensitive, private information.

Access to other peripheral equipment may also facilitate intrusions. Unsecured output and removable media devices, such as printers and disk drives, may give intruders the opportunity to generate copies of sensitive information that can be physically removed from your organization's premises.

In addition to periodically inspecting hardware as recommended below, you may need to conduct inspections in response to suspected intrusions. Watch for evidence of activities that indicate unusual access to your network, as described in Section 6.3.

6.6.1 Audit All Systems and Peripherals Attached to the Network Infrastructure

Periodic (for example, monthly) visits to physically examine equipment attached to the network should not be announced, so that unauthorized equipment cannot be hidden before the auditors arrive.

Using your documented hardware inventory, described in Section 5.3.12, identify any hardware that is missing, not in its designated location, unexpected, or extra.

6.6.2 Probe for Unauthorized Modems

Conduct a daily probe for unauthorized modems attached to your organization's telephone lines. You can do this using daemon dialer tools.[5] Because this process causes all dialed telephones to ring, we recommend that it be done outside normal working hours. However, even this approach will cause telephones that have been forwarded to ring.

---

5. Refer to the article "Sweeping Changes for Modem Security" (King 00) at *http://www.infosecuritymag. com/articles/june00/features1.shtml.*

6.6.3 Probe All Internal Network Segments to Identify Unauthorized Hardware

Examine daily (1) unauthorized devices attached to your network, (2) any new or unexpected IP or MAC addresses, and (3) any new or unexpected network ports on switches.

You can do this using public domain tools such as ARPWATCH[6] and a variety of commercial network management software packages.

Identify any hardware that is missing, not in its designated location, unexpected, or extra.

6.6.4 Look for Unexpected Routes Between the Organization's Network and External Networks

Daily, examine the network traffic logs for connections that originate outside your network and are destined for addresses outside your network. Traffic that moves in this way could indicate that an unauthorized computer is connecting to one of your hosts.

If possible, compare the network traffic logs from individual hosts/workstations with network traffic logs from the firewall host(s). Discrepancies or mismatches could indicate that traffic is being routed through unsecured connections or gateways directly to the individual host, bypassing your organization's firewalled Internet connection.

6.6.5 Policy Considerations

Your organization's networked systems security policy should do the following:

- Require the maintenance of documented hardware inventories
- Require the maintenance of a documented network topology
- Specify the authority and responsibility of designated security personnel to (1) perform physical audits of installed hardware and software and (2) establish network connections and routes
- Specify what kinds of hardware and software users are permitted to install on their workstations

---

6. Available at *ftp://ftp.ee.lbl.gov/*. ARPWATCH is only effective for hosts attached to your local area network, as external hosts are represented by your router/firewall.

6.7 Look for Signs of Unauthorized Access to Physical Resources

Although we tend to think of the information in networked computer systems as being in electronic form, we should remember that this information is held on physical media—CD-ROMs, tapes, disks, paper—that are subject to physical compromise by theft, destruction, corruption, or unauthorized duplication. To ensure the security of your network, you should also ensure the physical security of its components by periodically inspecting them for possible compromise.

In many organizations, designated personnel are responsible for the physical security of the premises. However, as a system or network administrator, you are often in a unique position to notice signs of physical access to system resources.

If a document or electronic storage medium is stolen, the confidentiality and availability of the information it contains is lost. Even if the item is recovered, you won't know the extent to which its contents have been copied and disseminated. Also, you won't know whether the information it contains has been corrupted or altered. Furthermore, if the compromised information is critical to security (e.g., user passwords, internal network addresses, or system configuration data), your entire network is potentially threatened by more damaging intrusions.

Therefore, it is just as important for you to keep track of physical resources and to promptly detect attempts at physical intrusion and access as it is for you to track and protect your electronic resources.

You may want to consider encrypting all backup and other selected electronic media in the event that your site, an offsite data storage site, or a disaster recovery site is physically compromised.

6.7.1 Check All Physical Means of Entrance or Exit

Perform this check daily, looking for signs of tampering, trespassing, or attempted trespassing. Keep in mind that intruders have many strategies for obtaining confidential or security-critical documents. For example, they may steal discarded copies of reports, console logs, system printouts, or other sensitive data. They search through trash containers or Dumpsters to find carelessly discarded physical copies. They may also attempt to steal backup or archive tapes, whose disappearance may not be noticed for some time.

6.7.2 Check Physical Resources for Signs of Tampering

Perform this check daily. For example, inspect locks or seals on hardware cabinets, review console logs, and monitor paper usage.

6.7.3 Perform a Physical Audit of All Movable Media

We recommend performing an audit weekly if possible. Ensure that write-disabled media continue to be so. Note that, as a complementary practice, you should also audit the contents of the media for electronic integrity.

6.7.4 Report All Signs of Unauthorized Physical Access

Report signs of unauthorized physical access to your organization's internal security point of contact. Such intrusion includes access to offsite data storage and disaster recovery sites.

6.7.5 Policy Considerations

Your organization's networked systems security policy should require the tagging and inventory of all physical computing resources as described in Section 5.3.12, and should specify how to respond when a physical intrusion has been detected

6.8 Review Reports of Suspicious System and Network Behavior and Events

In security-conscious organizations, users will report suspicious events and behaviors. As a system or network administrator, you should use those reports, along with information you gather, to help identify possible intrusions. When appropriate, you should also use external sources of information, such as reports from incident response teams, to help you decide whether or not you need to augment your monitoring and incident analysis efforts. Potential sources are listed in Chapter 1.

Recruiting users and external contacts to assist you in security monitoring greatly extends your ability to detect intrusions, potentially enabling you to detect intrusions of which you were previously unaware. Not only does this step increase the number of people alert to possible intrusions, but these individuals can often be more aware of the "normal" behavior of their personal computing environments than you are. Many intrusions are not discovered until someone with day-to-day experience using a particular system notices something unusual. Users are susceptible to intruder-initiated social engineering attempts (for example, to obtain passwords or to gain physical access) and need to understand how to identify and report these.

Intruders often compromise multiple systems when they attack a target site. At each compromised system, there may be telltale signs of intrusive activities that users of the system discover. Although a single user report may not be sufficient evidence of an intrusion, analysis of several reports may reveal a pattern of attack under way. By consolidating users' reports of suspicious system behaviors, you may also be able to determine the extent of the attacks against your networked systems.

Administrators from other organizations may contact you if they have reason to believe that an intrusion into their systems may involve or affect your organization. Always thoroughly investigate any reports you receive from incident response teams, such as the CERT/CC, to determine if an intrusion has in fact occurred at your site. If your network environment supports connections to external networks, it is possible that your systems may have been compromised and are serving as unwitting participants in a large-scale attack (such as a distributed DoS attack[7]) against several sites.

6.8.1 Perform "Triage" upon Receipt of a Report

Immediately gather as much information as necessary to make an initial assessment of whether there has been a probable intrusion and if so how severe it seems to be. You may need to make direct contact with the user to get a description of what was observed. Also acquire any records or data from logging, monitoring, or other data collection mechanisms that illustrate the problem. If the information clearly indicates an intrusion attempt, investigate it immediately.

---

7. Refer to CERT advisories on this subject at the CERT web site.

A report should include the following information:

- Contact information for the individuals discovering the problem and any responsible parties involved (such as the system administrator)
- Target systems and networks and all of their characteristics, such as operating system versions and IP addresses
- The purpose of the systems under attack, including the types of services and applications they provide, as well as an indication of the importance or criticality of the system
- Any evidence of intrusion, including methods of attacks used, vulnerability exploited, source IP address of attacker, and network contact information for this address
- A list of parties to notify, such as legal, other technical, management, and public relations

Refer also to the CERT tech tip *Incident Reporting Guidelines* at the CERT web site.

6.8.2 Evaluate, Correlate, and Prioritize Each Report

On a regular basis (daily, if possible), review all user and external reports. These include new reports, reports currently under investigation, and any reports that remain unresolved after investigation. Look for correlations or patterns among the reports. Prioritize and schedule investigations of all reports based on your assessment of their severity. If the suspicion proves unfounded, close the report and provide feedback to the user who reported the problem.

6.8.3 Investigate Each Report or Set of Related Reports

Based on the nature of the report, you may need to contact other users to document their observations. You may also need to verify the integrity of directories and files (as described in Section 6.5), examine your system and network logs (as described in

Sections 6.3 and 6.4), examine processes on affected systems (as described in Section 6.4), and install additional monitoring mechanisms to identify the cause of the anomalous behavior.

Document and report your findings. Regardless of the outcome of your investigation, record your findings and report them to the users who submitted the reports, the system and network administrators, the security personnel in your organization, and other appropriate individuals as specified in your organization's policies.

6.8.4 Policy Considerations

Your organization's networked systems security policy should establish the following guidelines:

- Users should immediately report any unexpected or suspicious system behavior to their designated security official and system administrator.

- Users should immediately report any physical intrusions to networked systems or offline data storage facilities to their designated security official and system administrator.

- System administrators should investigate each reported suspicious activity to determine whether it represents an intrusion.

- System administrators should notify users in advance of any changes that will be made to the systems they use, including software configurations, data storage and access, and revised procedures for using systems as a result of the changes.

6.9 Take Appropriate Actions

Upon discovering unauthorized, unexpected, or suspicious activity, you may need to (1) initiate your intrusion response procedures as described in Chapter 7 and (2) determine if the activity should be reflected in your characterization baseline, alerting, or other data collection mechanisms. Refer to Section 5.3 for information on developing a characterization baseline.

Identifying unauthorized or suspicious activities and then not taking appropriate follow-up actions will perpetuate any damage or other negative consequences. These consequences include possible loss of integrity, availability, or data confidentiality, as well as legal liability. In addition, these activities are likely to recur, placing your systems at considerable risk in the future.

6.9.1 Document Any Unusual Behavior or Activity That You Discover

Over time, you may see recurring kinds of unusual or suspicious activity. Maintaining records of these activities and noting your conclusion on their causes will help you and others to understand new occurrences more quickly and accurately.

For example, in *Network Intrusion Detection* Northcutt (99) writes:

> To detect and classify a coordinated attack (one coming from or going to multiple locations), it helps to have a database of all traffic and techniques to complement your signatures (of known attacks). Without a database of traffic that covers a time window of at least a couple months, there is no way to determine whether this activity [that you are now investigating] has been going on and simply hasn't been detected, or whether it is a new pattern. (p. 171)

Northcutt also recommends creating a directory to store data traces. The data traces can be examined when investigating an unknown attack pattern.

6.9.2 Investigate Each Documented Anomaly

Ask yourself the following questions:

- Is the apparent anomaly the result of a legitimate new or updated characteristic of your system? (e.g., the unexpected process is executing a recently added administrative tool)

- Can the anomaly be explained by the activities of an authorized user? (e.g., the user really was in Cairo last week and connected to the network; a legitimate user made a mistake)

- Can the anomaly be explained by known system activity? (e.g., there was a power outage that caused the system to reboot)

- Can the anomaly be explained by authorized changes to programs? (e.g., the mail log showed abnormal behavior because the system programmer made a mistake when the software was modified)

- Did someone attempt to break into your system and fail?

- Did someone break in successfully? Do you have the data that will tell you what he or she did?

6.9.3 Recognize the Iterative Nature of Analysis and Investigation

Often, you will observe an initial indication of suspicious behavior but will not have sufficient information to determine what occurred. In such cases you can take a number of steps:

- Look for past occurrences of similar behavior and study the results of that investigation.
- Formulate and ask different questions to better identify what data will best reveal what happened.
- Modify the configuration of selected data collection mechanisms to collect additional data or better filter and select from existing data (refer to Section 5.3 for further guidance).
- Add new data collection mechanisms.

6.9.4 Initiate Your Intrusion Response Procedures

If any activity or event cannot be attributed to authorized or explicable activity, initiate your intrusion response procedures immediately, as described in Chapter 7. Report such occurrences to your organization's designated security point of contact.

6.9.5 Update the Configuration of Alert Mechanisms

Updating the configuration of alert mechanisms is warranted if a previous event notification that occurred via logs, error reports, statistics reports, or another data collection mechanism is now of a sufficiently high priority.

The reverse is also true. An event that is reported as an alert all of the time may become less important and need to be changed to be captured as an error report.

6.9.6 Update All Characterization Information

Refer to Section 5.3 for a definition of typical characterization information. You need to reflect on what you learn from reviewing any unusual activity or event. This is important in four situations:

1. An unusual activity occurs frequently enough for you to consider it normal and expected, so that you should add it to an asset's characterization baseline.

2. A new activity has occurred and needs to be added to an asset's characterization baseline.

3. A previously normal or expected activity now needs to be considered suspicious or unexpected.

4. A previously normal or expected activity should be dropped from consideration for analysis altogether.

6.9.7 Update Logging and Data Collection Mechanism Configurations

Updating logging and data collection mechanism configurations is necessary to reflect information on new attack methods. Refer to Sections 5.3 (logging and data collection mechanisms) and Chapter 1 (information sources on new attack methods) for further guidance.

6.9.8 Dispose of Every Reported Event

You must somehow dispose of every reported event, either by resolution and closure, by deciding not to pursue it further unless it becomes more critical, or by taking no immediate action but preserving the event to see if it recurs or contributes to a pattern.

6.9.9 Policy Considerations

Your organization's networked systems security policy should do the following:

-   Specify the actions to be taken following the discovery of unexpected, unusual, or suspicious activity

-   Require the actions prescribed to be actually performed

-   Specify the responsibilities and authority of designated systems administrators and security personnel to take the prescribed actions

Chapter 6 Checklist

Practice	Step Number	Step Description	Yes	Partial	No
P6.2: Ensure That the Software Used to Examine Systems Has Not Been Compromised	S6.2.1	Policy considerations			
P6.3: Monitor and Inspect Network Activities	S6.3.1	Notify users			
	S6.3.2	Review network alerts			
	S6.3.3	Review network error reports			
	S6.3.4	Review network performance			
	S6.3.5	Review network traffic			
	S6.3.6	Policy considerations			
P6.4: Monitor and Inspect System Activities	S6.4.1	Notify users			
	S6.4.2	Review system alerts			
	S6.4.3	Review system error reports			
	S6.4.4	Review system performance statistics			
	S6.4.5	Monitor process activity and behavior			
	S6.4.6	Monitor user behavior			

(continued)

Chapter 6 Checklist (*cont.*)

Practice	Step Number	Step Description	Yes	Partial	No
	S6.4.7	Monitor for the presence of network sniffers			
	S6.4.8	Run network mapping and scanning tools			
	S6.4.9	Run vulnerability scanning tools on all systems			
	S6.4.10	Policy considerations			
P6.5: Inspect Files and Directories for Unexpected Changes	S6.5.1	Verify integrity			
	S6.5.2	Identify unexpected changes and their implications			
	S6.5.3	Policy considerations			
P6.6: Investigate Unauthorized Hardware Attached to the Network	S6.6.1	Audit all systems and peripherals attached to the network infrastructure			
	S6.6.2	Probe for unauthorized modems			
	S6.6.3	Probe all internal network segments to identify unauthorized hardware			
	S6.6.4	Look for unexpected routes between the organization's network and external networks			
	S6.6.5	Policy considerations			

Practice	Step Number	Step Description	Yes	Partial	No
P6.7: Look for Signs of Unauthorized Access to Physical Resources	S6.7.1	Check all physical means of entrance or exit			
	S6.7.2	Check physical resources for signs of tampering			
	S6.7.3	Perform a physical audit of all movable media			
	S6.7.4	Report all signs of unauthorized physical access			
	S6.7.5	Policy considerations			
P6.8: Review Reports of Suspicious System and Network Behavior and Events	S6.8.1	Perform "triage" upon receipt of a report			
	S6.8.2	Evaluate, correlate, and prioritize each report			
	S6.8.3	Investigate each report or set of related reports			
	S6.8.4	Policy considerations			
P6.9: Take Appropriate Actions	S6.9.1	Document any unusual behavior or activity that you discover			
	S6.9.2	Investigate each documented anomaly			

(continued)

Chapter 6   Checklist (*cont.*)

Practice	Step Number	Step Description	Yes	Partial	No
	S6.9.3	Recognize the iterative nature of analysis and investigation			
	S6.9.4	Initiate your intrusion response procedures			
	S6.9.5	Update the configuration of alert mechanisms			
	S6.9.6	Update all characterization information			
	S6.9.7	Update logging and data collection mechanisms configurations			
	S6.9.8	Dispose of every reported event			
	S6.9.9	Policy considerations			

Chapter 7

Responding to Intrusions

Most organizations are not adequately prepared to respond to intrusions. They are likely to address the need to respond only after a breach occurs. The result is that when an intrusion is detected, many decisions are made in haste and can reduce an organization's ability to do the following:

- Understand the extent and source of an intrusion
- Protect sensitive data contained on systems
- Protect the systems, the networks, and their ability to continue operating as intended
- Collect information to gain a better understanding of what happened, without which actions may inadvertently be taken that can further damage your systems
- Return systems to normal operation
- Support legal investigations

Even if you have sophisticated prevention measures in place, intrusions can happen. In this chapter, we describe practices to be implemented independent of the size, type, or severity of an intrusion or of the methods used to gain access. The significant event is that an intruder has gained unauthorized access to your systems or data and this access has been detected.

7.1 Overview

These practices are intended primarily for system and network administrators, managers of information systems, and security personnel responsible for networked information resources.

They are applicable to your organization if your networked systems infrastructure includes any of the following items:

- Host systems providing services to multiple users (file servers, time-sharing systems, database servers, Internet servers, etc.)

- Local area or wide area networks

- Direct connections, gateways, or modem access to and from external networks, such as the Internet

We recommend that you read all of the practices in this chapter before taking any action. To implement the practices successfully, it is important that you understand the overall context and relationships among them.

In addition, once you read the practices in the Handle category (see Table 7.1), it is easier to understand the response preparation practices described in Section 5.5. If you are currently dealing with an intrusion, you may want to skip the preparation practices and move immediately to Section 7.2 Analyze all available information. Once you have taken necessary response steps, we recommend that you review and implement the preparation practices (Section 5.5).

7.1.1 The Need to Respond to Intrusions

You will not know what to do in the event of an intrusion if the necessary response procedures, roles, and responsibilities have not been *defined and exercised in advance*. The absence of systematic and well-defined procedures can lead to the following consequences:

- Extensive damage to data, systems, and networks due to failure to take timely action to contain an intrusion, resulting in increased costs, loss of productivity, and loss of business

- The possibility of an intrusion affecting multiple systems both inside and outside your organization because staff did not know whom else to notify and what additional actions to take

- Negative exposure in the news media that can damage your organization's stature and reputation with your shareholders, your customers, and the community at large

- Possible legal liability and prosecution for failure to exercise an adequate standard of due care when your systems are inadvertently or intentionally used to attack others

7.1.2 An Approach for Responding to Intrusions

The order in which response practice steps are to be executed and the time relationships among practices are shown in Figure 7.1. An intrusion occurs at time "T1," and the response process is complete at time "Tn." Practice titles are abbreviated in this description. The full titles can be found in Table 7.1.

The steps in the Policies (Section 5.2) and Select Tools (Section 5.5) practices help you prepare to respond to an intrusion. Ideally, you should implement them prior to exposing your networks and systems to intruders. You can implement them any time during or after executing response procedures, except when the compromised status of systems involved in an intrusion prevents you from taking recommended preparatory steps. You should examine and exercise the steps called out in these two practices on an ongoing basis, as tools, methods, policies, and procedures change.

At time T1, you need to execute the steps in the Analyze practice (Section 7.2). Once some initial analysis is completed, you then execute the steps in the Communicate (Section 7.3) and Collect and Protect (Section 7.4) practices. From this point on (T2), the steps in the Analyze, Communicate, and Collect and Protect practices occur throughout the process and should be executed in parallel as events dictate.

Execute the steps in the Contain practice (Section 7.5) after initial analysis is complete and then iteratively reexamine the steps in the Contain practice coincident with executing the steps in the Analyze practice. In other words, every insight gained through analysis may cause you to take a different containment step or alter what you did previously. Execute the steps in the Eliminate practice (Section 7.6) after the first round of containment actions occur. Then iteratively reexamine the steps in the Eliminate practice coincident with taking further Analyze and Contain actions, for the reasons stated above.

Ideally, you perform the steps in the Return practice (Section 7.7) after the Eliminate steps are complete. And the steps in the Lessons practice (Section 7.8) should take place shortly after returning your systems to normal operation.

To reflect this set of practice relationships, we group practices into two categories as shown in Table 7.1:

1. Handling an intrusion
2. Taking necessary follow-up steps to ensure that your security practices are improved. This will result in a more secure operational environment that is based on what you learned as you responded to an intrusion.

Table 7.1   Responding to Intrusions Practice Summary

Approach	Practice	Reference
Handle	Analyze All Available Information	Section 7.2; page 273
	Communicate with Relevant Parties	Section 7.3; page 278
	Collect and Protect Information	Section 7.4; page 282
	Contain an Intrusion	Section 7.5; page 285
	Eliminate All Means of Intruder Access	Section 7.6; page 289
	Return Systems to Normal Operation	Section 7.7; page 293
Improving	Implement Lessons Learned	Section 7.8; page 296

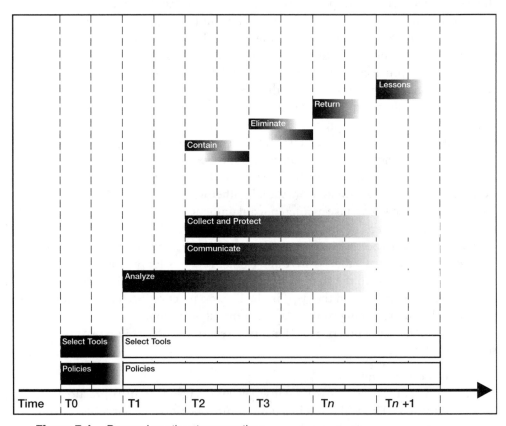

Figure 7.1   Respond practice steps over time

7.2 Analyze All Available Information

Once you have been alerted by your intrusion detection mechanisms or another trusted site that an intrusion has been detected, you first need to determine to what extent your systems and data have been compromised and then take action. Information, as collected and interpreted through analysis, is key to your decisions and actions while executing response procedures.

The purpose of analysis is to obtain the following information:

- What attacks were used to gain access
- What systems and data were accessed by an intruder
- What an intruder did after obtaining access
- What an intruder is currently doing when an intrusion has not been contained or eliminated

Other organizations may notify you that they have found evidence (such as a log file produced by an intruder tool that shows all successful connections) that your systems have been attacked from their systems, or that they have detected attacks on their systems originating from your systems. You may also receive such a report from a response team that coordinates the response effort of affected sites.

During the analysis, you may be tempted to actively collect additional information about the systems an intruder used to attack your systems. Such attempts can alert an intruder to your activities, however. In the event that the attacking system belongs to another organization, active data collection may itself be interpreted as intruder activity.

Therefore, the value of collecting as much information as possible needs to be balanced against the possible risk of intruders recognizing that their activities have been detected. Some intruders may panic and attempt to delete all traces of their activities, further damaging the systems you are trying to save. Others may not return, in which case any follow-up information you planned to collect the next time they entered your system will no longer be obtainable.

In order to deal with an intrusion effectively, you need to determine its scope and impact and prioritize your intended actions. You can do this only when you have analyzed all available information. For example, your actions may depend on the level of access an intruder gained and the extent of your confidence that your analysis of the intruder's access level is correct.

This practice assumes you have previously performed the steps identified in Chapters 5 and 6.

7.2.1 Capture and Record System Information

Capture and record system information that may be lost or not captured during the execution of your backup procedure, including the following:

- All current network connections
- All current processes
- Active users currently logged on
- All open files (files may be deleted if a process exits when the network is disconnected)
- Any other volatile data that would be lost, such as memory or cache

7.2.2 Back Up the Compromised Systems

Make at least two full backups of the system or systems that have been identified as compromised, as well as the user data on those systems. Do so using hardware-write-protectable or write-once media.

Preserve the backup media in a secure location. They may be reinstalled on other test systems for further analysis, and the data may be used for system recovery.

To protect the backup as evidence, preserve the second backup media in a secure location and preserve the chain of custody (as described in Section 7.4). Do not use this copy for any operational task.

In specific instances or for critical environments, the backups are used to reinstall the compromised system on other hosts and hard drives, while the original hosts and hard drives are preserved as evidence. This approach preserves the original environment most accurately, even though it may alert an intruder and require significant hardware resources.

Be aware of the following and plan accordingly:

- Unusually high levels of disk activity that occur during backups may alert an intruder.
- An intruder may have installed a Trojan horse that will delete log files. An example of this is modification of the system backup program so that if it cannot ping a router when it (the backup program) is executing, it destroys the disk. If you take the system offline and try to back it up, all logs may be lost. Refer to Section 7.6 for suggested ways to deal with this situation.

7.2.3 Isolate the Compromised Systems

You can isolate the compromised systems by taking one of the following actions:

- Transferring the backup files to a test system that is isolated from your operational systems and restoring the compromised system(s) on the test system
- Disconnecting the compromised systems and performing analysis on those systems directly, keeping in mind that this will destroy the original source of information

See also Section 6.2 for further details on alternatives for examining compromised systems.

7.2.4 Search on Other Systems for Signs of Intrusion

Intruders regularly establish more entry points into a network once they have gained initial access. Whenever an attack or an intrusion is detected, you need to check all other systems that are "similar" to the system that was accessed.

"Similar" can have various meanings depending on your operational environment. It can refer to any of the following:

- Systems that are in the same IP address range or are on the same network segment. Intruders perform scans across large ranges of IP addresses to locate security vulnerabilities.
- Systems that are in the same "trusted" domain. These systems provide access to users from other systems within the same domain without further authentication.
- Systems that have at least one network service in common. Intruders often check for well-known services such as DNS, FTP, HTTP, and SMTP.
- Systems that have the same operating system.
- Systems that share the same file system by providing file system space to any compromised system or using file system space from any compromised system.

7.2.5 Examine Logs

Attacks often leave trace information that can lead the analyst to the system that was used (or abused) by an intruder. Such traces include log and audit files, files left behind by an intruder, or information about the use of servers and services on other systems used in moving through the network. This trace information can be used to search for other events or connections originating from that system that were previously unnoticed. In this way, you can identify other systems to which an intruder gained access.

Firewall, network monitor, and router logs often remain intact and contain valuable information—even if an intruder gains local access, manages to get administrator privileges, and deletes the local system logs to hide the information about the attack method, the intrusion itself, and the access methods used. These programs and devices, if properly configured, record connections and message traffic generated by an intruder. The logs that they each produce may reveal intruder activity. For example, firewall log files can be configured to store information about the source of any message, its destination, and characteristics of connections such as the amount of data transferred.

Using information from the previous step (including date, time, and systems attacked), you can locate related records in these logs that reveal more detailed information about an intrusion or information missed altogether. Look for similar connections, including connections coming from the same source or going to the same destination.

Building a complete picture can be a tedious task. Log formats of many systems are not compatible, and no general-purpose tools currently exist that chronologically synchronize logs produced by multiple systems. However, there are monitoring tools that will collect information from multiple systems and consolidate the logs produced by those systems. In addition, the timing source and time zone used by systems may differ. Protocols such as NTP (Network Time Protocol) can be used to synchronize the time for multiple systems.

Refer to *Network Intrusion Detection: An Analyst's Handbook* (Northcutt 99) for further information on analyzing network traffic to gain a better understanding of intruders' actions.

7.2.6 Identify the Attacks Used to Gain Access

You should search the local logs of the compromised systems for information that reveals what kind of attack an intruder used, in addition to making use of logs produced by firewalls, routers, and network monitors.

Usually, intruders attempt a number of different attacks or scan for the presence of one particular vulnerability before they gain initial access. Depending on how your systems are configured to detect signs of intrusions, look for the following on your system and network logs:

- Denied access messages (if an intruder tried to guess passwords)
- Messages pointing to old vulnerabilities such as the UNIX sendmail `wiz` command

- Blocked accesses to specific services collected by an installed tool such as TCP wrapper

You may also find date, time, and source in the logs, which can be quite useful.

After gaining access, an intruder may try to delete all logs or specific log entries. Therefore, it is possible that you will not find any useful entries. Sometimes the deletion of log entries is detectable. If it is, it tells you that something suspicious has happened to your system and that you need to conduct further analysis.

7.2.7 Identify What an Intruder Did

You need to understand how an intruder attacked and gained access to your systems. But just understanding the means of access will not reveal what the intruder actually did once access was gained. Without more information, you cannot identify what damage was done to systems and data. On many systems, you can easily identify attempts to write and modify files while unfortunately, due to its high volume, read access (of potentially sensitive data) is rarely captured.

In the absence of any further information, you should assume that once intruders gain access, they are able to obtain any data and access any service or program on the compromised system. That is, you need to assume the worst case for the purpose of assessing damage.

To identify what an intruder did, you can analyze various log files; compare cryptographic checksums of known, trusted files to those on the compromised machine; and use other intrusion detection and analysis tools.

It is particularly important to have a trusted cryptographic checksum as a point of comparison to detect if an intruder modified your operating system kernel. Intruders tend to leave behind three main types of traces:

1. Changes to log files to hide their presence
2. Actions to modify a system utility so that it does not list processes they started, to protect against easy recognition of installed back doors
3. Trojan horses, back doors, or new versions of system commands

Refer to Chapters 5 and 6 for more information on data that may reveal actions taken by an intruder.

7.2.8 Policy Considerations

Your organization's networked systems security policy should document the roles, responsibilities, authority, and conditions for the examination of data, systems, and networks suspected of having been compromised, as well as for the analysis of intrusions.

Your organization's information disclosure policy should indicate what information is shared with others and in what circumstances, as well as who has the authority to initiate information disclosure beyond what your policy specifies.

7.3 Communicate with Relevant Parties

Communicate with all parties who need to be made aware of an intrusion and its progress. Those with key roles in responding to an intrusion need to be kept informed at the appropriate times so that they can fulfill their responsibilities. You need to notify immediately the responsible mid-level and senior managers; your local computer security incident response team (CSIRT), if one exists; your public relations staff; and the affected system administrators, if they are not already involved, based on your organization's information dissemination policy (see the section on policy considerations below). For responses to intrusions that require management approval, the following decisions need to be made:

- Whether or not to close the breach and continue doing business
- Whether or not to continue to gather data on an intruder's activities (including protecting evidence associated with these activities)
- What quantity and type of information you should communicate
- Whom you need to inform

The process of executing your information dissemination procedures may include contacting users affected by an intrusion, security personnel, law enforcement agencies, vendors, and other CSIRTs external to your organization.

Designated staff members (both inside and outside your organization) cannot execute their responsibilities if they are not notified in a timely manner that an intrusion is occurring or has occurred and if they are not kept informed as an intrusion progresses. As a result, your systems, networks, and data may suffer greater damage (loss of confidentiality, integrity, availability) than if all those who needed to be involved had been informed as required.

Your organization may suffer loss of business or reputation if the public communication aspects of an intrusion are improperly handled.

It is important to keep communicating with other organizations about an intrusion. If they are experiencing unexpected system behavior caused by intruder actions, you may be able to gain information that will help you protect your own systems. For example, the system administrator of a site may contact you indicating that a system at your site is attacking them. An intruder may have compromised your system to hide his or her tracks and to launch an attack against the other organization.

You need to initiate communication with those in other parts of your organization whose systems may be vulnerable, such as managers and administrators, system administrators at external customer and collaborator sites, and other CSIRTs, to identify intruder behavior that you observe. You should do this regardless of the follow-up actions you intend to take.

Since communications actions may tip off an intruder, you should alter your normal communications procedures.

It is critical that you establish and exercise your information dissemination policy and procedures before an intrusion takes place so that all parties are aware of how they are to participate when an intrusion occurs. Doing so will help you learn how to speak to your contacts and describe what is happening in language that is meaningful for them.

Refer to the *CSIRT Handbook* (West-Brown 98) for more information on this subject, specifically Chapter 3.7 on interactions.

7.3.1 Follow Your Information Dissemination Procedures

Establish, use, and maintain specific points of contact in support of your information dissemination policy as described in the section on policy considerations below (name, title, organizational affiliation, telephone number, emergency pager numbers, e-mail address, fax number, means of secure communication, means of authentication). Getting to know these contacts before intrusions occur helps to make your response process more efficient.

Create, use, and maintain an intrusion notification call tree (listing the sequence of people to call and who will call whom) and other procedures for informing people quickly. Require your intrusion response team members to carry contact information with them at all times in the event they need to use it.

Share all information on a need-to-know basis and sanitize sensitive information if required.

7.3.2 Use Secure Communication Channels

Establish and use secure mechanisms for all communication as described in Section 5.5. Intruders can overhear or pick up communication, so carry out all communication relevant to an intrusion in a secure manner.

Use only communications that do not involve your systems or networks, such as phone and fax. Do not send e-mail from compromised systems or networks.

7.3.3 Inform Other Affected Sites

Inform upstream and downstream sites of attacks and intrusions. Upstream sites are those that were involved in an intrusion before your system became involved. Downstream sites are those that became involved after your site experienced an intrusion.

In the process of analyzing an intrusion, you can often gain information about systems not belonging to your organization that were compromised in one of the following ways:

- Used by an intruder to attack your systems
- Attacked by an intruder from your systems
- Used by an intruder to access your systems
- Accessed by an intruder from your systems
- Introduced by an intruder to serve as decoys or distractions (red herrings)

Such information is usually obtained from logs about connections attributed to an intruder or from remnant files left behind by an intruder. Remnant files may include scripts with the IP addresses of the attacked hosts or the output files of attack scripts an intruder neglected to delete.

You have a responsibility to inform the administrators of all other organizations about the involvement of their systems so that they can take the necessary steps to respond to the intrusion. These organizations include any ISPs that may have been involved in transmitting and receiving intruder messages. However, in the event of an ongoing legal investigation, your ability to inform other organizations may be restricted. For example, action on your part may affect the outcome of the investigation in some way; alternatively, users from the other organization may actually be the subject of the investigation.

7.3.4 Maintain Contact Information

Keep an accurate, detailed log of all contacts made and of the information exchanged. Make sure your system's point of contact information in the InterNIC whois database[1] and other public directories is up-to-date so that other sites can contact you if they detect involvement of your systems in an intrusion at their site. Use secure procedures for updating this critical information.

7.3.5 Policy Considerations

Your organization's networked systems security policy should include an information dissemination policy that identifies the following:

- Whom to notify in the event of an intrusion and in what order. The order of notification may depend on the type of intrusion or other circumstances. You should contact the responsible manager, your public relations point of contact, and your local response team immediately (shown as the first, second, and third items below). The remaining contacts are listed in no particular order:

  the responsible manager and other managers who need to be made aware

  public relations

  CSIRT, if one exists

  system and network administrator(s)

  security officer and personnel

  your site's Internet service provider (ISP)

  human resources (in the event of an employee intruder)

  help desk personnel (who may have to answer inquiries about an intrusion)

  legal counsel

  corporate investigations group, if one exists

  law enforcement agencies (local, state, federal[2])

  users

---

1. Refer to *http://rs.internic.net/whois.html.*

2. Refer to the CERT tech tip *How the FBI Investigates Computer Crime* at *http://www.cert.org/tech_tips/ FBI_investigates_crime.html.*

> vendors
>
> other CSIRTs outside your organization, for example, the team associated
> with your ISP, CERT/CC, your national CSIRT

- Specific roles and responsibilities for each contact within your organization, including their range of authority
- How much information should be shared with each class of contact and whether or not sensitive information needs to be removed or filtered prior to sharing it
- Whom to notify and when to notify them, using specified communication mechanisms (e.g., phone, e-mail, fax, pager), and whether or not these mechanisms need to be secure
- Who has the authority to initiate information disclosure beyond that specified in your policy

7.4 Collect and Protect Information

All information about the compromised system(s) and cause(s) of an intrusion needs to be captured and securely stored. This information may include system and network log files, network message traffic, user files, results produced by intrusion detection tools, analysis results, system administrator console logs and notes, and backup tapes that capture the state of the affected system both before and after intrusion. All information must be carefully collected, labeled, catalogued, and securely stored at each stage of intrusion analysis.

If you do not collect and protect this information, you may not be able to learn from the experience and improve your systems, their operation, and your staff capabilities. It will be difficult to interact knowledgeably with other CSIRTs. In the case of an internally generated intrusion, you may not be able to take appropriate action to educate, reprimand, or terminate an employee found responsible.

If you intend to prosecute an intruder, you need to have thorough and convincing evidence that has been protected through a secure chain-of-custody procedure that tracks who has been involved in handling the evidence and where it has been stored. Otherwise, the information you collect may not be considered valid evidence in a legal proceeding. Law enforcement officials and your legal counsel are good sources of advice about how and when to collect and protect critical information.

7.4.1 Collect All Information

Collect information about all relevant system and network logs from the compromised system(s), including written log records made by intrusion response staff, any other auditing information produced by tools, full backups, partial backups (snapshots), screen shots, videotapes, and photographs.

Document all information in a notebook that answers the questions who? what? where? when? why? and how? The answers should include the following information:

- The name of the system
- The date and time of each entry
- What actions were taken
- What was said
- Who was notified
- Who had access
- What data were collected
- What information was disseminated—to whom, by whom, when, and for what purpose
- What was submitted to legal counsel—to whom, by whom, and how it was verified (e.g., notarized)

Keep in mind that your notes may be subject to subpoena in any legal proceeding, so document responsibly. Make sure you use a separate notebook for each intrusion, so that if it is subpoenaed, it does not contain information about other intrusions.

7.4.2 Collect and Preserve Evidence

Designate a point of contact to be responsible for communicating with law enforcement and other external agencies. To ensure that evidence will be acceptable to the legal community, its collection should be done following predefined procedures in accordance with all laws and legal regulations. Also take the following steps:

- Document, use, and maintain a procedure for preserving the compromised system and any associated evidence in case of a criminal investigation.
- Whenever possible, analyze a replica of a compromised resource, not the original, to avoid inadvertently tampering with evidence.

- To ensure that replicating the compromised resource does not change the original, write-protect the original information before copying it.

- Document meticulously all actions intended to preserve the chain of custody that are performed by all participants from detection through analysis and response (refer to Sections 7.4.3 and 7.4.4).

- Ensure that all log files containing information regarding an intrusion are retained for at least as long as normal business records, and longer if an investigation is ongoing.

- Archive all information collected (listed in Section 7.4.1) to physically secure offline media.

In addition to taking all of the above steps, you should ensure that all critical information is duplicated and preserved both on site at your facility and off site in a secure location. This information includes policies, procedures, contact information, tools, critical data, configurations, databases, cryptographic checksums, and system backups. On-site alternative storage provides for quick access in the event of an emergency. Off-site storage safeguards the information in the event of a natural disaster (such as a fire or a flood).

Define and document a procedure for authorizing access to both on-site and off-site information so that you can access it quickly in case of an emergency.

7.4.3 Preserve the Chain of Custody of Evidence

The chain of custody of evidence is preserved by having verifiable documentation indicating the sequence of individuals who have handled a piece of evidence and the sequence of locations where it was stored (including dates and times).

To establish a proven chain of custody, you must be able to account for the evidence at all times and fully document the passage of evidence from one party to the next, and from one location to the next.

If your organization has a policy concerning chain of custody, ensure that your actions are in keeping with this policy.

7.4.4 Contact Law Enforcement

If you choose to keep your systems running and connected to collect more information about an intruder and an intrusion (as opposed to disconnecting or shutting down your systems), you may be liable if your system is used as a launch point to attack another site. You need to notify law enforcement immediately and take whatever action they advise to limit this liability.

Keep in mind that laws vary from country to country and state to state within the United States. You need to determine the legal requirements of the country from which you are operating—especially the laws that pertain to collecting and protecting evidence, chain of custody, and sufficiency of evidence for prosecution—and then implement the necessary procedures to meet those requirements.

7.4.5 Policy Considerations

Your organization's networked systems security response procedures should ensure that a provable chain of custody is maintained to protect potential evidence through, for example, the generation of a detailed action and decision log indicating who made each entry. This level of rigor is required even if you choose not to initiate an official legal investigation. Other affected organizations may decide to take action and request your assistance and any evidence you have collected, and such organizations may initiate legal proceedings against you if an intruder attacked their systems from yours.

7.5 Contain an Intrusion

Containment consists of short-term, tactical actions whose purpose is to stop an intruder's access to compromised systems, limit the extent of an intrusion, and prevent the intruder from causing further damage.

Containment actions can quickly inform users, customers, and/or business partners that an unexpected event that could interfere with their work is occurring; convey to the media that something is going on; and alert an intruder that his or her presence and activities have been detected.

Assuming you wish to contain an intrusion, your organization needs to decide whether or not to shut systems down or disconnect them from a network. These decisions require management involvement. However, if an intruder's activities are malicious, system administrators may need to take more immediate action. Therefore, the decision-making process and the level of authority required need to be articulated in your security policy and made operational in your procedures.

When making decisions, you need to take several factors into account:

- An overall assessment of the intrusion (scope, impact, damage)
- Any relevant results from the analysis, such as the origin of an intruder

- The goals and priorities of your organization that govern the response process
- Business continuity plans

Keep in mind that any changes to the compromised systems, including containment actions, may destroy information required to assess the cause of an intrusion. You need to exercise caution to ensure that you collect all necessary data to complete the analysis before making any system changes. Also ensure that you collect and protect all evidence that may be needed in a subsequent investigation.

When containing an intrusion your two main objectives are (1) to regain control of the systems involved to be able to analyze the problem further and return the systems to normal operation; and (2) to deny an intruder access and thus prevent further damage and possible additional interference.

While an intruder still has access, you cannot be sure that you will successfully eliminate this access capability and thus be able to return your systems to normal operation. Curtailing intruder access through containment actions is a short-term solution. This step then gives you the latitude to develop longer-term solutions once you have more detailed information.

Denying intruders access to your systems achieves three goals:

1. It protects against further damage that intruders can cause once they realize that you have detected their presence.
2. It prevents them from destroying valuable evidence and tampering with the system while you are analyzing it.
3. It prevents them from using your systems to attack other systems, thereby protecting you from liability as a result of damage claims by other organizations.

Containment thus provides a reasonable security solution until you have sufficient information to take more appropriate actions that address the vulnerabilities used to access your system and the damage done by the intrusion.

7.5.1 Temporarily Shut Down the System

You need to temporarily shut down the compromised system when there is no other means by which to deny the intruder access to the system. This action will prevent more serious damage and provide time to perform more detailed analysis. However, it will also deny access to legitimate users of the system. Therefore, we recommend that if possible, you do this only for a limited period of time.

Shutting down the compromised system may destroy important information needed for analysis. As an example, an intruder's programs may be available only in main memory if he or she deleted the files on the hard drive to avoid their detection. In an emergency, you need to be able to weigh the risk of further damage against the possibility of losing this information by shutting down.

7.5.2 Disconnect the Compromised System from the Network

Instead of shutting down a system, you can choose to (1) disconnect the local area network or corporate network to which the system is connected from the local or public networks the intruder is using or (2) disconnect the compromised system from the local network.

The first alternative ensures that the system and all communication with it are still available from within the organization. However, this may alter critical information on the compromised system as normal use continues and will limit access to other networks for those using the disconnected network.

The second alternative allows users of systems other than the compromised system to continue to access the public network. However, if you have incorrectly determined the scope of an intrusion (which may include other systems on the same local network), you run the risk of allowing the intruder continued access to that network and the remaining systems connected to it, which may also be compromised.

7.5.3 Disable Access, Services, and Accounts

Other computers that have access to a compromised file system can themselves become compromised as a result of accessing that file system. This problem can occur when an intruder-installed Trojan horse, virus, or other malicious code is executed by an unsuspecting user or is automatically invoked by a startup or exit routine. Therefore, you need to disable access to any file system that you suspect may be compromised. Note that the shared file system may not be resident on the compromised system. Access to it could be provided by another computer acting as the file server in response to requests from the compromised system.

In addition, disabling access to a compromised file system may have the effect of preventing intruder actions taken to delete evidence contained in files on the file system. This step also facilitates the analysis process by eliminating ongoing access (and further modification) to files on the file system

If you have performed sufficient analysis to limit the scope of an intrusion correctly to specific services, you should disable these services. Disabling services is especially critical if no patch is immediately available to eliminate the vulnerability that an intruder used. By disabling only the specific services the intruder used, you can continue to provide users on the system with access to all other services and to the system itself.

Although it is not a totally reliable containment action (an intruder may have other means of access), disabling the accounts or changing the passwords associated with the accounts that an intruder is using will terminate that access path if the account was the primary means used to gain access (versus the use of a vulnerability that bypassed user authentication).

7.5.4 Monitor System and Network Activities

Regardless of what other steps are taken, you need to monitor all system and network activities for unusual and suspicious events. You need to watch the network for attacks previously used by an intruder and connections coming from systems known to be used by an intruder.

This approach enables you to identify subsequent attempts by intruders to gain access more quickly and more easily. It may also reveal other access paths not previously identified, which you can then disable. Refer to Sections 6.3 and 6.4 for network and system monitoring guidance.

7.5.5 Verify That Redundant Systems and Data Have Not Been Compromised

If you are running hot, warm, or cold backups in support of your configuration redundancy policy (refer to Sections 5.2 and 4.24), you need to ensure that an intruder's actions have not been replicated, thereby affecting those systems and data.

In addition, ensure that any containment, elimination, and restoration steps you take on the primary system are also taken on your backup systems, including the elimination of vulnerabilities that were used by an intruder to gain access.

7.5.6 Policy Considerations

Your organization's networked systems security policy should specify the following:

•   The acceptable level of risk to business processes and the systems and networks that support them

- To what extent business processes and the systems and networks that support them must remain operational, even in the event of intrusions or attacks

- What additional systems that reside on local networks with compromised systems will be disconnected, even if they are known to be as yet unaffected. This is a preventive measure.

- Who is empowered to make a final decision and in what circumstances, and who has the authority to make decisions in situations not covered by the policy

- How to manage password compromises, including when and how to change passwords for all users and accounts at a specific site or on an organizational level

7.6 Eliminate All Means of Intruder Access

Complete eradication of the root cause(s) of an intrusion is a long-term goal that can be achieved only by implementing an ongoing security improvement process. In response to a specific intrusion, you need to ensure that the affected systems are protected against the same or similar types of access and attacks in the future, once an intrusion is contained and systems are returned to normal operation.

As part of a successful intrusion, intruders typically install back doors or other mechanisms for obtaining future access to the compromised system. This practice describes steps to eliminate this access to the greatest possible extent. These steps are likely sufficient if you have prepared properly, performed thorough analysis, and are able to identify all changes made by an intruder.

If you are not prepared, your only option is to reinstall the systems from original distribution media and restore all user data as far as possible. Many administrators may choose to reinstall the systems anyway, either to ensure that all intruder changes are eliminated or because they doubt the accuracy of the information they are relying on to identify such changes.

Intruders widely advertise compromised systems and regularly trade system addresses and access information in exchange for attack tools or similar information. Victims of intrusions indicate that intruders try to access their system addresses long after the original intrusion has occurred. Such addresses are not only distributed amongst intruders but are also available in databases accessible on the Internet.

You need to ensure that your systems are no longer vulnerable before returning them to service. Otherwise, they can be compromised by the same kind of attack that resulted in the successful intrusion. The absence of elimination actions undermines your ability to operate securely and in effect negates all efforts you may expend to respond to the original intrusion.

7.6.1 Change Passwords

Change all passwords on all systems to which the attacker may have had access. While we recommend taking this step in all cases, it is most important when there is evidence that an intruder may have had access to your password file or used a password sniffer tool that captures user passwords transmitted in clear text on the network.

You need to plan for the fact that executing and enforcing this step will create a fair amount of work for users and may confuse them. If passwords cannot be changed, another alternative is to lock out the compromised accounts and reassign new accounts.

7.6.2 Reinstall Compromised Systems

If you are insufficiently prepared, you probably do not have access to information such as cryptographic checksums (as described in Section 5.3) to verify the authenticity of the operating system version used on the compromised systems. In this case, you need to reinstall these systems from the original distribution media or from copies you trust.

After successful reinstallation of the operating system, you need to reinstall site-specific modifications to your systems, apply all relevant patches and bug-fixes, and ensure that these modifications do not introduce additional defects or vulnerabilities. One possible way of doing this is to execute a known series of system regression tests, if you have such a set of tests and prior test results are available for comparison.

7.6.3 Remove Any Means for Intruder Access

Use the results of intrusion analysis to determine the means by which an intruder gained access and the best way to eliminate them, for example:

- Known vulnerabilities for which patches are available; install the patches.
- The presence of malicious code (back door, Trojan horse) with an unknown and hidden function such as deleting log files or starting a service on unused ports to permit access without requiring a password; reinstall a trusted version of the affected software.
- The addition of new users to the list of authorized users, including levels of system privileges up to full privileges; reinstall a trusted version of your authorized users file.
- Setting new passwords for existing users; reinstall a trusted version of your password file.

- Weak or inadequate procedures (e.g., password setting and aging); update the procedures and enforce them.

- Corrupted configuration files containing, e.g., previously disabled entries (such as an *rshd* daemon entry within the *inetd.conf* configuration file on UNIX systems); correct them.

- Inspect all files executed at boot time for the presence of Trojan horses or back doors; reinstall a trusted version of files that contain such malicious code.

7.6.4 Restore Executable Programs and Binary Files from Original Distribution Media

You need to identify all files that have been added, changed, or deleted by an intruder, because you cannot determine what hidden functions may have been left behind or what critical functions may have been influenced by these changes. For executable files (including nonbinary files such as UNIX shell scripts) and other binary files (such as libraries), verify cryptographic checksums to ensure that the files were not compromised.

Detailed logging or audit information about files accessed and programs executed by an intruder makes this step much easier by allowing your staff to concentrate on specific files instead of all existing and deleted files.

7.6.5 Review System Configurations

System configuration files include the following types of data:

1. User accounts
2. System services and their configuration
3. Audit and monitoring facilities
4. Access control lists

Compare all system configuration files with authoritative copies of these files, or compare cryptographic checksums with trusted checksums collected before an intrusion. If authoritative copies are available, you may choose to overwrite the current set of files with these copies.

In the absence of trusted copies or checksums, you need to review all files manually. Clearly, this will take significant time and resources. The review can be effectively conducted as a peer review performed by multiple system and network administrators or by members of your response team.

7.6.6 Correct System and Network Vulnerabilities

Determine whether you have uncorrected system and network vulnerabilities and correct them if necessary. Pay particular attention to vulnerabilities for which exploit scripts and tools exist within the intruder community and where vendor solutions are available as patches or hot-fixes.

You can conduct a security audit or evaluation of your systems by executing public domain or vendor tools (such as SATAN[3], SAINT, and SARA for UNIX systems); alternatively, you can arrange for external experts to check for the presence of known vulnerabilities.

7.6.7 Improve Protection Mechanisms

All protection mechanisms (such as firewalls) should be reviewed and their configurations adjusted based on what you learn in responding to a successful intrusion. Pay particular attention to the following aspects:

- Determine whether protection mechanisms need to be configured differently (such as by changing or adding new IP addresses to the router filter for allowing or disallowing connections).

- Determine whether protection mechanisms need to be placed in a new or additional location on your network that was previously unprotected or insufficiently protected.

- Review available information on vulnerabilities, patches, and new versions of your protection mechanism software, ensuring that your configurations are up to date.

7.6.8 Improve Detection Mechanisms

Update your detection mechanisms, such as intrusion detection systems and other types of intrusion reporting tools (refer to Section 5.3.15 and Table 5.3) to ensure that similar attacks are detected by these mechanisms in the future. Perform the following analysis and take appropriate actions.

---

3. SATAN (System Administrator Tool for Analyzing Networks) is available at *ftp://ftp.porcupine.org/ pub/security/*.

1. Determine whether detection mechanisms need to be configured differently (such as by adding in new attack patterns to be detected or changing logging options).
2. Determine whether detection mechanisms need to be placed in a new or additional location on your network that was previously insufficiently covered.
3. Review and update the conditions under which your detection mechanisms generate alerts to system and network administrators and the forms of the alert (e-mail, phone, pager, printouts, etc.).
4. Review available information on vulnerabilities, patches, and new versions of your detection mechanism software, ensuring that your configurations are up to date.

7.6.9 Policy Considerations

Your organization's networked systems security policy should establish the following guidelines:

- Regular checks should be made for the presence of system and network vulnerabilities.

- There should be timely evaluation and selective installation of patches and other corrections that you need to operate securely.

- People need to stay informed about the constantly changing sequence of new alerts, security bulletins, and advisories, particularly as they affect your protection and detection mechanisms. This task can be very resource-intensive, so you need to be selective regarding information sources that you review regularly.

- Clearly assign roles and responsibilities within your organization to perform regular checks, install patches, and to stay current with new information.

- Protect password transmission across an untrusted network by encryption or the use of other secure authentication technologies such as one-time passwords, challenge-response approaches, or security tokens.

7.7 Return Systems to Normal Operation

Restoring and returning a compromised system to normal operation permits your staff to have access to that system again. This is best accomplished after you have eliminated all means by which an intruder might gain access. Doing so prevents the same or similar types of intrusions from occurring, or at the very least ensures timely detection and notification by your updated intrusion detection mechanisms.

Business reality may require that you return systems to operation before full intrusion analysis is completed and all corrections are made. This risk needs to be carefully managed and monitored. If you do need to do this, continue analysis and eliminate the intruder's access to your system as soon as possible, recognizing that your system is vulnerable to another occurrence of the same type of intrusion. Containing the intrusion becomes even more critical.

The purpose of this practice is to define steps to help you correct damage caused by an intruder or caused by the actions taken to contain an intrusion, such as disconnecting the compromised systems from your network. Details about restoring any specific business application or related service are beyond the scope of this practice, but these steps can be used in those cases as well.

One of the purposes of response procedures is to eliminate the vulnerabilities that allowed an intrusion to occur and to return affected systems to full operational status. If these systems cannot be successfully reinstated, the business operations that depend on them cannot be performed. The efforts to eliminate intruder access and analyze intruder activities to determine vulnerabilities are wasted if systems cannot be returned to service.

7.7.1 Determine the Requirements and Time Frame

You need to determine the requirements to be met and the priority they should have before you return the affected system to normal operations. This determination generally requires the involvement of senior management if the guidance is not specified as part of your policies and procedures.

If the requirements do not include completion of intrusion analysis and the elimination of vulnerabilities (due to a business-critical need to return the system to operations as soon as possible), continue analysis in parallel. Upgrade the system as soon as possible, recognizing that the system is vulnerable to another occurrence of the same type of intrusion until you do so. One way to mitigate the risk is to increase the level of monitoring and intrusion detection to ensure that a new intrusion does not go unnoticed.

7.7.2 Restore User Data

An intruder may have altered user data and application program areas, which can be done in a number of ways, including the following:

- Installing back doors to provide future access. For example, an intruder installs a program in a local user directory that is called each time the user logs in, providing an unprotected login shell that can be accessed by anyone via the Internet.

- Compromising user data to sabotage the user's work. For example, an intruder makes small changes to spreadsheets that go unnoticed. Depending on how the spreadsheets are used, this can cause minor to major damage.

Use the latest trusted backup to restore user data. For files that have not been compromised, consider using the backup that was made closest to the time an intrusion was detected to avoid user rework. This step should be undertaken with caution and only if you have a high level of confidence that restored user files were not compromised. Regardless, you need to encourage users to check for any unexpected changes to their files and warn them about the risk of compromise.

Users should review all restored data files that resided on the compromised system to ensure they were not affected by an intruder's activities.

All executables or binary files residing in user areas should be handled in the same way as system executables and binary files. If no authenticated, cryptographic checksum is available, you need to reinstall from the original distribution media.

7.7.3 Reestablish the Availability of Services and Systems

To eliminate the vulnerability exploited by the intruder, enable previously disabled services that are either known not to be vulnerable or have been corrected.

Enable only those services that are required by the users of the system (rather than enabling all available services).

Return previously compromised file systems to service after ensuring that all intruder modifications and malicious programs have been eliminated.

Reconnect the restored system to its local network. Where a local or corporate network containing the compromised system was previously disconnected from the public network used by an intruder, reconnect the local or corporate network.

Validate the restored system, executing a known series of regression tests where prior test results are available for comparison.

7.7.4 Watch for Signs of the Intruder's Return

In many cases, you can gather much more information about intruders when they attempt to return than you can immediately after an intrusion. This is particularly true if you have installed improved monitoring tools and procedures as a result of lessons learned from a previous intrusion.

Monitor for failed login attempts, attempts to access back doors, attempts to re-exploit the original vulnerability, and attempts to exploit new vulnerabilities. Each occurrence of these should be analyzed further.

Once a system is compromised and this fact becomes known in the intruder community, the system becomes a bigger target for future attacks. Improved monitoring may reveal new attacks more easily and provide the opportunity to defeat the attacker.

7.7.5 Policy Considerations

Your organization's networked systems security policy should specify the order in which system services are returned to operation. This precaution ensures that the order meets your business objectives and priorities while minimizing the impact on users whenever possible.

Actions to restore any specific business application or related service should be taken as recommended above.

7.8 Implement Lessons Learned

It is important to learn from the successful and unsuccessful actions taken in response to an intrusion. Capturing and disseminating what worked well and what did not will help reduce the likelihood of similar intrusions and will improve the security of your operation. This goal can be accomplished by performing a post-mortem review with all involved parties and communicating the results of the review.

Several additional tasks need to be performed in the aftermath of an intrusion. These include notifying any individuals or teams with whom you have been communicating about the outcome of an intrusion and putting in place monitoring mechanisms and security policy and procedure updates resulting from knowledge gained through lessons learned.

If your organization does not learn from the experience of responding to a successful intrusion, you will continue to operate at risk and will likely have to deal with the same or a similar type of intrusion again. Any successful intrusion indicates weaknesses in your systems, networks, and operations that provide opportunities to make them more secure. It may also point to an inadequate level of staff preparedness that can be remedied through additional training or other forms of skill development.

7.8.1 Complete Communication Steps

If further notification is required (per policies and procedure), execute this notification. Follow up with the sites you contacted previously.

Manage ongoing press aspects of an intrusion, if any. Do this in accordance with your information dissemination policy, as described in Section 7.3.

7.8.2 Hold a Postmortem Review Meeting

Hold a postmortem review meeting within three to five working days of completing the investigation of an intrusion with all involved parties. Otherwise, participants are likely to forget critical information.

Capture the following information:

- Did your detection and response processes and procedures work as intended? If not, where did they not work? Why did they not work?
- What methods of discovery and monitoring procedures would have improved your ability to detect and analyze an intrusion?
- What improvements to procedures and tools would have aided you in the response steps? For example, should you consider using updated router and firewall filters, different placement of firewalls, moving the compromised system to a new name or IP address, or moving the compromised machine's function to a more secure area of your network?
- What improvements would have enhanced your ability to contain an intrusion?
- What correction procedures would have improved your effectiveness in recovering your systems?
- What updates to policies and procedures would have allowed the response procedures to operate more smoothly?
- What topics should be addressed to improve user and system administrator preparedness?
- What areas for improving communication exist throughout the detection and response procedures?

Estimate the costs associated with an intrusion to support the business case for the level of investment you should make in security improvement. This estimate should include the approximate value of proprietary or sensitive information assets that may have been accessed by an intruder and the opportunity cost of unavailable systems (staff members unable to do productive work).

Document and review meeting results. Prepare a final report and brief senior management (CIO/CEO level) with these results for their review and comment. This action ensures that they are aware of the vulnerability of their systems and continue to be educated about these issues.

7.8.3 Revise Security Documents

Include any new, improved methods resulting from lessons learned in your current security plans, policies, procedures and user and administrator training.

Make sure that you are regularly reviewing the public, legal, and vendor information sources necessary to protect your systems from further attacks of this type, as described in Chapter 1. These sources regularly report current intruder trends, new attack scenarios, and tools that will improve the effectiveness of your response process.

7.8.4 Additional Steps

Determine whether or not to perform a new risk analysis based on the severity and impact of an intrusion.

Take a new inventory of your system and network assets. See Section 5.3 for further guidance.

Participate in investigation and prosecution, if applicable.

Chapter 7 Checklist

Practice	Step Number	Step Description	Yes	Partial	No
P7.2: Analyze All Available Information	S7.2.1	Capture and record system information			
	S7.2.2	Back up the compromised systems			
	S7.2.3	Isolate the compromised systems			
	S7.2.4	Search on other systems for signs of intrusion			
	S7.2.5	Examine logs			

Practice	Step Number	Step Description	Yes	Partial	No
	S7.2.6	Identify the attacks used to gain access			
	S7.2.7	Identify what an intruder did			
	S7.2.8	Policy considerations			
P7.3: Communicate with Relevant Parties	S7.3.1	Follow your information dissemination procedures			
	S7.3.2	Use secure communication channels			
	S7.3.3	Inform other affected sites			
	S7.3.4	Maintain contact information			
	S7.3.5	Policy considerations			
P7.4: Collect and Protect Information	S7.4.1	Collect all information			
	S7.4.2	Collect and preserve evidence			
	S7.4.3	Preserve the chain of custody of evidence			
	S7.4.4	Contact law enforcement			
	S7.4.5	Policy considerations			
P7.5: Contain an Intrusion	S7.5.1	Temporarily shut down the system			
	S7.5.2	Disconnect the compromised system from the network			
	S7.5.3	Disable access, services, and accounts			
	S7.5.4	Monitor system and network activities			

(continued)

Chapter 7 Checklist (*cont.*)

Practice	Step Number	Step Description	Yes	Partial	No
	S7.5.5	Verify that redundant systems and data have not been compromised			
	S7.5.6	Policy considerations			
P7.6: Eliminate All Means of Intruder Access	S7.6.1	Change passwords			
	S7.6.2	Reinstall compromised systems			
	S7.6.3	Remove any means for intruder access			
	S7.6.4	Restore executable programs and binary files from original distribution media			
	S7.6.5	Review system configurations			
	S7.6.6	Correct system and network vulnerabilities			
	S7.6.7	Improve protection mechanisms			
	S7.6.8	Improve detection mechanisms			
	S7.6.9	Policy considerations			
P7.7: Return Systems to Normal Operation	S7.7.1	Determine the requirements and time frame			
	S7.7.2	Restore user data			
	S7.7.3	Reestablish the availability of services and systems			
	S7.7.4	Watch for signs of the intruder's return			
	S7.7.5	Policy considerations			

Practice	Step Number	Step Description	Yes	Partial	No
P7.8: Implement Lessons Learned	S7.8.1	Complete communication steps			
	S7.8.2	Hold a postmortem review meeting			
	S7.8.3	Revise security documents			
	S7.8.4	Additional steps			

Appendix A

Security Implementations

A.1 Overview

This Appendix contains detailed descriptions (called implementations) that elaborate on specific steps in the technology-neutral practices described in Chapters 2–7. Implementations provide procedural and tool-based guidance for accomplishing one or more steps described in a practice for a specific operating system environment. Given that CERT/CC expertise is heavily oriented to the UNIX environment, we have developed and selected implementations for a commonly installed UNIX operating system—Sun Solaris.

These implementation examples are intended to be illustrative in nature and do not necessarily reflect the most up-to-date operating system versions. The most current versions of over 50 implementations are available on the CERT web site. New implementations are added regularly, and existing implementations are updated periodically.

This appendix includes the following implementations. These examples were selected as those most broadly applicable to the practices contained in this book and those most frequently referenced by user inquiries and via the CERT web site.

A2. Installing, Configuring, and Using Tripwire to Verify the Integrity of Directories and Files on Systems Running Solaris 2.x

This implementation describes capturing a file and directory characterization baseline based on cryptographic checksums using the Tripwire tool, as described in Chapter 5. The implementation also describes how to use Tripwire to capture cryptographic checksums for current files and directories and compare these to the trusted baseline, identifying all changes for further review and analysis as called out in Chapter 6.

A3. Installing, Configuring, and Operating the Secure Shell (SSH) on Systems Running Solaris 2.x

This implementation describes one approach for ensuring secure, encrypted communication using the SSH tool in support of several of the practices described in Chapters 2 and 3.

A4. Understanding System Log Files on a Solaris 2.x Operating System

A5. Configuring and Using Syslogd to Collect Logging Messages on Systems Running Solaris 2x

A6. Installing, Configuring, and Using Logsurfer 1.5 to Analyze Log Messages on Systems Running Solaris 2.x

The above three implementations describe various aspects of logging and approaches for filtering log files for data of interest in support of practices described in Chapters 5 and 6.

A7. Installing, Configuring, and Using Spar 1.3 on Systems Running Solaris 2.x

The spar tool supports the ability to review and understand process accounting data, which is one way of identifying suspicious behavior as described in Chapters 5 and 6.

A8. Installing and Operating Tcpdump 3.4 on Systems Running Solaris 2.x

A9. Writing Rules and Understanding Alerts for Snort,
a Network Intrusion Detection System

Snort and tcpdump are two commonly used, public-domain tools that provide the ability to filter, select, and analyze network traffic. Detecting unusual or unexpected network traffic, as described in Chapters 5 and 6, can point to the presence of an intruder.

A.2 Installing, Configuring, and Using Tripwire to Verify the Integrity of Directories and Files on Systems Running Solaris 2.x

Tripwire is a file system integrity-checking program for UNIX operating systems. To use it, you first must build a configuration file that designates the directories and files that you want to verify and the attributes you want to have verified for each. You then run Tripwire (with the initialize option) to create a database of cryptographic checksums that correspond to the files and directories specified in the configuration file.

To protect the Tripwire program, configuration file, and initialized database against corruption, be sure to transfer them to a medium that can be designated as physically write-protected, such as a disk or CD-ROM. This read-only version then becomes the authoritative reference program, configuration, and data, which you can reliably use to test the integrity of directories and files on your system.

In addition to one or more cryptographic checksums representing the contents of each directory and file, the Tripwire database also contains information that allows you to verify the following:

- Access permissions and file mode settings, including effective execution settings
- Inode number in the file system
- Number of links
- User ID of the owner
- Group ID of the group of users to which access may be granted
- Size of the item
- Date and time the item was last accessed, the last modification made to the item, and the creation date and time associated with the item's inode

For any system, you want to verify the integrity of all critical operating system directories and files, plus any other directories and files that you consider sensitive or not subject to change under normal conditions. Pay particular attention to executable programs, daemons, scripts, and the libraries and configuration files associated with them.

The default Tripwire configuration file for Solaris provides a good starting point, but you need to review and edit it carefully to reflect your system. Consult the `filesystem(5)` manual page for details of how the Solaris 2.x file system is organized, and for descriptions of directories containing files that you should verify.

When choosing which attributes of files and directories to verify, you need to consider how they are used on your system. For example, you know that since your log files grow as events cause records to be written to them, verifying the constancy of the file size for these files does not make sense. However, monitoring changes to the size of system binaries or to access permissions for log files is probably warranted.

Effort Estimates

The time needed to retrieve the source code from the distribution site varies depending upon your connection speed. The source code is less than 283 KB (version 1.3.1-1). Building and installing Tripwire depends upon machine performance but on average will take less than ten minutes.

You will need to allocate several days of staff time to determine a comprehensive configuration suitable for your environment that is tailored to minimize the generation of any misleading or unnecessary messages. Extraneous messages that do not require your attention will show up during this initial period of use. You will need to make adjustments and tailor them to meet your reporting requirements as you go.

Tripwire database updates are required if new software or new releases are added to your system configuration. These actions may also require further tailoring of your Tripwire configuration.

Prerequisites

You can build and install Tripwire on many UNIX systems. To build Tripwire on your system, you need Internet access to retrieve the following software tools:

- An MD5[1] cryptographic checksum program
- GZIP[2] to uncompress the downloaded file
- PGP[3] to verify the authenticity of the software distribution
- A C compiler—either the Sun C Computer or the free GNU C Compiler[4]

Downloading and Verifying

The latest Academic Source Release (ASR) version of Tripwire (1.3.1-1) is available as `Tripwire-1_3_1-1_tar.gz` from *http://www.tripwiresecurity.com/products/index.cfml.*

See Additional Information below for guidance on open source and for-purchase versions.

Perform a file transfer from *http://www.tripwiresecurity.com/products/index.cfml* to download the Tripwire distribution.

Verify the authenticity of the Tripwire distribution using an MD5 checksum as shown below:

File to Download	MD5 Checksum
`Tripwire-1.3.1-1.tar.gz`	`31025a0649e8c5123877b30d13b62143`

If the computed cryptographic checksum of the download files does not correspond to the information above, verify that (1) your downloaded file names match those listed above and (2) your checksum program computes MD5 message digests.

---

1. Refer to the implementation titled *Using MD5 to verify the integrity of file contents*, available at *http://www.cert.org/security-improvement*, under UNIX implementations.

2. Available at *ftp://ftp.gnu.org/gnu/gzip/gzip-1.2.4a.tar.*

3. Available at *http://www.pgp.com.*

4. Available at *ftp://prep.ai.mit.edu/gnu/gcc/gcc-core-2.95.2.tar.gz.*

Install Tripwire

Choose a storage location with sufficient space for the Tripwire distribution. We recommend that you also download the Tripwire User Manual. It contains trouble-shooting suggestions and additional details that are beyond the scope of this implementation.

Unpack the Tripwire Distribution

First you need to unzip the Tripwire distribution:

```
$ gunzip Tripwire-1_3_1-1_tar.gz
```

To unpack the Tripwire distribution, use the system `tar` command:

```
$ tar xvf Tripwire-1.3.1-1_tar
```

This command creates a subdirectory named `tw_ASR_1.3.1_src`. Perform all operations within this subdirectory.

Several files exist in the created directory. One of these files is the Tripwire `README` file. It outlines the various strategies and settings for configuring and operating. `Ported,` another file, lists the platforms and operating systems to which Tripwire has already been ported. Find your OS in the list and note the system settings. You will use these to build Tripwire on your system. Once you have reviewed both the `README` and `Ported` files, you will better understand how to configure Tripwire for your specific system.

Choose the Right Operating System Settings

Change the `Makefile` to make sure it is correctly tuned for your system environment. To do so, edit the lines:

```
#CC     = cc             # common
CC      = gcc            # also common
```

to read:

```
CC      = cc             # common
#CC     = gcc            # also common
```

Choose the Path and Name of the Tripwire Configuration and Database Files

Edit the `./include/config.h` file, tailoring it to your specific system. Paths and names for Tripwire configuration files are specified in `./include/config.h`. Decide if you will use a disk or CD-ROM to store the Tripwire databases (as read-only) and specify the locations where Tripwire will look for its files.

Perform the following steps if you are using a floppy disk to store the Tripwire databases:

1. Insert the disk with the protect tab set to writable.

2. Format the disk:
   ```
   # fdformat -v /dev/rdisk
   ```

3. Create a file system on the floppy disk:
   ```
   # newfs -v /dev/rdisk
   ```

4. Create the /floppy mount directory:
   ```
   # mkdir /floppy
   ```

5. Mount the floppy disk as read-write:
   ```
   # mount -n /dev/disk /floppy
   ```

6. Create the /floppy/databases data directory:
   ```
   # mkdir /floppy/databases
   ```

If you prefer to use a CD-ROM, refer to other technical sources for its proper configuration and use. Once you have a working CD-ROM writer, it should act as any other media device with respect to its interaction with Tripwire.

Based on the assumption that the configuration files are stored locally and that the Tripwire databases are stored on a floppy disk, the following table lists the options that need to be adjusted within `./include/config.h`. Edit this file to reflect the recommendations below:

Option	Recommendation	Description
CONFIG_PATH	/etc	The directory where the Tripwire program looks for its configuration file
DATABASE_PATH	/floppy/databases	The directory where the Tripwire program searches for the databases

Create an Initial Version of Tripwire Configuration Files

Various templates for several operating systems are located in the `./config` directory as part of the distribution. Copy the default file for Solaris 2.x `tw.conf.sunos5` to the directory specified for the Tripwire configuration file location (see the previous step).

```
# cp config/tw.conf.sunos5 /etc/tw.config
```

Next, you need to edit the `/etc/tw.config` file (consult the `w.config.5` man page) to include any local system binaries, other critical files, and any additional files that you want to monitor.

After the configuration is finished, you can now build the Tripwire executable by specifying the make command:

```
$ make
```

Install the Tripwire Distribution

Start the installation using the command `make install` to place the Tripwire binary and man pages into the correct system directories. Perform this as system administrator using the root account. You can also place all necessary files into the desired directory manually as follows:

```
# cp man/siggen.8   /usr/local/man/man8/
# cp man/tripwire.8  /usr/local/man/man8/
# cp man/tw.config.5  /usr/local/man/man5/
# cp src/tripwire  /usr/local/bin/
# cp src/siggen   /usr/local/bin/
```

Testing Tripwire

The Tripwire distribution includes a script-driven testing suite that checks the build process. To run the testing suite, type the following command:

```
$ make test
```

This starts a script that tests your build of Tripwire against a copy of the Tripwire database in the `./test` directory. If all goes well, the output of the test matches the expected values that the script provides. For more information on the testing suite, consult the Tripwire User Manual.

For additional details on installation and configuration, consult the Tripwire User Manual, the README file, or the man pages.

Preparing to Use Tripwire

Once you have built and tested Tripwire, you need to address several additional topics that are important for the program's overall use. Not all files need the same level of protection. Tripwire comes with multiple cryptographic signature algorithms. Some execute more quickly than others, and some are more secure than others. (See the Tripwire User Manual for a discussion of the individual algorithms.) You will need to tailor your configuration files to reflect this trade-off between security and performance. Tripwire's default setting is to use two algorithms to calculate cryptographic checksums: MD5 and Snefru. Using MD5 alone should be sufficient for most files and directories.

Tripwire can be run in one of four modes:

1. Database generation
2. Database update
3. Interactive update mode
4. Integrity checking

Generate the Tripwire Database

Integrity checking requires a previously generated database against which to compare. Such a database is created by the tw.config file once you start database generation. Once you have configured the tw.config file as desired and have successfully installed Tripwire, insert the prepared floppy disk (disable write protection if necessary) and type the following commands:

```
# mount -n /dev/disk /floppy
# tripwire -initialize
```

The first command mounts the floppy. The second command creates a file named tw.db_<the local system's host name> within the directory /floppy/databases/. This file is the authoritative copy to which the Tripwire program refers when checking the file system's integrity for this host. You can use the automatic or interactive update modes to maintain this database whenever changes are made to the system that need to be reflected in the Tripwire database.

After completing database generation, place a copy of the Tripwire program and its configuration file on the same disk as the database to protect the Tripwire software and critical files. Restrict access via the ownership and permissions settings on the files written to the disk so that only the root user can read them. Having all files on a write-protected floppy disk allows you to easily identify any changes by comparing versions on the disk to an authoritative reference copy. Once this step is complete, unmount and eject the floppy disk. The commands to execute this step are as follows:

```
# cp /etc/tw.config /floppy
# cp /usr/local/bin/tripwire /floppy
# umount /floppy
```

Shift the write-protect tab on the disk to disable writing to it. This write-protected disk now represents your authoritative reference. Store this floppy in a physically secure location. Create an exact copy of the disk to work with so that you do not need to use the original.

Integrity Checking Using Tripwire

Obtain the read-only medium containing the authoritative reference from its physically secured storage. Make sure that write protection is enabled and mount the floppy disk as shown below:

```
# mount -n /dev/disk /floppy
# echo 'test' > /floppy/test
/floppy/test:  cannot create
```

If the file test exists after the last command, the floppy is not write-protected.

Compare each directory and file with its authoritative reference data. Identify any files whose contents or other attributes have changed. Execute Tripwire directly from the write-protected floppy, specifying which configuration (-c option) and database (-d option) files to use as follows:

```
# cd /floppy
# ./tripwire -c ./tw.config -d ./databases/tw.db_<the
  local system's host name>
```

Investigate any unexpected changes among those you have identified. If any changes cannot be attributed to authorized activities, initiate your incident response procedures immediately as described in Chapter 7. Report the incident to your internal security point of contact. Provide the Tripwire report as additional data if applicable.

Return the authoritative reference data to its physically secured storage. If all changes reported by Tripwire are as expected, follow your organization's procedures for securely updating the authoritative reference copy of the Tripwire database.

When you have completed a Tripwire scan and update process, don't forget to unmount the authoritative reference medium and return it to secure storage.

```
# umount /floppy
```

Tripwire Report Examples

Example 1: No changes have occurred

The output below shows that no changes have occurred in the files and directories being checked.

For this example, verbose mode (-v option) is enabled to illustrate Tripwire's scanning of each directory and file. The configuration is tailored to cover only files in the /etc directory.

```
# cd /floppy
# ./tripwire -v -c ./tw.config -d ./databases/tw.db_<the
  local system's host name>
### Phase 1: Reading configuration file
### Phase 2: Generating file list
./tripwire: /etc/dfs/sharetab: No such file or directory
./tripwire: /etc/hosts.equiv: No such file or directory
./tripwire: /etc/named.boot: No such file or directory
./tripwire: /etc/rmtab: No such file or directory
### Phase 3: Creating file information database
scanning: /etc scanning: /etc/TIMEZONE
scanning: /etc/aliases
scanning: /etc/autopush
scanning: /etc/clri
scanning: /etc/crash
scanning: /etc/cron
scanning: /etc/cron.d
scanning: /etc/cron.d/.proto
scanning: /etc/cron.d/logchecker
scanning: /etc/cron.d/queuedefs
scanning: /etc/cron.d/at.deny
scanning: /etc/cron.d/cron.deny
scanning: /etc/cron.d/FIFO

  (...additional output deleted...)
```

```
scanning:  /etc/nodename
scanning:  /etc/hostname.le0
scanning:  /etc/defaultrouter
scanning:  /etc/resolv.conf
scanning:  /etc/.mnttab.lock
scanning:  /etc/nsswitch.conf.OLD
scanning:  /etc/shadow.OLD
scanning:  /etc/openwin
scanning:  /etc/openwin/devdata
scanning:  /etc/openwin/devdata/profiles
scanning:  /etc/.obp_devices
scanning:  /etc/initpipe
scanning:  /etc/utmppipe
scanning:  /etc/ftpusers
scanning:  /etc/auto_global
scanning:  /etc/auto_o
scanning:  /etc/auto_u
scanning:  /etc/ethers
scanning:  /etc/printers.conf
scanning:  /etc/shells
scanning:  /etc/one-time.sh
scanning:  /etc/mkgroup
scanning:  /etc/mkpasswd
scanning:  /etc/mkshadow

### Phase 4: Searching for inconsistencies
### ### Total files scanned:      461
### Files added:                    0
### Files deleted:                  4
### Files changed:                454
# # #
### After applying rules:
### Changes discarded:            454
### Changes remaining:              0
# # #
```

In phase 4, Tripwire summarizes its findings, which show that 454 files have
changed in some way. According to the rules specified in the configuration file, however,
none of these changes is considered unexpected. The detected changes are probably
associated with the most recent read accesses to the files, which we have chosen to

ignore. If any files are modified unexpectedly, this modification is reported, as illustrated in Example 2.

Example 2: Changes have occurred

Example 2 illustrates typical output generated after a new user has been added. In phase 4, Tripwire reports five unexpected changes. In Example 1, where the unexpected occurred, reporting stopped after phase 4. In this example, phase 5 of the Tripwire report gives more information and shows the detected modifications.

```
# cd /floppy
# ./tripwire -c ./tw.config -d ./databases/tw.db_<the
  local system's host name>
### Phase 1: Reading configuration file
### Phase 2: Generating file list
./tripwire: /etc/dfs/sharetab: No such file or directory
./tripwire: /etc/hosts.equiv: No such file or directory
./tripwire: /etc/named.boot: No such file or directory
./tripwire: /etc/rmtab: No such file or directory
### Phase 3: Creating file information database
### Phase 4: Searching for inconsistencies
# # #
### Total files scanned:    463
### Files added:              2
### Files deleted:            4
### Files changed:          456
# # #
### After applying rules:
### Changes discarded:      455
### Changes remaining:        5
###
added: -rw---- root    0 Apr 22 16:21:14 2000
      /etc/.pwd.lock
added: -rw---- root    0 Apr 22 16:21:13 2000
      /etc/.group.lock
changed: drwxr-xr-x root 3584 Apr 22 16:21:14 2000 /etc
changed: -r—r—r— root 6982 Apr 22 16:20:58 2000
      /etc/passwd
changed: -r---- root 1571 Apr 22 16:20:59 2000
      /etc/shadow
```

```
### Phase 5: Generating observed/expected pairs for
changed files
# # #
### Attr Observed (what it is) Expected (what it should be)
# # #
============================================================
/etc
  st_mtime: Sat Apr 22 16:21:14 2000
           Sat Apr 22 14:00:09 2000
  st_ctime: Sat Apr 22 16:21:14 2000
           Sat Apr 22 14:00:09 2000
/etc/passwd
  st_ino: 74339                                        74305
  st_size: 6982                                        6932
  st_mtime: Sat Apr 22 16:20:58 2000
           Sat Apr 22 14:00:08 2000
  st_ctime: Sat Apr 22 16:20:58 2000
           Sat Apr 22 14:00:08 2000
 md5 (sig1): 1k0No.UNC9mCJglGMtPk4O
           0D5zziXYpwvXxOzy.DrYCx
 snefru (sig2): 0ENvBIiHddw3tJMRQUMFHy
           3ilRZc:dY2NFYLu3CAEXVI
/etc/shadow
  st_ino: 74305 74338
```

The first two lines of phase 4 of the report are listing new files that are created when the admintool is executed to add the new user. The next three lines represent previously existing directories and files that have changed as a result of the addition. Phase 5 shows the following modifications:

- Inode creation timestamps on the /etc directory
- Several attributes of the /etc/passwd file
- The inode number of the /etc/shadow file

It is evident that the contents of the /etc/passwd file changed, since its size and cryptographic checksums (MD5, Snefru) changed.

Example 3: Identify any missing files or directories

In both of the previous examples, phase 2 reports that four files are missing.

This reporting occurs because the files were specified in the configuration file at the time the Tripwire configuration was initialized, but they did not exist at the time the database was generated.

If files are deleted, the line specifying the number of files deleted is non-zero in phase 4:

```
### Files deleted: 4
```

Similarly, a more detailed entry indicates which file has been deleted:

```
deleted: -rw-r--- 0 36 Jul 3 10:48:26 2000
/etc/testdir/testfile
```

Depending on how you have configured the parent directory scan, more information can be reported to indicate any changes related to the directory where the missing file was previously located.

Example 4: Identify any new files and directories

If files or directories are added, this is indicated on the line specifying the number of files added in phase 4 of the Tripwire report:

```
### Files added: 2
```

As with missing or changed files, the names of the added files are also listed.

```
added:  -rw---- root  0  Apr  22  16:21:14  2000
     /etc/.pwd.lock
added:  -rw---- root  0  Apr  22  16:21:13  2000
     /etc/.group.lock
```

Additional Information

As stated above, the open source version is called Tripwire 1.3 ASR (Academic Source Release). It is the latest version available as source code for Solaris and other UNIX operating system variants. For this implementation, we assume that you are using this version.

Tripwire was originally developed in 1992 at Purdue University. Since that time, it has been downloaded and used by thousands of individuals and organizations. In 1998, Purdue transferred management of Tripwire to Tripwire Security Solutions, Inc. (TSS: *http://www.tripwiresecurity.com*). TSS currently offers multiple distributions of Tripwire for purchase and at no charge. Newer versions (newer than the version used in this implementation) are available for purchase. Because of operating system coverage (which now includes Windows/NT) and significant improvements in functionality, we recommend that you evaluate TSS versions for use in your environment. The latest version available for sale is version 2.2.1.

In addition, a free version of 2.2.1 is also available from Tripwire Security for Linux. According to their web page (*http://www.tripwiresecurity.com/downloads/index.cfml*), "Linux is officially supported on RedHat 5.2 and 6.0. Other distributed versions of Linux are not officially supported, but basic functionality has been verified on RedHat 6.1, and various distributions of Debian, Caldera, Open Linux, and SuSE systems using Linux kernel 2.0.36 or higher." If you operate Linux, we recommend that you retrieve and install this version of Tripwire. Note that the differences between 1.3.1 and 2.2.1 are so significant that the majority of this implementation does not accurately document version 2.2.1. Use Tripwire Security's documentation to guide you through that version's installation and operation.

A comparison between the for-purchase and no charge versions can be found at *http://www.tripwiresecurity.com/products/index.cfml.* The links for downloading either version for use with a UNIX operating system are contained at the bottom of the web page.

Other open source versions of Tripwire are available via the Internet. Generally, these non-TSS open source versions are not as well maintained. As a result, we recommend using the version available through TSS if you choose not to use the version used in this implementation.

A.3 Installing, Configuring, and Operating the Secure Shell (SSH) on Systems Running Solaris 2.x

This implementation describes the steps necessary to install and operate the SSH suite of security tools in the Solaris 2.x environment.

Most UNIX systems provide the Berkeley r-commands (`rlogin`, `rsh`, and `rcp`) and the telnet program for establishing sessions between two networked hosts. These programs rely on the Domain Name Service (DNS) for host-level authentication, and either a login/password or DNS-based trust for user-level authentication. Intruders can easily fabricate the information necessary to gain access to resources to which they should not have access. In addition, all network traffic between hosts connected with any of these programs is entirely in the clear, including the user name and password exchange. Therefore, intruders can sniff the network and view or copy the traffic exchanged between hosts—including, but not limited to, abuse of any user name and password combination—to log in to a networked host.

The SSH suite of security-enhancing tools addresses the problem of host and user authentication by using strong public key cryptography and the problem of cleartext data transmission by using strong data encryption.

There will come a time when all network traffic will be encrypted and strong DNS and IP security will be widespread, eliminating the need for security tools like SSH. Until that time comes, SSH is a strong defense against network sniffing, DNS spoofing, and IP spoofing.

Effort Estimates

The time needed to retrieve the source code from the distribution site varies depending upon your connection speed. The source code is less than 532 KB (version 2.3p1). Building and installing SSH depends upon machine performance but on average will take less than 20 minutes.

Determining a comprehensive configuration suitable for your environment and tailored to your security requirements will take some additional time and may require minor adjustments once you are familiar with the programs in your operational environment.

If users are forced to use strong public-key-based authorization, individual users will need to have associated public keys located on each server they want to access. Such key management will likely require some ongoing attention from system administrators, as users may not have the necessary access when SSH replaces other applications for remote access.

Prerequisites

SSH can be built and installed on many UNIX systems. To build SSH on your system, you need Internet access to retrieve the following software tools:

- An MD5[5] cryptographic checksum program
- GZIP[6] to uncompress the downloaded file

---

5. Refer to the implementation titled *Using MD5 to verify the integrity of file contents*, available at *http://www.cert.org/security-improvement*, under UNIX implementations.

6. Available at *ftp://ftp.gnu.org/gnu/gzip/gzip-1.2.4a.tar*.

- PGP[7] to verify the authenticity of the software distribution
- A C compiler, either the Sun C Computer or the free GNU C Compiler[8]
- The ZLIB library[9] for compression functions
- The OpenSSL library[10] for cryptographic functions
- TCP Wrapper[11]

Downloading and Verifying

Download the OpenSSH Distribution

Perform a file transfer from one of the sites listed on *http://www.openssh.com/ portable.html.* Make sure to download the companion, detached PGP signature file.

Verify the Authenticity of the OpenSSH Distribution

To do this, you need the PGP public key from "Damien Miller <dmiller@ilogic. com.au>" within your own PGP public-key ring. You can get a copy of his key by searching one of the known PGP public-key servers such as *http://pgpkeys.mit.edu: 11371.* The key ID is 0x11B5748F. However, in our most recent attempt, we found that this key had expired, so we recommend also performing the MD5 check described below.

A match with his digital signature ensures that the software was downloaded successfully without modification. To verify the digital signature, issue the following command in the directory containing the downloaded files:

```
$ pgp openssh-2.3.0p1.tar.gz.sig
```

If the signature doesn't match, verify that (1) your downloaded file names match those listed above and (2) you have included the needed PGP key in your public key ring.

---

7. Available at *http://www.pgp.com.*

8. Available at *ftp://prep.ai.mit.edu/gnu/gcc/gcc-core-2.95.2.tar.gz.*

9. Available at *http://www.pinfo-zip.org/pub/infozip/zlib/.*

10. Available at *http://www.openssl.org/source/.*

11. Refer to the implementation titled *Installing, Configuring, and Using tcp Wrapper to Log Unauthorized Connection Attempts on Systems Running Solaris 2.x,* available at *http://www.cert.org/security-improvement* under UNIX implementations.

If you are unable to verify the authenticity using PGP, you can verify the distribution using an MD5 checksum as shown below:

File to Download	MD5 Checksum
openssh-2.3.0p1.tar.gz	b3d53dfb45da6e7bf88aaaf65b528aac
openssh-2.3.0p1.tar.gz.sig	dc34e26359b2f0c3a3bc0de8bd5ab722

If the computed cryptographic checksum of the download files does not correspond to the information above, verify that (1) your downloaded filenames match those listed above and (2) your checksum program computes MD5 message digests.

Building

Choose a location that has sufficient space for the OpenSSH distribution.

Unpack the OpenSSH Distribution

First you need to unzip the OpenSSH distribution:

```
$ gunzip openssh-2.3.0p1.tar.gz
```

To unpack the OpenSSH distribution, use the system tar command:

```
$ tar xvf openssh-2.3.0p1.tar
```

This command creates a subdirectory named openssh-2.3.0p1. All operations are to be performed within this subdirectory.

Several files exist in the created directory. One of these files is the OpenSSH INSTALL file. It outlines the requirements and various settings for configuration and installation. Another file is named README. It gives background information on this distribution and references for more information about the SSH protocol.

Choose the Right Configuration Settings Prior to Compile Time

A configuration script configure, provided with the distribution, generates a tailored Makefile. You need to specify several options prior to executing the configure script:

```
$ ./configure  —with-tcp-wrappers  —sysconfdir=/etc/ssh
```

Option	Description
—with-tcp-wrappers	Enable the use of the TCP wrapper library to protect against some attacks coming from non-authorized IP addresses.
—with-syssconfdir	Path to the subdirectory containing the OpenSSH configuration files, public keys and host keys.

Generate the OpenSSH Executables and Man Pages

After the configuration is finished, you can now build the executable and generate the tailored man pages by specifying the make command twice:

```
$ make
$ make manpages
```

Testing Before Installation

No pre-installation test suite comes with OpenSSH.

Installation

To place the OpenSSH binaries, templates for configuration files, and man pages into the correct system directories, start the installation using the make install command as the system administrator using the root account. You can also place all necessary files into the right directory manually as follows:

```
# cp ssh_config.out /etc/ssh/ssh_config
# cp sshd_config.out /etc/ssh/sshd_config
# cp ssh /usr/local/bin/ssh
# ln -s /usr/local/bin/ssh /usr/local/bin/slogin
# cp ssh-keygen /usr/local/bin/ssh-keygen
# cp ssh-agent /usr/local/bin/ssh-agent
# cp ssh-add /usr/local/bin/ssh-add
# cp scp /usr/local/bin/scp
# cp sshd /usr/local/sbin/sshd
# cp ssh.1.out /usr/local/man/man1/ssh.1
# ln -s /usr/local/man/man1/ssh.1
      /usr/local/man/man1/slogin.1
```

```
# cp ssh-keygen.1.out /usr/local/man/man1/
     ssh-keygen.1
# cp ssh-agent.1.out /usr/local/man/man1/ssh-agent.1
# cp ssh-add.1.out /usr/local/man/man1/ssh-add.1
# cp scp.1.out /usr/local/man/man1/scp.1
# cp sshd.8.out /usr/local/man/man8/sshd.8
# cp sftp-server.8.out /usr/local/man/man8/
     sftp-server.8
```

All files installed in /usr/local/bin and in /usr/local/sbin should be set to mode 755, and all documentation files installed in /usr/local/man should be set to mode 644. The /etc/ssh/ssh_config and /etc/ssh/sshd_config files should also be mode 644.

As the system runs, the /usr/local/sbin/sshd daemon creates /etc/ssh/sshd_pic and stores its process ID in that file. If /etc/ssh/sshd_pic exists, then its contents are overwritten with the new process ID each time sshd starts.

Generate the Host Keys

If you already have host keys from an older installation, you can continue to use them. Both RSA and DSA are effective and secure public key algorithms. However, from a security perspective we recommend using the DSA-based version 2 protocol instead of the RSA-based version 1 protocol, due to problems with this earlier protocol.

The version you select depends on the client software in use at your site. For example, if you have a larger number of Windows 95/98/NT clients that support only the old version 1 protocol, you need to support that version. If, on the other hand, you are building a new service, use the new version 2 protocol.

If you are supporting RSA-based version 1 protocol clients, you should plan to update them. Once you have switched to the version 2 protocol, make sure to remove the RSA key files /etc/ssh/ssh_host_key and /etc/ssh/ssh_host_key. pub to prohibit any further use.

To continue using existing keys, place the files within the /etc/ssh/ directory with the same file name as before. (Do not issue the commands listed below, as they will override your existing files!)

If you are not updating an existing SSH or OpenSSH installation, you will not have a public-key pair associated with the host. To create the public-key pair, you have to issue one or both of the following commands. The two commands shown below create two different pairs suitable for the old version 1 protocol and the new version 2 protocol. Create only the pair that you need.

To support the old, RSA-based version 1 protocol use

```
# ssh-keygen -b 1024 -f /etc/ssh/ssh_host_key -N ""
```

For support of the new, DSA-based version 2 protocol use

```
# ssh-keygen -d -f /etc/ssh/ssh_host_key_dsa -N ""
```

For user keys, a passphrase (as described below) is needed to protect the private key stored in the user's ~/.ssh directory; this is not required or supported for host keys (Option -N).

Both the /etc/ssh/ssh_host_key and the /etc/ssh/ssh_host_key_ dsa files must be mode 400 and must belong to the root account. Note that sshd disables the particular version if the specific file is group/world-accessible. The /etc/ssh/ssh_host_key.pub /etc/ssh/ssh_host_key_dsa.pub files should be mode 644.

Start and Stop the sshd Daemon

As a final step, you need to be able to start and stop the server on system reboots and on demand. Install the following script into /etc/init.d/sshd. Make hard links to /etc/rc0.d/K57sshd, /etc/rc1.d/K57sshd and /etc/rc2.d/S99sshd (see the man pages init (1M) and init.d for more information).

```
#! /bin/sh
#
# start/stop the secure shell deamon
# Make links to get sshd start/stoped at the right time:
# /etc/rc0.d/K57sshd
# /etc/rc1.d/K57sshd
# /etc/rc2.d/S99sshd

case "$1" in

'start')
    # Start the ssh deamon
      if [ -f /usr/local/sbin/sshd ]; then
       echo "starting SSHD daemon"
          /usr/local/sbin/sshd &
     fi
     ;;
```

```
'stop')
      # Stop the ssh deamon
        PID=`/usr/bin/ps -e -u 0 | /usr/bin/fgrep sshd |
                                /usr/bin/awk '{print $1}'`
      if [ ! -z "$PID" ] ; then
              /usr/bin/kill ${PID} 1/dev/null 2&1
      fi
      ;;

*)
      echo "usage: /etc/init.d/sshd {start|stop}"
      ;;

esac
```

Testing After Installation

To check whether the sshd daemon is actually working, execute the following tests:

Start the sshd Daemon

As root, start the daemon with the following command:

```
# sh /etc/init.d/sshd
```

Inspect /var/adm/message for log entries similar to the following:

```
Nov 23 19:24:23 host1 sshd[526]: Server listening on
                                 0.0.0.0 port 22.
Nov 23 19:24:23 host1 sshd[526]: Generating 768 bit RSA
                                 key.
Nov 23 19:24:24 host1 sshd[526]: RSA key generation
                                 complete.
```

These entries indicate that the server is running and is listening for connections on port 22 and that it has generated a 768-bit RSA key. The number of the listening process is in brackets. That number must match the contents of /etc/ssh/sshd_pic.

```
$ more /etc/ssh/sshd_pic
526
```

Connect to the sshd Daemon Using Telnet

Connect to the daemon with telnet. If sshd is running and accepting connections, you should see the message shown below. If you are updating your installation, verify that the displayed version number corresponds to the installed version.

```
$ telnet localhost 22
Trying 127.0.0.1...
Connected to localhost.
Escape character is '^]'.
SSH-1.99-OpenSSH_2.3.0p1
^]
telnet z
Suspended
$ ps -e -u 0 | grep sshd
526 ? 0:51 sshd
1057 ? 0:01 sshd
$ %%
telnet localhost 22
^]
telnet q
Connection closed.
$ ps -e -u 0 | grep sshd
526 ? 0:51 sshd
```

Stop the sshd Daemon

As root, stop the daemon with the following command:

```
# sh /etc/init.d/sshd stop
```

Configuring

The initial /etc/ssh/ssh_config and /etc/ssh/sshd_config files may need to be changed from their installed values. While ssh_config controls the use of the client programs (all programs installed into /usr/local/bin, most notably ssh, slogin and scp), sshd_config controls the server program /usr/local/sbin/sshd. We provide some recommendations for both files below. This approach allows authentication of users based only on their public keys.

You can implement an alternative model based on user authentication using ordinary passwords. We provide an outline of the changes to accommodate this approach.

Configure the ssh_config File

The `ssh_config` file is the per user configuration file used by the SSH client. Note that this file's values are installed after the user-specific file, located in ~.ssh/config. From the comments shown below, note that any configuration value is only changed the first time it is set. This means that the user's values can override the values given here. This may, however, disable the user's ability to gain access, depending on the configuration of the remote host the user wants to connect to (for example, the user specifies an incompatible cipher to ensure confidentiality not supported by the server).

We recommend that all configurable values be set so that the program's results are more predictable during version upgrades, a time when program defaults can change. Refer to the man page `ssh (1)` for a detailed explanation of all available values. We concentrate here on values that may have an impact on the security of the overall configuration.

You can further tailor the configuration files by using sections bracketed by "Host" specifications. Such a section applies only to hosts that match one of the patterns given in the specification. "*" and "?" can be used as wildcards in the patterns to be matched. A single "*" as a pattern can be used to provide global defaults for all hosts.

Option	Recommendation	Description
BatchMode	No	BatchMode may be necessary for the execution of scripts, etc., but should be disabled by default.
CheckHostIP	Yes	Enables checking whether the IP address of a server has changed. Such a change may indicate an attack.
Cipher	Blowfish	Cipher to use for version 1 encryption. Blowfish provides good security and performance.
Ciphers	Blowfish-cbc	Cipher to use for version 2 encryption.
DSAAuthentication	Yes	DSA authentication is attempted only if a DSA key exists for the user.

(continued)

Option	Recommendation	Description
FallBackToRsh	No	Otherwise the client tries to connect via the rsh client whenever a connection to the sshd daemon on the remote server is refused.
ForwardAgent	No	Setting this value to "yes" is necessary to make use of the authentication agent. Refer to the man page `ssh-agent (1)` for further information.
ForwardX11	No	Otherwise X11 connections are automatically redirected over the secure channel.
GatewayPorts	No	No remote hosts are allowed to connect to a local forwarded port.
PasswordAuthentication	No	Disables the use of password authentication.
Protocol	2,1	The order of precedence of version 1 and version 2 protocol. As version 2 provides better security, the recommended order is "2" followed by "1." If you are not using version "1" at all, just list "2" here.
RhostsAuthentication	No	RhostAuthentication is not secure. A value of "yes" slows down the client; "no" is recommended.
RhostsRSAAuthentication	No	RhostsRSAAuthentication is based on host keys only and is therefore not recommended. It is no longer supported in the version 2 protocol.
RSAAuthentication	Yes	RSA authentication is attempted only if an RSA key exists for the user.
StrictHostKeyChecking	Yes	Disables any automatic addition of host keys to the user's files indicating any known hosts. If the host key has changed, the connection is refused. This provides maximum protection against attacks.

Configure the `sshd_config` File

The `sshd_config` file is the per-system configuration file used by the `sshd` daemon.

We recommend that all configurable values be set so that the program's results are more predictable during version upgrades, a time when program defaults can change. Refer to the man page `sshd(8)` for a detailed explanation of all available values. We concentrate here on values that may impact the security of the overall configuration.

You need to make three specific changes as part of ongoing maintenance:

- `AllowHosts`: Change this to the list of hosts and domains that are allowed to connect to your server.
- `AllowUsers`: Change this to the list of users who can connect to your server.
- `ListenAddress`: This directive lists the IP address(es) where the sshd daemon listens for incoming connection requests. For multi-homed hosts, including those with dial-in IP access, you may want to define the interfaces that `sshd` listens to.

Option	Recommendation	Description
Ciphers	Blowfish-cbc	Cipher to use for version 2 encryption.
DSAAuthentication	Yes	DSA authentication is allowed.
IgnoreRhosts	Yes	`.rhosts` and `.shosts` in user directories are ignored.
IgnoreUserKnownHosts	Yes	Known hosts contained in user specific files are ignored.
PasswordAuthentication	No	Password authentication is not allowed. Users are authenticated based on keys only.
PermitEmptyPasswords	No	When password authentication is allowed, this specifies whether login to accounts with empty passwords is allowed.
PermitRootLogin	Without-password	Root login is allowed with a user key for root only.

(continued)

Option	Recommendation	Description
Protocol	2,1	The order of precedence of version 1 and version 2 protocol. As version 2 provides better security, the recommended order is "2" followed by "1." If you are not using version "1" at all, just list "2" here.
RhostsAuthentication	No	RhostAuthentication is not secure. A value of "yes" slows down the client; "no" is recommended.
RhostsRSAAuthentication	No	RhostsRSAAuthentication is based on host keys only and is therefore not recommended. It is no longer supported in the version 2 protocol.
RSAAuthentication	Yes	RSA authentication is allowed. If you do not need version 1, set the value to "no."
StrictModes	Yes	Strict checks on ownership and access rights for all user files are enabled. This avoids attacks based on insufficient protection of such files.

Setting Up a User Account

To set up an SSH-enabled user account, you first need to create the necessary keys.

Create a Version 1 User Key

The program `ssh-keygen` is used to create user keys. The user needs to enter a passphrase twice to protect the private key against unauthorized use. This passphrase is provided prior to any use.

```
$ ssh-keygen
Generating RSA keys:  Key generation complete.
Enter file in which to save the key
    (/home/jdoe/.ssh/identity):
```

```
Enter passphrase (empty for no passphrase):********
Enter same passphrase again:********
Your identification has been saved in
/home/jdoe/.ssh/identity.
Your public key has been saved in
/home/jdoe/.ssh/identity.pub.
The key fingerprint is:
76:37:9d:a6:cb:f8:8e:c1:4c:9d:65:8b:aa:3d:7b:d6
     jdoe@host1
```

This produces two files:

```
$ ls -la ~/.ssh
total 4
drwx---    2 jdoe       csd           1024 Nov 22 00:16 .
drwx---   23 jdoe       csd           1024 Nov 21 23:51 ..
-rw----    1 jdoe       csd            529 Nov 22 00:16
                                           identity
-rw-r—r—   1 jdoe       csd            333 Nov 22 00:16
                                           identity.pub
```

Create a Version 2 User Key

The program ssh-keygen is used to create version 2 user keys but executes longer than for version 1 keys. The user needs to enter a passphrase twice to protect the private key against unauthorized use.

```
$ ssh-keygen -d
Generating DSA parameter and key.
Enter file in which to save the key
     (/home/jdoe/.ssh/id_dsa):
Enter passphrase (empty for no passphrase):********
Enter same passphrase again:********
Your identification has been saved in
     /home/jdoe/.ssh/id_dsa.
Your public key has been saved in
     /home/jdoe/.ssh/id_dsa.pub.
The key fingerprint is:
fd:cf:32:64:b1:5d:6e:e0:b3:ba:eb:5b:74:41:ee:94
     jdoe@host1
```

This produces two more files (assuming that the user has created the version 1 keys first):

```
$ ls -la ~/.ssh
total 6
drwx---    2 jdoe       csd            1024 Nov 24 21:41 .
drwx---   23 jdoe       csd            1024 Nov 24 21:24 ..
-rw----    1 jdoe       csd             736 Nov 24 21:41 id_dsa
-rw-r-r-   1 jdoe       csd             604 Nov 24 21:41
                                           id_dsa.pub
-rw----    1 jdoe       csd             529 Nov 22 00:16
                                           identity
-rw-r-r-   1 jdoe       csd             333 Nov 22 00:16
                                           identity.pub
```

Transfer Public Keys to Remote Hosts

Users create their public/private-key pairs with `ssh-keygen` as outlined above. Once these are created, the public keys `~/.ssh/identity.pub` and / or `~/.ssh/id_dsa.pub` need to be transferred to the user's directory on all machines where they wish to log in as `~/.ssh/authorized_keys` (for version 1) and as `~/.ssh/authorized_keys2` (for version 2). However, since the public keys have not yet been installed on these machines, `ssh` apparently cannot be used to make this transfer. This transfer requires system administrator assistance.

System administrators at large sites find it difficult to maintain and distribute public keys. As a result, many sites do not require public-key-based authentication but allow password authentication, given that SSH encryption avoids cleartext password transmissions over insecure networks. The changes to accommodate this approach are outlined below.

Accessing a Remote Host

Once an administrator stores the required public keys as authorized keys, the user can use ssh to connect to a remote host. In order to do so, the user needs to provide the passphrase that was given as the key was created:

```
$ ssh remotehost
Enter passphrase for RSA key 'jdoe@host1':********
Last login: Wed Nov 22 00:36:42 2000 from host1
[jdoe@remotehost ~]$
```

The user has now established an encrypted connection to the remote host and has been authenticated using strong public-key cryptography.

Configuring for Password Authentication

You need to update `ssh_config` and `sshd_config` to allow password authentication. If you use this setup, users are not required to use public-key authentication, but they can still do so at any time.

Change the following entry in both configuration files from "no" to "yes":

Option	Recommendation	Description
PasswordAuthentication	Yes	Password authentication is allowed. Users are authenticated based on their established passwords.

For `sshd_config`, we strongly recommend that you not change the following two entries from the recommended values:

Option	Recommendation	Description
PermitEmptyPasswords	No	When password authentication is allowed, this specifies whether login to accounts with empty passwords is allowed.
PermitRootLogin	Without password	Root login is allowed with a user key for root only. Consider disabling any root login by setting the value to "no." In such cases, users may gain root privileges via su. All users authorized to do so should use public key authentication instead of password authentication.

Keep in mind that `sshd_config` changes need to be made on all remote hosts to which users want to connect.

Access a Remote Host

Once the `ssh` tools are available on the local host and `sshd` is running on the remote host, users can use `ssh` to connect to that remote host. The user needs to provide the remote password. The password is encrypted as part of establishing the network connection.

```
$ ssh remotehost
jdoe@remotehost's password:********
Last login: Wed Nov 22 00:36:42 2000 from host1
[jdoe@remotehost ~]$
```

The user has now established an encrypted connection to the remote host and has been authenticated using strong public-key cryptography.

Tripwire Configuration

This section presents the Tripwire configuration for the SSH system once it is installed. Almost all files are read-only, and none of their attributes should change. One exception is `/etc/ssh/ssh_pid`. The process ID file changes each time the daemon starts.

In addition, you may need to perform maintenance on the `/etc/ssh/ssh_config` and `/etc/ssh/sshd_config` files to change various configuration options. All of these files only change when you change them, and any other changes are unexpected.

```
@@define DYNAMIC                    E+pinugc-sam0123456789

/var/run/ssh_pid                            @@DYNAMIC

@@define BINARY                     E+pinugsamc1-023456789

/etc/init.d/sshd                            @@BINARY
/etc/ssh/rc0.d/K57sshd                      @@BINARY
/etc/ssh/rc1.d/K57sshd                      @@BINARY
/etc/ssh/rc2.d/S99sshd                      @@BINARY
/etc/ssh/known_hosts                        @@BINARY
/etc/ssh/ssh_host_key                       @@BINARY
/etc/ssh/ssh_host_key.pub                   @@BINARY
/etc/ssh/ssh_host_key_dsa                   @@BINARY
/etc/ssh/ssh_host_key_dsa.pub               @@BINARY
/etc/ssh/ssh_config                         @@BINARY
/etc/ssh/sshd_config                        @@BINARY
```

```
/usr/local/bin/ssh                      @@BINARY
/usr/local/bin/slogin                   @@BINARY
/usr/local/bin/ssh-keygen               @@BINARY
/usr/local/bin/ssh-agent                @@BINARY
/usr/local/bin/ssh-add                  @@BINARY
/usr/local/bin/scp                      @@BINARY
/usr/local/sbin/sshd                    @@BINARY
/usr/local/man/man1/ssh.1               @@BINARY
/usr/local/man/man1/ssh-keygen.1        @@BINARY
/usr/local/man/man1/ssh-agent.1         @@BINARY
/usr/local/man/man1/ssh-add.1           @@BINARY
/usr/local/man/man1/scp.1               @@BINARY
/usr/local/man/man1/slogin.1            @@BINARY
/usr/local/man/man8/sshd.8              @@BINARY
/usr/local/man/man8/sftp-server.8       @@BINARY
```

Normal maintenance may also cause the `/etc/ssh/known_hosts` file to change if you use host authentication. You need to make changes to this file when you add or remove host keys or when you replace the old keys for a host by new ones. If you plan to change this file, include the following line into your Tripwire configuration:

```
/etc/ssh/known_hosts                    @@BINARY
```

Additional Resources

We recommend that you stay current with the SSH suite of security tools by consulting the following additional resources:

- The OpenSSH FAQ, available at *http://www.openssh.com/faq.html.*

- The SSH FAQ, available at *http://www.tigerlair.com/ssh/faq/.* This site lists other sites where the FAQ is mirrored. You should check the FAQ often for advice.

- The SSH News Group. The news group comp.security.ssh is available at *http://www.deja.com/=liszt/dnquery.xp?query=-g%20comp.security.ssh.* You should read this frequently to find out about software updates and review questions and answers from SSH users.

A.4 Understanding System Log Files on a Solaris 2.x Operating System

The /var System Directory

Solaris systems use the /var directory to store logs and other local files so that the operating system can support other directories being mounted as read only, sometimes from file servers elsewhere on the network. The /var directory is thus often on a partition that is local to the system.

All of the log files described below can be found in subdirectories under /var. There may be other application-specific log files that you will also need to inspect. However, it is beyond the scope of this implementation to describe all of the log files that you might want to inspect for your specific Solaris installation.

Because log files often provide the only indication of an intrusion, intruders often attempt to erase any evidence of their activities by removing or modifying the log files. For this reason, it is very important that your log files be adequately protected to make it as difficult as possible for intruders to change or remove them.

/var/adm

This directory is usually also available as a symbolic link named /usr/adm. In earlier versions of the UNIX operating system, /usr/adm was a directory that contained most of the administrative log files, along with a number of other configuration tools and files useful for the administration of the operating system.

adm/log/asppp.log

This is the log file associated with the Asynchronous PPP Link Manager aspppd(1M), a user-level daemon that works in concert with the IP-Dialup driver (ipdcm) and PPP streams module (ppp(7M)) to provide IP network services over an analog modem using dialed voice-grade telephone lines.

The log file is text based, and the level of logging is based on an entry in the /etc/asppp.cf file or a command line argument to aspppd. See the man page aspppd(1M) for specific information about this file and the available logging levels.

adm/utmp, adm/utmpx, /adm/wtmp, and adm/wtmpx

These files contain user and accounting information that is recorded when a user logs in, logs out, or starts a new shell process with an application such as xterm or screen. Records written to these log files by the managing application contain account activity for the system.

The data in these files are written as binary data, so they must be read by a tool specifically designed to read such data, for example, last(1) and who(1). See the system man pages for last(1) and who(1) for additional information on the data and display formats available with these tools.

adm/lastlog

This binary log file stores information about a user who has logged into the system. It is kept up-to-date by utilities such as login(1) and in.uucpd(1M). The data are viewable with tools such as last(1), who(1), and finger(1). Refer to the system man pages for more information.

adm/sulog

The sulog file is a record of all attempts by users on the system to execute the su(1M) command. Each time su(1M) is executed, an entry is added to the sulog file.

The format of this human-readable text file includes date, time, success/failure (+/-), and both the current and requested account. The following is a sample excerpt from a sulog file:

```
SU 08/28 11:41 - pts/1 jxk-root
SU 08/28 11:41 + pts/1 jxk-root
SU 09/14 13:05 + pts/0 thimbl-root
SU 09/14 14:58 + pts/0 thimbl-root
SU 09/16 13:52 + pts/0 thimbl-root
SU 09/16 15:16 + pts/2 thimbl-guest
SU 10/19 14:17 - pts/2 marchok-root
SU 10/19 14:17 + pts/2 marchok-root
```

adm/messages

This file is a catch-all log file for a number of messages from the UNIX kernel as well as for other logging applications such as `syslogd`. The file is formatted as an ASCII text file, and entries are usually one record per line, with new entries appended to the end of the file.

The following is a sample excerpt from a messages file. Each pair of lines shown below appears as one line in the file:

```
Oct 31 04:05:01 unix.fghij.net syslogd:restart
Oct 31 04:05:02 unix.fghij.net named[112]: unapproved
     query
from  [10.10.0.1].32768 for "loghost.local.net"
Oct 31 04:05:02 unix.fghij.net named[112]: unapproved
query from [10.10.0.1].32768 for "loghost.local.net"
Oct 31 04:05:42 unix.fghij.net printd[207]: send_job
     failed job 203
(lw_land@lw.fghij.net)check status
Oct 31 04:06:00 unix.fghij.net sendmail[14602]: EAA14602:
     from=ih_cron,
size=456, class=0, pri=30456, ...
Oct 31 04:06:01 unix.fghij.net sendmail[14604]: EAA14602:
     to=ih_cron,
delay=00:00:01, xdelay=00:00:00, ...
Oct 31 04:06:42 unix.fghij.net printd[207]: send_job
     failed job 203
(lw_land@lw.fghij.net) check status
Oct 31 04:07:42 unix.fghij.net printd[207]: send_job
     failed job 203
(lw_port@lw.jghij.net)check status
```

Note that the messages file can get very large quickly and should be rotated regularly to ensure that it does not consume too much local disk space.

/var/log

This log directory is sometimes used to store miscellaneous log files, including log files created by syslog for messages that are not written to `/usr/adm/messages` or to the system console.

Syslog Files

Often a number of miscellaneous syslog files are written to /var/log for logging events that are not logged elsewhere such as main, news, and user events. You can view the events that are written to this directory (or any other log files) by reviewing the syslog config file /etc/syslog.conf. For example, the following syslog. conf file writes several specific log files to the /var/log directory:

```
#
      syslog configuration file (loghost)
      #
      #output to console
      *.err;mail,kern.notice;daemon,auth.debug;user.info
            /dev/console
      #output to local file "messages" for automatic log
            file analysis
      *.err;auth,daemon,mark,kern.debug;mail,user.notice
            var/adm/messages
      #output to local files for archiving messages of
            potential interest
      auth.debug    /var/log/auth.log
      daemon.debug /var/log/daemon.log
      lpr.debug     /var/log/lpr.log
      mail.debug    /var/log/mail.log
      news.debug    /var/log/news.log
      uucp.debug    /var/log/uucp.log
      user.debug    /var/log/user.log
      #
      #end of /etc/syslog.conf
      #
```

log/sysidconfig.log

This log file is created by the sysidconfig(1M) command, which executes system configuration applications or defines a set of system configuration applications. Specific information about this and other related system configuration tools can be found in the system man pages for sysidconfig.

/var/cron

This directory contains the files that you would find associated with the system's cron(1M) and at(1) functions.

cron/log

This file contains log entries for cron(1M) and at(1) jobs that have been run on the local machine. This file is a text file that lists the command that was run, at what time, and as what user. The following sample log file contains both a cron and at job entry:

```
> CMD: /usr/lib/uucp/uudemon.hour
> uucp 14572 c Mon Nov 9 19:11:00 1998
< uucp 14572 c Mon Nov 9 19:11:00 1998
> CMD: 910656780.a
> root 14592 a Mon Nov 9 19:13:00 1998
< root 14592 a Mon Nov 9 19:13:01 1998
```

Other Log Directories under /var and Elsewhere

There are other tools that may have specific log directories under /var. It is beyond the scope of this implementation to attempt to catalog even a collection of the most popular ones such as ftp and samba. We recommend that you familiarize yourself with the specific log files for all such applications and review them regularly.

A.5 Configuring and Using Syslogd to Collect Logging Messages on Systems Running Solaris 2.x

Syslogd(8) is a collecting mechanism for various logging messages generated by the kernel and applications running on UNIX operating systems.

Although this daemon is installed by default, its configuration should be adjusted to specify what messages are to be stored in what files or forwarded to another loghost on the local network. The default syslogd configuration usually does not reflect the full set of installed application programs and does not support the desired logging priorities.

This section describes how to configure and use syslogd on the Sun Solaris operating system, version 2.x.

Understand the syslog Function

Every message handed over to syslogd is assigned a level of importance, consisting of the facility—the system component from which the message originated, e.g., the mail system—and the priority—the severity of the message, e.g., a warning. The configuration lists combinations of priority and facility and specifies actions related to these combinations.

Understand Facilities and Priorities

Based on its configuration, syslogd performs a given action for all messages with a specified priority (or higher) and facility (see tables below). By using the facility, you can log messages generated by different system components with different priorities.

The values of both parameters (priority, facility) are described in detail on the `syslog(3)` man page as shown below:

Facility	Description
auth	Used by authorization systems (login)
cron	Used for the cron and at systems
daemon	System/network daemons
kern	Produced by kernel messages
lpr	Printing system
mail	Mail system
mark	Internally used for time stamps
news	Reserved for the news system
user	Default facility, used for any program
uucp	Reserved for the uucp system
local0..7	Reserved for local use

Priorities are listed from lowest to highest as shown below:

Priority	Description
debug	Normally used for debugging
info	Informational messages
notice	Conditions that may require attention
warning	Any warnings
err	Any errors
crit	Critical conditions like hardware problems
alert	Any condition that demands immediate attention
emerg	Any emergency condition

Understand the Associated Actions

Actions are associated with combinations of facilities and priorities. They specify what to do with the actual log messages that match a given combination as shown below:

Action (example)	Description
/dev/console	Send messages to devices
/var/adm/messages	Write messages to files
@loghost	Forward messages to a loghost
fred, user1	Send messages to users
*	Send messages to all logged-in users

Understand Protection Mechanisms for Log Files

Different approaches are available to provide adequate protection for collected messages:

- Forward a set of specified messages to a loghost, which provides additional security for the stored messages.

- Write a set of specified messages to a write-once medium like a WORM (write once, read many) device to avoid any corruption or manipulation, which might include the deletion, insertion, or change of any single message.
- Write a set of specified messages to a printer to create a paper trail of the most important messages.

Define the Appropriate Data Storage Location

Before establishing the configuration, you need to decide which messages are stored in what files, on what hosts, and what other actions you want to initiate. You need to address two situations:

1. Local hosts store some messages for normal system administration purposes and forward any message to a central loghost for monitoring and added security. On local systems, the directory /var/adm/ is used to store log message files.
2. A central loghost stores all messages based on the logging policies. On loghosts, the directory /var/log/ is used to store log message files.

Although these situations might be quite different, the same clear and simple set of rules can be applied throughout the entire network. The following items describe a policy to handle various log messages in a consistent way:

Display Important Information on the Console

The following messages should be written to the console:

- All messages with priority err or higher
- All messages with priority notice for the more critical facilities kern and mail

In addition, all messages from daemons (daemon) and the authentication components (auth) should be displayed (this implies priority debug or higher).

Collect All Messages for Further Processing

One file should be used to collect all important log messages. This file is then used as an input source for log file processing/filtering programs such as swatch[12] or logsurfer (Section A.6). The file name used for this file is usually messages.

---

12. The swatch implementation is titled *Installing, Configuring, and Using Swatch to Analyze Log Messages on Systems Running Solaris 2.x* and is available at *http://www.cert.org/security-improvement* under UNIX implementations.

All messages should be written to a single file if they are priority err or higher. For the facilities `auth`, `daemon`, `mark`, and `kern`, all messages with priority `debug` and higher should be saved to the same file. In addition, the facilities `user` and `mail` should also be saved there if the message has priority `warning` or higher.

Collect Messages Separately for Important Facilities

All messages for more important facilities like `lpr`, `mail`, `daemon`, and `auth` are written to separate files to produce a complete chronology of events for these facilities. The file names used for these files are usually the name of the facility with the extension .log, e.g., `daemon.log`.

Forward All Messages to a Central Loghost

All messages should be sent to a central loghost to provide consistent processing of all messages for all local hosts. On the loghost, all messages are handled as described above.

All messages forwarded to the loghost should be written to disk to build a complete picture of all events in one location. This assumes that there is sufficient disk space to do so.

It is not possible to differentiate between local and nonlocal messages. As a result, the rules stated above apply to both categories.

Prepare Files to Store Log Messages

You need to create and configure files that reflect the actions you intend for storage of logging messages.

Create the Necessary Files to Store Different Log Messages

You need to create log files and directories manually before their first use if they do not already exist. Existing files should be rotated so that all log files start at the same time and are consistent with one another. This is especially important if the same messages can be written to two or more files.

Check Permissions of Log Files and Directories Used to Store Log Files

You should restrict access to log files and their associated directories. Only system and network administrators should have read access. You should limit write access to `root` (syslogd runs with root privileges).

Routinely Rotate All Log Files

Ensure that log files are routinely rotated to prevent the consumption of all available disk space with historical and outdated messages. See the implementation on rotating log files[13] for more information.

Set Up Other Selected Mechanisms to Deal with Log Messages

If specific protection measures are required (e.g., print a subset of all log messages, write the messages on a write-once medium like a WORM drive), these should be initiated. Implementation details are very dependent on the selected mechanisms, so they are not addressed here.

Prepare and Use the Log Files' Configuration

The next step is to set up your configuration files. Small systems typically have one configuration file for both the local hosts and the loghost. The risk in this approach is that if one local host is compromised, the intruder can also determine the setup of the loghost by analyzing the configuration file. Two examples are provided that reflect the recommended setup. The rules consist of facility-priority combinations and an action separated by a special character (not a blank). More details on additional configurations are available from the man page `syslog.conf(4)`.

Prepare the Hostname for the Loghost

Implementing the rule stating that all messages are to be forwarded to a loghost relies on setting the name loghost as the hostname. This is accomplished by providing `loghost` as the alias or hostname within the file `/etc/hosts` via the domain name system (DNS) or other mechanisms such as the network information service (NIS).

Prepare the Configuration File for Local Hosts

The configuration file `/etc/syslog.conf` is as follows:

```
#
# syslog configuration file (local hosts)
#
# output to console
```

---

13. This implementation is titled *Using newsyslog to Rotate Files Containing Logging Messages on Systems Running Solaris 2.x* and is available at *http://www.cert.org/security-improvement* under UNIX implementations.

```
*.err;mail,kern.notice;daemon,auth.debug;user.info
    /dev/console
# output to local file "messages" for automatic log file
    analysis
*.err;auth,daemon,mark,kern.debug;mail,user.notice
    /var/adm/messages
# output to local files for archiving messages of
    potential interest
auth.debug      /var/adm/auth.log
daemon.debug    /var/adm/daemon.log
lpr.debug       /var/adm/lpr.log
mail.debug      /var/adm/mail.log
# forward to loghost
mark.debug;*.debug   @loghost
# end of /etc/syslog.conf
```

Prepare the Configuration File for the Loghost

The configuration file /etc/syslog.conf is as follows:

```
#
# syslog configuration file (loghost)
#
# output to console
*.err;mail,kern.notice;daemon,auth.debug;
  user.info/dev/console
# output to local file "messages" for automatic log file
analysis (logsurfer)
*.err;auth,daemon,mark,kern.debug;
  mail,user.notice/var/log/messages
# output to local files for archiving messages of
  potential interest
auth.debug      /var/log/auth.log
daemon.debug    /var/log/daemon.log
lpr.debug       /var/log/lpr.log
mail.debug      /var/log/mail.log
news.debug      /var/log/news.log
uucp.debug      /var/log/uucp.log
user.debug      /var/log/user.log
# end of /etc/syslog.conf
```

Inform the Current Process About the Configuration Change

The signal SIGHUP must be sent to an executing process to initiate the use of an updated configuration file. In addition, the process closes all previously opened log files and opens the newly specified log files, as follows:

```
# kill -SIGHUP `cat /etc/syslogd.pid`
```

Additional Steps

The steps above have described the process for handling log messages, implementing them in a syslog configuration, and activating the configuration. Additional steps are needed to fully satisfy security requirements.

Make Use of Mark Messages (Time Stamps)

Mark messages should be turned on to make it easier to analyze the timeline of messages and to identify possible gaps within the log archives.

Mark messages are generated by syslogd after a predefined time period. Other periods can be specified during the syslogd startup.

To activate mark messages, you need to edit the script file that starts syslogd. The file /etc/init.d/syslog must be edited within the start section. In the following example, syslogd is called to set a mark interval of ten minutes, as follows:

```
/usr/sbin/syslog -m 10 1>/dev/console  2>&1
```

If only -m is stated, the default interval is 20 minutes.

Thereafter, the current syslogd must be stopped and restarted by the following command sequence:

```
# /etc/init.d/syslog   stop
# /etc/init.d/syslog   start
```

All messages sent between stopping and starting syslogd will be lost.

Test the Configuration

A program called logger(1) is used to test the configuration. Any facility and priority combination can be specified on the command line, as follows:

```
# /usr/ucb/logger -p mail.warning -t sendmail "this is
the test for mail.warning"
```

This sets the facility set to `mail` and the priority to `warning`. The message is logged as coming from the program `sendmail`.

Protect the Integrity of the Configuration Files

An authoritative copy of the configuration files should be transferred to a write-protected medium to protect it from being compromised. The configuration files should be included in any integrity-checking procedure such as the use of Tripwire (as described in Section A.2).

Integrity-checking procedures that compare cryptographic checksums are of limited use for log files due to the regular addition of new records. It is more useful to compare access permissions, file mode settings, and the user ID of the owner of the current log files with those that are part of your previously stored expected state.

Additional Information

Provide Sufficient Disk Space

You need to provide sufficient disk space to be able to store all desired log messages. The required space is dependent on the configuration and system disk utilization. You need to review the size of log files after establishing the initial configuration and after a series of configuration changes. We recommend that you manually control the size of the log files over a period of time so that you can adjust as necessary.

Keep Denial-of-Service Attacks in Mind

You need to plan for DoS attacks. An intruder can create messages that consume all available disk space. After all available disk space is used, no new messages can be stored, and as a result you may lose the intruder's attack pattern as well as critical messages.

Other services can be compromised to fill the available disk space, so the syslog files should be stored in a separate partition to avoid any confusion or overlap with other services (e.g., the spool directories for printers, e-mail servers).

Another type of DoS attack can occur when the processing load on a system generating log messages is high, possibly preventing the system from storing or forwarding log messages to a loghost as a result. You need to consider resource loading both for systems generating log messages and systems serving as loghosts. You should minimize the placement of other services on servers performing as loghosts.

Even if sufficient system resources are available, log messages might not be forwarded to the loghost. The syslogd protocol is based on the UDP (User Datagram Protocol) network service. Network DoS attacks can result in single log message packets not reaching the loghost, with no notification to the generating host.

There Is No Authentication of Log Messages

Access to the syslogd process should be prohibited to protect against messages created by external network users. This ban on access can be accomplished by filtering packets at the interface between any public network (e.g., the Internet) and the local network. There is no need to accept any syslog message from outside the internal network. Filtering should apply to any internal destination address.

Local users are usually able to create arbitrary log messages using utilities like logger (1). There is no protection against this threat when using syslog.

Identify New syslog Messages

Every application produces different messages in varying formats when using syslog. As a result, it is usually very difficult to know all possible messages (their format, the priority and facility) in advance. We recommend initially storing every log message produced by a given application and then reviewing the results, so that you become familiar with the output. Once this goal has been accomplished, you can usually identify those messages that are most useful for detecting signs of intrusion through the use of application program documentation, man pages, or source code (if available).

If you develop new application programs, you need to include the format and meaning of each log message in the design documentation.

Tools such as swatch or logsurfer can be configured to watch for specific messages and act upon them. Known expected messages can be stored in a database for comparison purposes. Unknown messages can be written to a separate file for later review.

A.6 Installing, Configuring, and Using Logsurfer 1.5 to Analyze Log Messages on Systems Running Solaris 2.x

Many programs log messages that are of potential interest from a security and system administrative perspective. syslogd (as described in Section A.5) is the conventional method for capturing important messages from applications and servers. Typically, no support tools are provided for online analysis of these messages; swatch[14] or logsurfer can be used for this purpose.

Logsurfer was developed to address many of the underlying problems of swatch. The following differences should be considered in your tool selection process:

---

14. This implementation is titled *Installing, Configuring, and Using swatch to Analyze Log Messages on Systems Running Solaris 2.x* and is available at *http://www.cert.org/security-improvement* under UNIX implementations.

- Swatch pattern matching is restricted to single lines, while logsurfer can collect sets of messages by defining expressions for so-called "contexts." A context is defined by all information belonging to it. Each line of a log file can become part of different contexts.

- Swatch rules are static; with logsurfer new rules can be inserted as matches are made.

- Logsurfer is written in C, while swatch is a PERL script.

- Logsurfer supports ease of administration for tasks such as reopening log files or writing a process ID into a file.

This implementation describes how to download, install, and configure the logsurfer tool, version 1.5, on the Sun Solaris operating system, version 2.x.

Effort Estimates

The time needed to retrieve the source code from the distribution site varies depending upon your connection speed. The source code is less than 646 KB (version 1.5). Building and installing logsurfer depends upon machine performance but on average will take less than ten minutes.

Coming up with a comprehensive configuration suitable for your environment and tailored to minimize any misleading or unnecessary message will likely require several months of effort. In particular, messages that do not occur during "normal" business will show up now and then and will require further tailoring.

If new software or new releases are deployed, messages might change or new messages might be generated. This will also require further tailoring.

Prerequisites

You can build and install logsurfer on many UNIX systems. To build logsurfer on your system, you need Internet access to retrieve the following software tools:

- An MD5[15] cryptographic checksum program
- PGP[16] to verify the authenticity of the software distribution
- A C compiler, either the Sun C Computer or the free GNU C Compiler[17]

---

15. Refer to the implementation titled *Using MD5 to Verify the Integrity of File Contents*, available at *http://www.cert.org/security-improvement* under UNIX implementations.

16. Available at *http://www.pgp.com*.

17. Available at *ftp://prep.ai.mit.edu/gnu/gcc/gcc-core-2.95.2.tar.gz*.

Downloading and Verifying

The latest release of logsurfer is available via anonymous ftp from *ftp://ftp.cert.dfn.de/pub/tools/audit/logsurfer/*. Perform a file transfer from *ftp://ftp.cert.dfn.de/pub/tools/audit/logsurfer/logsurfer-1.5.tar.*

To verify the authenticity of the logsurfer distribution using PGP, you also need the detached PGP signature file, available from *ftp://ftp.cert.dfn.de/pub/tools/audit/logsurfer/logsurfer-1.5.tar.asc.* You need the PGP public key from "Ruediger Riediger, DFN-CERT <riediger@cert.dfn.de>" within your own PGP public-key ring. You can get a copy of this key from the DFN-CERT web site (*http://www.cert.dfn.de/*). A match with his digital signature ensures that the software was downloaded successfully without modification. To verify the digital signature, issue the following commands in the directory containing the downloaded files:

```
$ pgp logsurfer-1.5.tar.asc
```

If the signature doesn't match, verify that (1) your downloaded filenames match those listed above and (2) you have included the needed PGP key in your public-key ring.

If you are unable to verify the authenticity using PGP, you can verify the distribution using an MD5 checksum as shown below:

File to Download	MD5 Checksum
ftp://ftp.cert.dfn.de/ pub/tools/audit/logsurfer/ logsurfer-1.5.tar	6e5b25f4a64368560e9452c3414c623d

If the computed cryptographic checksum of the download files does not correspond to the information above, verify that (1) your downloaded filenames match those listed above and (2) your checksum program computes MD5 message digests.

Install logsurfer

To unpack the logsurfer distribution, use the system tar command:

```
$ tar xvf logsurfer-1.5.tar
```

This command creates a subdirectory named `logsurfer-1.5`. All operations are to be performed within this subdirectory.

A configuration script `configure`, provided with the distribution, generates a `Makefile` and the header file `config.h` that contains all of the information necessary to build and install the logsurfer binary file. You need to specify several options when executing this script:

```
$ ./configure —prefix=/usr/local —with-etcdir=/etc
```

Option	Description
--prefix	Path to subdirectory containing all locally installed programs, libraries, etc.
--with-etcdir	Path to subdirectory containing the logsurfer configuration file

Logsurfer uses the GNU `regex` library, which is integrated into the configuration; no additional component needs to be installed.

After the configuration is finished, you can build the binary logsurfer by specifying the `make` command:

```
$ make
```

To place the logsurfer binary and the man pages into the correct system directories, start the installation with the `make` command as system administrator using the root account as follows:

```
# cp man/logsurfer.1 /usr/local/man/man1/
# cp man/logsurfer.conf.4 /usr/local/man/man4/
# cp src/logsurfer /usr/local/sbin/
```

To install the `start-mail` script, you need to execute the following commands. This script is normally used for delivery of e-mail messages related to logsurfer actions:

```
# cp contrib/start-mail/start-mail /usr/local/sbin/
# chmod 750 /usr/local/sbin/start-mail
```

Configure logsurfer

The following sections provide the information you need to prepare the logsurfer configuration so that it reflects your log-processing requirements.

Understand Limitations

Logsurfer can start external programs, which may impact system performance. For example, logsurfer can send e-mail to users (based on a configuration rule) directly or invoke sendmail to do this. The mailer can be called to deliver e-mail immediately. You need to be careful to ensure that in the case of a message flood, logsurfer does not initiate a sendmail flood as well. Start the mailer specifying a "queue only" mode option (which stores the mail messages in a spool directory) to avoid the potential for this type of DoS attack. However, in the event of a serious attack, this option may lead to a delayed report, giving the attacker greater opportunity to suppress reporting and thereby hide the attack.

If using "queue only" mode causes long delays, the README file explains how to use a specific flag, set at compile time, that results in the spool queue being cleared at more frequent intervals.

Check the use of regular expressions within each configuration before using the configuration in a production system. You may end up collecting more log messages than expected if you use submatches to build new regular expressions. Characters such as "." can cause problems. For example, if some.host.name is specified as a submatch, this matches itself but it also matches some+host@name and all other strings with arbitrary characters between some, host, and name.

Understand the Configuration File Structure

Each line starting with the character "#" is considered a comment and is not processed. Each line starting with a white space (TAB or space) is considered a continuation of the previous line. All other lines are interpreted as the beginning of a new rule.

Each configuration rule consists of six mandatory fields and one optional field. Fields are separated by white spaces. More details are explained in the man page logsurfer(4):

Field	Explanation
1. match_regex	This field determines what lines match the rule. Use POSIX regular expressions, as defined within egrep (1), to describe the pattern.
2. not_match_regex	Unless this field is specified as " - ", it is considered to be a regular expression that excludes any line matched by match_regex.

(continued)

Field	Explanation
3. `stop_regex`	Unless this field is specified as `"-"`, the rule is deleted from the list of active rules if the line matches this regular expression.
4. `not_stop_regex`	If the line matches `stop_regex` and the fourth field is not specified as `"-"`, the rule is not deleted.
5. `timeout`	Time duration in seconds. The rule does not time out if "0" is specified.
6. `continue` (optional)	If the keyword "continue" is specified, the remaining rules in the configuration files are considered instead of having the matching process terminated with the current line (the default condition).
7. `action`	This field specifies the action of a rule by one keyword (explained below) along with optional arguments.

Understand the Use of Quotes

You can use submatches of regular expressions to define new contexts or to invoke other actions. These are defined in `egrep` (1). You need to use quotes correctly to ensure that the action is executed as intended. There are three ways to use quotes:

Quotes	Explanation
string	The string is terminated at the first whitespace (TAB or space).
'string'	The string is terminated at the first single quote (') following the initial one. The content between opening and closing quotes is matched.
"string"	The string is terminated at the corresponding double quote ("). The backslash character \ is used as an escape character. \" specifies a double quote without ending the quoted string.

Understand the Actions Available for Rules

The following actions are available:

Action	Explanation
ignore	No further processing is done. Matching lines are ignored from that rule on.
exec	At least one argument must be specified that identifies the program to be called. More arguments can be passed. Variables describing submatches of the match_regex are also allowed.
pipe	Similar to the exec action, this calls an external program to process the matching lines but passes these lines via stdin.
open	This action opens a new context if one does not already exist. See below for more information regarding the use of contexts.
delete	This deletes an existing context without forcing the action related to this context to be executing.
report	The specified contexts are fed as standard input to the program specified by the first argument.
rule	New rules can be created "on the fly." See below for more information about the concept of creating new rules.

You must specify all external programs using a full pathname. Execution of external programs is started in the background so that the logsurfer process is not impacted.

Understand Contexts

Single log messages and sets of log messages can relate to a single event or set of related events. Sending single messages to an administrator by e-mail is not efficient and makes it more difficult for the administrator to know what is happening. Most of the time, the administrator can understand the situation only by inspecting the log file and analyzing messages in context. This being the case, logsurfer was developed to collect a set of log messages based on regular expressions. Default actions are associated with each context. These are executed after a specified time period or after a specified number of log messages are collected. The opening of a context ensures that there is a defined end to a context. The context is also available for further processing such as sending it as a report to an e-mail address. The regular pattern that specifies the match pattern is used as the "name" for a context and is used to reference it within other rules.

Each context consists of six mandatory fields. Fields are separated by white spaces. More details are explained in the man page `logsurfer(4)`:

Field	Explanation
1. `match_regex`	This field determines what lines match the context.
2. `not_match_regex`	Unless this field is specified as `"-"`, it is considered to be a regular expression that excludes any line matched by `match_regex`.
3. `line_limit`	This value defines the maximum number of lines that are to be stored within the context. It is always useful to define a limit to avoid DoS attacks.
4. `timeout_abs`	This value in seconds defines how long the context is considered active before the default action is executed.
5. `timeout_rel`	In addition to the absolute timeout, the default action is executed if a relative timeout (in seconds) is defined and no new log message is added to the context within that time period.
6. `default_action`	The specified action is carried out whenever the maximum number of lines, or the absolute or relative timeout, is reached. All actions except open, delete, and rule are available.

Understand the Concept of Dynamic Rules

One of the most powerful features of logsurfer is the ability to create new rules as needed. This is especially useful when a specific recurring message (such as "file system full") needs immediate attention but only requires an alert to be sent once per hour. This can be achieved by sending mail to the administrator and including a new rule to ignore the same message over a specified time period.

The advantage of dynamic rules is that you can redefine at run-time which events are "of interest." For example, if a telnet connection from a given host is denied, you might want to review all other events related to this host.

To initiate a new rule, use the following action syntax:

Field	Explanation
1. rule_keyword	The keyword rule initiates the creation of a new rule.
2. position	This specifies the position of a rule (see below).
3. new_rule	This specifies the new rule in the same syntax as explained above for all rules.

Position	Explanation
before	The new rule is added before the actual rule.
behind	The new rule is added behind the actual rule.
top	The new rule is added as the first rule.
bottom	The new rule is added as the last rule.

Understand the Handling of a Single Log Message

For each log message, a sequence of procedures is executed:

- The message is stored within each context when it matches match_regex unless it matches not_match_regex.
- The message is compared to the rules in their actual order. When the first rule matching the match_regex line occurs, the given action is executed unless the message matches not_match_regex. No other rules are compared unless the keyword continue is specified.
- The message is compared to all rules. If the message matches the stop_regex rule but not the not_stop_regex rule, the rule is deleted.
- The timeout value of all rules is analyzed. If a timeout is reached, the rule is deleted.

- The relative and absolute timeout values of all contexts are analyzed. If a timeout is reached, the context is deleted and the default action is processed.

By default, logsurfer stops searching for another matching rule after the first matching rule is found, so the order of rules is important. Rules that specify messages to ignore and rules that address frequently occurring messages should appear early in the configuration definition.

Create the Initial Configuration

The most difficult part of the logsurfer setup is defining an acceptable, workable initial configuration that reflects your log-processing interests. To achieve an effective configuration, you need to analyze messages of interest from operational log files. You can then determine what actions you need to take based on this experience. Use the `egrep(1)` program to help define effective rule patterns and test each regular expression to ensure that it operates as intended.

If you are using swatch, you can start with its configuration as a starting point for logsurfer. You can achieve the same results with swatch and logsurfer if you do not use dynamic rules and contexts. It takes some effort to change swatch's regular expressions and the specification of rules, but starting with this configuration allows for a smoother transition to logsurfer. New logsurfer features can be added as the need arises.

Examples

Several sample rules are provided in this section to illustrate how you can use logsurfer. The volume and type of logged messages depend on the specifics of the installed software and the configuration of syslogd as described in Section A.5.

For this example, we assume that the following supporting tools are installed on your system. All of these are available at the CERT web site, *http://www.cert.org/security-improvement,* under UNIX implementations.

- tcp wrapper
- rshd and rlogind from logdaemon
- login from logdaemon
- rpcbind from tcp wrapper

The logsurfer configuration is stored in `/etc/logsurfer.conf`. The program `safe_finger` is part of the tcp wrapper distribution and is used in the example to determine what users are responsible for handling specific log messages. The program `start-mail` is part of the logsurfer distribution (subdirectory `contrib`) and allows you to specify the subject of and recipient for email messages.

```
#----------------------------------------------------------
#  /usr/local/etc/logsurfer.conf
#----------------------------------------------------------

# each tcp wrapper connect messages  will start a context
#----------------------------------------------------------

' .*\[[0-9][0-9]*\]: connect from (.*@|)(.*)' '.*:
connect from (.*@|) ([^]*.local.net\localhost)' - - 0
      CONTINUE open "^.{19,}$3" - 4000 86400 0 ignore

# tcp-wrapper refused messages
#----------------------------------------------------------

' .*\[[0-9][0-9]*\]: refused connect from (.*)' 'refused
connect from 10\.0\.1\.' - - 0
      CONTINUE open "^.{19,}$2" - 4000 86400 0 ignore

' ([^ .]*)(.local.net|) .*\[[0-9][0-9]*\]: refused
connect from (.*)'  - - - 0
      CONTINUE rule before " .*\\[[0-9][0-9]*\\]: refused
connect from $4" - - - 300 ignore

' ([^ .]*)(.local.net|) .*\[[0-9][0-9]*\]: refused
connect from (.*)' - - - 0
      exec "/usr/sbin/safe_finger @$4 |
/usr/local/sbin/start-mail logsurfer \"$2: tcpd:
(backtrack for $0)\""

# unverified hostnames...

' (.*)\[([0-9][0-9]*)\]: warning: can.t verify hostname:
gethostbyname\([^ ]*\) failed' - - - 0
      open " ([^ .]*)(.local.net|) $2\\\[$3\\\]: " - 100
600 10
      pipe "/usr/local/sbin/start-mail logsurfer \"$2:
tcpd: unverified hostname\""

# rpcbind
#----------------------------------------------------------
```

```
' rpcbind: refused connect from ([^        ]*)' '
connect from [^]*.local.net|localhost)' - - 0
      CONTINUE open "^.{19,}$2" - 4000 86400 0 ignore

' ([^ .]*)(.local.net|) rpcbind: refused connect from
([^ ]*) ' - - - 0
      CONTINUE report "/usr/local/sbin/start-mail
logsurfer \"$2: rpcbind: connection refused\""
"^.{19,}$4"

' ([^ .]*)(.local.net|) rpcbind: refused connect from
([^ ]*) ' - - - 0
      CONTINUE rule before " rpcbind: refused connect
from $4" - - - 300 ignore

' ([^ .]*)(.local.net|) rpcbind: refused connect from
([^ ]*) ' - - - 0
      exec "/usr/local/sbin/safe_finger @4 |
/usr/local/sbin/start-mail logsurfer \"$2: rpcbind:
(backtrack)\""

# login
#----------------------------------------------------------

# report login failures on the modem line
'modem.local.net login\[[0-9][0-9]*\]: .* LOGIN FAILURES
ON term/a' - - - 0
      pipe "/usr/local/sbin/start-mail logsurfer \"MODEM:
login: LOGIN FAILURES ON term/a\""

# always report multiple login failures/refused on direct
lines

' ([^ .]*)(.local.net|) login\[[0-9][0-9]*\]: .* LOGIN
FAILURES* ON' - - - 0
      pipe "/usr/local/sbin/start-mail logsurfer \"$2:
login: LOGIN FAILURES\""

' ([^ .]*)(.local.net|) login\[[0-9][0-9]*\]: LOGIN
REFUSED ON' - - - 0
      pipe "/usr/local/sbin/start-mail logsurfer \"$2:
login: LOGIN REFUSED\""

# trace back login attempts over the network
```

```
' ([^ .]*)(.local.net|) login\[[0-9][0-9]*\]: .* LOGIN
(FAILURES*|REFUSED) FROM ([^ ]*)' - - - 0
      exec "/usr/sbin/safe_finger @5 |
/usr/local/sbin/start-mail logsurfer \"$2: login: remote
login errors\""

# ignore regular logins

' login\[[0-9][0-9]*\]: login on (console) as
user1|user2|user3|user4|user5)$' - - - 0
      ignore

' login\[[0-9][0-9]*\]: ROOT LOGIN  ON console' - - - 0
      ignore

# report all other login stuff

' ([^ .]*)(.local.net|) login\[[0-9][0-9]*\]: ' - - - 0
      pipe "/usr/local/sbin/start-mail logsurfer \"$2:
login: unknown login message\""

# ftpd
#---------------------------------------------------------
'ftpd\[([0-9][0-9]*)\]: connection from' - - - 0
      open "ftpd\\[$2\\]:" - 4000 10800 1800 ignore

'ftpd\[([0-9][0-9]*)\]: failed login from ([^ ]*)
\[([0-9.]*)\]' - - - 0
      report "/usr/local/sbin/start-mail logsurfer
\"ftpd: failed login\""
      "ftpd\\[$2\\]:" "^.{19,}$3" "^.{19,}$4"

'ftpd\[([0-9][0-9]*)\]: cmd failure - not logged in'
- - - 0
    rule before
    "ftpd\\[$2\\]: FTP session closed" - '.*' - 1800
          report "/usr/local/sbin/start-mail logsurfer
\"ftpd: cmd failure\"" "ftpd\\[$2\\]:"

'ftpd\[([0-9][0-9]*)\]: FTP session closed' - - - 0
    delete "ftpd\\[$2\\]:"

# ***** other messages
#---------------------------------------------------------
```

```
# ***** here more rules will be usually included to
ignore unimportant
# ***** messages or to handle the specific needs of other
servers and
# ***** applications.

# default - everything else is of potential interest
#-----------------------------------------------------
'.*' - - - 0
      pipe "/usr/local/sbin/start-mail logsurfer \"unknown
message: $0\""

#-----------------------------------------------------
# End of file: logsurfer.conf
#-----------------------------------------------------
```

Complete the logsurfer Setup

After installing the logsurfer software and creating the initial configuration, you need to perform several additional administrative tasks and initiate automatic startup.

Prepare a Separate User ID

The logsurfer process does not require `root` privileges to read the relevant log files, so do not use the root account. Create a separate user ID for logsurfer execution (such as "logsurfer").

If read access to the log files is restricted to a group of system administrators (for example, SA), include logsurfer in this group. If the group has more privileges than necessary for logsurfer, create a new group that includes the SA group and logsurfer. Set the access privileges for the log files to the new group.

Creating a separate user ID is even more important if logsurfer is set up to write the process ID into a file. The home directory of the user logsurfer can be used to store the error log or other data recorded by the program.

Prepare the Needed E-mail Addresses

Include e-mail aliases (not specific user IDs) in the logsurfer configuration if e-mail is used to alert system personnel. This makes it easier to maintain the configuration when users are added and removed.

Set up aliases or mailing lists for each group that needs to receive messages from logsurfer. All unknown messages should be sent to an administrative account for manual inspection and considered for inclusion in an updated logsurfer configuration.

Create a Specific Startup File

You can automatically start up logsurfer using the script /etc/init.d/logsurfer. The script supports starting and stopping the logsurfer process. Keep in mind that hard links (see init (1M) and init.d) have to be created to control changes that occur whenever the system status changes.

These scripts are executed with root privileges. Execute the su command to change the privileges to the previously created user ID ("logsurfer"). This limits any exposure and potential damage if problems occur during logsurfer execution.

```
#!/bin/sh
#

pid=`/usr/bin/cat -s /users/logsurfer/logsurfer.pid`
user=`/usr/bin/id|/usr/bin/sed 's/.*(\(.*\)) .*/\1/'`

# test if listed process is still active

if [ "${pid}" != "" ]; then
    pid=`/usr/bin/ps -p ${pid} | /usr/bin/grep  -w
logsurfer | \
    /usr/bin/awk '{print $1}'`
fi

# handle the option specified

case "$1" in
      'start')
          # start the logsurfer process

          if [ "${pid}" != "" ]; then
              /usr/bin/echo '\nLogsurfer System is already
initialized.'
              exit 0
Logsurfer System initialized.'
              exit 0
          fi

          # stop the actual process
```

```
            /etc/init.d/logsurfer stop

            # wait a while

            /usr/bin/sleep 5

            # start a new process

            /etc/init.d/logsurfer start

            ;;              fi

            if [ -f /usr/local/sbin/logsurfer -a -f
/etc/logsurfer.conf ];
                    then /bin/su - logsurfer -c
"/usr/local/sbin/logsurfer \
                -c /etc/logsurfer.conf \
                -d /users/logsurfer/logsurfer.dump \
                -f /var/adm/messages \
                -l `/usr/bin/wc -l < /var/adm/messages` \
                -p /users/logsurfer/logsurfer.pid  \
                  /users/logsurfer/logsurfer.error 2&1
</dev/null &"
            else

                /usr/bin/echo '\nNo Logsurfer program or
configuration found.'
            fi
            ;;

       'newstart')
            # restart the logsurfer process

            if [ "${pid}" = "" ]; then
                /usr/bin/echo '\nNo

       'stop')
            # stop all logsurfer processes

            if [ "${pid}" = "" ]; then
                /usr/bin/echo '\nNo Logsurfer System
initialized.
                exit 0
            fi

            /usr/bin/kill ${pid}
```

```
        /usr/bin/rm /users/logsurfer/logsurfer.pid
        ;;

    *)
        /usr/bin/echo "Usage: /etc/init.d/logsurfer {
start | newstart | stop }"
        ;;

esac
```

This script is executed during the next status change or at startup unless explicitly initiated.

Restart logsurfer after Rotation of Log Files

Logsurfer opens a specific file to read every new line appended to this file. Logsurfer needs to be informed if the file is no longer used by `syslog` (occurs as a result of log file rotation using newsyslog[18]). The running process must receive a signal `SIGHUP` as shown below to initiate logsurfer's reopening of the file. Make the current process ID available within a specific file using the `-p` <pidfile> option.

```
#!/bin/sh
#
# /usr/lib/newsyslog - rotate log files (loghost)
#

[...]

/bin/kill -HUP `/usr/bin/cat /etc/syslogd.pid`

# ensure a restart of logsurfer

/bin/kill -HUP `/usr/bin/cat
/users/logsurfer/logsurfer.pid`

# end of file /usr/lib/newsyslog
```

Tripwire Configuration

The following is the Tripwire configuration for the installed logsurfer files:

---

18. Available at *http://www.cert.org/security-improvement* under UNIX implementations.

```
@@define BINARY                       E+pinugsamc1-023456789

/etc/logsurfer.conf                   @@BINARY
/etc/init.d/logsurfer                 @@BINARY
/usr/local/man/logsurfer.1            @@BINARY
/usr/local/man/logsurfer.conf.4       @@BINARY
/usr/local/sbin/start-mail            @@BINARY
/usr/local/sbin/logsurfer             @@BINARY
```

A.7 Installing, Configuring, and Using Spar 1.3 on Systems Running Solaris 2.x

Spar (Show process accounting records) is a freely available tool used to process the accounting records on UNIX systems that are generated when the tool is enabled. The program parses information from the accounting records created by `accton` by using command line expressions to query accounting logs and translating them into human-readable form. Spar is similar to the Solaris `lastcomm` program but requires less processor time to return queries.

Spar is a useful security tool for system administrators. It preserves raw data to aid in determining if unauthorized processes have been executed. For example, you can use spar to create a process baseline for later comparisons by recording the normal execution of system processes. This helps you characterize the normal behavior of a system and ultimately recognize behaviors that fall outside normal or expected bounds.

Effort Estimates

Time to retrieve the README and archive files from the distribution site will vary depending on connection speed. The expected time is five seconds or less with a T1 connection. Building and installing spar usually takes around 30 seconds, depending on machine performance.

Prerequisites

Spar can be built and installed on many UNIX systems. The following list is taken from the INSTALL file that comes with the spar distribution:

```
spar is known to compile and run on:

SunOS 4.x, SunOS 5.x

spar should also compile on:

AIX 3.x
IRIX 4.x
HPUX 7.x
NeXT 3.x
```

To build and run spar on your system, you need Internet access to retrieve the software and the following software tools:

- An MD5[19] cryptographic checksum program
- GZIP[20] to uncompress the downloaded file
- A C compiler; either the Sun C Computer or the free GNU C Compiler[21]
- Solaris 2.6 process accounting packages, SUNWacctu and SUNWacctr

Downloading and Verifying

Download the following files into the same directory and verify their checksums with an MD5 checksum program.

File to Download	MD5 Checksum
`spar.README` (from *http://www.zcu.cz/ftp/ mirrors/security-tamu/*)	`546e9c1a182fe41b693dbf53da4e3843`
`spar-1.3.tar.gz` (from *http://www.zcu.cz/ftp/ mirrors/security-tamu/*)	`362dffbbe9844d0046f08c0ae18eeffa`

---

19. Refer to the implementation titled *Using MD5 to Verify the Integrity of File Contents*, available at *http://www.cert.org/security-improvement* under UNIX implementations.

20. Available at *ftp://ftp.gnu.org/gnu/gzip/gzip-1.2.4a.tar.*

21. Available at *ftp://prep.ai.mit.edu/gnu/gcc/gcc-core-2.95.2.tar.gz.*

Building

Unpack the spar distribution with

```
# gunzip -c spar-1.3.tar.gz | tar xf -
```

This creates a directory named `spar-1.2`.
Link to the appropriate `config.h` file.

```
# rm -f config.h
# ln -s config/sunos5.h config.h
```

You should review the Makefile to ensure that there are no configuration variables set that you do not want as part of the build. In particular, make sure that the specified compiler (for example, cc) is the one that you want and that the compiler options are set appropriately for your site. On Solaris 2.x, the defaults should produce a satisfactory build. Build spar with

```
# make
```

Testing Before Installation

To test the correct operation of spar, execute spar with no options from the install location, as follows:

```
# ./spar
```

You should receive output to the terminal similar to the following:

```
02/02/2000 12:21:36 P  accton  root  tty:100.0 00:00
00:00  00:00:00
02/02/2000 12:36:15 F  cron    root  <notty>   00:00
00:00  05:01:00  KILL
02/02/2000 12:47:28 FP snmpdx  root  <notty>   00:00
00:00  05:00:03  KILL
```

Installation

You may want to choose a directory for the spar binary, such as `/usr/local/bin`, that is not part of the standard OS binary tree instead of copying it to `/sbin`. The spar binary and man page can be copied directly to their respective subdirectories without additional install steps. For example, copy spar to `/usr/local/bin/` and `spar.1` to

/usr/local/man/man1/. You should check their ownership and file protections once they have been copied to ensure that they cannot be modified or executed by unprivileged accounts.

Configuration

The spar program does not require you to configure any of the distribution files. Procedures for configuring dependent services related to spar are described in the following section.

Turn on Process Accounting

The spar tool requires that process accounting be turned on and assumes that the process accounting information is written to the file /var/adm/pacct. If you have not already enabled process accounting on your system and are not familiar with how to do so, see the implementation *Enabling Process Accounting on Systems Running Solaris 2.x,* available at *http://www.cert.org/security-improvement* under UNIX implementations.

Test the spar System

Once spar has been installed and process accounting turned on, you can issue basic commands and see output that is similar to what follows.

The following spar command prints information on processes run by root from a tty

```
# spar -e 'user=root && tty != notty {print}'
```

and produces output similar to the following:

```
10/19/1999 14:34:48    F    sh       root   pts/0   00:00
    00:00 00:00:00
10/19/1999 14:34:52         ls       root   pts/0   00:00
    00:00 00:00:00
10/19/1999 14:36:09         accton   root   pts/0   00:00
    00:00 00:00:00
10/19/1999 14:36:31    F    which    root   pts/0   00:00
    00:00 00:00:00
10/19/1999 14:36:31         which    root   pts/0   00:00
    00:00 00:00:00
10/19/1999 14:34:37    P    sh       root   pts/0   00:00
    00:00 05:15:44
```

Using spar

Common Use

Spar is run with or without options from the command line. Under basic execution with no options, spar returns ASCII output to the terminal, similar to

```
02/02/2000 12:21:36  P accton    root    tty:100.0  00:00
       00:00 00:00:00
02/02/2000 12:36:15 F  cron       root    <notty>    00:00
       00:00 05:01:00 KILL
02/02/2000 12:47:28 FP snmpdx     root    <notty>    00:00
       00:00 05:00:03 KILL
```

Recommended Use

Spar is more useful when combined with other command line options such as -e {script}. This option allows spar to run with an inline script. For example, spar could be executed to report only those processes that root or another privileged user has run, between specified dates and times, and from what locations. See the spar man page, spar -h (help), or below for more advanced options.

Advanced Use

Spar can be combined with other tools, or its output can be compared against the output of other tools, to create a more complete picture of system processes and to help recognize unexpected events.

Use with Other Commands

When integrated with native text tools, spar can be used to immediately return possible potential security events of interest. The following are some examples of combined use:

```
# spar -e 'user=root {print}' | grep passwd
# spar -e 'user=root {print}' | grep useradd
```

Advanced Examples

While these examples use spar to track down privileged commands by using an expression in conjunction with the grep command, using advanced expressions with spar can help to capture those processes running under abnormal circumstances. Examples of abnormal events or occurrences might be the following.

(1) Processes executed by users or administrators not within the normal business hours and on weekends, for example:

```
# spar -r -e 'time=18:00:00 || time<=08:00:00
  {print}'
# spar -r -e 'date=01/01/2000 || date<=02/02/2000
  {print}'
```

(2) Processes executed by users from remote locations, for example:

```
# spar -r -e 'tty=notty'
```

Automated Use

Process accounting records log information to the file `/var/adm/pacct` (or other specified file). Newsyslog[22] can be used to rotate the accounting logs on a periodic basis to keep the logs down to a manageable size for use with spar. Spar can therefore be automated through addition of the tool to a daily or weekly `cron` job where the tool is set to search for specific expressions as mentioned above.

Integration with Other Administrative/Security Tools

When compared with the output of other security tools, spar's output can do the following:

1. Corroborate a security event that happened by returning the process and user information of the event
2. Identify discrepancies when processes that are reported by programs such as top, sps, and ps are not properly logged by process accounting

Tripwire Configuration

The following is the Tripwire configuration for the spar program once installed. Only two files, the spar executable and `spar (1)` man page, require monitoring by Tripwire. In addition, files necessary to implement process accounting in the Solaris OS should be monitored.

---

22. Refer to the implementation titled *Using newsyslog to Rotate Files Containing Logging Messages on Systems Running Solaris 2.x,* available at *http://www.cert.org/security-improvement.*

The following files should not change, as any changes are unexpected:

```
@@define BINARY              E+pinugsamc1-023456789

/usr/local/bin/spar          @@BINARY

/usr/local/man/man1/spar.1   @@BINARY
```

A.8 Installing and Operating Tcpdump 3.4 on Systems Running Solaris 2.x

Tcpdump is a tool for network monitoring and one of the best-known sniffers for UNIX. Built with the libpcap (packet capture library) interface,[23] tcpdump collects information from packets on the network, including those intended for other host machines. Tcpdump does this through a network interface card's ability to enter into promiscuous mode where the tool then dumps packet header information depending on the Boolean expression being applied.

Tcpdump helps you characterize the normal behavior of a system and ultimately recognize those behaviors that fall outside the normal bounds. Note that tcpdump only *aids* in the collection of information about network traffic (types of traffic, connections, etc.) appearing on a network segment; the administrator must still analyze whether the network traffic is within normal boundaries. Therefore, one of the key uses of tcpdump is to gather information about the normal behavior of a network's traffic and then filter out the known traffic patterns in an attempt to identify unusual or unexpected traffic that warrants further investigation.

Effort Estimates

Time to retrieve the archive files from the distribution site will vary depending on connection speed. Expected time is under 30 seconds for both files via a T1 connection. Building and installing tcpdump will take some time depending on machine performance. The expected time is less than five minutes.

---

23. Refer to the implementation titled *Installing libpcap to Support Network Packet Tools on Systems Running Solaris 2.x,* available at *http://www.cert.org/security-improvement,* under UNIX implementations.

Prerequisites

Tcpdump can be built and installed on many UNIX systems. This software is known to compile and run on

AIX, BSDI, DG-UX, FreeBSD, HP-UX, IRIX, Linux, NetBSD, OpenBSD, SCO, Solaris, SunOS, True64 UNIX, UNIX, Ultrix, and Unixware

To build and run tcpdump on your system you need Internet access to retrieve the following software tools:

- An MD5[24] cryptographic checksum program
- GZIP[25] to uncompress the downloaded file
- A C compiler; either the Sun C Computer or the free GNU C Compiler[26]

Downloading and Verifying

Download the following files into the same directory (i.e. `/tmp`) and verify their checksums with an MD5 checksum program.

File to Download	MD5 Checksum
`http://www.tcpdump/org/` `release/tcpdump-3.5.2.tar.gz`	`61f221d8a81893fbd4efa89f8426e145`
`http://www.tcpdump.org/` `release/libpcap-0.5.2.tar.gz`	`1138682b9bef56c8c9986346645f7216`

If the computed cryptographic checksum of the download files does not correspond to the information above, verify that (1) your downloaded file names match those listed above and (2) your checksum program computes MD5 message digests.

---

24. Refer to the implementation titled *Using MD5 to Verify the Integrity of File Contents,* available at *http://www.cert.org/security-improvement,* under UNIX implementations.

25. Available at *ftp://ftp.gnu.org/gnu/gzip/gzip-1.2.4a.tar.*

26. Available at *ftp://prep.ai.mit.edu/gnu/gcc/gcc-core-2.95.2.tar.gz.*

Building

Unpack the libpcap and tcpdump distribution under the same parent directory (i.e. /tmp) with

```
# /usr/local/sbin/gunzip -c libpcap-0.5.2.tar.Z |
  /usr/sbin/tar xf -
# /usr/local/sbin/gunzip -c tcpdump-3.5.2.tar.Z |
  /usr/sbin/tar xf -
```

This unpacks the compressed archives and creates directories named libpcap-0.5 and tcpdump-3.5 respectively. If necessary, enter the libpcap-0.5 and tcpdump-3.5 directories and read the respective INSTALL files.

Next, enter the libpcap-0.5 directory and build libpcap with

```
# ./configure
# /usr/ccs/bin/make
```

Next, enter the tcpdump-3.5 directory and build tcpdump with

```
# ./configure
# /usr/ccs/bin/make
```

Testing Before Installation

To test the correct operation of tcpdump, change to the root user and execute tcpdump with no options from the pre-install location, with

```
# ./tcpdump
```

You should receive output to the terminal similar to the following:

```
Tcpdump: listening on pcn[x]
09:39:00.806655 hosta.domain.org.138
  123.123.123.123.138: udp 212
09:39:00.816435 hosta.domain.org.138
  123.123.123.123.128: udp 210
09:41:38.234360 arp who-has hostb.domain.org tell
  hosta.domain.org
09:41:38.235053 arp reply hostb.domain.org is-at
  xx:xx:xx:xx:xx:xx
```

```
10:02:07.770265 hosta.domain.org.32841
  hostc.domain.org.domain: 10557+ (31)
10:02:07.780248 hostc.domain.org.domain
  hosta.domain.org.32841: 10557 NxDomain* 0/1/0 (86) (DF)
```

Hit Ctrl-C to escape the tool; you should receive messages similar to the following:

```
^C
7 packets received by filter
```

Installation

Next, change to the root user and install tcpdump with

```
#  /bin/su root
#  /usr/ccs/bin/make install
#  /usr/ccs/bin/make install-man
```

The tcpdump binary, `tcpdump`, installs to `/usr/local/sbin/tcpdump` and the manual page, `tcpdump.1`, installs to `/usr/local/man/man1/tcpdump.1`. After installation, you should check their ownership and file protections to ensure that they cannot be modified or executed by unprivileged accounts. Our recommendations are to maintain access controls defined by the creator, as follows:

```
tcpdump     Mode 550 with owner bin and group sys
tcpdump.1   Mode 444 with owner bin and group sys
```

Testing After Installation

To test the correct operation of tcpdump after installation, follow the steps mentioned in the Testing Before Installation section above, naming the absolute path of the tool. Again, you must be the root user to execute tcpdump, for example:

```
#  /bin/su root
#  /usr/local/sbin/tcpdump
```

Configuration

The tcpdump program does not require configuration of any of the distribution files.

Using tcpdump

Common Use

Tcpdump is run with or without options from the command line. Under basic execution with no options, tcpdump returns ASCII output to the terminal describing the network traffic, including the following:

- Timestamp [hh:mm:ss.xxxxxx]
- Interface [pcn{0,1, 2, ...}, lo]
- Direction of the traffic [>,<]
- Protocol [tcp, udp, arp, . . .]
- Resolved/unresolved address(es)
- Media access control (MAC) address
- Other information (dependent on traffic type)

Recommended Use

Tcpdump is more effective when used to examine specific network traffic passing by a promiscuous host. This filtering requires that command line arguments be supplied to tcpdump at execution. For example, tcpdump could be executed to return only that traffic that pertains to a specific protocol, host, or connection.

The following information presents options, primitives, and expressions that may be passed to tcpdump at the command line at execution. This information was reproduced from the `tcpdump(1)` manual pages.

Option	Description
-a	Attempt to convert network and broadcast addresses to names.
-c	Exit after receiving `count` packets.
-d	Dump the compiled packet-matching code in a human readable form to standard output and stop.
-dd	Dump packet-matching code as a C program fragment.
-ddd	Dump packet-matching code as decimal numbers (preceded with a count).
-e	Print the link-level header on each dump line.

Option	Description
-f	Print "foreign" Internet addresses numerically rather than symbolically (this option is intended to get around serious brain damage in Sun's yp server #151; usually it hangs forever translating nonlocal internet numbers).
-F	Use `file` as input for the filter expression. An additional expression given on the command line is ignored.
-i	Listen on `interface`. If unspecified, tcpdump searches the system interface list for the lowest numbered, configured up interface (excluding loopback). Ties are broken by choosing the earliest match.
-l	Make stdout line buffered. Useful if you want to see the data while capturing it. E.g., "tcpdump -l	tee dat" or "tcpdump -l dat & tail -f dat".
-m	Load SMI MIB module definitions from file `module`. This option can be used several times to load several MIB modules into tcpdump.
-n	Don't convert addresses (i.e., host addresses, port numbers, etc.) to names.
-N	Don't print domain name qualification of host names. E.g., if you give this flag then tcpdump will print "nic" instead of "nic.ddn.mil".
-O	Do not run the packet-matching code optimizer. This is useful only if you suspect a bug in the optimizer.
-p	Don't put the interface into promiscuous mode. Note that the interface might be in promiscuous mode for some other reason; hence, '-p' cannot be used as an abbreviation for 'ether host {local-hw-addr} or ether broadcast'.
-q	Quick (quiet?) output. Print less protocol information so output lines are shorter.
-r	Read packets from `file` (which was created with the -w option). Standard input is used if file is " - ".
-R	Assume ESP/AH packets to be based on specification (RFC1825 to RFC1829). If specified, tcpdump will not print replay prevention field. Since there is no protocol version field in ESP/AH specification, tcpdump cannot deduce the version of ESP/AH protocol.
-s	Snarf snaplen bytes of data from each packet rather than the default of 68 (with SunOS's NIT, the minimum is actually 96). 68 bytes is adequate for IP, ICMP, TCP and UDP but may truncate protocol information from name

(continued)

Option	Description
	server and NFS packets (see below). Packets truncated because of a limited snapshot are indicated in the output with "[|proto]", where `proto` is the name of the protocol level at which the truncation has occurred. Note that taking larger snapshots both increases the amount of time it takes to process packets and effectively decreases the amount of packet buffering. This may cause packets to be lost. You should limit `snaplen` to the smallest number that will capture the protocol information you're interested in.
-T	Force packets selected by "expression" to be interpreted as the specified type. Currently known types are `rpc` (Remote Procedure Call), `rtp` (Real-Time Applications protocol), `rtcp` (Real-Time Applications control protocol), `vat` (Visual Audio Tool), and `wb` (distributed White Board).
-S	Print absolute, rather than relative, TCP sequence numbers.
-t	Don't print a timestamp on each dump line.
-tt	Print an unformatted timestamp on each dump line.
-v	(Slightly more) verbose output. For example, the time to live and type of service information in an IP packet is printed.
-vv	Even more verbose output. For example, additional fields are printed from NFS reply packets.
-vvv	Even more verbose output. For example, telnet `SB...SE` options are printed in full. With `-X` telnet options are printed in hex as well.
-w	Write the raw packets to `file` rather than parsing and printing them out. They can later be printed with the -r option. Standard output is used if file is "`-`".
-x	Print each packet (minus its link level header) in hex. The smaller of the entire packet or `snaplen` bytes will be printed.
-X	When printing hex, print ascii too. Thus if `-x` is also set, the packet is printed in hex/ascii. This is very handy for analysing new protocols. Even if `-x` is not also set, some parts of some protocols may be printed in hex/ascii.
Expression	selects which packets will be dumped. If no expression is given, all packets on the net will be dumped. Otherwise, only packets for which expression is "true" will be dumped.
	The expression consists of one or more primitives. Primitives usually consist of an ID (name or number) preceded by one or more qualifiers. There are three different kinds of qualifier:

Qualifier	Description
type	Specify what kind of thing the id name or number refers to. Possible types are host, net and port. E.g., 'host foo', 'net 128.3', 'port 20'. If there is no type qualifier, host is assumed.
dir	Specify a particular transfer direction to and/or from id. Possible directions are src, dst, src or dst and src and dst. E.g., 'src foo', 'dst net 128.3', 'src or dst port ftp-data'. If there is no dir qualifier, src or dst is assumed. For "null" link layers (i.e., point to point protocols such as slip) the inbound and outbound qualifiers can be used to specify a desired direction.
proto	Restrict the match to a particular protocol. Possible protos are ether, fddi, ip, arp, rarp, decnet, lat, sca, moprc, mopdl, tcp and udp. E.g., 'ether src foo', 'arp net 128.3', 'tcp port 21'. If there is no proto qualifier, all protocols consistent with the type are assumed. E.g., 'src foo' means '(ip or arp or rarp) src foo' (except the latter is not legal syntax), 'net bar' means '(ip or arp or rarp) net bar' and 'port 53' means '(tcp or udp) port 53'.

Primitive	Description
dst host host	True if the IP destination field of the packet is host, which may be either an address or a name.
src host host	True if the IP source field of the packet is host.
host host	True if either the IP source or destination of the packet is host. Any of the above host expressions can be prepended with the keywords ip, arp, rarp, or ip6 as in ip host host which is equivalent to ether proto \ip and host host If host is a name with multiple IP addresses, each address will be checked for a match.
ether dst ehost	True if the Ethernet destination address is ehost. Ehost may be either a name from /etc/ethers or a number (see ethers (3N) for numeric format).
ether src ehost	True if the Ethernet source address is ehost.
ether host ehost	True if either the Ethernet source or destination address is ehost.

(continued)

Primitive	Description
gateway host	True if the packet used host as a gateway, i.e., the Ethernet source or destination address was host but neither the IP source nor the IP destination was host. Host must be a name and must be found in both /etc/hosts and /etc/ethers. (An equivalent expression is ether host [ehost] and not host [host], which can be used with either names or numbers for [host] / [ehost].)
dst net net	True if the Ipv4/v6 destination address of the packet has a network number of net. Net may be either a name from /etc/networks or a network number (see networks (4) for details).
src net net	True if the Ipv4/v6 source address of the packet has a network number of net.
net net	True if either the Ipv4/v6 source or destination address of the packet has a network number of net.
net net mask mask	True if the Ipv4/v6 address matches net with the specific net-mask. May be qualified with src or dst. Note that this syntax is not valid for IPv6 net.
net net/len	True if the Ipv4/v6 address matches net with a netmask len bits wide. May be qualified with src or dst.
dst port port	True if the packet is ip/tcp or ip/udp and has a destination port value of port. The port can be a number or a name used in /etc/services (see tcp(4P) and udp(4P)). If a name is used, both the port number and protocol are checked. If a number or ambiguous name is used, only the port number is checked (e.g., dst port 513 will print both tcp/login traffic and udp/who traffic, and port domain will print both tcp/domain and udp/domain traffic).
src port port	True if the packet has a source port value of port.
port port	True if either the source or destination port of the packet is port. Any of the above port expressions can be prepended with the keywords tcp or udp, as in tcp src port port, which matches only tcp packets whose source port is port.

Primitive	Description
less `length`	True if the packet has a length less than or equal to `length`. This is equivalent to: `len <= length`.
greater `length`	True if the packet has a length greater than or equal to `length`. This is equivalent to: `len = length`.
ip proto `protocol`	True if the packet is an ip packet (see `ip(4P)`) of protocol type `protocol`. `Protocol` can be a number or one of the names `icmp`, `igrp`, `udp`, `nd`, or `tcp`. Note that the identifiers `tcp`, `udp`, and `icmp` are also keywords and must be escaped via backslash (\), which is \\ in the C-shell. Note that this primitive does not chase protocol header chain.
ip6 proto protocol	True if the packet is an IPv6 packet of protocol type protocol. Note that this primitive does not chase protocol header chain.
ip6 protochain `protocol`	True if the packet is an IPv6 packet and contains protocol header with type `protocol` in its protocol header chain. For example, `ip6 protocol 6` matches any IPv6 packet with TCP protocol header in the protocol header chain. The packet may contain, for example, authentication header, routing header, or hop-by-hop option header, between IPv6 header and TCP header. The BPF code emitted by this primitive is complex and cannot be optimized by BPF optimizer code in tcpdump, so this can be somewhat slow.
ip protochain `protocol`	Equivalent to `ip6 protochain protocol`, but this is for IPv4.
ether broadcast	True if the packet is an Ethernet broadcast packet. The `ether` keyword is optional.
ip broadcast	True if the packet is an IP broadcast packet. It checks for both the all-zeroes and all-ones broadcast conventions, and looks up the local subnet mask.
ether multicast	True if the packet is an Ethernet multicast packet. The `ether` keyword is optional. This is shorthand for `'ether[0] & 1 != 0'`.

(continued)

Primitive	Description
ip multicast	True if the packet is an IP multicast packet.
ip6 multicast	True if the packet is an IPv6 multicast packet.
ether proto `protocol`	True if the packet is of ether type `protocol`. Protocol can be a number or a name like `ip`, `ip6`, `arp`, or `rarp`. Note these identifiers are also keywords and must be escaped via backslash (\ ). [In the case of FDDI (e.g., `'fddi protocol arp'`), the protocol identification comes from the 802.2 Logical Link Control (LLC) header, which is usually layered on top of the FDDI header. Tcpdump assumes, when filtering on the protocol identifier, that all FDDI packets include an LLC header, and that the LLC header is in so-called SNAP format.]
decnet src `host`	True if the DECNET source address is `host`, which may be an address of the form "10.123", or a DECNET hostname. [DECNET hostname support is only available on Ultrix systems that are configured to run DECNET.]
decnet dst `host`	True if the DECNET destination address is `host`.
decnet host `host`	True if either the DECNET source or destination address is `host`.
ip, ip6, arp, rarp, decnet	Abbreviations for `ether proto p` where `p` is one of these protocols.
lat, moprc, mopdl	Abbreviations for `ether proto p` where `p` is one of the above protocols. Note that tcpdump does not currently know how to parse these protocols.
tcp, udp, icmp	Abbreviations for `ip proto p` where `p` is one of these protocols.
[expr] [relop] [expr]	True if the relation holds, where [relop] is one of <, >=, <=, =, !=, and [expr] is an arithmetic expression composed of integer constants (expressed in standard C syntax), the normal binary operators [+, -, *, /, &, |], a length operator,

Primitive	Description
	and special packet data accessors. To access data inside the packet, use the following syntax:

```
proto [ expr : size ]
```

Proto is one of `ether`, `fddi`, `ip`, `ip6`, `arp`, `rarp`, `tcp`, `udp`, or `icmp`, and indicates the protocol layer for the index operation. Note that the tcp, udp, and upper-layer protocol types apply only to IPv4, not IPv6 (this will be fixed in the future). The byte offset, relative to the indicated protocol layer, is given by [expr]. [Size] is optional and indicates the number of bytes in the field of interest; it can be one, two, or four, and defaults to one. The length operator, indicated by the keyword `len`, gives the length of the packet.

For example, `'ether[0] & 1 != 0'` catches all multicast traffic. The expression `'ip[0] & 0xf != 5'` catches all IP packets with options. The expression `'ip[6:2] & 0x1fff = 0'` catches only unfragmented datagrams and frag zero of fragmented datagrams. This check is implicitly applied to the tcp and udp index operations. For instance, `tcp[0]` always means the first byte of the TCP header, and never means the first byte of an intervening fragment.

Applying command line arguments to tcpdump at execution allows you to begin to characterize the normal behavior of packets traversing your network. Specifically, tcpdump will allow you to recognize the normal patterns of traffic on your network by producing the types of protocols used, internal to external connections made, and inbound and outbound traffic to and from specific hosts. Again, the tool only enables you to collect information about network traffic; the formation of heuristics and the notion of an expected norm are your responsibility as the administrator. The following examples allow you to begin to form the heuristics of normal behavior.

Examples of Recommended Use

To display all inbound and outbound packets from the host [hostA.dom.org]:

```
# tcpdump host host.dom.org
```

To display packets between host [hostZ.domain.org] and either [hostB.dom.org] or [hostC.dom.org]:

```
# tcpdump host hostA.dom.org and \( hostB.dom.org or
   hostC.dom.org \)
```

To display all IP packets between [hostZ.dom.org] and any host except [hostA.dom.org]:

```
# tcpdump ip host hostZ.dom.org and not hostA.dom.org
```

To display all packets between local hosts and hosts at network [domB.org]:

```
# tcpdump net domB.org
```

To display all ftp traffic through the Internet gateway [GateA] (note that the expression is quoted to prevent the shell from misinterpreting the parentheses):

```
# tcpdump 'gateway GateA and (port ftp or ftp-data)'
```

Advanced Use

Once tcpdump has been applied and you have observed the normal types of traffic and protocols on your network, you can begin to use tcpdump to identify unusual or unexpected traffic. Tcpdump can be used to filter for and recognize abnormal traffic, for example:

- By applying options that filter out the observed, normal traffic between hosts
- By applying options that filter the network for traffic that should never exist on your network (such as "spoofed" ip traffic)

Advanced Examples

These examples use tcpdump to filter network traffic by using advanced expressions and help you to recognize abnormal traffic passing by or destined for your system.

To display start and end packets (SYN and FIN packets) of each TCP conversation involving a nonlocal host:

```
# tcpdump 'tcp[13] & 3 != 0 and not src and dst net
[localnet]'
```

To print traffic that does not have a local host as its source or destination (note that if your network has only one gateway between you and one other network, this traffic should never traverse your local network):

```
# tcpdump ip and not net [localnet]
```

To display IP packets longer than 576 bytes sent through gateway snup:

```
# tcpdump 'gateway snup and ip[2:2]  576'
```

To display IP broadcast or multicast packets that were not sent via Ethernet broadcast or multicast:

```
# tcpdump 'ether[0] & 1 = 0 and ip[16] = 224'
```

To display all ICMP packets that are not echo requests/replies (i.e., not ping packets):

```
# tcpdump 'icmp[0] != 8 and icmp[0] != 0'
```

Integration with Other Administrative/Security Tools

Compared with the output of other security tools, tcpdump's output can do the following:

1. Corroborate that a security activity has happened (through traffic logs) or is happening by displaying network traffic that may relate to a security event
2. Identify discrepancies and possible security events when network traffic is displayed but open network connections are misreported by programs such as top, lsof, and ps.[27]

Tripwire Configuration

The following is the Tripwire configuration for the tcpdump program once installed. Only two files, the tcpdump executable and `tcpdump(1)` man page, require monitoring by Tripwire. In addition, files necessary to implement process accounting in the Solaris OS should be watched.

The following files should not change, and any changes are unexpected:

```
@@define BINARY               E+pinugsamc1-023456789

/usr/local/bin/tcpdump        @@BINARY
/usr/local/man/man1/tcpdump.1 @@BINARY
```

---

27. Refer to implementations available at *http://www.cert.org/security-improvement*, under UNIX implementations.

Acknowledgments

The author would like to thank the developers of tcpdump and the authors of the tcpdump manual page. Many of the examples provide in this document can be directly attributed to the developer's information accompanying the tcpdump source distribution.

A.9 Writing Rules and Understanding Alerts for Snort, a Network Intrusion Detection System

Snort[28] is a lightweight network intrusion detection system created by Martin Roesch. Snort is based on the libpcap[29] packet capture library, commonly used in many TCP/IP traffic sniffers and analyzers. According to the Snort web site, the program "can perform protocol analysis, content searching/matching, and can be used to detect a variety of attacks and probes, such as buffer overflow, stealth port scans, CGI attacks, SMB probes, OS fingerprinting attempts, and much more."

Snort has a real-time alerting capability, with alerts being sent to syslog, a separate "alert" file, or as a WinPopup message via Samba's smbclient.

This implementation covers the basic steps to obtain and install the Snort intrusion detection system on your computer. We examine how to write Snort rules and describe how you can validate generated alerts. This document does not cover basic or advanced use of the Snort system, customization of the installation, or configuration of the logging and alerting system; nor does it answer such questions as where to deploy Snort in your network environment. For details on these subjects, ports to other operating systems, plug-ins for reporting, and prebuilt rule sets, consult the Snort web site.

Effort Estimates

Time to retrieve the necessary archive files from the distribution site will vary depending on connection speed. The expected time is a minute or less with a high-speed con-

---

28. Refer to *http://www.snort.org*.

29. Refer to the implementation titled *Installing libpcap to support network packet tools on systems running Solaris 2.x*, available at *http://www.cert.org/security-improvement*, under UNIX implementations.

nection. Building and installing Snort usually takes a minute or two, depending on machine performance.

Prerequisites

Snort can be built and installed on many UNIX systems. The following list is taken from the Snort web site:

Snort is known to compile and run on

```
Sparc: SunOS 4.1.x, Solaris, Linux, and OpenBSD
x86: Linux, OpenBSD, FreeBSD, NetBSD, and Solaris
M68k/PPC: Linux, OpenBSD, NetBSD, Mac OS X Server
```

Snort should also compile on

```
AIX, IRIX, HPUX, Tru64
```

To build and run Snort, you need Internet access to retrieve the software and the following software tools:

- An MD5[30] cryptographic checksum program
- GZIP[31] to uncompress the downloaded file
- A C compiler; either the Sun C Computer or the free GNU C Compiler[32]
- libpcap library installed (as described in the CERT implementation referenced above)

Downloading and Verifying

Download the following files into the same directory and verify their checksums with an MD5 checksum program.

---

30. Refer to the implementation titled *Using MD5 to Verify the Integrity of File Contents*, available at *http://www.cert.org/security-improvement*, under UNIX implementations.

31. Available at *ftp://ftp.gnu.org/gnu/gzip/gzip-1.2.4a.tar*.

32. Available at *ftp://prep.ai.mit.edu/gnu/gcc/gcc-core-2.95.2.tar.gz*.

File to Download	MD5 Checksum
`http://www.snort.org/` `Files/snort-1.6.3.tar.gz` Source distribution for UNIX	5d628b08c0bf42af3affc9fcfca7ea69
`http://www.snort.org/` `Files/snort-1.6.3-` `sol-2.6-sparc-local` Pre-compiled distribution for Solaris 2.6	ca491ade76253700860a6e2ac9259874

If the computed cryptographic checksum of the download files does not correspond to the information given above, verify that (1) your downloaded filenames match those listed and (2) your checksum program computes MD5 message digests.

Building

The pre-compiled Solaris 2.6 distribution may be installed using the pkgadd program. If you are unfamiliar with pkgadd or distrust supplied packages and wish to examine the source code, we recommend installing the program using the following procedure.

Unpack the Snort source distribution.

The compressed file can be uncompressed using the GNU gunzip utility and unpacked using the system tar command:

```
# gunzip -c snort-1.6.3.tar.gz| tar xvf -
```

This creates a directory named `snort-1.6.3`. Change to this subdirectory because all remaining operations are performed there.

You should review the INSTALL file to ensure that there are no other prerequisites before compiling the program. Additionally, configure-time switches are listed in this file, which allow such configurations as "flexible-response" and SMB alerting.

Now, configure and make the program with

```
# /bin/sh ./configure
# /usr/ccs/bin/make
```

Testing the Snort System Before Installation

To test the correct operation of Snort, execute Snort with the following options from the install location, as follows:

```
# ./snort -c ./snort-lib -v -i hmex
```

You should receive output to the terminal similar to that produced by tcpdump (as described in Section A.8): date and time stamp, unresolved source IP, source port, unresolved destination IP, destination port, and other protocol specific information.

Installation

Now install the program and manual pages with the following command. You should check the file ownerships and file protections once they have been copied to ensure that they cannot be modified or executed by unprivileged accounts, and that they reflect the security policy of your organization.

```
# /usr/ccs/bin/make install
```

Create a Directory for Snort Log Files

Create a separate directory where the Snort log and alert files will be stored. Note that this directory will contain connection information that may expose potential intrusions and attempted attacks of your network. We recommend that you restrict access to this directory as shown below. We further recommend that you store this directory within the /var directory because /var usually contains other log information:

```
# /bin/mkdir /var/adm/snort
# /bin/chmod 700 /var/adm/snort
```

Test the Snort System After Installation

Test Snort by following procedures similar to those under the section on testing before installation above. To get help on command line options to Snort, issue the following from the command line:

```
# ./snort -?
```

Writing Rules

Snort Rules and Examples

Snort allows you to write rules describing the following:

- Well-known and common vulnerability exploitation attempts
- Violations of your security policy
- Conditions under which you think a network packet(s) might be anomalous

Through the use of an easy-to-understand and lightweight rule-description language, Snort rules can be both flexible and robust, written for both protocol analysis and content searching and matching.

Two basic guiding principles must be kept in mind when writing Snort rules:

- Rules must be completely contained on a single line.
- Rules are divided into two logical sections, the *rule header* and the *rule options*. The rule header contains the rule's action, protocol, source and destination IP addresses and CIDR (Classless Inter-Domain Routing) block, and the source and destination ports information. The rule option section contains alert messages. It also contains information about which parts of the packet you should inspect to determine if you should take the rule action.

An sample rule:

```
alert tcp any any -> 192.168.1.0/24 111
(content:"| 00 01 86 a5|"; msg: "mountd access";)
```

Example 1: Sample Snort Rule

This rule describes an alert that is generated when Snort matches a network packet with all of the following attributes:

- TCP packet
- Sourced from any IP address on any port
- Destined for any IP address on the 192.168.1.0 network (24 describes the CIDR block and netmask used) on port 111.

The text up to the first parentheses is the *rule header*:

```
alert tcp any any -> 192.168.1.0/24 111
```

The section enclosed in parenthesis is the `rule options`:

```
(content:"|00 01 86 a5|"; msg: "mountd access";)
```

The word(s) before the colons in the *rule options* section are called *option keywords*. These keywords may appear once, as with "content" in Example 1 above, or multiple times, as shown in Example 2 below.

```
alert tcp any any -> any 21 (content:"site exec";
content:"%"; msg:"site exec buffer overflow attempt";)
```

Example 2: Sample Snort Rule

The above rule illustrates an FTP vulnerability. The keyword "content" appears twice because the two strings that "content" describes are not concatenated but appear at different locations within the packet(s). For this rule to be violated, the content of a packet(s) must contain character strings, "site exec" and "%."

The *rule options* section is not specifically required by any rule; it is used for the sake of making tighter definitions of packets to collect or to issue an alert.

Elements of an individual rule are treated as forming a logical AND statement. The complete collection of rules in a Snort rules library file (i.e., snort-lib) are treated as forming a larger logical OR statement.

Basics in Writing Snort Rules

Rule Actions: The *rule header* contains the information that defines the "who, where, and what" of a packet, as well as what to do when a packet occurs with all the attributes indicated in the rule. The first field in a rule is the rule action. The rule action tells Snort what to do when it finds a packet that matches the rule criteria. There are three available actions in Snort: alert, log, and pass.

```
alert - generates an alert using the selected alert
     method, and then logs the packet
log - logs the packet
pass - drops (ignore) the packet
```

Protocols: The next field in a rule is the protocol. There are three IP protocols that Snort currently analyzes for suspicious behavior: TCP, UDP, and ICMP. In the future there may be more, such as ARP, IGRP, GRE, OSPF, RIP, and IPX.

IP Addresses: The next portion of the rule header deals with the IP address and port information. The keyword "any" may be used to define any address. Snort does not have a mechanism to provide hostname lookup for the IP address fields in the rules file. The addresses are formed by a straight numeric IP address and a CIDR block. The CIDR block indicates the netmask that should be applied to the rule's address and any incoming packets that are tested against the rule. A CIDR block mask of /24 indicates a Class C network, /16 a Class B network, and /32 a specific machine address. For example, the address/CIDR combination 192.168.1.0/24 would signify the block of addresses from 192.168.1.1 to 192.168.1.255. Any rule that used this designation for, say, the destination address would match on any address in that range. The CIDR designations give us an easy way to designate large address spaces with just a few characters.

In Example 1 above, the source IP address was set to match for any computer communicating, and the destination address was set to match on the 192.168.1.0 Class C network. A negation operator can be applied to IP addresses. This operator tells Snort to match any IP address except the one indicated by the listed IP address. The negation operator is indicated with a "!". For example, an easy modification to the initial example is to make it alert on any traffic that originates outside of the local network with the negation operator, as shown in Example 3.

```
alert tcp !192.168.1.0/24 any -> 192.168.1.0/24 111
(content: "|00 01 86 a5|"; msg: "external mountd
  access";)
```

Example 3: Example IP Address Negation Rule

This rule's IP addresses indicate "any TCP packet with a source IP address not originating from the internal network and a destination address on the internal network."

Port Numbers: Port numbers may be specified in a number of ways, including "any" ports, static port definitions, ranges, and by negation. "Any" ports is a wildcard value, meaning literally any port. Static ports are indicated by a single port number, such as 111 for portmapper, 23 for telnet, or 80 for http. Port ranges are indicated with the range operator ":". The range operator may be applied in a number of ways, such as in Example 4.

```
log udp any any -> 192.168.1.0/24 1:1024
```

Log UDP traffic coming from any port and destination ports ranging from 1 to 1024.

```
log tcp any any -> 192.168.1.0/24 :6000
```

Log TCP traffic from any port going to ports less than or equal to 6000.

```
log tcp any :1024 -> 192.168.1.0/24 500:
```

Log TCP traffic from privileged ports less than or equal to 1024 going to ports greater than or equal to 500.

Example 4: Port Range Examples

The negation operator "!" may be applied against any of the other rule types (except "any," which would translate to none). For example, if for some reason you wanted to log everything except the X Windows ports, you could do something like the rule in Example 5.

```
log tcp any any -> 192.168.1.0/24
!6000:6010
```

Example 5: Example of Port Negation

Direction Operator: The direction operator "->" indicates the orientation, or "direction," of the traffic that the rule applies to. The IP address and port numbers on the left side of the direction operator designate traffic coming from the source host, and the address and port information on the right side of the operator designate destination host. There is also a bidirectional operator, which is indicated with a "<>" symbol. This tells Snort to consider the address/port pairs in either the source or destination orientation. This is handy for recording and analyzing both sides of a conversation, such as telnet or POP3 sessions. An example of the bidirectional operator being used to record both sides of a telnet session is shown in Example 6.

```
log !192.168.1.0/24 any <> 192.168.1.0/24 23
```

Example 6: Snort Rules Using the Bidirectional Operator

In Example 6, any traffic on any port originating from outside the internal network (192.168.1.x) with a destination of the internal network on the telnet port (23) is logged. Reciprocally, any telnet traffic originating from the internal network with a destination outside the internal network to any port is logged. Therefore, both sides of a telnet connection are logged.

Snort Alerting

Snort Alerts and How We Trust Them

Alerting, part of the Alerting and Logging subsystem, is activated at run time through the use of command-line options. In this section, we do not discuss these options, as they are detailed in documentation on the Snort web site. Instead, we describe how you, the system administrator, can verify that a Snort-generated alert is valid.

To fully trust an intrusion detection system alert, you must be able to examine three complementary data points:

1.   A rule representing behavior you know or suspect of being anomalous
2.   An alerting message warning you of a rule violation or of particular behavior
3.   A network packet (or series of packets) causing the rule violation

In lieu of having all three components, you must be able to relate the network packet to at least one of the following:

1.   The alerting message (of the proposed intrusion or intrusion attempt)
2.   The rule violated (of the proposed intrusion or intrusion attempt)

If neither of these relationships occurs, you are precluded from characterizing the security event as a positive or negative. The network packet(s) is a critical point of examination, and without the actual, tangible packet(s) we cannot investigate whether a rule is violated or whether an alerting message displays a positive occurrence of violation to our security policy. Therefore, because Snort allows you to configure various levels of alerting and logging, we recommend that Snort be set up to log the offending packets causing the rule violation and to record the alerts in separate files.

Snort Alerts and Logs

When Snort inspects a network packet and detects a match between a rule (describing a violation) and the network packet, Snort sends an alerting message to the user-defined facility and/or logs the packets causing the rule violation. The alerts

> *may either be sent to syslog, logged to an alert text file in two different formats, or sent as WinPopup messages using the Samba smbclient program. The syslog alerts are sent as security/authorization messages that are easily monitored with tools such as logsurfer [as described in section A.6]. WinPopup alerts allow event notifications to be sent to a user-specified list of Microsoft Windows consoles running the WinPopup software. There are two options for sending the alerts to a plain text file: full and fast alerting. Full alerting writes the alert message and the packet header information through the transport layer protocol. The fast alert option writes a condensed subset of the header information to the alert file, allowing greater performance under load than full mode. There is a fifth option to completely disable alerting, which is useful when alerting is unnecessary or inappropriate, such as when network penetrations tests are being performed.*

Similarly, logging can be set up to

log packets in their decoded, human-readable format to an IP-based directory structure, or in tcpdump [refer to section A.8] binary format to a single log file. The decoded format logging allows fast analysis of data collected by the system. The tcpdump format is much faster to record to the disk and should be used in instances where high performance is required. Logging can also be turned off completely, leaving alerts enabled for even greater performance improvements.

To put this into perspective, let's examine the logging and alerting areas of a system. For this discussion, the system sends alerts to the syslog facility and the offending network packet(s) to an IP-based directory structure. All alerts are logged via `syslog` to a file called `alerts` in the file `/var/adm/snort/alerts`. Any alerting message found in this file will have corresponding offending network packets logged in the same directory as the alert file but under the IP address of the source packet.

Using the rule in Example 1 above:

```
alert tcp any any -> 192.168.1.0/24 111
(content:"|00 01 86 a5|"; msg: "mountd access";)
```

When Snort inspects and matches the above rule to an offending network packet(s), an alerting message is sent to `syslog` stating that a "mountd access" violation has occurred. This message is recorded in the file `/var/adm/snort/alerts` and the actual network packet(s) causing the alert to be recorded in a file based on the source IP address of the offending packet(s), (i.e. `/var/adm/snort/a.b.c.d`).

Some problems may occur when filtering log entries into an IP-named file. For one, multiple alerts may involve one IP address. Under this condition, the offending packets violating each unique rule are sent to the same IP-named file; and mapping the specific alert to the offending packet(s) then demands a search and locate approach that could be time-consuming.

Snort Integration with Other Administrative/Security Tools

Snort's output can be used in concert with the output of other security tools to do the following:

1. Corroborate a security event that happened by returning the process and user information of the event
2. Identify discrepancies when processes are reported by programs such as ntop and tcpdump.

Tripwire Configuration

The following is the Tripwire configuration for the Snort program once installed. Only a few files—the Snort executable, `Snort(8)` man page, and the Snort alert file—require monitoring by Tripwire. In addition, files necessary to implement the software (i.e., libpcap) and the `/var/log/snort/` directory should be monitored.

The following files should not change, as any changes are unexpected:

```
@@define BINARY                    E+pinugsamc1-023456789

/usr/local/bin/snort               @@BINARY
/usr/local/man/man8/snort.8        @@BINARY
/var/log/snort/alerts              @@BINARY
```

Acknowledgments

The author would like to thank the developers of Snort and the author(s) of the Snort web site (*http://www.snort.org/*). Many of the examples and some documentation were reproduced in part and can be directly attributed to the developer's information as posted on the Snort web site. The section titled Basics in Writing Snort Rules was taken in part from the web document *Writing Snort Rules: How to Write Snort Rules and Keep Your Sanity* by Martin Roesch.

Appendix B

Practice-Level Policy Considerations

Security policies define the rules that regulate how your organization manages and protects its information and computing resources to achieve security objectives. Security policies and procedures that are documented, well known, and visibly enforced establish expected user behavior and serve to inform users of their obligations for protecting computing assets. Users include all those who access, administer, and manage your systems and have authorized accounts on your systems. They play a vital role in implementing your security policies.

This appendix contains additional details on candidate topics to be addressed in an organization's or site's security policies. In addition, all policy considerations that appear with each practice throughout this book are repeated here, by chapter and by practice section. Having this material in one location may aid you in reviewing and selecting policy topics and generating policy language.

Chapter 1: Introduction

An effective information security policy should have the following characteristics:[1]

- Be designed with a long-term focus.
- Be clear and concise.
- Be understandable and supported by all stakeholders.
- Be role-based.
- Be independent of positions or titles.
- Be realistic.
- Be implementable and enforceable.
- Specify areas of responsibility and authority.
- Include separation of duties.
- Release system administrators from responsibility for risks they should not manage.
- Enable system administrators to operate with management authority when needed, for example, providing limited, well-defined conditions under which users' e-mail may be read, traffic monitoring, etc.
- Be well defined.
- Be supported by well-established standards, guidelines, and procedures.
- Be kept up-to-date.

Any user (general, administrator, manager, etc.) should be able to answer the following questions about his or her organization's security policy:

- Where are your organization's security policies defined?
- Who is involved in establishing security policy?
- Who is responsible for monitoring compliance to your security policy?
- To whom is the security policy disseminated? How is it disseminated? How is receipt acknowledged?
- How often is the security policy updated? How are updates disseminated and acknowledged?

---

1. The majority of material in this Overview section is taken from the CERT one-day course *Concepts and Trends in Information Security,* specifically the course module on Information Security Policy. This course was developed in 1999 and is offered periodically. Check the SEI (*http://www.sei.cmu.edu*) and CERT web sites for course schedule information.

Examples of topics covered in an effective information security policy include the following

- Computing purchasing guidelines
- Privacy
- Access—least privilege
- Accountability
- Authorization
- Authentication
- Identification
- Auditing
- Availability
- Network traffic
- Violations reporting
- Communications
- Redundancy
- Resources
- Risk reduction

Chapter 2: Securing Network Servers and User Workstations

Section 2.2: Address Security Issues in Your Computer Deployment Plan (NS, UW)

Your organization's networked systems security policy should receive the following built-in protections:

- A detailed computer deployment plan should be developed, implemented, and maintained whenever computers are being deployed (or redeployed).
- Access to your deployment plan should be given only to those who require the information to perform their jobs.
- All new and updated computers should be installed, configured, and tested in a stand-alone mode or within test networks (i.e., not connected to operational networks).

- All computers should present a warning banner to all users indicating that they are legally accountable for their actions and that by using the computer they are consenting to having their actions logged.

- All computers (both workstations and servers) should be configured securely prior to deployment.

Section 2.3 Address Security Requirements When Selecting Servers (NS)

Your organization's networked systems security policy should require a security evaluation (including vulnerability assessment) as part of your computing and network technology selection procedures.

Section 2.4: Keep Operating Systems and Applications Software up to Date (NS, UW)

Your organization's networked systems security policy should require system administrators to monitor the need for necessary security-related software updates and install them in a timely manner.

Section 2.5: Stick to Essentials on the Server Host Machine (NS)

Your organization's networked systems security policy should require two important protection mechanisms:

1. Individual network servers, including public servers, should be configured to offer only essential services.
2. Each network service should be on a dedicated, single-purpose host wherever possible.

Section 2.6: Stick to Essentials on the Workstation Host Machine (UW)

Your organization's networked systems security policy should require all workstations to be configured with only essential software and all other software to be disabled or removed.

Section 2.7: Configure Network Service Clients to Enhance Security (UW)

Your organization's workstation acceptable use policy should provide users with a clear explanation of the following:

- The precautions they should observe when using a web browser (for example, should Java and ActiveX be enabled or disabled?)

- The circumstances, if any, in which they may download and execute software from other hosts (inside or outside your organization)

- The limitations, if any, on the kinds of information that may be included in electronic mail

Section 2.8: Configure Computers for User Authentication (NS, UW)

A password policy should cover five elements:

1. Length—it is common to specify a minimum length of eight characters.
2. Complexity—it is common to require passwords to contain a mix of characters, that is, both uppercase and lowercase letters and at least one nonalphabetic character.
3. Aging—how long a password may remain unchanged. It is common to require users to change their passwords periodically (every 30–120 days). The policy should permit users to do so only through approved authentication mechanisms.
4. Reuse—whether a password may be reused. Some users try to defeat a password-aging requirement by changing the password to one they have used before.
5. Authority—who is allowed to change passwords.

Your organization's networked systems security policy should have the following characteristics:

- It should describe under what conditions an account is created and deleted. This description should cover what account actions are taken (disabled, deleted, transferred) and how files are handled when an employee, contractor, or vendor who has an account no longer works for your organization.

- It should require appropriate authentication of all users on all computers that can access information assets, including users of network services hosted by your servers.

- It should include an appropriate password policy.
- It should prohibit users from recording and storing passwords in places that could be discovered by intruders.

When writing a password policy, remember that requiring users to have complex passwords may result in the undesired situation where users write their passwords on paper that they keep near the computer (often stuck to the machine) or with personal papers (in a wallet, purse, or briefcase). If that paper is observed, lost, or stolen, it creates a potential vulnerability.

If a password policy is especially difficult to follow, it creates in users a desire to find ways around it. This attitude can negatively influence users' compliance with other aspects of security policies.

Your organization's acceptable use policy for workstations should require that users shut down or lock their unattended workstations.

Section 2.9: Configure Operating Systems with Appropriate Object, Device, and File Access Controls (NS, UW)

Your organization's networked systems security policy should specify the following:

- Access privileges and controls for the information that will be stored on computers.
- How to access files that have been encrypted with a user key. This information is very important when that user no longer works for your organization.
- Access privileges and controls for administrative users, such as

  the authority and conditions for reading other users' e-mail

  access to protected programs or files

  disruption of service under specific conditions

  a ban on sharing accounts

  a ban on the unauthorized creation of user accounts

  the authority and conditions for using vulnerability testing tools

Section 2.10: Configure Computers for File Backups (NS, UW)

Your organization's networked systems security policy should do the following:

- Require the creation of a file backup and restoration plan
- Inform users of their responsibilities (if any) for file backup and recovery

Section 2.11: Use a Tested Model Configuration and a Secure Replication Procedure (UW)

None.

Section 2.12: Protect Computers from Viruses and Similar Programmed Threats (NS, UW)

Your organization's workstation acceptable use policy or security policy for networked systems should do the following:

- Define users' authority (or lack thereof) to download and/or install software on the computer.
- Specify who has the responsibility to scan for and eradicate viruses—users or system administrators—and where to scan to include workstations, servers, and gateways.
- Prohibit users from running executable files that they have received as e-mail attachments or downloaded from untrusted sites. If such a file needs to be run, it should be run on a host that is isolated from your operational systems. The host should not contain sensitive information, and the file should be run through virus detection tools. In addition, determining the file originator, if possible, will aid in determining the level of trust.

Section 2.13: Configure Computers for Secure Remote Administration (NS, UW)

Your organization's networked systems security policy should do the following:

- Require the use of secure procedures for administration of network servers and workstations

- Specify the circumstances under which third parties (vendors, service providers) are permitted to administer your systems remotely and how such administration is to be conducted

Section 2.14: Allow Only Appropriate Physical Access to Computers (NS, UW)

Your organization's networked systems security policy should indicate the following:

- Who is or is not allowed to install new hardware or modify existing hardware in a computer
- The circumstances in which users may or may not use storage devices with removable media
- The circumstances in which users may take storage media or printed information away from your site
- The need for network servers to be deployed in physically secure locations and for the access list to these locations to be kept short
- The circumstances in which third parties (vendors, service providers) are permitted to physically access your systems and how such access is to occur

Section 2.15: Develop and Roll Out an Acceptable Use Policy for Workstations (UW)

Elements of an Acceptable Use Policy

The policy should cover all of the information technologies that your staff are likely to use. The policy needs to address corporate data, network access, and use of workstations, portable computers, home computers, modems, software packages, etc.

An acceptable use policy for workstations is best developed as part of an overall site security policy. Your policy should specify the following:[2]

- Workstations a user may or may not use
- Hardware changes the user may make
- Software the user may install or remove

---

2. Refer also to Policy Considerations in sections 2.7, 2.8, and 2.12.

- What kinds of work the user may perform on the workstation (such as manipulation of classified data or conducting personal business)
- Network services the user may or may not use
- Information the user may or may not transmit across the network (such as in electronic mail)
- User responsibilities to operate the workstation securely, such as performing administrative tasks
- What kinds of configuration changes users may or may not make if they are given higher levels of privilege
- A ban on sharing of accounts
- The need to comply with your password policy.
- Guidelines for accessing unprotected programs or files
- A ban on breaking into accounts and systems
- A ban on cracking passwords
- A ban on disruption of service
- Consequences for noncompliance

Chapter 3: Securing Public Web Servers

Section 3.2: Isolate the Web Server

Your organization's networked systems security policy should establish the following guidelines:

- Your public servers should be placed on subnets separate from external public networks and from your internal network.
- Servers providing supporting services for your public servers should be placed on subnets separate from external public networks, from your public servers, and from your internal networks.
- Routers and firewalls should be configured to restrict traffic between external public networks and your public servers, and between your public servers and internal networks.
- Routers and firewalls should be configured to restrict traffic between servers providing supporting services for your public server and external public networks, your public server, and your internal networks.

Section 3.3: Configure the Web Server with Appropriate Object, Device, and File Access Controls

Your organization's networked systems security policy should require public servers to be configured to take maximum advantage of all available object, device, and file access controls to protect information as identified elsewhere in your security policy.

Your organization's information access control policy should address information residing on any public server, including web servers.

Section 3.4: Identify and Enable Web-Server-Specific Logging Mechanisms

None.

Section 3.5: Consider Security Implications for Programs, Scripts, and Plug-ins

Your organization's networked systems security policy should require a security evaluation (including vulnerability assessment) as part of your web server software selection procedures.

Section 3.6: Configure the Web Server to Minimize the Functionality of Programs, Scripts, and Plug-ins

Your organization's networked systems security policy should require a security evaluation (including vulnerability assessment) as part of your web server software selection and/or implementation procedures.

Section 3.7: Configure the Web Server to Use Authentication and Encryption Technologies

Your organization's networked systems security policy should mandate the review of all information prior to its posting on your public web site and ensure that access to sensitive or restricted information via the web site is protected at the level required.

Section 3.8: Maintain the Authoritative Copy of Your Web Site Content on a Secure Host

Your organization's networked systems security policy should establish the following guidelines:

- Identical, authoritative copies of all information residing on public servers should be securely maintained. This information includes the current version of public server content as well as previous versions and their update/transfer history. Include the transfer date, time, user ID, reason for the transfer, and any related observations.

- The transfer of authoritative content to public servers should use strong authentication and encryption.

Chapter 4: Deploying Firewalls

Section 4.2: Design the Firewall System

Your organization's networked systems security policy should address the following topics:

- The risks you are trying to mitigate with the firewall (i.e., the information assets and resources you are trying to protect and the threats that you are trying to protect against based on the security requirements that specify how these assets are to be protected)

- The services you intend to offer to untrusted networks from your protected network (these could be offerings to the Internet or to other internal networks)

- The services you intend to request from untrusted networks via your protected network (these could be requests to the Internet or to other internal networks)

- All incoming and outgoing network traffic must go through the firewall (that is, no traffic that bypasses the firewall is permitted, for example by using modems)—or conversely, specific loopholes are permitted and under what conditions (such as through the use of modems, tunnels, or connections to ISPs)

When offering and requesting services, your policy should ensure that you allow network traffic only if it is (1) determined to be safe and in your interests and (2) minimizes the exposure of information about your protected network's information infrastructure.

Section 4.3: Acquire Firewall Hardware and Software

None.

Section 4.4: Acquire Firewall Training, Documentation, and Support

None.

Section 4.5: Install Firewall Hardware and Software

Your organization's networked systems security policy should establish the following guidelines:

- Timely evaluation, selection, and installation of patches and other corrections that you need to operate securely

- Access to the firewall system by authorized personnel only via authorized, strongly authenticated mechanisms

- Installation of the firewall system in an environment isolated from your operational networks

- Regular backups of your firewall system

Section 4.6: Configure IP Routing

Your organization's networked systems security policy should (1) require that configuring IP routing for your firewall system be performed in an environment isolated from your operational networks and (2) specify what connectivity is to be permitted, explicitly stating that all other connectivity is denied.

Section 4.7: Configure Firewall Packet Filtering

Your organization's networked systems security policy should state that (1) all network traffic that is not explicitly permitted should, by default, be denied and (2) configuration of packet filtering for your firewall system must be performed in an environment isolated from your operational networks.

You should take care to minimize the amount and usefulness of information about your information infrastructure disclosed to those outside the firewall by addressing the following points in your policy:

- Limit the use of your organization's internal networks and services by users who are not members of your organization. If you are providing services specifically for use by nonmembers (such as access to your public web site), your policy should require that they be isolated from your internal systems. This decreases your risk even if one of the services is vulnerable to attack because access is strictly controlled.

- Address access requirements by members of your organization who are located on untrusted networks, such as mobile users on the Internet and employees located at a business partner's site. You may need to allow mechanisms to be implemented granting these people appropriate access through the firewall system to your internal networks or systems. If so, require the use of strong authentication and encryption.

The following is an example of a text-based firewall policy to protect a local user workstation on the ABC network. It assumes that all traffic not explicitly permitted is denied:

Permit all traffic to and from local host.

Permit all inbound ssh traffic.

Permit all AFS client traffic (AFS is the site file system).

Permit all Kerberos 4 client traffic.

Permit all Kerberos 5 client traffic.

Permit all DNS client traffic.

Permit all NTP client traffic to ntp1.abc.org.

Permit all NTP client traffic to ntp2.abc.org.

Permit all NTP client traffic to ntp3.abc.org.

Permit all syslog traffic to log-server.abc.org.

Permit all ICMP traffic.

Permit fragments from ABC networks inbound.

Permit all outbound TCP connections.

The following is an example of a text-based firewall policy to protect a public web server. Like the example above, it assumes that all traffic not explicitly permitted is denied:

Permit all traffic to and from local host.

Permit all inbound web (http and https) traffic.

Permit all inbound ssh traffic.

Permit all AFS client traffic.

Permit all Kerberos 4 client traffic.

Permit all Kerberos 5 client traffic.

Permit all DNS client traffic.

Permit all NTP client traffic to ntp server.

Permit all syslog traffic to logging server.

Permit all ICMP traffic.

Section 4.8: Configure Firewall Logging and Alert Mechanisms

Your organization's networked systems security policy should establish the following guidelines:

- Your firewall system should record all significant activity (such as administrative changes and attempts to breach filter rules) by doing thorough auditing and logging.

- Configuration of the logging and alert mechanisms for your firewall system should be performed in an environment isolated from your operational networks.

- Designated administrators should be notified of suspicious behavior that can be detected by the firewall system. Such behavior would include events related to the firewall system, such as failed login attempts and requests to disable filter rules.

- Guidelines should be specified for handling archived log information, deciding how long information should be retained, and discarding log information.

Section 4.9: Test the Firewall System

Your organization's networked systems security policy should establish the following guidelines:

- The firewall system should be tested in an environment isolated from your operational networks.

- The firewall system should be retested after every configuration change and periodically using the regression test suite.
- The regression test suite should be kept up-to-date to exercise the current firewall system configuration.
- The inventory of all applications software, operating systems, supporting tools, and hardware should be kept up to date.
- Monitoring of all network and systems, including your firewall system, should be performed on a regular basis.

Section 4.10: Install the Firewall System

Your organization's networked systems security policy should ensure that the firewall system installation/deployment plan and schedule are consistent with your site infrastructure business plan and schedule of infrastructure upgrades.

Section 4.11: Phase the Firewall System into Operation

Your organization's networked systems security policy should do the following:

- Require your users to be notified of firewall system service outages in advance
- Specify the person to be notified in the event of firewall system anomalies once deployment is complete

Chapter 5: Setting Up Intrusion Detection and Response Practices

Section 5.2: Establish Policies and Procedures (for Intrusion Detection and Response)

Document the important and critical information assets and the level of protection (confidentiality, availability, integrity) required for each. Designations for the level in question may range from "cannot be compromised under any circumstances" (maximum protection) to "contains no sensitive information and can be easily restored" (minimal protection).

Document the types of threats or events that indicate possible signs of intrusion, as well as how you intend to respond to them if they are detected. Possible types of threats include the following:

- Attempts (either failed or successful) to gain unauthorized access to a system or its data
- Unintended and unauthorized disclosure of information
- Unwanted disruption or denial of service
- The unauthorized use of a system to process, store, or transmit data
- Changes to system hardware, firmware, or software characteristics without the knowledge or consent of you or of the asset owner

Recognize that some threats are difficult to protect against if your systems are connected to the Internet. You need to determine what actions you will take if these occur. Threats of this type include the following:

- Resource starvation, such as e-mail bombing (sending a large volume of electronic messages to a targeted recipient until the system fails) and flood attacks (e.g., filling a channel with garbage, thereby denying others the ability to communicate across that channel or to the receiving host). These may result in the loss of availability, i.e., denial of service.
- Programmed threats, such as new viruses not yet detected and eliminated by virus-checking tools, and malicious software in the form of CGI scripts, plugins, servlets, or applets
- Intruders probing or scanning your systems with the intent to exploit any vulnerabilities they discover for use in attempting an intrusion

Document the requirement to establish and maintain secure, reliable configuration information for all assets that represent your known, expected operational state. This includes taking inventory and tagging all physical computing resources. Periodically compare this information with your current state to determine if anything has been altered in an unexpected way.

If a critical machine is compromised as a result of an intrusion, having redundant equipment in place enables you to restore service quickly while preserving all of the evidence on the compromised machine, and to perform ongoing analysis. You need to describe, for example, where and when to use hot, warm, and cold backups. Ensure that this configuration redundancy policy is consistent with your business continuity policy and document it.

Establish guidelines and rules at the management level for responding to intrusions. These guidelines and rules can be categorized as follows:

Priority and Sequence of Actions

Document the priority and sequence of actions to be taken when dealing with an intrusion. Actions necessary to protect human life and safety are likely to have priority over those that ensure operational and service continuity, protect classified and sensitive data, or prevent damage to systems. Document the factors that can alter the priority and sequence of actions, for example, time, additional information (such as the extent of an intrusion), and awareness that an intrusion you are analyzing interacts with one or more other intrusions.

A number of actions can be taken:

1. Deny access to an intruder, possibly by disconnecting the affected system from the network and shutting down the system.
2. Contain an intrusion and limit the actions of an intruder.
3. Continue operation to gather additional information.
4. Restore the affected system.

For the last action, you need to specify the order in which services will be restored, if this is a consideration (for example, restore your e-mail service before restoring FTP). This step ensures that the order meets your business objectives and priorities while minimizing negative effects on users whenever possible.

Authority to Act

This guideline should indicate what types of responses to an intrusion require management approval and which are preapproved.

Document the circumstances in which you need authorization to (1) stay connected to pursue an intruder by gathering additional information, (2) protect your systems by disconnecting and shutting down, or (3) conduct covert monitoring of network traffic and file access.

Ensure that the individuals or team responsible for intrusion response have preauthorization from management to disconnect from the network and shut down the affected system(s), if appropriate. This will cause a denial of service on the affected assets until they are returned to operation.

Document the necessary authority and actions to be taken in dealing with intrusions involving remotely connected computers used by your employees and vendors if these actions differ from those taken for other types of intrusions.

Intrusion Response Resources

Determine how you will structure, staff, and support your intrusion response activity. One option is to create a computer security incident response team (CSIRT). For this option, determine if the team will be distributed across organizational units or centralized within one unit and/or at one site. Identify the roles to be filled by team members based on your organization's security policies and procedures. Identify qualified people to assume these roles and determine how much of their time will be devoted to team activities. Ensure that you have a knowledgeable team trained and in place to handle the full intrusion response process.

If you choose not to create a CSIRT, ensure that all response roles and responsibilities are clearly assigned to system and network administrators, security personnel, and other staff.

Section 5.3: Identify Characterization and Other Data for Detecting Signs of Suspicious Behavior

Your organization's networked systems security policy should require your system administrators to create an accurate, reliable, and complete characterization of those assets you have selected. This should be done when they are first created and at well-defined events when you modify, add to, and replace elements of your systems or determine that the characterization of normal, expected behavior needs to change.

Section 5.4: Manage Logging and Other Data Collection Mechanisms

Your organization's networked systems security policy should establish the following guidelines:

- You should document a management plan for handling log files. This plan should include what to log, when and why to log, where to log, and who is responsible for all aspects of the plan.

- Approved sources should be identified for acquiring tool software (Internet, shareware, purchased from vendor, etc.) and acceptable use practices related to tools.

Section 5.5: Select, Install, and Understand Tools for Response

Your organization's networked systems security policy should establish the following guidelines:

- Designated system and network administrators, and response team members should be trained in the use of intrusion response tools and environments. This training should include participation in response practice drills or simulations using the tools and environments.

- The inventory of all applications software, operating systems, supporting tools, and hardware should be kept up-to-date.

- Quick access to backups should be available in an emergency, even if they are stored at a remote site. This requirement may include defining procedures that give specific managers the responsibility to authorize such access.

- Staff members dealing with an intrusion should be able to gain access to restricted systems and data. This policy may include

    specifying how staff access is granted and how they will obtain administrator passwords and encryption keys

    establishing the authority for staff access

    establishing the authenticity of the staff member obtaining access

    requiring all access to be documented and tracked

Chapter 6: Detecting Signs of Intrusion

Section 6.2: Ensure That the Software Used to Examine Systems Has Not Been Compromised

Your organization's networked systems security policy should specify the level of verification that is required when examining each class of data and service provided by the organization's systems.

Section 6.3: Monitor and Inspect Network Activities

Your organization's networked systems security policy should specify the following:

- The need for users to be notified that you will monitor network activities
- Your objectives for monitoring
- Which data streams will be monitored and for what purposes
- The responsibilities and authority of system administrators for handling notifications generated by monitoring and logging software
- What forms of unexpected network behavior users should watch for and the need to report any such behavior to their designated security officials and system administrators

Section 6.4: Monitor and Inspect System Activities

Your organization's networked systems security policy should specify the following:

- The need for users to be notified that process and user activities will be monitored and state the objective of such monitoring
- The responsibilities and authority of designated systems administrators and security personnel to examine systems, processes, and user activity for unexpected behavior
- What forms of unexpected behavior users should watch for and require users to report any such behavior to their designated security officials and system administrators.
- What software and data users and administrators are permitted to install, collect, and use, with explicit procedures and conditions for doing so
- What programs users and administrators are permitted to execute and under what conditions

Section 6.5: Inspect Files and Directories for Unexpected Changes

Your organization's networked systems security policy should establish the following guidelines:

- Users should be notified that files and directories will be examined and informed of the objective of such examinations.
- The responsibilities and authority of designated systems administrators and security personnel to examine files and directories on a regular basis for unexpected changes should be specified.

- Users should report any unexpected changes to their software and data files to system administrators or your organization's designated security point of contact.

Section 6.6: Investigate Unauthorized Hardware Attached to the Network

Your organization's networked systems security policy should do the following:

- Require the maintenance of documented hardware inventories
- Require the maintenance of a documented network topology
- Specify the authority and responsibility of designated security personnel to (1) perform physical audits of installed hardware and software and (2) establish network connections and routes
- Specify what kinds of hardware and software users are permitted to install on their workstations

Section 6.7: Look for Signs of Unauthorized Access to Physical Resources

Your organization's networked systems security policy should require the tagging and inventory of all physical computing resources, and specify how to respond when a physical intrusion has been detected.

Section 6.8: Review Reports of Suspicious System and Network Behavior and Events

Your organization's networked systems security policy should establish the following guidelines:

- Users should immediately report any unexpected or suspicious system behavior to their designated security official and system administrator.
- Users should immediately report any physical intrusions to networked systems or offline data storage facilities to their designated security official and system administrator.
- System administrators should investigate each reported suspicious activity to determine whether it represents an intrusion.

- System administrators should notify users in advance of any changes that will be made to the systems they use, including software configurations, data storage and access, and revised procedures for using systems as a result of the changes.

Section 6.9: Take Appropriate Actions

Your organization's networked systems security policy should do the following:

- Specify the actions to be taken following the discovery of unexpected, unusual, or suspicious activity
- Require the actions prescribed to be actually performed
- Specify the responsibilities and authority of designated systems administrators and security personnel to take the prescribed actions

Chapter 7: Responding to Intrusions

Section 7.2: Analyze All Available Information

Your organization's networked systems security policy should document the roles, responsibilities, authority, and conditions for the examination of data, systems, and networks suspected of having been compromised, as well as for the analysis of intrusions.

Your organization's information disclosure policy should indicate what information is shared with others and in what circumstances, as well as who has the authority to initiate information disclosure beyond what your policy specifies.

Section 7.3: Communicate with Relevant Parties

Your organization's networked systems security policy should include an information dissemination policy that identifies the following:

- Whom to notify in the event of an intrusion and in what order. The order of notification may depend on the type of intrusion or other circumstances. You should contact the responsible manager, your public relations point of contact, and your local response team immediately (shown as the first, second, and third items below). The remaining contacts are listed in no particular order.

the responsible manager and other managers who need to be made aware

public relations

CSIRT, if one exists

system and network administrator(s)

security officer and personnel

your site's Internet service provider (ISP)

human resources (in the event of an employee intruder)

help desk personnel (who may have to answer inquiries about an intrusion)

legal counsel

corporate investigations group, if one exists

law enforcement agencies (local, state, federal[3])

users

vendors

other CSIRTs outside your organization, for example, the team associated with your ISP, CERT/CC, your national CSIRT

- Specific roles and responsibilities for each contact within your organization, including their range of authority

- How much information should be shared with each class of contact and whether or not sensitive information needs to be removed or filtered prior to sharing it

- Whom to notify and when to notify them, using specified communication mechanisms (e.g., phone, e-mail, fax, pager), and whether or not these mechanisms need to be secure.

- Who has the authority to initiate information disclosure beyond that specified in your policy.

Section 7.4: Collect and Protect Information

Your organization's networked systems security response procedures should ensure that a provable chain of custody is maintained to protect potential evidence through, for example, the generation of a detailed action and decision log indicating who made each

---

3. Refer to the CERT Tech Tip *How the FBI Investigates Computer Crime,* available at *http://www.cert. org/tech_tips/FBI_investigates_crime.html.*

entry. This level of rigor is required even if you choose not to initiate an official legal investigation. Other affected organizations may decide to take action and request your assistance and any evidence you have collected, and such organizations may initiate legal proceedings against you if an intruder attacked their systems from yours.

Section 7.5: Contain an Intrusion

Your organization's networked systems security policy should specify the following:

- The acceptable level of risk to business processes and the systems and networks that support them
- To what extent business processes and the systems and networks that support them must remain operational, even in the event of intrusions or attacks
- What additional systems that reside on local networks with compromised systems will be disconnected, even if they are known to be as yet unaffected (this is a preventive measure)
- Who is empowered to make a final decision and in what circumstances, and who has the authority to make decisions in situations not covered by the policy
- How to manage password compromises, including when and how to change passwords for all users and accounts at a specific site or on an organizational level

Section 7.6: Eliminate All Means of Intruder Access

Your organization's networked systems security policy should establish the following guidelines:

- Regular checks should be made for the presence of system and network vulnerabilities.
- There should be timely evaluation and selective installation of patches and other corrections that you need to operate securely.
- People need to stay informed about the constantly changing sequence of new alerts, security bulletins, and advisories, particularly as they affect your protection and detection mechanisms. This task can be very resource-intensive, so you need to be selective regarding information sources that you review regularly.
- Clearly assign roles and responsibilities within your organization to perform regular checks, install patches, and to stay current with new information.

- Protect password transmission across an untrusted network by encryption or the use of some other secure authentication technologies, such as one-time passwords, challenge-response approaches, or security tokens.

Section 7.7: Return Systems to Normal Operation

Your organization's networked systems security policy should specify the order in which system services are to be returned to operation. This precaution ensures that the order meets your business objectives and priorities while minimizing the impact on users whenever possible.

Section 7.8: Implement Lessons Learned

None.

Bibliography

General

Alberts, Christopher J., et al. "Health Information Risk Assessment and Management: Toolkit Section 4.5." *CPRI Toolkit: Managing Information Security in Health Care, Version 2,* 2000. Online:
http://www.3com.com/healthcare/securitynet/hipaa/4_5.html.

Alberts, Christopher J., et al. *Operationally Critical Threat, Assets, and Vulnerability Evaluation*^{SM}*(OCTAVE*^{SM}*) Framework, Version 1.0.* (CMU/SEI-99-TR-017). Pittsburgh, PA: Software Engineering Institute, Carnegie Mellon University, 1999. Online:
http://www.sei.cmu.edu/publications/documents/99.reports/99tr017/ 99tr017abstract.html.

Allen, Julia, et al. "Improving the Security of Networked Systems." *Crosstalk: The Journal of Defense Software Engineering,* vol. 13, no. 10. October 2000a. Online:
http://www.stsc.hill.af.mil/Crosstalk/crostalk.html.

Allen, Julia, et al. *Security of Information Technology Service Contracts* (CMU/SEI-SIM-003). Pittsburgh, PA: Software Engineering Institute, Carnegie Mellon University, 1998. Online:
http:// www.cert.org/security-improvement/modules/m03.html.

Allen, Julia, et al. *State of the Practice of Intrusion Detection Technologies.* (CMU/SEI-99/TR-028). Pittsburgh, PA: Software Engineering Institute, Carnegie Mellon University, 1999. Online:
http://www.sei.cmu.edu/publications/ documents/99.reports/99tr028/99tr028abstract.html.

Allen, Julia, and Kossakowski, Klaus-Peter. *Securing Network Servers* (CMU/SEI-SIM-010). Pittsburgh, PA: Software Engineering Institute, Carnegie Mellon University, 2000b. Online:
http:// www.cert.org/security-improvement/modules/m10.html.

Allen, Julia, and Stoner, Ed. *Detecting Signs of Intrusion* (CMU/SEI-SIM-009). Pittsburgh, PA: Software Engineering Institute, Carnegie Mellon University, 2000c. Online:
http://www.cert.org/security-improvement/modules/m09.html.

423

Anderson, Ross. "Why Cryptosystems Fail." *First Conference on Computer and Communications Security.* Association for Computing Machinery (ACM), Virginia, 1993. Online:
http://www.cl.cam.ac.uk/users/rja14/wcf.html.

Anonymous. *Maximum Security: A Hacker's Guide to Protecting Your Internet Site and Network.* Indianapolis, IN: Sams.net Publishing, 1997. Online:
http://mx.nsu.ru/Max_Security/.

Bejtlich, Richard. "Interpreting Network Traffic: A Network Intrusion Detector's Look at Suspicious Events," 1999. Online:
http://packetstorm.securify.com/papers/IDS/intv2-8.pdf.

CERT Coordination Center Tech Tips:

Denial of Service Attacks, 1999. Online:
http://www.cert.org/tech_tips/denial_of_service.html.

Frequently Asked Questions About Malicious Web Scripts Redirected by Web Sites, 2000. Online:
http://www.cert.org/tech_tips/malicious_code_FAQ.html.

How the FBI Investigates Computer Crime, 2000. Online:
http://www.cert.org/tech_tips/FBI_investigates_crime.html.

How to Remove Meta-Characters from User-Supplied Data in CGI Scripts, 1999. Online:
http://www.cert.org/tech_tips/cgi_metacharacters.html.

Intruder Detection Checklist (UNIX), 2000. Online:
http://www.cert.org/tech_tips/intruder_detection_checklist.html.

Steps for Recovering from a UNIX Root Compromise, 2000. Online:
http:// www.cert.org/tech_tips/root_compromise.html.

Understanding Malicious Content Mitigation for Web Developers, 2000. Online:
http://www.cert.org/tech_tips/malicious_code_mitigation.html.

Windows NT Intruder Detection Checklist, April 2000. Online:
http://www.cert.org/tech_tips/win_intruder_detection_checklist.html.

Comer, Douglas E. *Internetworking with TCP/IP, Vol. 1: Principles, Protocols, and Architecture.* 3rd edition. New York: Prentice-Hall, 1995.

Computer Security Institute, "2000 CSI/FBI Computer Crime and Security Survey," *Computer Security Issues and Trends,* vol. VI, no. 1, Spring 2000.

Dunigan, Tom, and Hinkel, Greg. "Intrusion Detection and Intrusion Prevention on a Large Network: A Case Study." Proceedings of the First Workshop on Intrusion Detection and Network Monitoring, Santa Clara, CA. April 9–12, 1999. Online:
http://www.usenix.org/publications/library/proceedings/detection99/full_papers/dunigan/dunigan_html/index.html.

Ferguson, P., and Senie, D. RFC 2267 Network *Filtering: Defeating Denial of Service Attacks which Employ IP Source Address Spoofing.* Internet Engineering Task Force, 1998. Online:
http://www.ietf.org/rfc/rfc2267.txt.

Firth, Robert, et al. *An Approach for Selecting and Specifying Tools for Information Survivability.* (CMU/SEI-97-TR-009). Pittsburgh, PA: Software Engineering Institute, Carnegie Mellon University, 1997. Online:
http://www.sei.cmu.edu/ publications/documents/97.reports/97tr009/97tr009abstract.html.

Fithen, William, et al. *Deploying Firewalls.* (CMU/SEI-SIM-008). Pittsburgh, PA: Software Engineering Institute, Carnegie Mellon University, 1999. Online:
http:// www.cert.org/security-improvement/modules/m08.html.

Ford, Warwick, and Baum, Michael. *Secure Electronic Commerce.* Prentice-Hall, 1997. Internet Engineering Task Force, 1999.

Franks, J., et al. *RFC 2617 HTTP Authentication: Basic and Digest Access Authentication.* Online:
http://www.ietf.org/rfc/rfc2617.txt.

Fraser, Barbara, ed. *RFC 2196 Site Security Handbook.* Internet Engineering Task Force Network Working Group, 1997. Online:
http://www.ietf.org/rfc/rfc2196.txt.

Garfinkel, S., and Spafford, G. *Practical UNIX and Internet Security.* 2d edition. Sebastopol, CA: O'Reilly & Associates, Inc., 1996.

Garfinkel, Simon, and Spafford, Gene. *Web Security & Commerce.* Sebastopol, CA: O'Reilly & Associates, 1997.

Guttman, B., and Bagwill, R. *Internet Security Policy: A Technical Guide -Draft.* Gaithersburg, MD: NIST Special Publication 800-XX, 1997. Online:
http://csrc.nist.gov/isptg/html.

Howard, John. *An Analysis of Security Incidents on the Internet: 1989–1995.* Pittsburgh, PA: Carnegie Mellon University, 1997. Online:
http://www.cert.org/research/JHThesis/Start.html.

Howard, John, and Longstaff, Tom. *A Common Language for Computer Security Incidents.* (SAND98-8997). Albuquerque, NM: Sandia National Laboratories, 1998.

Kessler, Gary C. "Web of Worries." *Information Security* (April 2000). Online:
http://www.infosecuritymag.com/.

King, Nathan. "Sweeping Changes for Modem Security," 2000. Online:
http://www.infosecuritymag.com/articles/june00/features.shtml.

Kossakowski, Klaus-Peter, et al. *Responding to Intrusions* (CMU/SEI-SIM-006). Pittsburgh, PA: Software Engineering Institute, Carnegie Mellon University, 1999. Online:
http:// www.cert.org/security-improvement/modules/m06.html.

Kossakowski, Klaus-Peter, and Allen, Julia. *Securing Public Web Servers* (CMU/SEI-SIM-011). Pittsburgh, PA: Software Engineering Institute, Carnegie Mellon University, 2000. Online:
http:// www.cert.org/security-improvement/modules/m11.html.

Larson, Eric, and Stephens, Brian. *Web Servers, Security & Maintenance.* Prentice Hall, 2000.

Laurie, Ben, and Laurie, Peter. *Apache: The Definitive Guide.* Sebastopol, CA: O'Reilly & Associates, 1997.

Maiwald, Eric. "Automating Response to Intrusions." The Fourth Annual UNIX and NT Network Security Conference. Orlando, FL: The SANS Institute, October 24–31, 1998.

Marchany, Randy. "Incident Response: Scenarios and Tactics." The Fourth Annual UNIX and NT Network Security Conference. Orlando, FL: The SANS Institute, October 24–31, 1998.

McCarthy, Vance. "Web Security: How Much Is Enough?" *Datamation.* January 1997.

Mead, N. R., Lipson, H. F., and Sledge, C.A. "Toward Survivable COTS-Based Systems," *Cutter IT Journal,* vol. 14, no. 2 (February 2001): 4–11.

Mead, Nancy, et al. *Survivable Network Analysis Method* (CMU/SEI-2000-TR-013). Pittsburgh, PA: Software Engineering Institute, Carnegie Mellon University, 2000. Online:
http://www.sei.cmu.edu/publications/documents/00.reports/00tr013.html.

National Institute of Standards and Technology. *Internet Security Policy: A Technical Guide,* 1998. Washington, DC. Online:
http://csrc.nist.gov/isptg

Newsham, Tim, and Ptacek, Tom. "Insertion, Evasion, and Denial of Service: Eluding Network Intrusion Detection," 1998. Online:
http://www.snort.org under Security Info.

Northcutt, Stephen. "Computer Security Incident Handling: Step-by-Step." The Fourth Annual UNIX and NT Network Security Conference. Orlando, FL: The SANS Institute, October 24–31, 1998.

Northcutt, Stephen. *Network Intrusion Detection: An Analyst's Handbook.* Indianapolis, IN: New Rider, 1999.

Pethia, Richard. "Internet Security Issues: Testimony Before the U.S. Senate Judiciary Committee." Pittsburgh, PA: Software Engineering Institute, Carnegie Mellon University, May 25, 2000. Online:
http://www.cert.org/congressional_testimony/Pethia_testimony25May00.html.

Pichnarczyk, Karyn, Weeber, Steve, and Feingold, Richard. *Unix Incident Guide: How to Detect an Intrusion.* (CIAC-2305 R.1). Livermore, CA: Lawrence Livermore National Laboratory, Department of Energy Computer Incident Advisory Capability, December 1994. Online:
http://ciac.llnl.gov/ciac/documents/CIAC- 2305_UNIX_Incident_Guide_How_to_Detect_an_ Intrusion.pdf.

Power, Richard. "1999 CSI/FBI Computer Crime and Security Survey." *Computer Security Journal,* vol. XV, no. 2. San Francisco: Computer Security Institute, 1999.

Ranum, Marcus. "Some Tips on Network Forensics." *Computer Security Institute,* 198 (September 1999): 1–8.

Reavis, Jim. "Do You Have an Intrusion Detection Response Plan?" *Network World Fusion,* (September 13, 1999). Online:
http://www.nwfusion.com/newsletters/sec/0913sec1.html.

Rubin, Aviel, and Geer, Daniel. "A Survey of Web Security." *IEEE Computer* (September 1998).

Rubin, Aviel, Geer, Daniel, and Ranum, Marcus. *Web Security Sourcebook.* New York: John Wiley & Sons, 1997.

Ruiu, Dragos. "Cautionary Tales: Stealth Coordinated Attack HOWTO," 1999. Online:
http://www.nswc.navy.mil/ISSEC/ CID/Stealth_Coordinated_Attack.html.

Russell, Deborah, and Gangemi, Sr., G. T. *Computer Security Basics.* Sebastopol, CA: O'Reilly & Associates,1991.

SANS Institute. *Computer Security Incident Handling Step by Step Guide,* Vol. 5. May 1998.

SANS Institute. "How to Eliminate the Ten Most Critical Internet Security Threats: The Experts' Consensus," Version 1.32, 2000. Online:
http://www.sans.org/topten.htm.

SANS Institute. *Solaris Security Step-by-Step Guide Version 1.0,* 1999. Information on how to acquire this guide is available at *http://www.sansstore.org.* Supporting guidance on hardening Solaris systems is available at *http://www.sans.org/newlook/resources/hard_solaris.htm.*

SANS Institute. *Windows NT Security: Step-by-Step.* 2d edition, 2000. Information on this guide is available at *http://www.sans.org/newlook/publications/ntstep.htm.* Information on how to acquire this guide is available at *http://www.sansstore.org.*

Schneier, Bruce. *Applied Cryptography.* 2d edition. New York: John Wiley & Sons, Inc.,

Schultz, Eugene. "Effective Incident Response." The Fourth Annual UNIX and NT Network Security Conference. Orlando, FL: The SANS Institute, October 24–31, 1998.

Seifried, Kurt. "Creating and Preventing Backdoors in UNIX Systems." *SecurityPortal* (June 28, 2000). Online:
http://www.securityportal.com/closet/closet20000628.html.

Sellens, John. "System and Network Monitoring." ; *login:* 25, 3 (June 2000).

Simmel, Derek, et al. *Securing Desktop Workstations* (CMU/SEI-SIM-004). Pittsburgh, PA: Software Engineering Institute, Carnegie Mellon University, 1999. Online:
http://www.cert.org/security-improvement/modules/m04.html.

Soriano, Ray & Bahadur, Gary. "Securing Your Web Server." *Sys Admin* (May 1999).

Spainhour, Stephen, and Quercia, Valerie. *Webmaster in a Nutshell.* Sebastopol, CA: O'Reilly, 1996.

St. Johns, M. *RFC 1413 Identification Protocol,* Internet Engineering Task Force, February 1993. Online:
http://www.ietf.org/rfc/rfc1413.txt.

Stein, Lincoln. *The World Wide Web Security FAQ,* 1999. Online:
http://www.w3.org/Security/Faq.

Stein, Lincoln. *Web Security: A Step-by-Step Reference Guide.* Reading, MA: Addison-Wesley, 1998.

Stevens, W. Richard. *TCP/IP Illustrated, Vol. 1: The Protocols.* Reading, MA: Addison-Wesley, 1994.

Summers, Rita C. *Secure Computing.* New York: McGraw-Hill, 1997.

West-Brown, Moira, Kossakowski, Klaus-Peter, and Stikvoort, Donald. *CSIRT Handbook.* (CMU/SEI-98-HB-001). Pittsburgh, PA: Software Engineering Institute, Carnegie Mellon University, 1998. Online:
http://www.sei.cmu.edu/publications/documents/98.reports/98hb001/98hb001abstract.html.

Wood, Charles Cresson. *Information Security Policies Made Easy Version 7.* Baseline Software, Inc., 2000. Information on how to acquire this book is available at *http://www.baselinesoftware.com.*

Firewall References (Chapter 4)

General

Cheswick, William R., and Bellovin, Steven M. *Firewalls and Internet Security.* Reading, MA: Addison-Wesley, 1994.

Cooper, Deborah, and Pfleeger, Charles. "Firewalls: An Expert Roundtable." *IEEE Software,* New York: IEEE, September/October 1997.

Goncalves, Marcus. *Firewalls Complete.* New York: McGraw Hill, 1998.

Hall, Eric. "Internet Firewall Essentials." *Network Computing Online.* Manhasset, NY: CMP Media, Inc., November 1996. Online:
  http://www.networkcomputing.com/netdesign/wall1.html.

International Computer Security Association. *Third Annual Firewall Industry Guide,* 1998. Online:
  http://www.icsa.net/html/communities/firewalls/buyers_guide/index.shtml.

Lodin, Steve, and Schuba, Christoph. "Firewalls Fend Off Invasions from the Net." *IEEE Spectrum.* New York: IEEE, February, 1998.

Luk, Ellis, et al. *Protect and Survive: Using IBM Firewall 3.1 for AIX.* 3rd edition. Research Triangle Park, NC: IBM, 1998. Online:
  http://www.redbooks.ibm.com.

SC Magazine. "Firewalls Market Survey" (April 1999). Online:
  http://www.infosecnews.com.

Zwicky, Elizabeth, Cooper, Simon, and Chapman, D. Brent. *Building Internet Firewalls.* 2d edition. Sebastopol, CA: O'Reilly & Associates, June 2000.

Specific Firewall Technologies

Avolio, Blask. "Application Gateways and Stateful Inspection: A Brief Note Comparing and Contrasting." Trusted Information Systems, Inc., 1998. Online:
  http://www.avolio.com/apgw+spf.html.

Check Point Software Technologies Ltd. "Stateful Inspection Firewall Technology Tech Note," 1998. Online:
  http://www.checkpoint.com/products/technology/stateful1.html.

Detecting Intrusions

Escamilla, Terry. *Intrusion Detection: Network Security Beyond the Firewall.* New York: Wiley Computer Publishing, 1998.

Architecture Trade-off Analysis

Kazman, Rick, et al. "The Architecture Tradeoff Analysis Method." Proceedings of the Fourth IEEE International Conference on Engineering of Complex Computer Systems (ICECCS). Monterey, CA: IEEE, August 1998: 68–78.

Kazman, Rick, et al. "Experience with Performing Architecture Tradeoff Analysis." Proceedings of ICSE 21. Los Angeles, CA: ACM Press, May 1999.

Linux Systems

Grennan, Mark. *Firewalling and Proxy Server HOWTO, Version 0.4.* November 8, 1996. Online:
http://metalab.unc.edu/LDP/HOWTO/Firewall-HOWTO.html.

Lenz, Patrick, et al. Online:
http://freshmeat.net.

RedHat. RedHat software. Online:
http://www.redhat.com.

Russell, Paul. Linux *IPCHAINS-HOWTO, Version 1.0.5.* October 27, 1998. Online:
http://metalab.unc.edu/LDP/HOWTO/IPCHAINS-HOWTO.html.

Abbreviations

ACK	Acknowledgment
ACL	Access Control List
ARP	Address Resolution Protocol
ASCII	American Standard Code for Information Interchange
BIOS	Basic Input/Output System
BOOTP	Boot Protocol
CA	Certificate Authority
CEO	Chief Executive Officer
CERIAS	Center for Education, Research, and Information Assurance Security
CIO	Chief Information Officer
CGI	Common Gateway Interface
CLF	Common Log Format
COAST	Computer Operations, Audit, and Security Team
CPU	Central Processing Unit
CSIRT	Computer Security Incident Response Team
DDOS	Distributed Denial Of Service
DoS	Denial of Service
DG	Default Gateway
DHCP	Dynamic Host Configuration Protocol

DMZ	Demilitarized Zone
DNS	Domain Name System (Service)
EDI	Electronic Data Interchange
EEPROM	Electrically Erasable Programmable Read-Only Memory
ELF	Extended Log Format
ERP	Enterprise Resource Planning
FIRST	Forum of Incident Response and Security Teams
FTP	File Transfer Protocol
GUI	General User Interface
HAVAL	Hashing Algorithm with Variable Length
HTML	HyperText Markup Language
HTTP	HyperText Transfer Protocol
ICMP	Internet Control Message Protocol
IDS	Intrusion Detection System
IETF	Internet Engineering Task Force
IP	Internet Protocol
IPX	Internetwork Packet Exchange
IRC	Internet Relay Chat
ISP	Internet Service Provider
LAN	Local Area Network
LDAP	Lightweight Directory Access Protocol
MAC	Media Access Control
MD5	Message Digest 5
NAT	Network Address Translation
NIS	Network Information System
NTP	Network Time Protocol
OS	Operating System
OSPF	Open Shortest Path First
PERL	Practical Extraction and Report Language
PGP	Pretty Good Privacy
PKI	Public Key Infrastructure
RAM	Random Access Memory

RCS	Revision Control System
RFC	Request for Comment
RIP	Routing Information Protocol
RPC	Remote Procedure Call
RSH	Remote Shell
SAINT	Security Administrator's Integrated Network Tool
SARA	Security Auditor's Research Assistant
SATAN	System Administrator Tool for Analyzing Networks
SCCS	Software Configuration Control System
SET	Secure Electronic Transaction
SHA	Secure Hash Algorithm
S/HTTP	Secure HyperText Transport Protocol
SMTP	Simple Mail Transfer Protocol
SNMP	Simple Network Management Protocol
SOCKS	(general-purpose application proxy)[1]
SPAK	Send PAcKets
SQL	Structured Query Language
SSH	Secure SHell
SSL	Secure Socket Layer
SYN	Synchronize
TCL	Tool Command Language
TCP	Transmission Control Protocol
TEMPEST	Transient ElectroMagnetic Pulse Emanation Standard
TLS	Transport Level Security
UDP	User Datagram Protocol
URL	Uniform Resource Locator
VLAN	Virtual Local Area Network
VPN	Virtual Private Network
WORM	Write Once, Read Many
WWW	World Wide Web

---

1 Refer to *http://www.socks.nec.com.*

Index

The SEI Series in Software Engineering

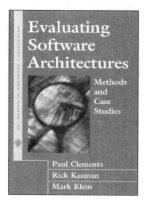

Evaluating Software Architectures

Methods and Case Studies

Paul Clements, Rick Kazman, and Mark Klein

This book is a comprehensive, step-by-step guide to software architecture evaluation, describing specific methods that can quickly and inexpensively mitigate enormous risk in software projects. The methods are illustrated both by case studies and by sample artifacts put into play during an evaluation: viewgraphs, scenarios, final reports—everything you need to evaluate an architecture in your own organization.

0-201-70482-X • Hardcover • 304 Pages • ©2002

Software Product Lines

Practices and Patterns

Paul Clements and Linda Northrop

Building product lines from common assets can yield remarkable improvements in productivity, time to market, product quality, and customer satisfaction. This book provides a framework of specific practices, with detailed case studies, to guide the implementation of product lines in your own organization.

0-201-70332-7 • Hardcover • 576 Pages • ©2002

The People Capability Maturity Model

Guidelines for Improving the Workforce

Bill Curtis, William E. Hefley, and Sally A. Miller

Employing the process maturity framework of the Software CMM, the People Capability Maturity Model (People CMM) describes best practices for managing and developing an organization's workforce. This book describes the People CMM and the key practices that comprise each of its maturity levels, and shows how to apply the model in guiding organizational improvements. Includes case studies.

0-201-60445-0 • Hardback • 448 Pages • ©2002

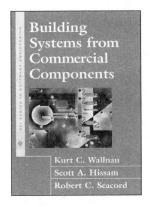

Building Systems from Commercial Components
Kurt C. Wallnau, Scott A. Hissam, and Robert C. Seacord

Commercial components are increasingly seen as an effective means to save time and money in building large software systems. However, integrating pre-existing components, with pre-existing specifications, is a delicate and difficult task. This book describes specific engineering practices needed to accomplish that task successfully, illustrating the techniques described with case studies and examples.

0-201-70064-6 • Hardcover • 416 pages • ©2002

CMMI Distilled
A Practical Introduction to Integrated Process Improvement
Dennis M. Ahern, Aaron Clouse, and Richard Turner

The Capability Maturity Model Integration (CMMI) is the latest version of the popular CMM framework, designed specifically to integrate an organization's process improvement activities across disciplines. This book provides a concise introduction to the CMMI, highlighting the benefits of integrated process improvement, explaining key features of the new framework, and suggesting how to choose appropriate models and representations for your organization.

0-201-73500-8 • Paperback • 240 pages • ©2001

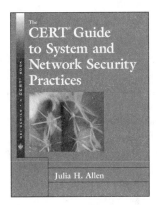

The CERT Guide to System and Network Security Practices
By Julia H. Allen

The CERT Coordination Center helps systems administrators secure systems connected to public networks, develops key security practices, and provides timely security implementations. This book makes CERT practices and implementations available in book form, and offers step-by-step guidance for protecting your systems and networks against malicious and inadvertent compromise.

0-201-73723-X • Paperback • 480 pages • ©2001

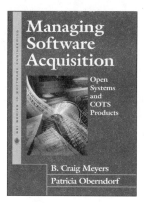

Managing Software Acquisition
Open Systems and COTS Products
B. Craig Meyers and Patricia Oberndorf

The acquisition of open systems and commercial off-the-shelf (COTS) products is an increasingly vital part of large-scale software development, offering significant savings in time and money. This book presents fundamental principles and best practices for successful acquisition and utilization of open systems and COTS products.

0-201-70454-4 • Hardcover • 288 pages • ©2001

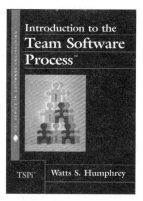

Introduction to the Team Software Process
Watts S. Humphrey

The Team Software Process (TSP) provides software engineers with a framework designed to build and maintain more effective teams. This book, particularly useful for engineers and students trained in the Personal Software Process (PSP), introduces TSP and the concrete steps needed to improve software teamwork.

0-201-47719-X • Hardcover • 496 pages • ©2000

CMM in Practice
Processes for Executing Software Projects at Infosys
Pankaj Jalote

This book describes the implementation of CMM at Infosys Technologies, and illustrates in detail how software projects are executed at this highly mature software development organization. The book examines the various stages in the life cycle of an actual Infosys project as a running example throughout the book, describing the technical and management processes used to initiate, plan, and execute it.

0-201-61626-2 • Hardcover • 400 pages • ©2000

Measuring the Software Process
Statistical Process Control for Software Process Improvement
William A. Florac and Anita D. Carleton

This book shows how to use measurements to manage and improve software processes within your organization. It explains specifically how quality characteristics of software products and processes can be quantified, plotted, and analyzed, so that the performance of software development activities can be predicted, controlled, and guided to achieve both business and technical goals.

0-201-60444-2 • Hardcover • 272 pages • ©1999

Cleanroom Software Engineering
Technology and Process
Stacy Prowell, Carmen J. Trammell, Richard C. Linger, and Jesse H. Poore

This book provides an introduction and in-depth description of the Cleanroom approach to high-quality software development. Following an explanation of basic Cleanroom theory and practice, the authors draw on their extensive experience in industry to elaborate the Cleanroom development and certification process and show how this process is compatible with the Capability Maturity Model (CMM).

0-201-85480-5 • Hardcover • 400 pages • ©1999

Software Architecture in Practice
Len Bass, Paul Clements, and Rick Kazman

This book introduces the concepts and practice of software architecture, not only covering essential technical topics for specifying and validating a system, but also emphasizing the importance of the business context in which large systems are designed. Enhancing both technical and organizational discussions, key points are illuminated by substantial case studies.

0-201-19930-0 • Hardcover • 480 pages • ©1998

Managing Risk
Methods for Software Systems Development
By Elaine M. Hall

Written for busy professionals charged with delivering high-quality products on time and within budget, this comprehensive guide describes a success formula for managing software risk. The book follows a five-part risk management road map designed to take you from crisis to control of your software project.

0-201-25592-8 • Hardcover • 400 pages • ©1998

Software Process Improvement
Practical Guidelines for Business Success
By Sami Zahran

This book will help you manage and control the quality of your organization's software products by showing you how to develop a preventive culture of disciplined and continuous process improvement.

0-201-17782-X • Hardcover • 480 pages • ©1998

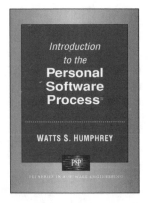

Introduction to the Personal Software Process
By Watts S. Humphrey

This workbook provides a hands-on introduction to the basic discipline of software engineering, as expressed in the author's well-known Personal Software Process (PSP). By applying the forms and methods of PSP described in the book, you can learn to manage your time effectively and to monitor the quality of your work, with enormous benefits in both regards.

0-201-54809-7 • Paperback • 304 pages • ©1997

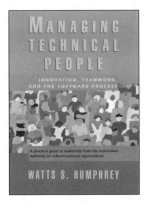

Managing Technical People
Innovation, Teamwork, and the Software Process
By Watts S. Humphrey

Drawing on the author's extensive experience as a senior manager of software development at IBM, this book describes proven techniques for managing technical professionals. The author shows specifically how to identify, motivate, and organize innovative people, while tying leadership practices to improvements in the software process.

0-201-54597-7 • Paperback • 352 pages • ©1997

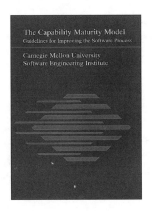

The Capability Maturity Model
Guidelines for Improving the Software Process
By Carnegie Mellon University/Software Engineering Institute

This book provides the authoritative description and technical overview of the Capability Maturity Model (CMM), with guidelines for improving software process management. The CMM provides software professionals in government and industry with the ability to identify, adopt, and use sound management and technical practices for delivering quality software on time and within budget.

0-201-54664-7 • Hardcover • 464 pages • ©1995

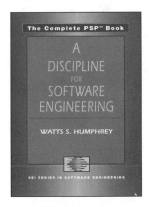

A Discipline for Software Engineering
The Complete PSP Book
By Watts S. Humphrey

This book scales down to a personal level the successful methods developed by the author to help managers and organizations evaluate and improve their software capabilities—methods comprising the Personal Software Process (PSP). The author's aim with PSP is to help individual software practitioners develop the skills and habits needed to plan, track, and analyze large and complex projects, and to develop high-quality products.

0-201-54610-8 • Hardcover • 816 pages • ©1995

Software Design Methods for Concurrent and Real-Time Systems
By Hassan Gomaa

This book provides a basic understanding of concepts and issues in concurrent system design, while surveying and comparing a range of applicable object-oriented design methods. The book describes a practical approach for applying real-time scheduling theory to analyze the performance of real-time designs.

0-201-52577-1 • Hardcover • 464 pages • ©1993

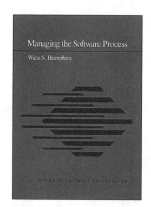

Managing the Software Process
By Watts S. Humphrey

This landmark book introduces the author's methods, now commonly practiced in industry, for improving software development and maintenance processes. Emphasizing the basic principles and priorities of the software process, the book's sections are organized in a natural way to guide organizations through needed improvement activities.

0-201-18095-2 • Hardcover • 512 pages • ©1989

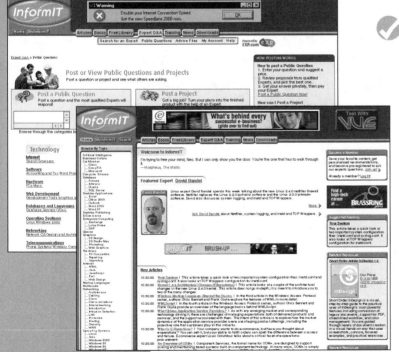